W9-BZM-223

An Exemplary Citizen

Letters of Charles W. Chesnutt
1906–1932

An Exemplary Citizen

Letters of
Charles W. Chesnutt
1906-1932

Edited by
Jesse S. Crisler
Robert C. Leitz, III
Joseph R. McElrath, Jr.

Stanford University Press
Stanford, California
2002

Stanford University Press
Stanford, California
© 2002 by the Board of Trustees of the
Leland Stanford Junior University
Printed in the United States of America

ISBN 0-8047-4508-0 (cloth : alk. paper)

This book is printed on acid-free, archival-quality paper

Original printing 2002

Last figure below indicates year of this printing:
11   10   09   08   07   06   05   04   03   02

Designed and typeset at Stanford University Press in 10/13 Sabon

Frontispiece: Charles W. Chesnutt and his daughter Helen,
photograph courtesy of the Western Reserve Historical Society,
Cleveland, Ohio

In loving memory
ANDREW LYON CRISLER
5 May–16 May
1980

Acknowledgments

———◆·◆———

This volume would not have been possible without the kind assistance of Charles W. Chesnutt's grandson John C. Slade and his permission to publish the letters made available to us at the Fisk University Library, the Western Reserve Historical Society Library, the Beinecke Rare Book and Manuscript Library of Yale University, the Moorland-Spingarn Research Center of Howard University, the Manuscripts Division of the Library of Congress, the Houghton Library of Harvard University, the Schomburg Center for Research in Black Culture of the New York Public Library, and the Rowfant Club.

For funding of this project we are indebted to the Collaborative Research Program of the National Endowment for the Humanities and to Florida State University, Brigham Young University, and Louisiana State University, Shreveport.

We also thank the following individuals who assisted us in our research. Gregory Martinson, Esq., identified and clarified the significance of all of the legal decisions to which Chesnutt refers. Anthony W. C. Phelps, Archivist of the Rowfant Club, searched for and discovered several previously unknown letters written by and to Chesnutt, as well as assisted us with research on the many Ohioans addressed and cited in the letters. Three other Clevelanders who went well beyond the call of duty to aid the good cause were Carl Weitman of the Rowfant Club, Ann Sindelar of the Western Reserve Historical Society Library, and Stephen J. Zietz, Head, Fine Arts and Special Collections Section of the Cleveland Public Library. At the Fisk University Library Ann Allen Shockley and Beth Howse cheerfully answered our queries and made research in the Special Collections room a pleasure.

Contents

Preface

This annotated edition of letters written by Charles W. Chesnutt stands as yet another of many recent testimonies to the historical significance of a man who was not only a pioneer in the African-American literary tradition but one of the most talented American authors of his generation. Born in 1858 and living until 1932, he enjoyed some popularity at the turn of the century, but by the time of his death he was largely forgotten by the reading public at large. Since the 1960s, however, there has been an outpouring of interpretive studies of his contributions to both imaginative literature per se and social thought concerning the relationship between the races during the Reconstruction and the period that came to be known as the Jim Crow era by the end of the nineteenth century. The novels and short stories Chesnutt saw published have all been reprinted; if not on display in bookstores, they are easily found in most libraries. Those writings that were not published before 1932 are now rapidly being made available; the demand for the products of his hand is keen, and what once seemed unimaginable—that "everything" he penned would appear in print—now appears inevitable.

This is the second collection of his letters to appear since 1997 when *"To Be an Author": Letters of Charles W. Chesnutt, 1889–1905* (Princeton University Press) was prepared by two of the present editors, McElrath and Leitz. Joining this team in 1999 for *Charles W. Chesnutt: Essays and Speeches* (Stanford University Press) was Crisler; and, as with the previous two volumes in this series, the present one attempts both to render accurately what Chesnutt intended to communicate to his contemporaries between 1906 and 1932 and to provide in notes the information necessary for understanding the references and allusions in the letters that may not be immediately intelligible to the majority of modern readers.

The intent of the editors when selecting letters for publication was to present all that promised to reveal Chesnutt's character and to disclose the wide variety of his interests, activities, and accomplishments between 1906 and 1932. Unless otherwise indicated, these were written at home or at his business office in Cleveland, Ohio. Few have to do directly with his affairs as the head of a stenographic and court reporting firm since such communications are typically terse statements of terms for services to be rendered and billings for work performed. That the number of these documents extant is relatively small suggests that his correspondence had previously passed through a selection process— with Chesnutt himself and, after his death, his daughter Helen M. Chesnutt determining how he would be represented to posterity in the major collections of his papers at Fisk University and the Western Reserve Historical Society. The letters seen here, then, deal mainly with these more telling subjects: life within Chesnutt's immediately family; his personal relationships with individuals in Cleveland and across the nation; his interest in race relations world-wide and both the laws and folkways affecting them in the United States; his efforts as an individual to ameliorate the conditions faced by African Americans in Cleveland and elsewhere; his participation in local civic-betterment and reform-minded national organizations, as well as in social and professional groups; his study of African-American history and culture; and— of course—his points of view on both the figure he cut as a turn-of-the-century literary phenomenon and his later activities as a prose fiction writer, essayist, and public speaker.

Some of the letters transcribed and edited are represented in two or more forms produced by Chesnutt and his typists: drafts, the versions sent, complete carbon copies, and incomplete carbons. When possible, we have selected for publication the letter received by a correspondent. The majority of the source-texts, however, exist in one form only: they are typescript carbon copies. The single sources also include publications in which the sole surviving texts of letters were either printed in full or quoted in part.

Normally following the edited texts of the letters appear two symbols indicating the kind of source-text employed and its location. For example, "*TCU*: TNF" first identifies the source as a typescript carbon copy, unsigned; then, following the colon, we specify the Library of Congress symbol for the Fisk University Library. All such symbols, as well as abbreviations of book titles frequently referenced in the notes, will be seen in our list of "Symbols Employed in This Edition." If a letter was not located in a collection but transcribed from a published source, the publication is named.

We have editorially emended the source-texts in a conservative manner according to Chesnutt's discernible intentions and in light of the sophistication he displays not only in his letters but the holographs and typescripts of his non-epistolary writings. The majority of unintended readings appear to have been typographical errors ("pycholgy" for "psychology" or "send it it to you"). Chesnutt's typists were also most likely responsible for the misspelling of "existence" as "existance" and of "prominent" as "prominant." That Chesnutt dictated some letters and did not carefully enough proofread the typed original or carbon copy may also explain "effect" and "greatful" instead of the intended word choice "affect" and the correct spelling "grateful."

On a case-by-case basis, we have responded to the omission of a word or words one normally expects to see in a phrase. On occasion, Chesnutt deliberately writes in a formulaic business or legal manner, *e.g.,* succinctly declaring "I wish to acknowledge receipt of copy of record in the Randolph cases . . . ." Editorially emended only are readings that cannot be construed as in the same category, such as "he glanced over it casually, and suggested that it was written rather in argumentative vein." The intended phase appears to have been "in an argumentative vein." But there are other errors that appear authorial in origin and the result of misrecollection or misunderstanding on Chesnutt's part, such as the surname "Loudin" being rendered as "Louden," "Storey" as "Story," and "Micheaux" as "Morceau." Finally, Chesnutt was not the first or last to err with a phonetic spelling of the name of Scotland's capital city: "Edinboro."

Chesnutt's punctuation practices may sometimes appear irregular, smacking of nineteenth-century usages prior to the popularization of a grammar-based system. Commas, for example, may function as the equivalent of breath-marks in a musical score, rather than set off phrases and clauses in the manner they do today. As antiquated for American readers is the appearance of a comma or period at the right of a closing quotation mark. We have emended only when essential punctuation is lacking and when an error is obvious, as in the interrogative "Will you kindly procure and send me one."

Regularization is both minimal and conventional according to the standards for printed texts in Chesnutt's time. We have italicized and added the appropriate accent marks to foreign language words, phrases, and abbreviations. Italicized, too, were the following which sometimes appeared within double quotation marks: the names of ships; and the titles of books and pamphlets, works of art such as paintings and musical compositions, films, and periodicals.

The reader will want to note in advance that there are three peculiarities to be seen in the edited letters. First, Chesnutt rarely signed the typescript carbon copies used as source-texts; thus his signature will often be found absent. Second, only the first page of a typescript carbon copy of some letters is extant. Ellipses at the ends of such letters do not indicate our deliberate editorial elisions but the unavailability of the remainders of their texts. Finally, the texts of letters derived from Helen M. Chesnutt's 1952 biography, *Charles Waddell Chesnutt: Pioneer of the Color Line*, were editorially truncated by her. Ellipses seen in these letters indicate her omissions.

The reader will note that no letters written in 1911 and 1918 appear in this volume. None for either year is extant.

Symbols Employed in this Edition

———◦◦◦———

The following indicate the kinds of source-texts from which the edited letters were derived:

ALS   Autograph letter, signed

TCS   Typed carbon copy, signed

TCU   Typed carbon copy, unsigned

TDU   Typed draft, unsigned

TLS   Typed letter, signed

TLU   Typed letter, unsigned

Pioneer Helen M. Chesnutt, *Charles Waddell Chesnutt: Pioneer of the Color Line* (Chapel Hill: University of North Carolina Press, 1952).

The symbols for the locations of letters are:

CtY   Beinecke Rare Book and Manuscript Library, Yale University

DHU   Moorland-Spingarn Research Center, Howard University

DLC   Manuscripts Division, Library of Congress

MH   Houghton Library, Harvard University

NN-Sc   Schomburg Center for Research in Black Culture, New York Public Library

OClWHi   Western Reserve Historical Society Library

Rowfant Archives of the Rowfant Club

TNF   Fisk University Library

The abbreviated titles of books cited in the explanatory notes are:

Essays and   *Charles W. Chesnutt: Essays and Speeches*, ed. Joseph R.
Speeches   McElrath, Jr., Robert C. Leitz, III, and Jesse S. Crisler
                (Stanford: Stanford University Press, 1999).

Letters   *"To Be an Author": Letters of Charles W. Chesnutt,*
                1889–1905, ed. McElrath and Leitz (Princeton: Princeton
                University Press, 1997).

Pioneer   See source-text symbols above.

Introduction

Born a "Free Man of Color" in 1858, Charles Waddell Chesnutt would live to see this vital distinction become an anachronism. By 1932, when he died in the city of his birth, the once-commonplace phrase would require deciphering not only in Cleveland, Ohio, but even in the South. The majority of Americans were then two or three generations removed from times in which one carefully distinguished thus between slaves and free men of color—or, immediately after the Civil War, between one who was born free and the freedman who had been "shot free" by Union soldiers. Whites of 1932 were unfamiliar not only with the abbreviation "F.M.C." but with like terminology and imagery known and used by ancestors who had either despised or cheered on the abolitionists before and during the war. Lost to history, too, for the vast majority of whites and blacks were the angry rhetoric and figurative language employed after the Civil War by Radical Republican congressmen such as Thaddeus Stevens and Charles Sumner who acted in a punitive manner to "reconstruct" the Southern states they characterized as conquered provinces. As was Chesnutt himself by 1932, this was all part of a past that, in the face of the Great Depression, received little if any attention from the native-born or recent immigrants and their children.

On the other hand, if 1930s Americans paid attention they *could* see as clearly as Chesnutt did the segregationist effects of the "fire-eater" speeches delivered from the 1870s into the 1890s by Southern Democrats determined to redeem "their" South. Likewise, they *could* note that current were the same epithets for and caricatures of the African American used by the Redemptionists—or, as Chesnutt termed them, the Bourbon Southern politicians urged on by "rednecks," "crackers," and "buckras" to restore the antebellum status quo. But, relatively few were paying attention then to the historical roots of white racism or were aware that they were participating in a longstanding linguistic tradition when they denigrated "darkies," "niggers," and "coons." What Chesnutt knew from over six decades of personal experience was, for most, as irrelevant as the African-American literary tradition for which he was a major pioneer figure from the 1880s through the turn of the century. Despite the attention given the Harlem Renaissance by sophisticates in the 1920s, this tradition remained as "invisible" to the mass of Americans as was the remarkable body of artful writing Chesnutt bequeathed to posterity when he died at 74 years of age.

Long before 1932, at the turn of the century, Chesnutt learned first-hand just how indifferent a large white subgroup—the ever-burgeoning body of novel-readers—had already become to the subject he found galvanic. It was then termed "The Negro Problem," to which he turned again and again in his prose fictions, essays, and speeches from 1885 on. Or, more specifically, he discovered by the early 1900s just how jaded this readership had become since Harriet Beecher Stowe published *Uncle Tom's Cabin* serially in 1851–52 and then as a book with sales of over 300,000 copies in 1852 alone. A half-century later Chesnutt's fifth book and second novel, *The Marrow of Tradition* (1901), was advertised by his publisher as the modern equivalent of Stowe's sympathy-inducing portrait of conditions in the South. It was, indeed, Chesnutt's long-standing intention to write this kind of novel, not only to mollify white attitudes toward African Americans but to establish himself as a professional author with an annual income at least equal to that yielded by the stenography and court reporting firm he founded in Cleveland in the late 1880s. Stowe served a noble cause and became wealthy doing so; why could not he, too?

His logic was sound so far as it went, and *Marrow* was a graphic exposé of post-Reconstruction racism offering scenes as sensational as Eliza's flight across the Ohio River with her son Harry in her arms in the pages of *Cabin*. Chesnutt's white-supremacist villains in North Carolina, for example, were as unspeakable as *Cabin*'s Haley, the slave trader intent upon capturing and selling Eliza's four-year-old boy. But Chesnutt did not take into account the real-world situation as it had more recently developed during the Jim Crow era. Attitudes among book-buyers, simply stated, had changed.

Initially, it appeared that Chesnutt's hope for a new career as a full-time man of letters was at last realized. The majority of the reviews were decidedly positive.[1] Yet, in 1901 and 1902 *Marrow* sold only slightly better than his two 1899 collections of short stories (*The Conjure Woman* and *The Wife of His Youth and Other Stories of the Color Line*), his biography (*Frederick Douglass*, 1899), and the two other novels that saw print during his lifetime (*The House Behind the Cedars*, 1900, and *The Colonel's Dream*, 1905).[2] At the same time that fewer than four thousand copies of Chesnutt's 1901 indictment of a barbaric South were purchased,[3] the white-supremacist novelist Thomas Dixon, Jr., was beginning to enjoy his hugely successful stint as a writer of polemical best-sellers. Thus, a second anachronism related to Chesnutt must be noted, this one having to do with the kind of prose fiction that he wrongly assumed would appeal to a mass readership. In 1901 he proffered post-Reconstruction victims who were African-American. Dixon—now viewed as a distinctly inferior artist—instead portrayed *white* victims of the Reconstruction in *The Leopard's Spots* (1902) and *The Clansman* (1905); and, declared Chesnutt in 1916, he "made a fortune prostituting his talent to ignoble uses."[4] That his anti-African-American perspective, rather than Chesnutt's point of view, struck a responsive chord was confirmed again in 1915 when *The Clansman* served as the base-text for the silent film *Birth of a Nation*.[5]

A later measure of the kind will be seen in Chesnutt's correspondence begun in 1920 concerning the cinematic adaptations given his

[1] See Ken Johnson, "The Contemporaneous Response to Charles W. Chesnutt: A Study of the Book Reviews," Ph.D. dissertation, Florida State University, 2000.

[2] When *The Marrow of Tradition* was published in mid-October 1901, the following sales for 1899–1900 had been recorded by Houghton, Mifflin & Co. (Houghton, Mifflin papers, Houghton Library, Harvard University): *The Conjure Woman*, 1,775 copies; *The Wife of His Youth*, 1,579 copies. By the end of 1901, the firm had sold 82 and 103 more, respectively. In 1900, 2,001 copies of *The House Behind the Cedars* were purchased, with 993 more sold in 1901. Sales figures for *Frederick Douglass* are not available. It went through four printings (size unknown) by 1912, and Chesnutt commented in 1916 that it was "still in active demand" (see the 16 October 1916 letter to E. J. Lilly). But he never cited the number of copies purchased. The Doubleday, Page & Co. record for sales of *The Colonel's Dream*, too, is not available; but, in the same letter to E. J. Lilly, Chesnutt described it as "the least successful of my books."

[3] At the close of 1902, Houghton, Mifflin had sold 3,387 copies; there were no sales in 1903–5.

[4] See 16 October 1916 to E. J. Lilly.

[5] Despite his reverence for the U.S. Constitution and its amendments, Chesnutt actively sought to prevent screenings of this film. See 23 November 1915 to Frank B. Willis and 3 April 1917 to Munson A. Havens.

tragic mulatta novel *The House Behind the Cedars*. It was released as a silent film in 1925 and as a "talkie" retitled *Veiled Aristocrats* in 1932. From the African-American film-maker Oscar Micheaux he received a grand total of $400 in royalties—out of the $500 promised him. But, in fact, he banked even less than this since 25% went to the 1900 publisher of *House*: Chesnutt, that is, earned the present-day equivalent of roughly $4,500. No "white" interest in films of this sort was assumed by Micheaux, who showed them in theaters for African Americans only.

In the early 1850s, then, Harriet Beecher Stowe happened to be in the right place at the right time. From the late 1860s through the '80s, George Washington Cable and Albion W. Tourgée, too, would enjoy less spectacular but still considerable success as indignant literary advocates of the African-American cause. Chesnutt, demonstrably as talented as—if not a better writer than—his three predecessors, was not born too late, but he certainly missed his opportunity. His parents having moved from Cleveland back to their home town of Fayetteville, North Carolina, after the Civil War, Chesnutt in his youth proved an intellectual prodigy there and began teaching while in his teens. He then channeled his extraordinary energy not into writing but advancement as an educator in the 1870s and early '80s. Emigrating to Cleveland in 1883, he continued to perfect his self-taught stenographic skills, and he read law, passing the Ohio Bar examination in 1887. He discovered by 1889 that stenography, rather than a legal practice, was where the earnings were for an African American, and thereafter he gave his working hours to developing and maintaining a clientele. He devoted only his leisure time to the writing of short stories, several of which brought him national visibility as they appeared between 1887 and 1899 in the *Atlantic Monthly*.[6]

The personal success and moral influence he hoped for were, however, not to be obtained by periodical publications but by books, particularly novels. Unfortunately, while the husband and father of four was quite understandably sticking with the "main chance" for his and the family's social and economic advancement—his flourishing business—the clock was ticking. He was already in his forties when he appeared on the national stage in 1899–1905 as a book-author, at a time

[6]See William L. Andrews, "A Bibliography of Charles Chesnutt's Published Works," *The Literary Career of Charles W. Chesnutt* (Baton Rouge and London: Louisiana State University Press, 1980), 279–86.

when widespread curiosity about and sympathy for the predicament of the African American appear to have been exhausted and perhaps become as tiresome to hear or read about as the endlessly debated import tariff and gold-to-silver ratio currency questions. Dead was the market for pro–African-American prose fiction of the kind that did not idealize "the good Negro" of yore in the manner of Thomas Nelson Page or picture him, à la Dixon, as the "big burly brute" intent upon not only social equality but inter-racial marriage and "black domination" in Southern political life. Again, the greater number of dominantly white book reviewers acknowledged Chesnutt's artistic prowess in his short stories and novels, and the more liberal celebrated the keen insight into "The Negro Problem" displayed by this "insider" and spokesman for the race. But, given Chesnutt's sales, that obviously carried little weight for a dominantly white readership not particularly interested in an African-American perspective on what it meant to be African-American.

"Success," of course, is a relative term. For example, in his post-1905 correspondence Chesnutt did not hesitate to refer to *The House Behind the Cedars* as the best-seller among his books, meaning *his* rather than *a* best-seller.[7] As is also clear in "Post-Bellum–Pre-Harlem," his 1930 essay concerning the publication of his first book in 1899, Chesnutt was fully aware of how remarkable his achievement was when viewed historically and in light of how poorly other African-American literary artists had fared in the nineteenth-century market-place.[8] By 1877, for example, Albery Allston Whitman had published two narrative poems of considerable length featuring non-white heroes dealing valiantly with the evils of slavery and abuses of Native Americans. Chesnutt was aware of him and his poetical narratives, but in 1896 even he could not remember Whitman's name or the titles of his major works when citing him in a letter describing African-American

[7]See 11 March 1912 to William H. Hudson where he relates that *House* is "still the most popular of my books and still has the largest sale." That year 67 copies of *House* were sold, while 19, 21, and 28 copies each of his other three Houghton, Mifflin volumes were purchased. *House* was out of print by 1918; and so Chesnutt later had to modify his claim, telling another correspondent in 1923 only that it is "my most popular work" (23 February 1923 to Carl Van Vechten).

[8]Chesnutt's essay appeared in a magazine whose subscribers were bibliophiles and literati: *Colophon*, 2, Part 5 (February 1931), n.p. Editor Elmer Adler invited Chesnutt to write the piece at the suggestion of Walter F. White; see 15 September 1930 to Elmer Adler, n. 1, and 15 November 1930 to Walter F. White, n. 2.

achievements in the arts and science.[9] The problem was that the mainstream American publishing industry was, in effect, a segregated one. Privately printed or produced by small commercial presses were the largely unadvertised and infrequently reviewed works of authors such as Harriet Jacobs, Whitman, William Easton, Frances E. W. Harper, and—before William Dean Howells sponsored him for publication by Dodd, Mead and Company in 1896—Paul Laurence Dunbar.

Chesnutt topped Dunbar when he crossed the color line in 1899 to be handled by presses superior to Dodd, Mead. Boston's Small, Maynard and Company published his *Frederick Douglass* in its "Beacon Biographies" series. The grand coup in Boston, though, was Chesnutt's winning the confidence of the most prestigious of American publishers, Houghton, Mifflin & Co. (later renamed Houghton Mifflin Company, as will be seen in Chesnutt's letters). In the short span of 1899–1901, it published no less than four of his books before reluctantly announcing, as it declined his manuscript for *The Colonel's Dream*, that it could not afford to continue marketing his unprofitable wares. Still, at this time, Chesnutt was the premier African-American novelist and short-story writer, he having bested Dunbar in both categories in the eyes of book reviewers and literary essayists. Thus, another distinguished publisher in New York City—Doubleday, Page & Co.—took a chance on him in 1905, giving Chesnutt another opportunity to prove himself a commercially viable author with *Dream*.[10]

[9]Chesnutt related that "a Texan has written an epic poem of more or less merit" in 1 February 1896 to S. Alice Haldeman, *"To Be an Author": Letters of Charles W. Chesnutt, 1889–1905*, ed. Joseph R. McElrath, Jr., and Robert C. Leitz, III (Princeton: Princeton University Press, 1997), 88; hereafter cited as *Letters*. McElrath and Leitz, too, could not name the poet, and James R. Hays first identified him in "Albery Allston Whitman (1851–1901), Epic Poet of African American and Native American Self-Determination," Ph.D. dissertation, Florida State University, 2000.

[10]In 1897–99, North Carolinian Walter Hines Page was Chesnutt's editor and mentor at *Atlantic Monthly* and in the offices of its publisher, Houghton, Mifflin. He took a special interest in Chesnutt, not only facilitating the publication of *The Conjure Woman* and *The Wife of His Youth* but counseling him at length as he developed the manuscript for *The House Behind the Cedars*. Page co-founded Doubleday, Page & Co. in late 1899; and, in 1905, he still had high hopes for the man who had once been his protégé. A less positive assessment of their relationship at the turn of the century was recalled with dismay by William Stanley Braithwaite in 1942: Chesnutt, Braithwaite related, was referred to in literary and publishing circles as "Page's darky" ("The House under Arcturus: An Autobiography," *Phylon*, 3 [Second Quarter 1942], 188).

When *The Marrow of Tradition* failed three years earlier, Chesnutt resigned himself to the notion that he could not afford pursuit of a full-time literary career. He had more or less withdrawn from stenographic work, living off of his savings in 1899–1901 as he gambled on producing a best-seller and lost. After returning to stenography and to writing on a part-time basis, he again saw a glimmer of hope for a commercial success, until the lackluster sales of *Dream* in 1905–6 proved the last straw. His expectations had again been raised: before the novel appeared in September 1905, Doubleday, Page had to do a second printing to accommodate the initial orders from booksellers. Then his hopes were dashed for the sixth time. Never thereafter does one see in his correspondence the suggestion that he might become a professional author. He would not submit another novelistic manuscript, "Paul Marchand, F.M.C.," to a publisher until 1921 when he was in his sixties.

This is not to say that Chesnutt stopped writing before the early 1920s or thereafter, though illness radically curtailed his activities in 1932. Even as the bad news about *Dream* was being confirmed in 1906, he had his pen in hand. As if addicted to the ideal of being a novelist somehow destined for grander—or, at least more—success, he will be seen relating in a July 1906 letter to his wife, then vacationing in England, that he had stayed home from the office for the day to work on an unnamed novel.[11] Through 1931 he produced new short stories, essays, and speeches; and, in addition to completing the manuscript "Paul Marchand, F.M.C.," he was working on another in 1928, "The Quarry." Neither was accepted by a publisher. These novels then joined four others that had met the same fate before 1906: they were filed away with "Mandy Oxendine," "The Rainbow Chasers," "A Business Career," and "Evelyn's Husband."

The publications of *Mandy Oxendine* and *The Quarry* in 1997 and 1998, respectively,[12] measure the now well-advanced "rediscovery" of Charles W. Chesnutt. That two university presses were at the same time working with different scholars to produce from manuscript competing 1998 and 1999 editions of *Paul Marchand, F.M.C.,*[13] for the

[11]See 5 July 1906 to Susan Utley Chesnutt.

[12]Ed. Charles Hackenberry (Champaign and Chicago: University of Illinois Press, 1997); ed. Dean McWilliams (Princeton: Princeton University Press, 1999).

[13]Ed. Matthew Wilson (Jackson: University Press of Mississippi, 1998); ed. Dean McWilliams (Princeton: Princeton University Press, 1999).

same expanding readership is, however, the more accurate indicator of a perceived importance greater than Chesnutt ever enjoyed during his lifetime. Virtually all of his short stories have been available in collections since 1974;[14] *The Journals of Charles W. Chesnutt* appeared in print in 1993,[15] and the first collection of his letters, *"To Be an Author": Letters of Charles W. Chesnutt, 1889–1905*, in 1997.[16] *Charles W. Chesnutt: Essays and Speeches* gathered his non-fiction in 1999;[17] and the history of the Chesnutt revival itself was the subject of a book published in 1999.[18]

True, Chesnutt lived to see what proved a distinctly minor revival, an "uncovering" of his publications he termed it, in his own time. In 1926, Carl Van Vechten made much of his art in his novel *Nigger Heaven*. The N.A.A.C.P. acknowledged his achievement with its Spingarn Award in 1928; and one of his books, *The Conjure Woman*, was ushered back into print in 1929. A yet more gratifying development occurred in 1930 when *New York Times* literary critic John Chamberlain began his "The Negro as Writer" essay for the *Bookman* thus: "Negro fiction in America properly commences with Charles Waddell Chesnutt, a Clevelander who is still living, but whose writing falls mainly into the period of the 'eighties and 'nineties."[19] Yet, when compared with the outpouring of books and articles on Chesnutt that began in the late 1960s, this earlier revival may more properly be termed a lapse in neglect.

Before Chesnutt could truly receive his just due, two historical developments that have occurred since the 1930s were required. The first had to do with another way in which the word anachronism relates to Chesnutt, as will be seen in how John Chamberlain felt he had to criticize at the same time as he celebrated Chesnutt in 1930. Declaring that Chesnutt-the-perceptive-truth-teller "blinks nothing," Chamberlain

[14]Short stories that had not previously appeared in books were collected by Sylvia Lyons Render in *The Short Fiction of Charles W. Chesnutt* (Washington, D.C.: Howard University Press, 1974).

[15]Ed. Richard Brodhead (Durham, N.C., and London: Duke University Press, 1993); hereafter cited as *Journals*.

[16]See n. 9.

[17]Ed. McElrath, Leitz, and Jesse S. Crisler (Stanford: Stanford University Press, 1999).

[18]*Critical Essays on Charles W. Chesnutt*, ed. McElrath (Boston: G. K. Hall, 1999).

[19]*Bookman*, 70 (February 1930), 603–11.

echoed the liberal white book-reviewers of the turn of the century who appreciated Chesnutt's penetrating analyses of race relations and racial discrimination. But unlike them, Chamberlain was uncomfortable lauding an author whose style, it had to be confessed, was dismayingly out-of-date, a lamentable throwback to the mid-nineteenth century. Chamberlain signalled that one has to suppress as best he can his aesthetic sense—"blank out" what he can of Chesnutt's primitive story-telling mannerisms—in order to take the positive measure of the man:

> One goes back to the archaic, quaintly flavored novels and stories of this pioneer with mingled appreciation and aesthetic blankness. Most of the Chesnutt plots hinge on such adventitious circumstances that the works of Thomas Hardy seem the very soul of the natural by comparison, but even in the stretches where the antique machinery creaks the loudest one reads with nothing but admiration for Chesnutt as a man. If his plot structure is definitely dated, the fault resides with the white models with which he worked in that era when the novel was designed to tell a story at all costs; and the spectacle of a Negro of the time working with any models at all and producing fiction with many good points is sufficient to compel applause.

While historically important as a pioneer in the African-American literary tradition and as a man who heroically rose above the limitations associated with being "a Negro of the time," Chesnutt as an artist displaying the shortcomings of pre-Modernist writers was dismissed by Chamberlain in much the same way as were other "period" artists such as too-sedate William Dean Howells, at one extreme, and too-flamboyant Frank Norris at another. Thus, before subsequent commentators could move beyond Chamberlain, toward our present, much less qualified appreciation of Chesnutt's art, the passage of time and the waning of Modernist prejudice against superseded literary conventions were essential. Requisite, that is, was historical distance.

Twentieth-century critics and the readers influenced by them who were thrall to Modernist literary values savaged, when they did not ignore, works that may generally be termed Victorian in their narrative voices, characterizations, plot constructions, and too obviously didactic authorial intentions. *Uncle Tom's Cabin* is a fustian case in point: when, in 1941, F. O. Matthiessen defined the "American Renaissance" of 1850–55, *Cabin* was *mentioned* only once.[20] But Matthiessen was kinder than most in his generation since Stowe, in fact, offended Mod-

---

[20]*American Renaissance: Art and Expression in the Age of Emerson and Whitman* (London and New York: Oxford University Press, 1941), 67. Stowe is referred to only as a best-selling popular writer.

ernist taste, and her "faults" were exactly the same as those of Chesnutt. Chesnutt was never a progressive artist, even by 1900 standards, and Chamberlain's loyalties were to writers like John Steinbeck. In 1936, when reviewing *In Dubious Battle*, he dubbed Steinbeck "the most versatile master of narrative now writing in the United States."[21] However, in a post-Modernism context—now, that is—*Cabin* is no longer anathema, nor is it any longer an occasion for quips and parodies among the smart set on university campuses. Its resurrection and the rehabilitation of its reputation are, simply stated, *faits accomplis*. What has made the difference—as it did when Felix Mendelssohn rediscovered J. S. Bach and T. S. Eliot decided that England's Metaphysical poets did not merit the disdain heaped upon them in the eighteenth century—is time, historical detachment, and the ability to recognize and appreciate the conventions of "period" art. The rule recently applied to French Academic painting of the nineteenth century, to the benefit of the once-scorned William Adolphe Bouguereau and Jean Léon Gérôme, is as simple as it is fair: given what the conventions employed were, how well were they employed?

With the beginning of the twenty-first century, Chesnutt has been fair-mindedly reevaluated as a moralistic romancer, rather than a modern realist, who exercised his imagination in the manner of other romance-writers such as Harriet Beecher Stowe, George Washington Cable, and Albion W. Tourgée—and, on the other hand, he has been recognized as a wit who sometimes displayed in his short stories a comedic genius worthy of comparison with Washington Irving's and Charles Dickens's.[22] Even his prophetic invocations of scripture have been forgiven him, given his A.M.E.Z. and, later, Episcopalian loyalties, as well as the now-accepted fact that his Bible-based declarations of principle and biblical imagery are part and parcel of the mid-Victorian cultural traditions in which he participated.

The other development, which made historical distancing much easier to achieve, was the Civil Rights movement of the 1950s and '60s, and particularly one of its spin-off benefits, the demand for a recovery and respectful interpretive reconstruction of African-American

---

[21]"Books of the Times," *New York Times*, 28 January 1936, 17.

[22]See McElrath's call for further refinement of the definitions of Chesnutt's historical situation as an author and his relationship to particular literary schools of his time: "Why Charles W. Chesnutt Is Not a Realist," *American Literary Realism*, 32 (Winter 2000), 91–108.

cultural history. The Chesnutt canon was, to say the least, apropos. Rapidly brought back into print was his prose fiction delineating ante-bellum plantation life via the recollections and charmingly pointed exaggerations of Uncle Julius McAdoo, the mulatto raconteur featured in *The Conjure Woman.* Spanning the Reconstruction, Redemption, and Jim Crow eras were the short stories and novels in which Chesnutt portrayed the conditions known by freedmen in the position of serfs, by upwardly mobile black entrepreneurs heeding the advice given by Booker T. Washington for advancement, and by their white allies and antagonists. Many of the essays and speeches recently brought together for the first time in a single volume reveal a Chesnutt who sedulously researched various aspects of "The Negro Problem" from the early 1880s on—protesting disfranchisement, peonage, and like violations of the civil rights of black citizens afforded by the Fourteenth and Fifteenth Amendments of the U.S. Constitution. His positive theme was that the rights conferred by these and the Thirteenth Amendment were absolute—no matter how interpreted by state legislatures and the courts to the disadvantage of African Americans. His plea was for understanding, compassion, and justice.

These non-fiction works also addressed both African-American cultural history and African-American contributions to American culture per se before and during the Harlem Renaissance. Complementing them in the present volume are the post-1905 letters to and about literary luminaries such as James Weldon Johnson, W. E. B. Du Bois, Jessie R. Fauset, Walter F. White, and Langston Hughes. But, most important, perhaps, for those wanting to reconstruct the whole of the African-American experience between 1858 and 1932, Chesnutt's letters and other writings reflect what it meant to be a sophisticated male, dedicated to the goal of integration and opposed to all "race pride" movements including black nationalism, who found ways to blunt and even transcend many of the effects of race prejudice to become a representative member of a truly understudied socio-economic subgroup, the very existence of which had received by the 1960s remarkably little attention from whites and much less than one might expect from African Americans themselves.[23] It would be difficult to find another business-

---

[23]Since the 1960s, remarkable progress has been made in this regard: see, for example, Willard B. Gatewood, *Aristocrats of Color: The Black Elite, 1880–1920* (Bloomington: Indiana University Press, 1990), and Kenneth L. Kusmer, *A Ghetto Takes Shape: Black Cleveland, 1870–1930* (Urbana: University of Illinois Press,

man of his time who so fully documented what it meant to be a member of America's black bourgeoisie.

Like the great man he lionized in *Frederick Douglass,* and like Booker T. Washington, who several times in his post-1905 letters invited Chesnutt to be his guest at his summer home in Huntington, Long Island, Chesnutt at the time of his death enjoyed an enviable lifestyle: he wanted for little after 1889. When relating in an 11 January 1927 letter that his earning power had diminished as he approached his seventies, Chesnutt told W. E. B. Du Bois: "For many years I made more money and lived better than any colored man in my city." But, in fact, his situation then was hardly an impoverished one. While reading his later complaints to several correspondents about the losses he had suffered because of the 1929 stock market crash, one will note in a 1931 letter that the Chesnutts were not quite so stressed as one might initially imagine. They took a maid with them when they left their 14-room house on Lamont Street—complete with a garage for their automobile—and vacationed for no fewer than nine weeks at their summer house in Idlewild, Michigan.[24] Put another way, by contemporaneous African-American standards and those of recent immigrants having experience of the kind represented by Upton Sinclair in *The Jungle* (1906), the gentleman who delighted in fishing for small-mouth bass at Idlewild was fabulously wealthy. Further, almost as well-off were many of the African Americans with whom he corresponded.

True, earlier in the century both Booker T. Washington and W. E. B. Du Bois gave much attention to signs of an emerging black middle-class, Washington with anecdotes based upon personal experience and Du Bois with statistics having to do with earnings and increasing rates of property ownership. But the sympathetic emphasis and focus in the twentieth century were dominantly upon the poor, the neglected, the dispossessed and disfranchised among African Americans. Chesnutt, who never fit into any of these categories, also wrote and spoke about this black underclass and how its status was being perpetuated. What he was uniquely qualified to do for his contemporaries, however, was facilitate empathy for blacks of his own upward-bound class and stimulate sympathy for those who had risen above the mass of blacks yet had good reason to speculate that their ambitions could not be so fully

---

1976). The latter is valuable for a second reason: it describes Chesnutt in the context of local black political, and especially civil-rights, activism of the period.

[24]See 17 November 1931 to Jessie Parks.

realized as those of their white counterparts—unless they "passed for white" or emigrated to Europe. What Chesnutt was also able to do, for us today, was provide in the letters his daughter Helen and he preserved a window through which we can see and appreciate what middle-class African-American life, as he knew it, was like in 1906–32.

A detailed portrait of Charles W. Chesnutt as he pursued literary fame, fortune, and ameliorative influence on American life up to 1906 was made possible by the voluminous correspondence from which *"To Be an Author": Letters of Charles W. Chesnutt, 1889–1905* was culled in 1997. The phrase quoted in the title was Chesnutt's in March 1881 when he declared to his journal, "It is the dream of my life—to be an author!"[25] Documented were the steps he took to realize this dream that once bordered upon being a grand obsession. Seen thus was his rise to and fall from grace in the eyes of the American publishing industry. The present collection of post-1905 letters does not permit the limning of so grandiose a goal or so dramatic a conception of himself motivating Chesnutt. For one thing, Chesnutt never again considered risking his profitable and highly respectable vocation for the sake of what clearly had to remain an avocation. For another, this eminently practical and disciplined man in middle age put his prose fiction writing in perspective in the same way that he had already his other interests, including his civic service activities in behalf of both black and white individuals and organizations. Stenographic transcription at business meetings and organizational conferences, court reporting and the taking of depositions, the preparation of legal papers by a stenographer especially trustworthy because of his study of the law—these were his full-time responsibilities until, in the early 1920s, he chose not to retire but to lighten his work-load by entering into a partnership with Helen C. Moore. Thus his surviving correspondence from 1906 and thereafter may disappoint readers with hagiographic inclinations who would like to find in Chesnutt a successor to his own heroes Frederick Douglass, John Brown, and Charles Sumner. They will look in vain in his post-1905 letters for justification of Frances Richardson Keller's choice of title for her 1978 biography *An American Crusade.*[26] More appropriate for Chesnutt than crusader is the epithet William

[25]*Journals,* 154; see also 124–26 and 139–40.
[26]*An American Crusade: The Life of Charles Waddell Chesnutt* (Provo, Utah: Brigham Young University Press, 1978).

Dean Howells chose in 1901 when deeming Booker T. Washington "An Exemplary Citizen."[27]

There were only 24 hours in each day for Chesnutt, many of which were given to his business and, as day followed day, the remainders were divided among family affairs, keeping up with his reading, writing fiction and non-fiction, public speaking and other forms of public service, and participation in clubs and associations both related and unrelated to race. As will be seen, Chesnutt served the good cause as public-spirited men in harmony with Progressive Era ideals did in the early twentieth century; indeed, he was a touchstone in this respect.[28] But he was not a minister who could dovetail political activism with conventional ministerial duties, a professor at a black college or university where research and professional service job requirements might be satisfied similarly, nor a full-time employee of the N.A.A.C.P. like William Pickens or Walter F. White. He was a professional of another kind and a civilian, so to speak, in the "war" against racial discrimination.

That Chesnutt's time was fully occupied by a wide variety of interests and obligations and that, for all of the gregariousness he displays in his letters, he was essentially a private person were cause for complaint by some in Cleveland's black community before 1906. Why was he not more "involved," like the editor of the *Cleveland Gazette*, Harry C. Smith, or Republican power-broker George A. Myers, or his cousin with a distinguished political career, John Patterson Green? His perceived standoffishness was addressed by Nahum D. Brascher of the *Cleveland Journal* when he reviewed *The Colonel's Dream* in 1905.[29] Chesnutt, he informed his black readership,

> is misunderstood by a great many people and consequently unjustly criticized. The criticism is for the most part local and due to the fact that Mr. Chesnutt is not a "mixer," in the political sense of that term. He is seldom seen at any gatherings among colored people and, for this reason, there is an impression that he is an enemy of the race and not a friend. Nothing could be farther from right. The race has no truer friend or better informed member on current conditions than Charles W. Chesnutt. Whether he is a "mixer" or not, is none of our business. Every man has a right to choose

[27]"An Exemplary Citizen" was the title of Howells's article published in *North American Review*, 173 (June 1901), 282–83.

[28]See Ernestine Williams Pickens, *Charles W. Chesnutt and the Progressive Movement* (New York: Pace University Press, 1994).

[29]"The Colonel's Dream," *Cleveland Journal*, 9 December 1905, 1.

his company. Mr. Chesnutt is a national man and not a local man; our esteem for him should be based on his national faithfulness to our cause. Through all his books, essays and addresses, as a member of the "Committee of Twelve," and in divers quiet ways, Mr. Chesnutt is loyal to the race.

How "loyal" he was—even at the national level—may again be questioned, especially in the early pages of this volume, if one has expectations like those of the readers Brascher chided. Chesnutt's preoccupation with "the race" and discrimination against its members will be seen throughout his letters. Yet, with so many other irons in the fire, his direct involvements with local and national groups of reformers were distinctly occasional.

In April 1905 Chesnutt was elected to membership on the Committee of Twelve for the Advancement of the Interests of the Negro Race, replacing W. E. B. Du Bois. How should we rate his performance? The correspondence through 1910 tells us that he was certainly not one of the leaders originating or implementing strategies for dealing with matters such as a proposed disfranchisement amendment to Maryland's constitution. He does not always answer queries from the Committee's secretary, Hugh M. Browne, in a timely fashion, this sometimes necessitating the writing of a second and, once, a third letter to him; and, on the whole, Chesnutt functions as no more than a part-time consultant, typically approving the decisions of the Committee members or authorizing others such as Booker T. Washington and Browne to do what they think best. When this individualist truly shines, it is not as a member of a committee nor as a representative of an organization such as the Cleveland branch of the N.A.A.C.P., but in situations in which he is the prime mover, as in 1913 when he manages Cleveland's Perry Centennial Commission's recognition of the African-American contribution to the winning of the War of 1812, or in 1914 when he solicits support from whites for the establishment of a settlement house in or near Cleveland's black neighborhood, or in 1917 when he personally investigates how African-American soldiers are being treated at their segregated training camp.

Later, when corresponding with the national office of the N.A.A.C.P., he projected a much more dynamic image than he did when a member of the Committee of Twelve, particularly when he was dealing with Walter F. White—though, again, he was functioning as an *ad hoc* consultant, either asked for information or requested to write public officials about matters of importance. For example, he was undeniably "loyal to the race" when he had the opportunity to aid a white with whom he presently did business and with whom he had maintained a friendly relationship and cordial correspondence for years. Newton D. Baker, the Mayor of Cleveland in 1912–16 and President Woodrow Wilson's Secretary of War in 1916–21, once sided with Chesnutt in opposition to a bill prohibiting inter-racial marriage in Ohio, invited him to contribute to the planning of the Perry Centennial celebration in Cleveland, and three times appointed him delegate to the National Conference on Charities and Corrections. In 1932 Baker was a possible U.S. Supreme Court nominee, and Walter F. White wrote Chesnutt concerning the position that the N.A.A.C.P. should take. While professing his reluctance to do so, Chesnutt on 10 February 1932 scotched any possible support from the N.A.A.C.P. on the grounds that Baker, whose origin was Southern, had privately expressed points of view that were inimical to African Americans. The "Southernness" of particular individuals was forgiven by Chesnutt on many occasions, but never when it even mildly recalled the barbaric attitudes he associated with the North Carolina of his youth.

Charles W. Chesnutt, F.M.C., no matter how affluent and acceptable to the whites among whom he moved so agreeably, never forgot what had transpired since the Reconstruction, and he never got over his intense dislike for Southerners who could not get over their intense dislike for African Americans—among whom his own wife and children were ineradicably numbered. The problem was less intense in the North. Still, when the Chesnutts vacationed at Idlewild, Michigan, they did so in a black summer resort locale. Chesnutt's genius—or his craft, or a cunning that brings to mind the congenial duplicity of Uncle Julius McAdoo—lay in negotiating for himself and his family a place on a high ground where vexations were minimal and the benefits of intercourse with both blacks and whites maximal. Indelibly African-American, his wife and children lived in dominantly white neighborhoods and were members of a white Episcopalian parish. But, not forgetting his roots, Chesnutt wrote checks for a local A.M.E.Z. church with which he maintained a relationship. Mrs. Chesnutt entertained fellow blacks at her home; she was also a member of a preponderantly white ladies social group that met regularly, the Brenton Circle. Son Edwin was graduated from Harvard, and Smith College was the alma mater of daughters Ethel and Helen; but all three were employed for varying lengths of time at Tuskegee Institute. Chesnutt was elected to an all-white Chamber of Commerce in 1912; when speaking for the local and national African-American communities, he graciously persuaded the Chamber to reject the recommendations of a subcommittee intent upon restricting black immigration to Cleveland in 1926. He knew how to get what he wanted for himself and his family—and what was morally right in this case—without burning his bridges behind him. In short, Chesnutt did not become a thrall to rage or prey to depression but pragmatically assessed the woefully imperfect world before him and, with his family, moved back and forth across the color line, implementing a program for obtaining and keeping the best that was within reach in his time.

Actually, the program in question was one articulated by another distinguished African American of his generation. The steps were: educate oneself; learn a marketable skill; put money in the bank; purchase property; and display congeniality, reliability, and probity in all of one's dealings with others. Chesnutt went beyond this, becoming a capable francophone, a connoisseur of high art, a philosophical adept, a literary man, and even a bibliophile admitted to the select company of Cleveland's Rowfant Club before which he delivered several papers on subjects such as the life and writings of poet François Villon and of novelist George Meredith. Booker T. Washington's plan for the advancement of the African American certainly did not include these extras; in fact, he advised against them in *Up from Slavery* (1901) and elsewhere as objectives likely to distract one from the accomplishment of the more basic requirements for obtaining the respect of whites and, ultimately, full civil rights. On this and other issues, Chesnutt and he disagreed, and their exchange of cordial but argumentative letters, begun at the turn of the century, continued into 1908—by which time they had fully aired their differences and amiability had become the constant.

One of the curious developments in mainstream African-American history is that Booker T. Washington and, after his death in 1915, his moderate successors did not *use* Chesnutt both as a paradigm for what was possible by way of integration for African Americans and as the proof positive that the myth of racial inferiority had been overturned. Chesnutt's earlier letters show that he "wanted it all"; the later letters in this volume repeatedly display the fact that he had earned the realization of his fondest dreams when a young man, save that of fame as a world-class novelist. Given Washington's work-ethic emphasis, it is remarkable that neither he nor other Bookerites held up Chesnutt as an inspirational icon. It was not until 1952 that the first monument of the kind was erected when *Charles Waddell Chesnutt: Pioneer of the Color Line* was written by his daughter Helen.[30]

Unfortunate also was another development, having to do with a falling out with William Dean Howells in late 1901, when Howells read *The Marrow of Tradition* and then wrote what Chesnutt took to be a negative review.[31] The two men never met or corresponded with each other again.[32] Howells, who would become a member of the N.A.A.C.P., had long been highly sympathetic to African Americans in his novels and in his literary essays. Had he lived past 1920, and had he come to know Chesnutt better, he would very likely have had to recant his declaration to a fellow-white novelist: after reading *Marrow*, he wrote to Henry Blake Fuller, "Good Lord! How such a negro must hate us."[33] Earlier, in 1901, when eulogizing Booker T. Washington as "an exemplary citizen" and before he reacted to the author of *Marrow* as a man with a chip on his shoulder, he bestowed a modicum of praise on Chesnutt as well.[34] But, had Howells had the opportunity to read the letters in the present volume, it is likely that he would have deemed Chesnutt the more significant figure. Washington, like Douglass, was a larger-than-life individual whose calling and life's work separated him from the common man, black and white, rich and poor. Chesnutt hoped once to rise to such an exalted, heroic status as a writer, but by 1906 circumstances had brought him down to earth where, as he pursued the prosaic career of stenographer, he more credibly modeled the attainable ideal that Howells envisioned for African Americans in a truly egalitarian society of the future.

Indeed, the "exemplary citizen" who wrote the letters in the present volume was, and is, a model figure for individuals of all ancestries and persuasions.

[30](Chapel Hill: University of North Carolina Press, 1952).

[31]"A Psychological Counter-Current in Recent Fiction," *North American Review*, 173 (December 1901), 872–88.

[32]The Howells-Chesnutt correspondence is treated in full in *Letters* and has been analyzed at length twice. See William L. Andrews, "William Dean Howells and Charles W. Chesnutt: Criticism and Race Fiction in the Age of Booker T. Washington," *American Literature*, 48 (November 1976), 327–39, and McElrath, "W. D. Howells and Race: Charles W. Chesnutt's Disappointment of the Dean," *Nineteenth-Century Literature*, 51 (March 1997), 474–99.

[33]10 November 1901 to Fuller, *Selected Letters of W. D. Howells, Volume 4: 1892–1901*, ed. Thomas Wortham *et al.*; vol. 24 of *A Selected Edition of W. D. Howells* (Boston: Twayne Publishers, 1981), 274.

[34] See n. 27.

An Exemplary Citizen

——◆——

Letters of Charles W. Chesnutt
1906–1932

To Booker T. Washington

January 8, 1906

Dear Dr. Washington:[1]

I have been very much gratified at observing the success of the campaign against the Poe Amendment in Maryland,[2] and in believing that the efforts of the Committee of Twelve had contributed to that end.[3] The Garrison celebration was a well-deserved tribute to the memory of the great anti-slavery agitator.[4] I suppose you saw what the *Independent* said last week about Garrison.[5]

I think you are competent to judge about the advisability of deferring the meeting to which you refer, and am quite willing to adopt your suggestion in regard to the matter. You are much better advised on the general race situation than I, and ought to be able to decide wisely when and where special efforts should be put forth.[6]

Yours very truly,

TCU: TNF

[1]Booker T. Washington (1856–1915), educator and key spokesperson for African Americans since the 1890s, was the founder of the Tuskegee Institute (1881) and served as its principal through the end of his life. Chesnutt's ongoing and sometimes argumentative correspondence with Washington was formally initiated in 1900; and they had by 1906 met several times, for example, when Chesnutt visited Tuskegee in February 1901 to attend the tenth annual Tuskegee Negro Conference (see "A Visit to Tuskegee," *Essays and Speeches*: 145–51). Their relationship involved more than a mutual interest in the condition of African Americans: daughter Ethel Perry Chesnutt Williams Beaman (1879–1958) taught history for a year at Tuskegee (1901–2); daughter Helen Maria Chesnutt (1880–1969) visited the Institute for a month in the summer of 1901, staying with the Washingtons; and son Edwin J. Chesnutt (1883–1939) served as one of Washington's assistants (1910–12). Chesnutt, in turn, was a regular financial contributor to Tuskegee and aided Washington and his representatives with fund-raising in Cleveland.

[2]John Prentiss Poe (1836–1909), dean of the University of Maryland Law School, drafted an amendment to Maryland's constitution which was intended to disfranchise African Americans. It was accepted by the General Assembly in 1904 and presented to the voters in the fall of 1905. It was defeated by nearly 35,000 votes, largely because of the efforts of Harry S. Cummings (1886–1917), an African-American lawyer and later politician in Baltimore who organized the Colored Voters Suffrage League against the amendment.

[3]Chesnutt became a member of the Committee of Twelve for the Advancement of the Interests of the Negro Race in 1905 (see 14 July 1906 to Hugh M. Browne, n. 1). The organization was formed in New York City in January

1904 by Booker T. Washington and his supporters. Washington served as chair, and Archibald H. Grimké (1849–1930) was treasurer. To defeat the proposed Maryland amendment, the Committee published and distributed in 1904–5 Grimké's *Why Disfranchisement Is Bad* and two unsigned pamphlets, *Voting Instructions to Maryland Voters* and *To the Colored Men of Voting Age in the Southern States: What a Colored Man Should Do to Vote.*

[4]On 10 December 1905 in New York City, Washington participated in a celebration of the hundredth anniversary of the birth of William Lloyd Garrison (1805–79), the abolitionist editor of *The Liberator*. Speaking also at Bethel Methodist Episcopal Church on West 25th Street was T. Thomas Fortune (1856–1918), editor of the *New York Age*. To commemorate the event, the Committee of Twelve published a leaflet entitled *Garrison Centenary, 1805–1905* (1905).

[5]Chesnutt here implies his disagreement with the editorial entitled "The Eulogies of Garrison," *Independent,* 59 (28 December 1905): 1550–51. It chided admirers for rewriting history by giving Garrison more credit than he merited.

[6]Chesnutt responds to Washington's letter of 2 January 1906 (TNF). Washington asked him to approve his decision to cancel a planned Committee of Twelve-sponsored meeting in New York City with the heads of various religious organizations, and he suggested that the Committee should instead report on its activities in February at the District of Columbia meeting of the Executive Committee of the Negro Young People's Christian and Educational Congress. Washington invited Chesnutt to express himself "freely and frankly" on this matter.

To Asa Z. Hall

February 2, 1906.

Dear Sir:—

I wish to thank you very much for the complimentary copy sent to me, with your card, of your novel *Stanton White*.[1] I have read it with much interest and pleasure, as one more note of protest against the chorus of detraction and defamation which has characterized the unkind, ungenerous, unchristian crusade against the common manhood rights of the Negro, which has been conducted so vociferously by a little clique of Southern leaders who have been poisoning the minds of the American people for the last ten or fifteen years.[2]

I hope the book will have a reception and a sale which its literary quality as well as its high moral purpose ought to warrant.

Sincerely yours,

TCU: TNF

[1]Asa Zadel Hall (1875–1965) was a Baptist minister and physician who, under the pseudonym of Harold Edson, wrote this 1905 novel subtitled *A Romance of the New South*.

[2]The Northern narrator of the novel, Harold Edson, visits the South with his college friend Stanton White. Their purpose is "to study at first hand the social conditions of the negro, and . . . to try to discover means for the uplift of this race." Edson describes their encounters with viciously racist whites who believe that "the negro is a beast" and with more liberal ones genuinely interested in helping African Americans to improve their lot. Edson recognizes the humanity of the African Americans he meets and the need to ensure their education and their opportunities for economic and social advancement. White has privately maintained the same point of view for good reason: near the novel's end he announces to a surprised Edson that he is a mulatto.

To Booker T. Washington

February 5, 1906.

My dear Dr. Washington:—

Miss Mary Kline, daughter of Mr. Virgil P. Kline, whom you know (I saw from the paper the other day that his salary as attorney for the Standard Oil is $50,000 a year), called at my office the other day to make a request of me, in fact two requests.[1]

There is being erected in this city a large private school, the Hathaway Brown school, and Miss Kline is one of a committee of the alumnae of the school who have agreed to raise the sum of $15,000 toward the new structure.[2] The greater part of it they have already secured by subscriptions, but they wish to get the remainder by bringing out a special magazine, which they hope to issue about a month hence. There will be an edition of eight or ten thousand copies, and it will circulate among the best people in this and other communities.

Miss Kline's requests were these: first, (probably out of courtesy and in order to pave the way for her other request) that I should make a contribution to the proposed magazine, which I promised to do;[3] second, whether I would write to you and ask if you would do the same. I know that you are a busy man, that your time is fully occupied, and that your words when you choose to put them on paper have a money value. But what could I do? I could only say that I would write to you and ask whether if you found time during the next few weeks, you could write something for Miss Kline's magazine. The subject is left entirely to yourself; she suggested that something about your school or about education would be entirely acceptable. It would give you an opportunity for a good ad in a quarter where it might be of service to your work, and it would confer a favor upon certain people who have the means to reciprocate.

Kindly let me know how you feel about this, whether you have the time or the inclination to do it, and oblige

Yours sincerely,

P.S. I mailed this letter to Tuskegee, but thinking you may be in New York, I send you this duplicate there. C.W.C.[4]

TLU, autograph postscript: DLC

[1]Mary Kline Pope (1877–1964) was in early 1906 the president of the newly organized alumnae association of Cleveland's Hathaway Brown School, from which she was graduated in 1896. Virgil P. Kline (1844–1917), of the law firm Kline, Carr, Tolles & Goff, was a long-term friend of Chesnutt's. In 1887, after he was admitted to the Ohio Bar, Chesnutt was employed by Kline's firm (then Henderson, Kline and Tolles). Washington had met Kline two years earlier during a visit to Cleveland; after making a presentation at Central High School on 13 January 1904, he was entertained at Kline's home.

[2]The school was founded in 1876 as an adjunct to Brooks Military School. Patrons had recently erected a sizeable building on Logan Street at East 97th and were now seeking to expand its facilities. Chesnutt's relationship with the school dated back to 2 February 1899. Its fourth owner and headmistress, Mary E. Spencer (?–1914), arranged for Chesnutt to read his then unpublished short story "The March of Progress" to a group of students and parents that evening.

[3]The sole issue of *Hathaway Brown Magazine*, dated 1 April 1906, went on sale on 25 April at 50¢ per copy. Chesnutt contributed the short story "The Prophet Peter" (pp. 51–66).

[4]In Washington's absence from Tuskegee, his secretary, Emmett J. Scott (1873–1957), responded to Chesnutt on 7 February 1906, expressing his confidence that Washington would want to "comply" with Chesnutt's request and relating that he would "see that the article is forthcoming at an early date" (TNF). Three days later, on 10 February 1906, Washington himself wrote Chesnutt that, once he returned to Tuskegee, he would be in a better position to tell him what he might do regarding Kline's request (TNF). Finally, with a brief note to Chesnutt dated 9 March 1906 (TNF), Washington enclosed a four-page typescript entitled "The Negro Rural School," which appeared in *Hathaway Brown Magazine* on pp. 68–70.

To Edwin J. Chesnutt

February 5, 1906

. . . Your mother has written a letter to Mrs. Hackley, which I enclose.[1] Please seal it and send it to her address, which you probably have. We were pleased to know that you had run across her, as she is a cheerful soul, will doubtless prove a congenial spirit, and tide you over any little period of loneliness or depression.[2]

I hope you had a pleasant passage, and that you are enjoying the sights of London. Keep your health always first in mind. It is that for which I sent you abroad. Have as good a time as you like, within the limits of strict economy, remembering that I am not carrying you, but merely boosting you along. . . .

We missed you very much for a day or two, but are getting a little bit adjusted to your absence. The whole family has become wonderfully fond of you since you left; in fact, I can scarcely restrain them from starting off to Europe immediately to look you up. Doubtless they will all swarm over during the summer. Much love and best wishes. . . .

Pioneer: 217

[1]Following his graduation from Harvard in June 1905, Chesnutt's only son, Edwin, failed to find suitable employment, despite numerous inquiries on his behalf made by his father. He was suffering from what Helen Chesnutt termed "a chronic catarrhal complaint" (*Pioneer*: 216). Edwin's sensitivity to racial prejudice may have had something to do with his sojourn in Europe (see 20 July 1906 to Edwin); but the trip abroad was financed by his parents primarily for the purpose of restoring him to health. Edwin sailed on 2 February, and Chesnutt is replying to his letter posted via a pilot boat.

[2]E. Azaliah Hackley, a friend of the Chesnutts, was in transit to France when Edwin met her. She was bound for Paris where she intended to study voice under Jean de Reszke (1850–1925), a distinguished Polish operatic singer and voice instructor.

To Little, Brown & Co.

February 17, 1906.

Dear Sirs:—

I thank you for your courtesy in sending me a copy of Mr. Reed's book, *The Brothers' War*.[1] I regret that it does not commend itself to me, nor could I commend it to others. Whatever quality of temperate statement it may possess in some regards, is counterbalanced by its extremely unjust and ungenerous attitude toward the Negro, to the writing down of whom the book is mainly devoted. It is the same old wolf in sheep's clothing. In spite of the legend on the cover, I do not think that 50 years hence, any one will write, and I feel quite sure that no one will publish a book devoted mainly to the justification of slavery, the glorification of the Ku Klux Klan, and a deification of Jefferson Davis and the gang of traitors who sought to destroy this Republic and perpetuate human slavery.[2]

I think the Negroes of this country are making very great progress, under great disadvantages, and that a very large part of the ninety-five per cent. whom Mr. Reed so uncharitably condemns to extinction, will win out in the struggle for life and larger opportunity.

Very truly yours,

TCU: TNF

[1]On 5 January 1906 (TNF), H[erbert]. F[ranklin]. J[enkins]. (1873–1941?), advertising manager for Little, Brown and Company, sought Chesnutt's opinion of this book by John C. Reed (1836–1910) concerning the Civil War. A copy was sent to Chesnutt under separate cover.

[2]Attempting to "explain the real causes and greater consequences of the bloody brothers' war," Reed addressed Northern readers: "Brothers and sisters of the north, you will never find your higher selves until you fitly admire the titanic fight which [Southerners] made for their sacred cause, and drop genuine tears over their heart-breaking failure." Chesnutt here responds to Reed's low opinion of abolitionists, those who promote "fusion" of the races, and the Fifteenth Amendment ("a stupendous blunder"). Reed championed the Ku Klux Klan as a widely misunderstood organization and heroic leaders of the South such as John C. Calhoun (1782–1850) and Jefferson Davis (1808–89).

To William H. Richards

February 21, 1906.

My dear Professor Richards:—

I am sorry I cannot be present at the Suffrage Meeting.[1] Were I there I could only say, as I shall ask you to say for me, that a disfranchised people is not a free people; the colored people of the United States, therefore, are not free. A people, part of whom are disfranchised, is not free; the American people, therefore, are not free. While the trend of political progress in every other civilized country of the world, has been, for the recent past, toward the extension of the suffrage, the

United States has gone backward. Seeking to disfranchise the Negro, the white people of the South have disfranchised vast numbers of themselves. I believe in manhood suffrage. Whoever by his labor, however humble, contributes to the wealth and revenue of the country—and that is every man who labors—should somehow have a voice in his own government. No man is fit to make laws for others without consulting them. Any limitation of the suffrage, however fair and specious in the abstract, which operates to deprive a great part of the population of a state or the nation of all direct representation in any law making or law administering body, and thereby leaves them without power to check in any degree the acts of those who make and administer the laws, is unjust and undemocratic; I wish I could say it is un-American. And when by the operation of such a system, the representation based on the number of the excluded class is openly, avowedly and shamelessly used by the usurping class to humiliate, degrade and further injure those whom they have robbed, a situation is created which calls for emphatic protest and ceaseless agitation until the wrong is righted. The Fifteenth Amendment, which declares that "The right of citizens of the United States to vote shall not be denied or abridged by the United States or any State on account of race or color," should be enforced both in the spirit and in the letter. If it be held by the Courts that the disfranchising constitutions of the South do not violate it, then the punitive clause of the Fourteenth Amendment should be enforced, and Southern representation reduced in proportion to the number of those disfranchised. There will then be fewer Negro-haters and Negro-baiters in Congress, to seek spectacular notoriety by abuse of their own constituents, and to trade their votes, in commercial legislation, for permission to maintain in their own States unlawful and unconstitutional forms of government.

The right of suffrage is fundamental to liberty. The poor and the unlettered need it even more than the rich and the learned, for these can in a measure take care of themselves without it. It is the plain man's only bulwark against oppression. He is not free without it; and if he be a black man, without it he cannot, as Dr. Du Bois[2] has well said, even earn a decent living in the land of his birth; he cannot get justice in the courts; and the traditional scorn of his color is intensified by the contempt which is felt for those who cannot defend themselves. The only hope for the future of the Negro of the South lies in the recovery of this right of which he has been deprived. To this end, those of us who love liberty should never cease to act, to agitate, and to seek by protest and

by argument, by every means at our command, the sympathy and support, for those thus wronged, of the great army of American people
who in their heart of hearts believe in the principles of democracy as
embodied in the Declaration of Independence and the amended Constitution of the United States.[3] The Negro is not without friends; they are
not dead, but only sleeping.[4] Their rights and their liberties are bound
up with the Negro's. Without their aid we can do little. Together we
can win our cause, which is not only the cause of the Negro, but the
cause of humanity.

Sincerely yours,

TCU: TNF

[1]William H. Richards (1856–?) was an attorney, a lecturer at the Howard
University Law School, and a past president of the Bethel Literary and Historical Association in Washington, D.C., before which Chesnutt had delivered
addresses on several occasions. On 8 February 1906 (TNF), he invited Chesnutt to speak on voting rights in the District of Columbia, offering to pay his
railroad fare.

[2]W. E. B. Du Bois (1868–1963) taught at Atlanta University (now Clark
Atlanta University) from 1897 to 1910. Since the publication of his *The Souls
of Black Folk* (1903), he had become an increasingly prominent spokesperson
for African Americans—especially those at odds with Booker T. Washington.

[3]The Fourteenth Amendment was ratified on 9 July 1868 and the Fifteenth
on 3 February 1870.

[4]Before restoring the daughter of Jairus to life, Jesus said to all who were
mourning, "Weep not; she is not dead, but sleepeth" (Luke 8:52).

To Edwin J. Chesnutt

March 6, 1906

. . . Am sorry you did not find better weather in northern Europe,
but I hardly expected you would find it warm. I don't understand why
your feet should have been wet; you surely had money enough to buy
rubbers, and you have yourself entirely to thank for not having dry
feet, the importance of which it seems to me would have occurred to
you with great force. If you had had some flannel underwear, as we
have vainly endeavored to induce you to get, you would not have
found it so chilly. I very much suspect that, after all, your health is a
matter in your own hands, and if you want to help yourself off the sur-
face of this earth or under it, you can very much contribute to that result by your own carelessness. . . .[1]

Had I known that you would have such disagreeable weather, I should have had you go from here directly to a Mediterranean port, and you could have worked northward in the summer, thereby saving the double trip. Your mother and Helen speak of coming over in the summer, and in fact are trying to secure passage, in which event you will be expected to meet them in France or England, and to act as their guide and attendant. . . .[2]

Pioneer: 219–20

[1]Edwin had written his parents from London, Paris, and the Riviera; see *Pioneer*: 217–19.

[2]Wife Susan Utley Perry Chesnutt (1862–1940), daughter Helen, and the Chesnutts' youngest child, Dorothy K. Chesnutt Slade (1890–1954), sailed to England on 23 June 1906 on the ship *Minneapolis*, arriving in London at St. Pancras station where Edwin duly met them.

To Augustus F. Hartz

March 11, 1906.

My dear Mr. Hartz:—

Received your telegram last evening as I was leaving office.[1] Sat up until midnight writing scenario, which I copied to-day, and enclose herewith.[2] It is quite a full synopsis, as the action and the lines are so closely connected, especially in the first act. I meant to have carried a scenario down to New York with me, but have probably written a better one as it is.[3] Knowing you to be a man of action, I shall hope to have news from you before long.[4]

Cordially yours,
Chas. W. Chesnutt.

P.S. If I can do anything more to further the enterprise, please let me know.

TCS: TNF

[1]Augustus ("Gus") F. Hartz (1843–1927) was a British actor who emigrated to the United States in 1863, settling in Cleveland in 1880. There he managed the Euclid Avenue Opera House for nearly four decades (1884–1920). While the telegram sent by Hartz to Chesnutt does not survive, a letter from him dated 8 March 1906 (TNF) specifies the terms for an acceptable play: $100 plus 5% for gross receipts up to $6,000 per week, and 8% if above $6,000. Hartz also mentions the possibility of an outright offer for ownership of the play.

[2]The "scenario" was for "Mrs. Darcy's Daughter" (TNF).

[3]Chesnutt was in New York City during the previous week. See 12 March 1906 to Booker T. Washington.

[4]On 14 March 1906 (TNF), Malcolm Douglas, a reader for the New Amsterdam Theatre owned by producers Marc Klaw (1858–1936) and Abraham Lincoln Erlanger (1860–1930), was not impressed by the synopsis: "It may be an excellent play, but the synopsis is one that would not make one particularly curious or anxious to read it." On 16 March 1906 (TNF), Hartz forwarded Douglas's letter to Chesnutt; then, a week later (TNF), he related that he had "nothing encouraging to write . . . as yet. Several theatrical men of more or less prominence have read [the] play, and all give the same opinion, that it is well written, well drawn, but as there is nothing new in it, they do not thing [*sic*] it would be a success."

To Booker T. Washington

March 12, 1906.

My dear Dr. Washington:—

I received yesterday the article for Miss Kline, and handed it to her this morning. She asked me to express her thanks to you, and we expect that the contribution will add materially to the interest and value of the publication.[1]

I was down in New York several days last week, and put up at the Manhattan Hotel. I inquired for you at the desk, and regretted that you did not come to the hotel while I was in the city. I presume you are very busy with the preparations for your anniversary, which I hope will prove an even greater success than the succession of successes which have marked the history of Tuskegee.[2]

Sincerely yours,
Chas. W. Chesnutt

TLS: DLC

[1]Washington had promised to write an article for the *Hathaway Brown Magazine* published in Cleveland; see 5 February 1906 to Washington, n. 4.

[2]Tuskegee Institute celebrated its 25th anniversay in 1906. On 16 March (TNF), Chesnutt declined a formal invitation to attend the ceremonies there, extending his "hearty congratulations" to Tuskegee for "the hold it has gained upon the public confidence" and both its "marvelous success" and "power for usefulness."

To Susan Utley Chesnutt

July 5, 1906

. . . I saw from the paper that the *Minneapolis* landed on Tuesday.[1] I fear Edwin did not meet you at the dock, but I hope you got safely up to London and that he looked after you properly.[2] The time distance between here and London is about six hours, and when I sit down to my meals I generally calculate what you folks are probably doing at the same moment.

I spent the Fourth in a somewhat humdrum way. It rained copiously the night before, and the grass was green and the trees fresh-looking. I decided to stay at home all day and write on my novel,[3] but after breakfast went down to get my mail, and called at Grant Street on the way back, where I found Ed, Ethel, and Charlie getting ready to go out to one of the parks to picnic.[4] I suggested that they come out to our house, which they did and brought their lunch along; Mrs. Gibson supplied them with coffee.[5] After lunch Ed and I went to the ball game; score 2 to 1 in favor of Cleveland as against Detroit. On the way home we bought some firecrackers for Charlie, who, by the way, cut up all day like the very old Harry.[6] When I went to shoot off the firecrackers he was "fwaid" and didn't want me to shoot off any more; so I gave the whole batch to Ed and told him to take them home and shoot them off where the crowd could enjoy them—there were not so very many.

I suppose you are now in the full enjoyment of your first impressions of the world's metropolis. Have a good time, while you have a chance. Mrs. Gibson is looking after my comfort and I am doing very well. I did a lot of hunting around for the flag yesterday and finally found it and hung it out. . . .

Pioneer: 221

[1]Susan, Helen, and Dorothy arrived in England on 3 July 1906, where Edwin Chesnutt was supposed to greet them (see 6 March 1906 to Edwin).

[2]They resided for the summer in a boarding house on Russell Square, taking trips from there to various English locales, Scotland, and France until 18 August when, without Edwin, they returned to the United States.

[3]Chesnutt had in hand at least four novelistic manuscripts—"Mandy Oxendine," "The Rainbow Chasers," "A Business Career," and "Evelyn's Husband"—and he may have begun another. He did not, however, submit a new one, "Paul Marchand, F.M.C.," for the consideration of a publisher until 1921 (see 8 October 1921 to Houghton Mifflin Company).

[4]In November 1902, Ethel Chesnutt married Edward C. Williams (1871–

1929), a librarian at Adelbert College of Western Reserve University and later at Howard University. "Charlie"—Charles Waddell Chesnutt Williams (1903–39)—was Chesnutt's first grandchild.

⁵Mary R. (?–1952) and David Gibson, friends of the family, stayed with Chesnutt in his home while his wife, son, and two unmarried daughters were abroad.

⁶That is, like the Devil.

To Horace Bumstead

July 14, 1906

My dear Dr. Bumstead:—

I am in receipt of your favor of recent date, enclosing me some literature in reference to Atlanta University,[1] and I have also received from time to time through the courtesy of the University various of the bulletins which it issues. I regret that I am unable to make any very substantial contribution to its expenses, but if the enclosed amount will be of any service, please accept it with my best wishes.[2]

I am glad to think I was of any service to the University on the occasion that you mention in your letter and assure you that it has always stood very high in my estimation and that I appreciated very much your own courtesy at the time of our acquaintance in New England.[3]

Yours sincerely,

TCU: TNF

[1]Horace Bumstead (1841–1919) served as president of Atlanta University (1888–1907) and had taught natural sciences and Latin there. An energetic advocate of the African American, he served during the Civil War as an officer commanding black troops in the Forty-third Massachusetts Regiment.

[2]Bumstead had sent Chesnutt a circular soliciting contributions. Dated 20 June 1906 (TNF), it noted the university's sound financial standing for the previous six years but called attention to the need for "some $10,000 more in donations" for the current year. At the bottom of the circular, Bumstead recalled the "readings" Chesnutt "so kindly gave" at the university "a few years ago"—an allusion to Chesnutt's visit to the institution on 22 February 1901 during his lecture tour of the South. On 20 July (TNF), Bumstead acknowledged Chesnutt's contribution of $10.

[3]In 1905 in Boston, Chesnutt attended a meeting of individuals interested in the welfare of Atlanta University; this fund-raising event was presided over by Bumstead.

To Hugh M. Browne

July 14, 1906.

My dear Professor Browne:—

I am in receipt of your favor of July 12th,[1] with reference to reprinting and circulating the address of Hon. William H. Fleming.[2] I read something about it and some extracts from it in the *Evening Post* about the time of its delivery.[3] And the quotations which you give would suggest that the spirit of the address is one which would make it a most excellent thing to place in as many hands as possible. I quite approve of the suggestion.

Yours very truly,

TCU: TNF

[1]Hugh M. Browne (1851–1923), principal of the Institute for Colored Youth of Philadelphia (now Cheney University of Pennsylvania), was secretary of the Committee of Twelve for the Advancement of the Interests of the Negro Race. On 12 April 1905 (TNF), he informed Chesnutt of his unanimous election to the Committee (not mentioning that W. E. B. Du Bois had resigned); on 2 June 1905 (TNF), Chesnutt accepted the position tendered.

[2]Browne wrote to Chesnutt on 10 (rather than 12) July 1906 (TNF) to convey the Committee's suggestion that it circulate Fleming's speech in pamphlet form. William Henry Fleming (1856–1944), a Georgia Democrat, served two terms in the U.S. House of Representatives (1897–1903) and failed to win a third. Moderate politically, Fleming delivered a speech before the Alumni Society of the University of Georgia in Athens on 19 June 1906: he argued against disfranchisement of African Americans, calling instead for an end to racial divisions in the state. Chesnutt appreciatively quoted Fleming in his November 1906 speech "The Age of Problems" (see *Essays and Speeches*: 250).

[3]"The Fair-Minded South," New York *Evening Post*, 28 June 1906, 6.

To Edwin J. Chesnutt

July 20, 1906

. . . I had two letters from the folks today, one from Susan and one from Helen. They say you do not eat enough to keep strong. Buck up, and eat your regular meals! I want you to get strong and healthy.[1]

I note what you say about your progress in shorthand, etc. It is very gratifying. Also note what you say about coming home.[2] I shall doubtless hear more from you on the subject—it is up to you. The climate is probably no better here than it was last winter, and the race prejudice is probably the same, though you may be better prepared to stand both.

Try to keep on good terms with the folks, and give them all the aid you can. *Eat plenty of nourishing food*; stay in the open air as much as possible and get strong—it takes a strong man to make a career in this strenuous world. . . .

Pioneer: 223

[1]Edwin apparently acted upon his father's 5 February 1906 directive to live "within the limits of strict economy" while in Europe. That "Ned is much better in health, but I am afraid he has been too economical in regard to what he eats" was his mother's report in her letter of 8 July 1906 (*Pioneer*: 222).

[2]Still concerned about discovering a suitable occupation for himself, Edwin began to study stenography. He returned to the United States in November 1906.

To Booker T. Washington

October 9, 1906.

My dear Dr. Washington:—

I am in receipt of your letter and telegram from Tuskegee, calling my attention to the meeting of the Committee of Twelve at the Stevens House on October 12th.[1] This is one of the meetings at which I should very much like to be present, and I regret exceedingly that I am tangled up here in a lawsuit which absolutely demands my presence during the whole of this week and very probably into the middle of next week; it is of a nature which does not permit of a substitute and I am therefore compelled to forego the privilege of attending the meeting.

I wish also to acknowledge your brief note calling my attention to the issue of the New York *World*, containing a review of the Atlanta horror.[2] I read with great interest Mr. H. G. Wells' article in *Harper's Weekly* on the "Tragedy of Color", and I think you will agree that my views and those of Mr. Wells are very much the same. I do not believe it possible for two races to subsist side by side without intermingling; experience has demonstrated this fact and there will be more experience along that line.[3] Another thing of which I am firmly convinced, in view of recent events, is that no system which excludes the Negro or any other class from the use of the ballot and leaves this potent instrument in the hands of the people who are alien to him in sympathy and interest, can have any healthy effect in improving his condition.[4] No subterfuge of equal qualifications and just application to black and white alike of disfranchising provisions, can overcome the solemn fact which is brought home every day by reading the newspapers that these state constitutions leave the Negro absolutely at the mercy of the white man.

I have never been able to see how any man with the interest of his people at heart could favor those abominations. I know that your heart is all right, but I think your very wise head is wrong on that proposition, and I should regard it as a much more hopeful day for the Negro in this country when you cease to defend them. There is no hope for the Negro except in equality before the law, and I suspect that hope will be deferred for many a day in the Southern States. At the same time I think nothing is lost and everything gained by insisting upon the principle. A man weakens his position immensely when he takes any attitude which justifies or excuses his oppressor.

I notice a great deal has been said by colored people about the Atlanta matter. And of course I have not failed to observe that those best qualified to speak, and whose utterances would carry most weight, have not been in a position to express themselves fully. I appreciate the difficulty of their situation. And so far as the mere matter of speech is concerned, discretion on the part of people who live and work in the South is imperative. I observe that a Georgia editor was expelled from that State for saying a few truthful things about the Jim Crow law in Savannah.[5] After all, the Northern press, with a surprising unanimity and vigor, has said the things which ought to have been said, much to the chagrin of the South, much to our satisfaction and I trust much to the enlightenment of Northern readers.

Negro leaders for some time to come are likely to lead a somewhat strenuous existence. They have my sympathy and will have any small support and cooperation that I can contribute.

With best wishes for a successful meeting of the Committee and of the Council,[6] at which you will doubtless be present to exercise a wise and restraining influence, I remain

Sincerely yours,
Chas. W. Chesnutt.

P.S. I presume you have been reading the "Autobiography of a Southerner" in the *Atlantic*. I don't know who wrote it (tho I presume you do.) It is great stuff, and shows a real insight into Southern conditions.[7]

C.W.C.

TLS, autograph postscript: DLC

[1]Washington had called for an emergency meeting of the Committee of Twelve at the Stevens House in New York City, sending Chesnutt both a letter and a telegram on 4 October 1906 (TNF). The cause was the Atlanta race riot that began on 22 September 1906 after several alleged assaults of white women by African-American males. Over the next five days 12 African Americans died and 70 others were wounded.

[2]Washington sent Chesnutt a brief note, dated 27 September 1906 (OClW-Hi), suggesting that he read "the [New York] Sunday World for a special account of the Atlanta affair." This lengthy analysis of the riot by Samuel M. Williams (1869–1959) was datelined "Atlanta, Ga., Sept. 29" ("Atlanta, after Its Debauch of Riot and Lynching, Turns with Fierce Ardor to the Work of Reform," New York *World*, 30 September 1906, "Editorial Section," 1). It detailed the immediate causes of the riot after noting "the modern proneness to exaggerate every incident into a case of assault" and the infrequency with which an African-American male "has a chance to explain or defend himself from the charge": "Thirteen cases of assault by negroes upon white women within two months around Atlanta were proclaimed by the local newspapers. Three of these were clearly proven cases. Of four others there was little doubt of the assailants' intention, though unsuccessful. In six cases there is room for doubt whether the negroes really intended assault, certainly no serious damage was done nor bodily harm inflicted." Williams then gave close attention to the socio-economic and race-discrimination factors motivating the whites "who thought it great sport this taking of human life in black skin."

[3]English novelist H. G. Wells (1866–1946) wrote a series of articles entitled "The Future in America" for *Harper's Weekly*, 50 (14 July–6 October 1906); his book with the same title was published in 1906. Chesnutt here refers to one of the installments subtitled "The Tragedy of Color," which appeared in the 15 September 1906 issue, 1317–19.

[4]Washington's forceful response to Chesnutt on this point dramatizes the degree to which the two men differed on the issue of the importance of the franchise. On 29 October 1906 (TNF), Washington retorted: "I have time to take only a minute to answer one point in your letter. I very much fear that you place too much reliance upon the ballot to cure evils that we are at present suffering. The ballot is valuable and should not be surrendered. Every man who can do so should vote, but in this connection, how do you account for the Atlanta riot, the worst that we have had in forty years? That occurred in practically the only Southern state where the Negro has not been disfranchised by reason of constitutional enactment."

[5]That the Reverend William J. White (1831–1913), editor and publisher of the *Georgia Baptist*, had been "the cause of incipient disturbances between the races" and that "a few years ago [he] was saved" by a locally prominent attorney "from injury and his office from destruction by a mob" was related in "Negro Editor Left Augusta," *Atlanta Constitution*, 26 September 1906, 4. White departed from Augusta, Ga.—"never to return"—on 25 September; the

immediate cause was the *Augusta Chronicle* having "strongly hinted that for the sake of his health Dr. White had better leave town" ("'Georgia Baptist' Man Driven Out of Augusta," *New York Age*, 27 September 1906, 1). White's criticism of the "Jim Crow" streetcar situation in Savannah, Ga., was noted in both the *New York Age* article and in "Call on the President," *Cleveland Gazette*, 13 October 1906, [1].

⁶On 4 October (TNF), Washington had related that the Afro-American Council would meet in New York City from 9 to 11 October and that he took it "for granted that" Chesnutt was "planning to be present at that meeting" as well.

⁷"Nicholas Worth" was the pseudonym of Walter Hines Page (1855–1918), Chesnutt's Houghton, Mifflin & Co. editor in 1897–99 and, after founding his own firm of Doubleday, Page & Co., the editor and publisher of Chesnutt's novel *The Colonel's Dream* (1905). His "Autobiography of a Southerner Since the Civil War" appeared in volume 98 of *Atlantic Monthly*, beginning in the July 1906 issue and ending in that for October. These installments were later included in *Autobiography of Nicholas Worth* (1909).

To Hugh M. Browne

November 3, 1906.

My dear Prof. Browne:—

I am in receipt of your favor of October 21st, and also of the copy of address on "Slavery and the Race Problem in the South," by Mr. Fleming.¹ I most heartily approve of its circulation among the leaders of opinion in the South. I should go a good deal further than Mr. Fleming, in some details, but the whole tone of his address is vastly in advance of current thought in the South, and the fundamental propositions of justice to the Negro and respect for the Constitution are so clearly and eloquently insisted upon, that I hope the words of this good man will not be without their weight in the councils of those Southern men who have the immediate fate of the Negro so largely in their hands.

Sincerely yours,

TCU: TNF

¹Enclosed with Browne's 22 (rather than 21) October 1906 letter to Chesnutt (TNF) was this Committee of Twelve pamphlet; see 14 July 1906 to Browne, n. 2.

To Booker T. Washington

November 3, 1906.

My dear Dr. Washington:—

I beg to acknowledge receipt of your letter of recent date. I note what you say about the franchise in Georgia, and while the riot occurred in Georgia, it was not because the Negroes had exercised the franchise or made any less progress or developed any less strength than elsewhere, but because of a wicked and indefensible effort to disfranchise them.[1]

I am quite aware that the Negro will not enjoy any large degree of liberty at the South until there has developed in that section a white party which is favorable to his enjoyment of the rights guaranteed by the Constitution of the United States. The rise of such men as Mr. Fleming indicates that this party, while small, is finding a voice. Surely no colored man can afford to demand less for his race than a white man is willing to concede, and as I read Mr. Fleming's pamphlet cursorily during a very busy week, he is willing to give them their rights under the Constitution. The scheme proposed in Georgia for the disfranchisement of the Negro is substantially that enacted in Alabama. This Mr. Fleming condemns. He uses this language: "Let us not in cowardice or want of faith needlessly sacrifice our higher ideals of private and public life."[2] Manhood suffrage is an ideal, already attained in this country except where the reactionary Southern States have qualified it. Surely in a country where every one else votes and the suffrage is freely conceded to foreigners in a great many States, including I believe Alabama, as soon as they declare their intention of becoming citizens, it is not only a great lapse from the ideal, but the rankest sort of injustice that any different rule should be applied to so numerous and important a class of the population as the Negro constitutes in the South. I think a little more anti-Negro agitation in the South will very likely result in an effort at the North to see, for the welfare of the whole country, that the Thirteenth,[3] Fourteenth and Fifteenth Amendments shall become not only the theoretical but the real law of the land. The practical difficulties I admit are enormous, but the value of equal citizenship is so great and so vital that it is worth whatever it may cost. Slavery was as deeply entrenched as race prejudice, yet it fell. And the sound of the trumpets you will remember shook down the walls of Jericho.[4]

If I wanted to answer with the *argumentum ad hominem*, with reference to the Atlanta riot, I could point out the fact that the riot occurred only a few days after your splendid object lesson of the Negro's progress in business and the arts of peace.[5] The fact of the matter is that this race problem involves all of the issues of life and must be attacked from many sides for a long time before it will approach anything like a peaceful solution. The American people will have to swallow the Negro, in punishment for their sins.[6] Doubtless the dose is a bitter one, but there is no other way out. It only remains for all of us to make the process as little painful as possible to all concerned.

One of your agents, Mr. Powell, has been operating around here for several weeks. I have shown him such small courtesies as I could during one of the busiest months of my life. And he tells me that he has been meeting with some encouragement.[7]

I have read a review somewhere of a book which is described as a very vicious attack on Tuskegee. I trust that this false and reckless publication has not done you any injury.

I also beg to thank you on behalf of myself and Mrs. Chesnutt, for the handsome little volume, *Putting the Most into Life*,[8] which you were good enough to send us. We shall prize it very highly.

Sincerely yours,

Chas. W. Chesnutt.

TLS: DLC

[1]See 9 October 1906 to Washington, n. 4.

[2]Fleming's speech at the University of Georgia in Athens had been published by the Committee of Twelve in pamphlet form as *Slavery and the Race Problem in the South with Special Reference to the State of Georgia* (1906); see 14 July 1906, n. 2, and 3 November 1906 to Hugh M. Browne.

[3]The Thirteenth Amendment, prohibiting slavery, was ratified on 6 December 1865.

[4]The account of the fall of Jericho is given in Joshua 6.

[5]Washington delivered an inspirational address to African Americans at the Mount Olivet Baptist Church in New York City on 20 September 1906, acknowledging their accomplishments and encouraging them to become "creators of enterprise" ("Washington Advises Negroes," New York *Sun*, 21 September 1906, 2).

[6]Lamentations 3:39.

[7]Clarence A. Powell was graduated from Tuskegee in 1891 and became a teacher of agricultural subjects at Slater Industrial Academy in Winston-Salem, N.C. Beginning in 1906 he represented Tuskegee in the North as one of several fund-raisers.

[8]Published in 1906 was this series of "Sunday evening talks" delivered by Washington to the Tuskegee students.

To Ida B. Wells-Barnett

November 3, 1906.

My dear Mrs. Barnett:—

I trust you will pardon my delay in answering your letter of several weeks since, but this has been the busiest month of my life, and I have just been able to attack my correspondence.[1]

I have read with interest of the Negro theatre in Chicago, and have been delighted with what I have read.

As to dramatizing my story, "The Wife of His Youth," I have always realized its dramatic character and have several times refused this permission to others with the intention of some time doing the work myself, as I am not altogether a novice at dramatic construction.[2] I should like to know a little more what your notion would be, to present it as a one-act play, or to undertake to develop it into a full evening's entertainment? A successful play is a very valuable asset, and it is always possible that a play might prove successful; if the "Wife of His Youth" contains such elements, I would not of course like to foreclose my own dramatic rights or lose the chance of making some more money out of the writings which by virtue of their appeal have not had and cannot hope for so wide a circulation as *The Clansman*[3] or books and plays which appeal to the baser side of humanity. I should like to correspond with you a little further about the matter before saying one way or the other.[4] Meantime believe me,

Cordially yours,

TCU: TNF

[1]Ida Bell Wells-Barnett (1862–1931) had taught school in Memphis in 1884–91. Provoked by lynchings and like abuses of African Americans, she turned to investigative journalism. The author of *Southern Horrors* (1892), *A Red Record* (1895), and *Mob Rule in New Orleans* (1900), she also chaired the Anti-Lynching League.

[2]See 11 March 1906 to A. F. Hartz, n. 4; Chesnutt is not known to have written a marketable play and is possibly referring to the "dramatic construction" of "The Wife of His Youth" (1898) and like prose narratives.

[3]*The Clansman: An Historical Romance of the Ku Klux Klan* (1905) was written by Baptist minister and white supremacist Thomas Dixon, Jr. (1864–1946). Like *The Leopard's Spots* (1902) and *The Traitor* (1907), it pictures black-white relations in the South in terms of heroic white resistance to pressures exerted by a "black dominance" movement.

[4]Neither Chesnutt nor Barnett is known to have prepared a dramatic ver-

sion of the short story. Permission for a 1907 adaptation and presentation in Chicago was, however, given later this year. See 21 December 1906 and subsequent letters to Celia Parker Wooley.

To Frederick R. Moore

November 15, 1906.

My dear Mr. Moore:—

I find on my desk a letter from you dated July last, requesting me to make a contribution to your magazine.[1] I must really beg your pardon for having neglected so long to answer it that the time for which you meant to use it has gone by. But I was so busily engaged with literary and other work at the time and since that it escaped my attention.[2] I beg to assure you that the seeming discourtesy was not intentional, and I hope at some future time to avail myself of the opportunity offered me.[3]

Sincerely yours,

TCU: TNF

[1]Frederick R. Moore (1857–1943) was a businessman, journalist, and politician who became editor of the *Colored American Magazine* in 1904 after Booker T. Washington purchased it. Three years later he became editor of *New York Age* when Washington and he became its owners. He served on the first board of directors of the National Urban League, which he co-founded in 1911, and he was appointed minister to Liberia under U.S. President William Howard Taft (1857–1930)—though he resigned from this position before even visiting that country. On 26 July 1906 (TNF), Moore wrote to Chesnutt, requesting a short statement "of one-hundred and fifty to two-hundred words" as part of a group of letters "from representative men of the race, suggesting what the Negro race can do along constructive lines to help itself and improve the condition as a whole."

[2]On the advice of Carrie Williams Clifford (1862–1934), honorary president of the Ohio State Federation of Colored Women's Clubs in 1905 and since 1886 wife of Ohio politician William H. Clifford (1862–1929), Moore would write to Chesnutt again on 12 December 1906 (TNF) to request a copy of "an excellent address" which Chesnutt had "recently delivered before a body of white people in Cleveland" for publication in his magazine. This was very likely "Age of Problems," delivered on 12 November 1906 to the Cleveland Council of Sociology; see *Essays and Speeches*: 238–52.

[3]Chesnutt is not known to have published anything in *Colored American*.

To Archibald H. Grimké

November 24, 1906.

My dear Mr. Grimké:

I have today forwarded to Hugh M. Browne, Secretary, N.Y. draft to my order, endorsed to him, as my contribution towards the expenses of printing and circulating Hon. William H. Fleming's oration, delivered June 19, 1906, at Athens, Ga.[1]

I am no hand at soliciting money for even the best of causes, and this contribution is made from my own pocket. Doubtless, others will be more successful. If there is any deficit, kindly let me know, and I will consider whether I can do anything further.

I read every week, or as often as they appear, your eloquent and forceful letters in the *New York Age*. I am beginning to feel more hopeful concerning the outcome of our problem. The Atlanta horror was, of course, a dreadful thing,[2] but the unanimous outburst of condemnation by the North, mainly concurred in by the South is a hopeful sign. The tree of liberty has always been watered with blood;[3] nor does it seem possible to escape the sacrifice. The successful efforts to head off Tillman[4] and Dixon,[5] here and there, are also encouraging. The strong protest of the united North and the Army against Mr. Roosevelt's cavalier treatment of the colored troops,[6] and the manner in which it has driven the colored people together and lent them voice, and made them friends, is a significant sign of the times.

Sincerely yours,
Charles W. Chesnutt

TCS: TNF

[1]See 14 July 1906, n. 2, to Hugh M. Browne and 3 November 1906 to Booker T. Washington concerning the Fleming pamphlet published by the Committee of Twelve. That Chesnutt sent his contribution to Committee secretary Browne, rather than treasurer Grimké, doubtless was the result of Browne's curt letter of 12 November 1906 (TNF), in which he reminded Chesnutt that members of the Committee of Twelve had agreed "to give or secure so much money as [they] can for the furtherance of the purpose of this committee," part of that purpose being the publication and distribution of Fleming's anti-disfranchisement pamphlet at a cost of $419 for 10,000 copies.

[2]See 9 October 1906, n. 1, to Booker T. Washington.

[3]Paraphrase of Thomas Jefferson (1743–1826), letter of 13 November 1787 to the American diplomat in London William S. Smith (1755–1816): "The tree of liberty must be refreshed from time to time with the blood of patriots and tyrants. It is its natural manure."

[4]Benjamin R. Tillman (1847–1918), former Confederate soldier and governor of South Carolina (1890–94), was U.S. Senator from South Carolina from 1895 until his death. A white supremacist, "Pitchfork Ben" advocated the repeal of the Fifteenth Amendment and justified lynching in cases of rape. In a speech delivered at Augusta, Ga., on 7 October 1906, he exhorted the South to take all steps necessary to maintain white dominance, predicting even worse violence than had been seen in the Atlanta riot should African Americans persist in their attempts to claim equality ("Race War Is Coming, Says Senator Tillman," *New York Times*, 8 October 1906, 1). An appearance before a meeting of African Americans in New York City a few days later resulted in severe criticism of his "savage fury" in "The Negroes and the South," *New York Times*, 12 October 1906, 8; the editorial charged him with a "vein of coarseness and brutality . . . [that] shocks and revolts all the decency of the American people whenever he gives it expression."

[5]See 3 November 1906 to Ida B. Wells-Barnett, n. 3.

[6]A race riot began in Brownsville, Tex., on 13 August 1906, when African-American soldiers of the Twenty-fifth U.S. Infantry stationed at nearby Fort Brown fired over 100 rifle shots in the streets of the town to protest a search of their quarters. The search followed an alleged attack by an African-American enlisted man on Mrs. Vane Evans at her Brownsville home. Killed by the gunfire was a bartender, Frank Natus; Joseph Domingo, the town's chief of police, was wounded. The immediate result of the incident—a War Department order, dated 20 August 1906, to relocate the troops to another post—was relatively minor. What followed was not. None of the soldiers, now stationed at Fort Bliss, Tex., would confess to having participated on 2 November 1906 in a second incident: saloon-keeper Alexander Johnson and Private Lewis were wounded; Private Matthews was killed. Nor would any reveal the names of fellow soldiers who had been involved. President Theodore Roosevelt (1858–1919) decided on 6 November 1906 to "discharge without honor" 160 of them. Both the public and ranking officers in the Army protested Roosevelt's decision, and a *New York Times* editorialist argued that dishonorable dismissal was both "beyond the authority of the President" and "in flat contravention of that provision of the Constitution which declares that no person shall be deprived of life, liberty, or property 'without due process of law'" ("Due Process of Law," *New York Times*, 16 November 1906, 1).

To Celia Parker Wooley

December 21, 1906.

Dear Mrs. Wooley:

Replying more fully to your letter of recent date with reference to using my story, "The Wife of His Youth," I give you that permission very willingly, upon the terms mentioned in your letter, namely, that the play made from it is to be used only under the auspices of the Frederick Douglass Center.[1] So far as destroying the manuscript is concerned, I would prefer that you send it to me when you are through with it. I have some notions of my own about how the story should be dramatized, and if I cannot go down there to see it,[2] I should at least like to read your version.

I am glad to know that a competent dramatic teacher will drill the company. My publishers have consented to this use of the story,[3] and, as I say, I am glad to do anything that will further the advancement of your very excellent work.

Thank you for the pamphlets containing your wise reflections.

Yours very truly,

TCU: TNF

[1]Unitarian minister Celia Parker Wooley (1848–1918) was a novelist, playwright, essayist, and social reformer who in 1904 co-founded with Fannie B. Williams (1855–1944) the Frederick Douglass Social Center, Chicago's first black settlement house. She wrote Chesnutt on 12 December 1906 (TNF), seeking permission to adapt the short story for performance at the Center.

[2]On 26 December (TNF), Wooley offered to pay Chesnutt's railway fare to Chicago for the proposed production in the spring.

[3]Permission was granted by Houghton, Mifflin & Co. on 17 December 1906 (TNF).

To Hugh M. Browne

March 22, 1907.

My dear Mr. Browne:—

I am in receipt of your letter of March 20th, enclosing copy of letter from Mr. Villard,[1] with reference to the article by Mr. Ray Stannard Baker.[2] I have n't seen the article, and am therefore not in a position to express any opinion concerning it, but from the fact that Mr. Washington wishes to distribute it, and Mr. Villard approves of the suggestion, I am very willing to accept their opinion upon the subject, and register my approval. I am glad to know that the oration by Mr. Fleming was productive of good results.[3] Something or other, I suspect chiefly the energetic manner in which the Northern press jumped upon the city of Atlanta for its conduct during the riot, has produced a lull in the persecution of the negro.

Very truly yours,

TCU: TNF

[1]Oswald Garrison Villard (1872–1949), grandson of William Lloyd Garrison, was the owner of and regularly wrote for the New York *Evening Post*, a newspaper sympathetic to African Americans and long a favorite of Chesnutt's. An ally of Booker T. Washington and active in fund-raising efforts in behalf of the Tuskegee Institute, he later helped found and served as an officer of the N.A.A.C.P.

[2]Enclosed with Browne's 20 March 1907 letter to Chesnutt (TNF) was a copy of a 16 March letter from Villard. Browne asked for Chesnutt's opinion of Villard's proposal that the Committee of Twelve publish as a pamphlet an article on the Atlanta Riot by Ray Stannard Baker (1870–1946): "Following the Color Line," *American Magazine*, 63 (April 1907), 563–79. (This was the first of five essays by Baker that in 1907 appeared under the same title in the April-August issues.) Villard thought that 5,000 copies would ensure "the widest circulation throughout the South." Browne noted that the proposal had already been endorsed by Booker T. Washington. The pamphlet published by the Committee was entitled *The Atlanta Riot* (1907).

[3]Chesnutt refers to a previous publication of the Committee, William H. Fleming's *Slavery and the Race Problem in the South*; see 3 November 1906 to Booker T. Washington.

To Celia Parker Wooley

March 22, 1907.

My dear Madam:—

I am in receipt of your favor of March 13th, with reference to the production, on April 1st, of the play made from my book, *The Wife of his Youth*.[1] I am delighted to know that you are making headway with it, and, so far as I know at present, I shall try to go down to see it. It is a little early for me to say positively that I will be there, as I have some other engagements along in that part of the month, but I hope to, and the chances are very much that I shall. With best wishes for your success in that and all your good work, I remain,

Very truly yours,

TCU: TNF

[1]Enclosing a circular advertising her dramatic adaptation of the short story "The Wife of His Youth" with her letter (TNF), Wooley specified 30 April 1907, rather than 1 April, as the date of performance at the Frederick Douglass Social Center in Chicago. The book to which Chesnutt refers is *The Wife of His Youth and Other Stories of the Color Line* (1899), the lead story of which is "The Wife."

To Booker T. Washington

March 23, 1907.

My dear Doctor Washington:—

I am in receipt of your favor of recent date, with reference to contributing toward the paying off of the mortgage on the Frederick Douglass home.[1] I shall be very glad to contribute at least the sum of $25.00 to this good purpose, and will look up the name of the treasurer in some of the newspapers, and either send it to him or to you about the latter part of the month. I have had a good many calls made upon me recently, local and otherwise, and am not able to contribute very largely, but the cause is a worthy one, and ought to meet with a generous response from a number of contributors. Frederick Douglass was the most conspicuous colored man of his generation, and ably and nobly held his own among the orators of the anti-slavery agitation.

I see that you have written a life of Frederick Douglass;[2] I hope to have the pleasure of reading it very soon. I have just written to Professor Browne, expressing my approval of the distribution of copies of Mr. Ray Stannard Baker's article.[3] I have n't seen the article, but I saw a preliminary announcement of the series. I told Professor Browne that I am willing to accept your opinion and Mr. Villard's, as to the advisability of distributing it in the South.

Cordially yours,
Chas. W. Chesnutt.

TLS: DLC

[1]On 5 March 1901 (TNF), Washington wrote from Tuskegee Institute, inviting Chesnutt to help in the amortization of the Frederick Douglass Homestead in Anacostia, Md. Douglass (1817–95)—orator, journalist, and diplomat—was the most distinguished African-American abolitionist of his generation. He was a major historical figure in Chesnutt's mind and a long-term personal influence; Chesnutt's biography *Frederick Douglass* (1899) was so laudatory that it was criticized by some reviewers for its adulatory tone.

[2]Apparently unaware of Chesnutt's biography, Washington gave his the same title, *Frederick Douglass*; see 22 November 1907 to Washington where Chesnutt registers his response to Washington's volume published in 1906.

[3]See 22 March 1907 to Hugh M. Browne.

To Hugh M. Browne

June 1, 1907.

My dear Professor Browne,

I beg to acknowledge receipt and thank you for an invitation to attend the commencement exercises of your Institute.[1] I regret that other engagements have rendered it impossible for me to be present. I received some little time ago a package of copies of the first of the Ray Stannard Baker articles in the *American Magazine*.[2] I mailed them to various gentlemen in this city to whom I thought they would prove interesting, and whose influence will be productive of good in that behalf.

Cordially yours,

TCU: TNF

[1]See 14 July 1906 to Hugh M. Browne, n. 1.
[2]See 22 March 1907 to Browne, n. 2.

To Booker T. Washington

July 11, 1907

My dear Dr. Washington:—

I write you this letter at the request of Mr. Nahum D. Brascher of this city. Mr. Brascher has for several years edited the *Cleveland Journal*, published in the interests of the colored people.[1] The *Journal*, while always a consistent advocate of the rights and interests of the race, has always been conservative in its tone, and has never indulged in any intemperate criticism of your policies or utterances. On the contrary, Mr. Brascher has been one of your ardent supporters and holds you in the highest esteem.[2]

This is of course but the prologue. Mr. Brascher's physician has advised him that a less rigorous climate than that of Cleveland would be of benefit to his health. His newspaper too, I think, is not especially prosperous. He would like if possible to secure an appointment, some time before the end of the year, to some position in the Congressional Library at Washington, and he has requested me to write and ask you if he might command your support and interest in this matter. Mr. Brascher is a young man of irreproachable character, ambitious for the best things, and entirely worthy of any sympathy or encouragement or interest which you can in any way extend him.[3]

Trusting you are well and that I may have the pleasure of seeing you during a visit I shall make to New York within a few weeks,[4] I remain

Sincerely yours,

Chas. W. Chesnutt.

TLS: DLC

[1]Nahum D. Brascher, born in Indiana and educated in Zanesville, O., moved to Cleveland late in the 19th century and found employment in real estate and advertising. He cofounded the Journal Publishing Company with Leroy Crawford (?–1954), real estate and insurance broker Welcome T. Blue (1867–1930), and Thomas Wallace Fleming (1874–1948), an attorney and Republican politician. Their company published the *Cleveland Journal* from 1903 to 1912.

[2]The Bookerite motto of the *Journal* was "Labor Conquers All Things."

[3]A copy of Washington's 15 July 1907 letter to Brascher (TNF) pledges assistance in the search for a suitable position. Brascher wrote to Chesnutt on 29 July 1907 (TNF), noting that he had heard from Washington and expressing the hope that Chesnutt would continue to press Washington in his behalf.

[4]See 1 August 1907 to Washington.

To Celia Parker Wooley

July 11, 1907

My dear Mrs. Wooley:—

I trust you will pardon me for not acknowledging sooner the receipt of copy of "our" play, which you were good enough to send me.[1] I have been exceedingly busy for several weeks, and out of town part of the time, and have n't time even now to go into the matter in detail as fully as I should like to. But I have read the manuscript with interest. It would not have been exactly my scheme of developing the story, but it is very cleverly done and I have seen a number of complimentary references to it in some of the newspapers published for colored people.

My own idea of dramatizing the story would not have taken the action back to the days of slavery, but would have begun with some preliminary development concerning the relations between Mr. Ryder and Mrs. Dixon, emphasizing the difference between Mr. Ryder and his old wife, and thereby of course enhancing the sacrifice which he made for a principle. It is quite likely, however, that your idea, being a broader one, is a better one. I am very glad that the play was produced. An author is always glad to have the children of his brain dressed up and presented to the world in flesh and blood. I hope to write to you further in regard to the matter.

With thanks for your courtesy and good wishes for your work, I remain

Sincerely yours,
Chas. W. Chesnutt.

TCS: TNF
[1]Wooley's dramatic adaptation of the short story "The Wife of His Youth" was performed on 30 April 1907 in Chicago; see 22 March 1907 to Wooley.

To Booker T. Washington

1 August 1907
My dear Dr. Washington—

Permit me to thank you for your hospitality in putting me up over night at your beautiful place. I enjoyed my brief visit immensely.[1]

While there I meant to speak to you about Mr. Brascher, and before I left I asked Mr. Cox[2] to say to you that Brascher is a very worthy fellow, who would be grateful and appreciative of anything you could do for him. He has a great deal of self-respect but is not at all conceited or vain. I hope to mention him when I see you again—I promised to *speak* to you about him and it is on my conscience.[3]

Shall be here all day Friday and probably Saturday, and shall be glad to talk with you further about your book—or any other subject.[4]

Yours cordially,
Chas. W. Chesnutt—

ALS: DLC
[1]In an undated letter on the stationery of Manhattan's Hotel Belleclaire, Chesnutt informed Washington that he would "be very glad to meet" with him (DLC). In consequence, he was Washington's house guest at Huntington, Long Island. Chesnutt then returned to the Belleclaire where he wrote the present letter.

[2]Julius Robert Cox (1867–1907), a former bookkeeper, became Washington's private secretary in 1904.

[3]Nahum D. Brascher did not receive the hoped-for appointment at the Library of Congress (see 11 July 1907 to Washington). He did, however, enjoy the patronage of Thomas W. Fleming, Cleveland's first African-American member of the City Council. Elected in 1909, Fleming arranged Brascher's appointment as a city storekeeper. In July 1917, he moved to Chicago where he was an editor for the Associated Negro Press.

[4]Washington's *The Negro in Business* was published in 1907. Possibly discussed instead was the work entitled *The Story of the Negro*, which appeared in 1909.

To Theodore E. Burton

Aug. 31, 1907

Dear Mr. Burton:

It would give me great pleasure to see you run for Mayor.[1] It might involve some sacrifice, but there would be compensations. To be the mayor of a great city in our days is to fill a very conspicuous and useful career, and to beat Johnson would be a national event.[2] You could do it—to the great benefit of Cleveland and the Republican Party.

Yours Cordially,
Chas. W. Chesnutt

TLS: OClWHi, Theodore E. Burton Papers

[1]Theodore E. Burton (1851–1929) was a member of the U.S. House of Representatives from Chesnutt's congressional district (1889–91, 1895–1909, and 1927–28) and served as U.S. senator in 1928–29. One of Chesnutt's long-term acquaintances, he assisted with the distribution of copies of *The Marrow of Tradition* (1901) among congressmen whom Chesnutt hoped to influence in 1902.

[2]Democrat Tom L. Johnson (1854–1911) was a wealthy Ohio manufacturer, admirer of the writings of social reformer Henry George (1839–97), and U.S. congressman (1891–95). He had been the mayor of Cleveland since 1901 and become a nationally-known figure because of his efforts to regulate public utilities and to diminish the power of the Republican political "boss" Mark A. Hanna (1837–1904). That a Burton victory would be "a national event" was due to Johnson's reputation; he was described as "the best mayor of the best governed city in America" by journalist Lincoln Steffens (1866–1936) in "Ohio: A Tale of Two Cities," *McClure's Magazine*, 25 (July 1905), 293–311.

To the Citizen's Committee of Cleveland

September 1, 1907.

Chairman Citizen's Committee:—

If I were at the meeting,[1] which I hope to be, but am likely to be kept away by a previous business engagement, I should say that the time had about come for colored voters to let it be understood by political parties that they appreciate the ballot as a means of defense of their rights and interests, and a weapon to punish those who ignore them. The Republican party has historic and well grounded claims upon the Negro vote, but in order to retain it, it must give that element of the party due recognition, in legislation and in practical politics. There can be no better time to make this plain than now. The colored vote will be needed in Northern elections from now on.

The local vote is large enough to demand recognition, and there should be a good man on the city ticket. Mr. Jacob E. Reed is an aspirant for the nomination of councilman-at-large. He is a good man, and would make a worthy representative, for whom I should be glad to vote.[2] If possible we should agree on some man, and ask that he be placed on the ticket, with the understanding that some other good man, who might be willing to step aside for the sake of harmony, be provided for otherwise—surely there ought to be room for two colored men somewhere under the city administration. If it is impossible to agree, fight it out in the convention, but let it be distinctly understood that the Republican party can no longer expect the colored vote to make bricks for it without straw[3]—in the way of protection of their rights, state and national, and a just recognition of their claims for consideration in the distribution of patronage.

Respectfully,

TCU: TNF

[1]The meeting of the Citizen's Committee and its date were not announced in the *Cleveland Gazette* or other Cleveland newspapers.

[2]Jacob E. Reed (1852–1935), who had moved to Cleveland from Pennsylvania two decades earlier, worked his way up from a variety of blue-collar jobs to co-ownership of a fish market by 1893. A prominent civic leader, Reed co-founded Cleveland's most socially distinguished African-American church, St. Andrew's Episcopal, in 1890; he would serve as the first vice-president of the Cleveland Association of Colored Men when it was organized in June 1908. Reed's candidacy for councilman-at-large was announced in "T. E. Burton Heads Ticket," *Cleveland Journal*, 14 September 1907, 1; but, as chairman of a mass meeting of African-American voters on 29 October 1907, he supported Thomas W. Fleming as a candidate for this office.

[3]Exodus 5:7.

To Will N. Harben

October 11, 1907.

Dear Sir:—

I have read with interest your *Mam' Linda*, a copy of which you were good enough to have sent me.[1] I must confess that I find all novels dealing with Southern race conditions painful reading—much as would be hospital reports, because, after all, conditions in the South are pathological—in spite of the fact that I have tried to write them. One is inclined to think, after reading one of them, that if the negroes of the South are very much inferior to the white people around them, they must be in a very bad way indeed.

But your novel ought to make for better conditions. It condemns injustice, exalts righteousness, and preaches the doctrine of fair play. It recognizes the essential wickedness of race prejudice, at least in its grosser and more brutal aspects, and it breathes a human sympathy which reaches beyond the borders of race, and recognizes the wider bond of humanity. I hope your ideal hero may prove to be a prototype whom many will seek to emulate, and that your novel may offset in some degree the literature of race hatred which has of late years flooded the land.[2] The marked passages in the pamphlet I enclose, suggest how great is the need of men like Carson Dwight.[3]

Cordially yours,

TCU: TNF

[1]Will N. Harben (1858–1919), a prolific novelist born in Georgia, had been a newspaperman and assistant editor for *The Youth's Companion* (1891–93) before turning exclusively to writing prose fiction. *Mam' Linda* (1907) is one of several works set in the fictional southern community of Darley.

[2]Carson Dwight, the protagonist of *Mam' Linda*, is a young white attorney whose belief that African Americans are not being treated fairly alienates him from his acquaintances in Darley. The tale ends happily: Dwight saves a falsely accused black man from the clutches of a mob, and he is subsequently elected to the house of representatives of his state.

[3]The pamphlet sent to Harben was not identified by Chesnutt here or elsewhere in his correspondence.

To the Editor of the *Cleveland Journal*

[26 October 1907]

Editor of *The Cleveland Journal*:

Colored voters should support Mr. Burton[1] for the same reasons that should influence other voters. He is an able, honest statesman, of tried powers, who would give Cleveland a conservative, economical and progressive administration. He is a Cleveland man, educated at Oberlin College, and imbued with the best traditions of that institution and of the Republican party. His proposed settlement of the street railroad question is practicable, just to all concerned, and will be of immediate benefit to all the people,[2] especially those who live in the Central and Quincy avenues district.[3]

This is a municipal election, and the local issues are large enough to stand alone. To those who seek to drag national issues into the campaign,[4] my answer would be that I am unable to see how the colored voters have anything to gain by turning away from their own party and that of their friends, to the party which, in those states where it is in control, is responsible for the disfranchisement and civic degradation of the Negro.

Yours sincerely,
Chas. W. Chesnutt

"Leading Citizens Endorse Burton," *Cleveland Journal*, 26 October 1907, 1.

[1]Theodore E. Burton; see 31 August 1907 to Burton, n. 1. Published with other statements by prominent African-American Clevelanders, Chesnutt's letter appeared under the subtitle "Burton Will Be Progressive."

[2]A major issue of the election was the regulation of streetcar fares: Burton proposed a rate of 3½¢ and Johnson 3¢.

[3]Principally African Americans.

[4]The national issue in question was whether the U.S. senator from Ohio Joseph B. Foraker (1846–1917) was supportive of or opposed to fellow-Republican Burton's candidacy. See 21 November 1907 to Hicks, n. 3.

To Lucius S. Hicks

November 21, 1907.

Dear Sir:—

Replying to yours of recent date,[1] I beg to say that the municipal campaign at Cleveland, which was over before I received your letter, was fought out on the street-car issue, by the respective opinions upon which nine-tenths of the whole vote, including even a larger proportion of the colored vote, was determined. The election was won by the popular low-fare candidate, Mr. Johnson, who has for years advocated three-cent street-railroad fare.[2]

I do not know anything about the deep-laid scheme for the elimination of Senator Foraker by means of Mr. Burton's candidacy for Mayor of Cleveland. If there was any such thing, it failed. From letters written by Senator Foraker and published during the campaign, it appeared that Senator Foraker favored Mr. Burton's election and expressed the wish that he might succeed.³ So far as Senator Dick is concerned, I imagine there is no doubt about his friendliness to the colored voter.⁴

Yours very truly,

TDU, revised by hand: TNF

¹After his graduation from the Boston Latin School (1896–1902), Lucius S. Hicks (1881–?) spent one year at Harvard and, at the time he wrote Chesnutt, was a law student at Boston University. He received the LL.B. degree in 1908 and was admitted to the Massachusetts Bar in 1909. Thereafter he practiced law in Boston and was active in local politics.

²See 26 October 1907 to the editor of the *Cleveland Journal*. Not only Tom L. Johnson but all of the Democrat candidates for municipal offices won; Johnson would complete his third term as mayor in 1909.

³Republican Joseph B. Foraker, former governor of Ohio (1885–89) and current U.S. senator (1897–1909), had been alleged by the Democrats in Cleveland to be a supporter of the Democrat candidates. The allegation appeared in newspapers across Ohio, and Foraker was obliged to write disclaimers to all of the Cleveland newspapers. Before Chesnutt rewrote it, the first sentence of this paragraph did not interpret the chicanery of the Democrats; it stated instead, "I do not know whether Mr. Burton was opposed to Senator Foraker."

⁴Charles Dick (1858–1945), a former member of the U.S. House of Representatives (1898–1904), was presently serving as U.S. senator from Ohio (1904–11). Chesnutt had no doubt about Senator Dick's attitude toward the African American because of his record as a progressive Republican; as Chairman of the Republican State Executive Committee in 1907, his orientation was well known to party stalwarts such as Chesnutt. Also, Chesnutt was very likely aware of Dick's political alignment following the 1906 Brownsville incident. Senator Foraker was sure that President Theodore Roosevelt made the wrong response when punishing 160 African-American soldiers by discharging them "without honor." (See 24 November 1906 to Archibald H. Grimké, n. 6.) Dick was of a like mind and in 1908 supported Foraker for the Republican presidential nomination, rather than William H. Taft who had been Roosevelt's Secretary of War when the Brownsville incident occurred. Chesnutt's concluding sentence originally did not include a reference to Dick. It read, "The colored vote in Cleveland was not large enough to have changed the issue of the election, even had it all been cast against Mr. Burton."

To Booker T. Washington

November 22, 1907.

My dear Dr. Washington:—

I wish to thank you, somewhat tardily, for the copy of your *Life of Frederick Douglass*, that you were good enough to send me.[1] It is a very well written and readable volume, although the "Bibliography" did omit to mention my little volume upon the same subject, in the Beacon Series of American Biographies, doubtless an oversight.

I was deeply grieved to learn only a day or two ago of the death of Mr. Cox, who, I imagine, was a very useful man, whom you will find it difficult to replace.[2] If you have it in mind, kindly extend my sympathy to Mrs. Cox when you see her.[3]

Professor Browne sent me the other day a copy of Mr. Carnegie's Edinburgh address, requesting my views upon it.[4] It is worthy of all commendation, except that I do not agree with him, or with you, if you are correctly quoted, that it is the "wiser course" to let the ballot for the Negro go, substantially, by default. We may not be able to successfully resist the current of events, but it seems to me that our self-respect demands an attitude of protest against steadily progressing disfranchisement and consequent denial of civil rights, rather than one of acquiescence. Georgia is gone, Oklahoma and Maryland will soon fall into line. I hope at least that Mason and Dixon's line will prove an impassable barrier.

But while I differ from you very earnestly and deeply on this point,[5] I must congratulate you on having won over to such active friendship for the Negro, so able and influential a citizen of the world as Mr. Carnegie.

Sincerely yours,
Chas. W. Chesnutt.

TLS: DLC

[1]On 26 March 1907 (TNF), Washington thanked Chesnutt for his promised contribution of $25 toward amortization of the Frederick Douglass home in Anacostia, Md. (see 23 March 1907 to Washington). He also enclosed a copy of his biography of Douglass.

[2]Chesnutt and Julius R. Cox met at Washington's residence in Huntington, Long Island, in July 1907. See 1 August 1907 to Washington.

[3]Gertrude L. Caldwell Cox was teaching fifth grade at Tuskegee when her husband died following an operation for appendicitis.

[4]Andrew Carnegie (1835–1919), steel magnate and philanthropist, contrib-

uted substantial funds in support of both Tuskegee and the Committee of Twelve. On 16 October 1907 he delivered an address, "The Negro in America," to the Philosophical Institution of Edinburgh—for which Washington's lieutenant, Emmett J. Scott, had provided information used by Carnegie. Hugh M. Browne sent Chesnutt a copy of Carnegie's address with a cover letter dated 13 November 1907 (TNF), in which he asked for immediate response regarding the desirability of publishing the speech as a Committee of Twelve pamphlet. When Chesnutt failed to reply, Browne wrote him again on 20 November 1907 (TNF) and a third time on 20 December 1907 (TNF) to inform him that the revised version of the address would be published.

[5]In the context of the Chesnutt-Washington correspondence dating back to 1900, Chesnutt is here sounding a note familiar to Washington: once again Chesnutt attacks the position on disfranchisement that he uniformly perceived as Washington's. Washington did not rebut until after he learned that Chesnutt had aired the same complaint in a letter to Hugh M. Browne. See 1 January 1908 to Washington.

To Booker T. Washington

Jan. 1, 1908[1]

My dear Dr. Washington:—

I received your long and interesting letter.[2] I shall be glad to thresh the ballot proposition over with you sometime.[3] As to the ballot, the importance of a thing is not to be measured by the number of times you do it. Some of the most important and vital things of life are done only once. A man is born only once, but on that act depends his whole life; he dies only once, which ends all his hopes and fears and usefulness. He marries only a few times.

The importance of the ballot is to me a paramount element of citizenship.[4] A man can earn his daily bread easier and bank more money with it than without it. You argue the question as though the Negro must choose between voting and eating. He ought to do both, and he can do both better together than he can do either alone. It is not the *act* of voting I speak of—it is the right of every citizen to have some part in the choice of those who rule him, and the only way he can express that choice is at the polls. It is just as effective if he votes once in five years as once a day. Would you maintain for a moment that the economic conditions in the South, which crush the Negro and drive away white immigration, would continue to exist if the Negroes could vote, and their votes were directed by intelligent leadership? If they could vote, and you with your power of leadership, would direct their votes in the right channel, do you believe their condition would not be materially improved? I do, and you do. It is not all of life to eat or to put money in the bank, but, as I say, a free man can do both of those things better than a mere praedial serf, yoked to the mule, with no concern in life but his belly & his back. If the colored people ever expect to cut any figure in this Republic they must not pitch their ideals too low; tho their feet must of course rest upon the earth, it should not be forbidden to them to lift their eyes to the Hills.[5]

Wishing you a Happy & prosperous New Year,

Cordially yours,
Chas. W. Chesnutt.

ALS: CtY

[1]Misdated 1907.

[2]Washington wrote to Chesnutt on 6 December 1907 (DLC), responding not to Chesnutt's direct criticism of his position on the franchise for African Americans (see 22 November 1907 to Washington) but to Chesnutt's restatement of his point of view in a letter to Hugh M. Browne that Washington had read in Boston. In this letter, Chesnutt was answering Browne's query: since Andrew Carnegie had asked for suggestions as to how his recent speech, "The Negro in America," might be improved by revision, did Chesnutt have any suggestions? Chesnutt was critical of both Carnegie and Washington. Washington thus wrote to Chesnutt, "In your letter [to Browne] you say: 'On one point, however, I do not at all agree with Mr. Carnegie or with Dr. Washington, whom he quotes, in holding it "the wiser course" to practically throw up the ballot, or the demand for it.'" Washington observed that "Mr. Carnegie has said no such thing," nor had he himself. Washington promised to send "a first class Alabama possum for . . . Christmas dinner" if Chesnutt could prove that he had ever made a statement of the kind.

[3]On 6 December, Washington invited Chesnutt to "thrash this out" with him "when we meet again."

[4]Chesnutt did not wait until he saw Washington again to "thrash this out" with him. He here initiates a point-by-point rebuttal of the clarifications of his position on voting rights that Washington offered in his 6 December letter. Washington explained, "there is no disagreement between you and me as to the importance of the ballot"; but some "of our people maintain that the ballot is a matter of first consideration in our present condition. This I do not agree with." Paramount instead is "the matter of earning your daily bread and banking your money." One votes, perhaps, once in two years, but one must make a living "every day in the year, except Sundays." Educating one's children and "attending church" are also more pressing needs. That is, concluded Washington, there "is something deeper in human progress than the mere act of voting."

[5]In Helen M. Chesnutt's typed copy of a now-unavailable draft of this letter (TNF), Chesnutt originally concluded with "it should not be forbidden to

them to lift their eyes to the stars." Perhaps deciding to respond playfully to Washington's 6 December observation that Chesnutt did not attend church regularly, he revised his conclusion to paraphrase Psalms 21:1: "I will lift up mine eyes unto the hills, from whence cometh my help."

To Charlotte Teller

April 22, 1908.

Dear Madam,

Replying to yours of March 28th,[1] I beg to say that I lived in the South a number of years when a child, and extending into manhood, and have kept pretty closely in touch all my life with the literature and current information regarding the negro in the United States, and I can assure you that I have never yet learned of any authentic instance of the practice of "voodoo." Indeed, the worship of the snake and the sacrifice of the "Goat without horns" are absolutely unknown to the American negro, nor have I ever heard the suggestion that it was ever practiced except possibly in early days in some modified form among the slaves of Louisiana. The stories of voodoo worship in Haiti and some of the West Indies are probably grossly exaggerated. They are like ghost stories—you never meet any one who saw a ghost, but someone who has seen someone whose brother's wife's cousin knew a man who had once seen a ghost. Of course there is a certain dramatic value to that sort of thing in fiction, but fiction to my mind ought to be, if not founded on fact, at least within the limit of probability. I am entirely convinced that if you make voodoo as I understand it play any large part in your story, it will be untrue to the facts or to the psychology of the negro mind. There are lingering superstitions in the remoter parts of the South concerning conjuration, "goophering", and things of that sort, but they are a very attenuated form of original African witchcraft or fetichism, and are little more than the current superstitions of ignorant white people in the same part of the country, from which it would be extremely difficult to differentiate them.

I note in your postscript you say that capitalism necessitates slavery. That opens up a large subject which one cannot discuss within the limits of a letter.[2]

Cordially yours,

P.S. I am unable to direct you to any source for information about voodooism. A reference to a good library catalogue or to *Poole's In-*

*dex*³ will probably disclose what you want; most of it is fleeting magazine articles, and, as I say, as a rule untrustworthy because not based on any accurate observation.

TCU: TNF
¹Charlotte Teller Hirsch (1876–?) was the author of *The Words of Paul: Drama in Four Acts* (1905), *Mirabeau: A Play in Five Acts* (1906), and another play, *The Sociological Maid* (1906). Her labor movement novel *The Cage* appeared in 1907. She is now renowned principally for her correspondence with Mark Twain, published as *S.L.C to C.T.* (1925). Having come across Chesnutt's "goopher" stories in *The Conjure Woman* (1899), Teller wrote him to request information on voodooism, one of the subjects of a story she was currently writing (TNF).

²After thanking Chesnutt on 24 April (TNF) for his courteous reply, Teller explained her brief remark on 28 March concerning the relationship between capitalism and slavery: "I am speaking, of course, as a Socialist, believing with those like Harriet Beecher Stowe and Phillips Brooks, that the wage slavery of the white man is not far less disgraceful than the old slavery of the black. We have to fight the system in this." Stowe (1811–96) is thus recalled as the author of *Uncle Tom's Cabin* (1851–52). Phillips Brooks (1835–93) was a prominent "broad-church" Episcopalian bishop who preached at Trinity Church in Boston; while a vigorous moralist, he is now remembered principally for his composition of the hymn "O Little Town of Bethlehem!" (1880).

³*Poole's Index to Periodical Literature* has been an essential reference work in libraries since its initial publication in 1883.

To Hugh M. Browne

April 22, 1908.

Dear Mr. Browne:—

I am in receipt of yours of April 13th, with reference to the copy of Mr. Carnegie's Edinburgh Address to be presented to him. It was a very happy thought, and I am entirely willing that a sub-committee shall sign for the Committee of Twelve.¹ It was a very friendly address, not as advanced a position perhaps as you and I would take,² but a tremendous advance from the common ordinary garden variety of opinion with reference to the negro; and the mere fact that Mr. Carnegie aligns himself as a friend of the race is extremely significant and valuable.³

Cordially yours,

TCU: TNF

[1]The Committee of Twelve had published Andrew Carnegie's recent speech concerning African Americans as the pamphlet entitled *The Negro in America, an Address Delivered before the Philosophical Institution of Edinburgh, 16 October 1907* (1907). On 13 April 1908 (TNF), Browne proposed that a leather-bound copy be signed by those members of the Committee who could be readily reached and then presented to Carnegie as soon as was practicable.

[2]See 22 November 1907 and 1 January 1908 to Booker T. Washington for Chesnutt's other thoughts concerning the address.

[3]Carnegie's alignment resulted in Browne's informing Chesnutt on 14 May 1908 (TNF) of what had transpired at a 3 May meeting of the Committee in the District of Columbia that Chesnutt did not attend: announced was Carnegie's contribution of $3,000 and his charge to the Committee to "gather, publish and distribute facts bearing on the progress of Negroes in America."

To Booker T. Washington

June 1, 1908.

My dear Dr. Washington:—

I received your letter, requesting me to reserve for you at the Hollenden Hotel, a room with a bath, for June 29th and 30th.[1] The manager stated that they would be glad to take care of you, but that they were not reserving rooms during the N.E.A. convention unless they were reserved for the whole period, to-wit: five days, beginning with the 29th. I told him that would be all right, that he should make the reservation, and since you were occupying the room for the first two days of the period, it would probably not remain vacant at all after you gave it up; but if there were any loss, I would guarantee it.[2] I hope this arrangement will meet your wishes.[3]

My family join me in regards to you and yours.[4]

Very sincerely yours,
Chas. W. Chesnutt

TLS: DLC

[1]Washington informed Chesnutt on 26 May 1908 (TNF) that he would address the National Education Association in Cleveland and asked him to make hotel reservations. Washington thanked him on 4 June 1908 (DLC) for his prompt attention to this request.

[2]In the same 4 June letter, Washington assured Chesnutt that he would assume the cost of the hotel stay.

[3]On 3 July at the Hippodrome Theater, Washington spoke to N.E.A. con-

ventioneers on "Negro Education and the Negro"; his text was published in the *Cleveland Journal*, 4 July 1908, 1.

⁴On 1 July 1908 (DLC), Washington thanked Chesnutt for the "many acts of thoughtful kindness" extended him and invited Chesnutt to visit him in Huntington, Long Island, where he planned to spend "a large part of the summer."

To Walter C. Camp

June 4, 1908.

Dear Sir:—

In your speech in response to the toast "The Yale Field", at the Yale dinner here a couple of weeks ago, you quoted certain fines imposed in the university in the past generation.¹ Observing that you were reading it and assuming that I could get the manuscript, I did not take it down. You will remember I spoke to you about the matter at the close of your speech. I am sending you herewith a copy of your remarks as I took them down, and if you will kindly fill in that gap and make any other changes that you care to, and return the copy to me, I shall be very much obliged. I also enclose you the memoranda which you handed me.²

Yours very truly,

TCU: TNF

¹This is a typical piece of business correspondence illustrating the nature of Chesnutt's work as a professional stenographer. Walter C. Camp (1859–1925) was graduated from Yale University in 1880. He studied at Yale Medical School for two years and then initiated a life-long business association with the New Haven Clock Co. In 1888, this executive began serving as Yale's athletic director and head football coach; he was also well known as the author of a number of football-related novels and handbooks on coaching. Chesnutt transcribed Camp's speech given at the fourth Dinner of Associated Western Yale Clubs, held in Cleveland on 23 May 1908 (see "Old Grads Have Good Time Here," Cleveland *Plain Dealer*, 24 May 1908, 1); other speakers at the banquet included soon-to-be-elected U.S. President William H. Taft and financier John Hays Hammond (1855–1936).

²Camp replied on 6 June 1908 (TNF), agreeing to edit the transcription, promising to send the information on fines, and asking where the speech was to be published. On 20 June (TNF), Chesnutt thanked him for his cooperation and related that he knew of no plan to publish the speech.

To William H. Richards

June 6, 1908

My dear Prof. Richards:—

Please excuse my delay in answering your letter of May 2nd.[1] May was about the busiest month of my life, and I have had to work up to things as rapidly as I could. I have n't decided whether I can go to Washington on the last day of September or the first Tuesday of October, but so far as things seem at present, I see nothing that would interfere with my visiting Washington at that time. I will therefore accept your invitation, and will keep the appointment unless something of very grave importance intervenes to prevent me. So far as I know at present either date will be equally convenient to me.

I trust that you are well, and shall look forward with pleasure to meeting you.[2]

Sincerely yours,

TCU: TNF

[1]Richards had invited Chesnutt to come to Washington, D.C., to initiate the 1908–9 Bethel Literary and Historical Association lecture series on either the last Tuesday in September or the first Tuesday in October (TNF).

[2]Chesnutt spoke before the Bethel Association on 6 October 1908; see 9 October 1908 to Edwin J. Chesnutt and to Reverdy M. Hall.

To Hugh M. Browne

June 6, 1908.

Dear Prof. Browne:—

I am in receipt of yours of June 3rd, with reference to the appointment of young man in Jackson, Miss., for sociological investigation. I think it is a very good idea. There ought to be material enough in that region to write an encyclopedia.[1]

Yours truly,

TCU: TNF

[1]On 3 June 1908 (TNF), Browne suggested that the results of the proposed investigation of conditions in Jackson could be published along with "statistical articles" in the yearbook issued annually at Tuskegee on the progress made during the previous year by African Americans. The Committee of Twelve subsequently hired Dudley Weldon Woodard (1881?–?), a mathematics teacher at Tuskegee (1907–14), to perform the study and published it as *Negro Progress in*

a Mississippi Town, being a Study of Conditions in Jackson, Mississippi (1909). Also cited in the title was a second essay included in the pamphlet, *Negro Banks of Mississippi* by Charles Banks (1873–1923), the 1904 founder of the Bank of Mound Bayou in the black community of Mound Bayou, Miss.

To James Ball Naylor

June 10, 1908.

My Dear Sir:—

I am in receipt in this morning's mail of your letter of June 8th, and also of autographed copy of your *Sign of the Prophet*, with the very clever sentiment inscribed on the fly-leaf, followed by your autograph.[1] It is a very handsome book and I shall certainly read it, not from any sense of compulsion but because I expect to enjoy it.

I am sending you by this mail a copy of my novel *The House Behind the Cedars*,[2] which I trust you may find interesting.[3] I join with you in the hope that our paths may sometime cross and that we may meet at the junction point.

Cordially yours,

TCU: TNF

[1] James Ball Naylor (1860–1945) was a physician, poet, and prolific novelist.

[2] Published in 1900.

[3] On 29 April 1908 (TNF), Naylor had proposed that Chesnutt and he exchange autographed copies of one of their books. On 6 June (TNF), Chesnutt agreed to the exchange, requesting one that he had not read, *The Sign of the Prophet: A Tale of Tecumseh and Tippecanoe* (1901).

To Hugh M. Browne

June 20, 1908.

Dear Prof. Browne:—

Pardon my delay in acknowledging receipt of yours of June 9th, with copy of address to the American people adopted by the bishops.[1] I see no objection to its publication, nor any good reason why it should be published. But I will very willingly abide by whatever decision is reached. If it is published, the proof ought to be pretty carefully read over by you or some other educated person. The names of the Christian Fathers are "balled up" somewhat. I am not able to see why Africa should be the scene of the great operations of the American Church; indeed, I am not greatly concerned about Africa except as an interesting foreign country.

The grammar of a certain passage at the bottom of page 2 which I have marked, is somewhat shaky.[2]

Trusting that you are well this hot weather and may enjoy a pleasant summer, I remain,

Sincerely yours,

TCU: TNF

[1]On 9 June 1908 (TNF), Browne sent Chesnutt a copy of "Address to the American People," written jointly by bishops of the A.M.E., A.M.E.Z., and C.M.E. churches, requesting Chesnutt's opinion on its suitability for publication by the Committee of Twelve.

[2]On 16 July (TNF), Browne reported that negative responses from other members of the Committee had resulted in the decision not to produce such a pamphlet.

To Mrs. Walter Sampson

August 8, 1908.

My dear Mrs. Sampson,

I reached home after a very interesting and instructive trip from Boston up through the White Mountains to Quebec, where I saw a very interesting and picturesque city and a considerable part of the festivities; thence to Montreal and up the St. Lawrence to the Thousand Islands to Toronto, and thence home, where I found my family in good health and spirits, having borne my absence wonderfully well.

Permit me to thank you and Mr. Sampson a little more formally for your kind hospitality during my brief visit to Boston.[1] I understand my sister Lillian is visiting your city and will probably be there when you receive this.[2] With best wishes, believe me

Cordially yours,

TCU: TNF

[1]Mr. and Mrs. Walter Sampson were Boston relatives of Chesnutt, Walter having also descended from the family of Chesnutt's maternal grandmother, Chloe Sampson.

[2]In the late 1880s, Chesnutt's youngest sister, Lillian Chesnutt Richardson (1871–1940), moved to Cleveland and worked for her brother for several years, first as a typist and then as a stenographer.

To Booker T. Washington

August 28, 1908.

My dear Dr. Washington,

I was duly in receipt of newspaper cutting containing your letter to the New York *World* on the subject of lynching.[1] I not only note the facts, with which I was already reasonably familiar through the newspapers, but I also note the direct and forceful manner in which you refer to them. It is a very wise and just presentment of a point of view which ought to be pressed upon the public consciousness, and I have no doubt whatever that coming from you it will have its weight.

I had a letter from my daughter Helen the other day, telling me that you paid a visit to Arundel-on-the-Bay, and seemed to enjoy yourself.[2] I hope you feel all the better for the social relaxation in which you have indulged during the summer.

Cordially yours,
Chas. W. Chesnutt.

TLS: DLC

[1]A race riot, triggered by the transfer of a prisoner accused of rape, occurred in Springfield, Ill., from 14 to 16 August 1908. Two African Americans, brothers Scott and George Donigan, were lynched, and seventy-five other blacks were injured before order was restored. Washington's condemnation of lynching as a "danger that threatens our civilization" appeared as "A Statement on Lynching," New York *World*, 20 August 1908, 9.

[2]While in Baltimore, where he wrote his statement on lynching, Washington visited the Chesapeake Bay resort at which Helen and Edwin Chesnutt were vacationing.

To Hugh M. Browne

September 16, 1908.

Dear Prof. Browne:—

I have your favor enclosing copy of story of work done by the colored people of Baltimore in waging war against saloons and dens of vice within the district where they reside. It outlines a very interesting story of self-help.[1] I cannot imagine a subject upon which a paper would be more profitable.

Yours truly,

TCU: TNF

[1]On 11 September 1908 (TNF), Browne suggested that the anti-vice war in Baltimore be the subject of a Committee of Twelve pamphlet, and on 15 September (TNF), he sent Chesnutt an outline for the project. Published before the year's end was *Work of the Colored Law and Order League, Baltimore, Md.* (1908) by James Henry Nelson Waring, Sr. (1861–1924), a graduate of Howard University's medical college (1888) and since 1903 the principal of the Baltimore Colored High and Training School.

To William English Walling

September 17, 1908.

Dear Sir:—

I wish to express my appreciation of the very fine article from your pen, in a recent number of the *Independent*, on the Springfield riot.[1] You are in the van of the movement for which you recognize the necessity—a movement to give the Negro equality—not any particular kind of equality, but simply equality, with whatever the word may justly imply. No man is free who is not as free as any other man. By that test the Negro must stand or fall; and the important thing for all of us, is not whether he shall stand or fall, but that he shall have an equal chance.

Cordially yours,

TCU: TNF

[1]Married to prominent socialist writer Anna Strunsky (1879–1964), William English Walling (1877–1936) was a Southerner opposed to racism who would co-found in 1909 the National Negro Committee, forerunner to the N.A.A.C.P. In "The Race War in the North," *Independent*, 65 (3 September 1908), 529–34, Walling charged the citizens of Springfield, Ill., with gross insensitivity to the dire situation in which their black fellow-townsmen had been placed as a result of the race riot that occurred there in August. See 28 August 1908 to Booker T. Washington.

To Ulysses L. Marvin

September 17, 1908.

My dear Judge:—

Some one sent me a copy of the *Ohio State Journal* containing a report of your address at St. Paul's Church in Columbus.[1] I can see, even from so brief an abstract, that you are about as radical on the subject as I am; and it is a case where the radicals of our way of thinking are right.[2] Mr. Ray Stannard Baker, in the concluding number of his series of well considered articles on the Negro, which have been running in the *American Magazine*, (it will appear in the October number, which will be out in a few days,)[3] reaches the same conclusion. He says:—

As a fundamental proposition, then, it will be found that the solution of the negro problem lies in treating the negro more and more as a human being like ourselves. Treating the negro as a human being, we must judge him, not by his color, or by any outward symbol, but upon his worth as a man. Nothing that fails of that full honesty and fairness of judgment in the smallest particular will suffice.[4]

You deserve the thanks of all good citizens, and I give you mine—I try to stay in that category.

Yours cordially,

TCU: TNF

[1]Ulysses L. Marvin (1839–1925) was a captain in the Fifth United States Colored Infantry during the Civil War who had served as a judge of the Circuit Court of Appeals of Northeastern Ohio for nearly two decades. His address delivered at the St. Paul A.M.E. Church in Columbus, O., was reported in "Unworthy of Men Is Racial Hatred," *Ohio State Journal*, 14 September 1908, 2. He declared that "the prejudice against the negro was groundless, unworthy, and unchristian" and that "upon investigation, he had found that in a majority of cases where race wars occurred the whites were to blame."

[2]Judge Marvin opposed disfranchisement of African Americans, deeming the Fifteenth Amendment, like the Thirteenth and Fourteenth, "wise."

[3]The article in question appeared in the September issue. See n. 4.

[4]After completing a series of five articles on African Americans for *American Magazine* (see 22 March 1907 to Hugh M. Browne, n. 2), Baker produced eight more pieces published in this monthly between February and September 1908. The one quoted here is "What to Do about the Negro," *American Magazine*, 66 (September 1908), 463–70. The same point made by Baker was enunciated by Judge Marvin: "the only solution of the race problem is for a man to be treated as what he is, good or bad, irrespective of his race or color, and that . . . the time would come in America when this solution would arrive."

To Edwin J. Chesnutt

October 9, 1908

. . . I went down to Baltimore last Saturday night, stayed there over Sunday and until Monday noon, met a number of fine people, including Dr. Waring, Mr. Bishop and Mr. Hughes.[1] I stopped at Dr. Hall's[2] and visited the high school Monday morning.[3] I then went on to Washington, was cordially received, and lavishly entertained. Lectured at the Bethel Literary Tuesday night[4] to a very large audience, among whom were all the best people, and strange to say pleased them all with my lecture, which was on "Rights and Duties,"[5] referring, of course, to the everlasting problem. I labored like a mountain in bringing forth my arguments, and was greatly relieved that no one seemed to regard them as a mouse[6]. . . .

Pioneer: 229

[1]Chesnutt arrived in Baltimore on 3 October and went to the District of Columbia on 5 October. James H. N. Waring was an educator (see 16 September 1908 to Browne, n. 1). William H. Bishop (1851–1918) held various clerical positions with the U.S. Department of Revenue office in Baltimore, eventually becoming the chief clerk. W. A. C. Hughes (1877–1940) had served since 1905 as the pastor of Baltimore's Sharp Street Memorial Methodist Episcopal Church.

[2]Dr. Reverdy M. Hall (1846–?) was a graduate of Howard University Medical College and practiced medicine in Baltimore. Chesnutt and he were well acquainted by the time the first surviving letter between the two men was written (Hall to Chesnutt, 18 November 1905 [TNF]). He stayed with the Chesnutts in late November 1905, when making a vacation excursion from Baltimore to the American West.

[3]The Baltimore Colored High and Training School, which was under the direction of Waring (see n. 1). Helen M. Chesnutt taught there for most of the 1901–2 academic year (*Pioneer*: 183–84).

[4]6 October 1908.

[5]See *Essays and Speeches*: 252–62.

[6]Paraphrase of Horace (Quintus Horatius Flaccus, 65–8 B.C.), *Ars Poetica*: "The laboring mountain scarce brings forth a mouse."

To Reverdy M. Hall

Oct. 9, 1908.

My dear Dr. Hall:—

I wish to thank you and Mrs. Hall most cordially for the charming hospitality extended to me in your beautiful home during my recent visit to Baltimore. I brought away the most pleasant impressions of your beautiful city, and they will long remain with me as a pleasant memory.

The people of Washington also exerted themselves to make my stay agreeable. Mr. and Mrs. Clifford, formerly of Cleveland, gave me a dinner party at which a number of the leading men were present and several ladies.[1] Dr. and Mrs. Francis entertained me at dinner,[2] and Mr. Cobb and Mr. Tyler invited me to a luncheon party at a cafe,[3] at which were Mr. Terrell[4] and several other gentlemen prominent in political life. I lectured to a large audience at the Metropolitan M.E. Church,[5] which included most of the prominent citizens; and strange to say, in spite of the various shades of opinion which they must have represented, succeeded in pleasing them all. My subject was "Rights and Duties", along the line, of course, of the ever- . . . .[6]

TCU, incomplete: TNF

[1]Carrie and William Clifford recently moved from Cleveland to Washington, D.C. William, a former member of the Ohio legislature (1894–95, 1898–99), had been appointed auditor in the War Department, where he served for over two decades. On 9 October (TNF), Chesnutt wrote letters of appreciation to the Cliffords and all of the others cited in the present letter.

[2]Dr. John R. Francis (1856–1913) was the owner of the Francis Sanatorium located on Pennsylvania Avenue, which specialized in obstetrics, gynecology, and surgery for women.

[3]James A. Cobb (1876–1958), a graduate of Fisk University and Howard University Law School, became an attorney in Washington in 1901 and served as special assistant to the Department of Justice (1907–15). Ralph Waldo Tyler (1859–1921), a former journalist with the *Columbus Evening Dispatch* (1884–1901) and *Ohio State Journal* (1901–4), was appointed auditor to the Naval Department by President Roosevelt in 1905.

[4]Robert H. Terrell (1857–1925), an attorney and educator in the District of Columbia, was appointed municipal judge in 1902 by President Roosevelt, in which position he served for the rest of his life.

[5]See 9 October 1908 to Edwin J. Chesnutt.

[6]One of Chesnutt's favorite terms for the subject of racial discrimination was "the everlasting problem." See 9 October 1908 to Edwin J. Chesnutt. The "eternal question" was another he used to express vexation; see 8 September 1924 to Judson Douglas Wetmore.

To Carrie W. Clifford

Oct. 9, 1908.

My dear Mrs. Clifford:—

I want to thank you and Mr. Clifford most cordially for your charming hospitality during my recent visit to Washington; I shall remember it for a long time. All my friends in Washington were cordial and appreciative, and left nothing undone to make my visit pleasant.[1]

I was especially pleased at the manner in which my address was received. To have evoked no word of dissent from an audience in which many different shades of opinion must have been represented, makes me feel that I must have come very near to the fundamental truths underlying our very difficult problem.

Mrs. Chesnutt and the family join me in regards to you and your family.

Sincerely yours,

TCU: TNF

[1]See 9 October 1908 to Edwin J. Chesnutt.

To Carrie W. Clifford

Oct. 15, 1908.

My dear Mrs. Clifford:—

I am in receipt of your interesting letter of October 9th.[1] I have no doubt that had you had time, you would have discussed my paper most interestingly on the night it was delivered. In fact, several said to me that the audience was just warming up to the discussion when the president, with righteous zeal for regularity of hours, adjourned the meeting.[2]

Thanks for the newspaper cutting enclosed. What you mention is no new thing.[3] Newspapers are looking for two things—something sensational, no matter how radical it is, or, in default of the sensational, something that will fit in with current public opinion and make pleasant reading. It is the fad nowadays to ignore the rights of the negro and emphasize his duties. The same rule is applied to whatever Mr. Washington says. He does emphasize the duties and says not a great deal about the rights, but what little he does say is practically ignored. That Mr. Washington is not indifferent to his rights may be gathered from the fact that when he makes a pilgrimage through a southern state, as he is doing in Mississippi at present, he hires a special car for himself and his party.[4]

I note the quotation from Mr. Baker's article. I read it and had it in my manuscript with some comment thereon, but do not remember whether I read it or not, my paper was so long. Agitation for rights is by no means foolish; where rights are denied it is a sacred duty; though of course it can be conducted in a foolish way. And of course you cannot hold Washington responsible for the language of Baker's article.[5]

You and I have no quarrels about the principle involved, nor about anything at all. Rights are fundamental—nothing can alter that fact.

I don't blame any one for becoming angry or impatient about the situation in this country. The only way for a colored person to keep calm about it is not to think about it. But there is a certain conservatism in discussion, and a certain philosophical point of view which I think quite as effective as hysterical declamation. But we need both— some to fan the flame and others to furnish the fuel.

With regards to Mr. Clifford, believe me

Sincerely yours,

TCU: TNF

[1]Clifford had written Chesnutt (TNF) on the stationery of the Niagara Movement and was identified in the letterhead as the secretary for women in the South. Founded in 1905 and disbanded in 1910, the Niagara Movement was a forerunner to the N.A.A.C.P.

[2]Helen M. Chesnutt omitted the second and third sentences of this paragraph when she published this letter (*Pioneer*: 230).

[3]The clipping is not extant. Clifford (TNF) summarized the main point of the article or editorial thus: whites are constantly advising African Americans to fulfill their obligations as citizens, and yet whites do not fulfill their own civic duty of protecting the civil rights of African Americans.

[4]Washington had just completed a 4–11 October speaking tour in Mississippi and Arkansas; see 19 October 1908 to Washington. Clifford had observed that "thinking Negroes must take issue with Dr. Washington" who continues to delineate the duties and obligations of African Americans while giving scant attention to their rights.

[5]In her letter to Chesnutt Clifford quoted from Ray Stannard Baker's article "What to Do about the Negro" (see 17 September 1908 to Ulysees L. Marvin, n. 3). She objected to Baker expressing a point of view in harmony with Booker T. Washington's, in part because his doing so would further increase factionalism within the black community. Baker had asserted that an African American should be judged solely on his "worth as a man." His corollary, though, was that "the Negro must not clamor for places he cannot fill" in American industry. Baker then quoted Washington: "The trouble with the Negro . . . is that he is all the time trying to get recognition, whereas what he should do is get something to recognize." What Clifford most deplored was how Baker concluded his treatment of the subject. He had written, "Instead of foolish agitation for the enforcement of rights which the Negro is not yet in most instances ready to use with wisdom, how wise is Booker T. Washington, emphasizing duties and responsibilities, asking his people to prepare themselves for their rights."

To William S. Bennet

Oct. 17, 1908.

Dear Sir:—

May I call your attention as Chairman of the Speakers' Bureau of the Republican National Committee,[1] to the fact that there is considerable restlessness, not to say disaffection, among the colored vote in this state and in this city, growing partly out of the Brownsville affair,[2] and partly out of a feeling that the party has neglected the rights and interests of the race? While not a politician, I am more or less of a student and observer of race and political affairs. I think, however, that if properly handled this feeling can be largely counteracted before the election. Good speakers who can point out how little is to be expected from the Democratic party, how much, after all, the Republican party has done which it might have left undone, and how very much safer the rights of the Negro will be under any sort of Republican administration than under any sort of a Democratic administration, would be effective in stemming this very real dissatisfaction.

Speakers who are not office holders would probably be more effective, since their views would seem to rest more upon principle than upon self-interest. Several prominent colored office . . . .

TCU, incomplete: TNF

[1] At this time, New Yorker William S. Bennet (1870–1962) was also a member of the U.S. House of Representatives. He served from 1905 to 1911 and returned to Congress for another term in 1915–17.

[2] See 24 November 1906 to Archibald H. Grimké, n. 6.

To Booker T. Washington

Oct. 19, 1908.

My dear Doctor Washington:—

I was reading yesterday in a copy of the *Boston Transcript* for October 12, I think was the date, an account of a lynching in Mississippi, where the victims were left hanging beside the railroad track where you would pass on your way from one town to another. The statement was coupled with utterances ascribed to Mr. Vardaman and others that if you made half a dozen more speeches in Mississippi there would be a good many more lynchings.[1]

I was very sorry to read this. Things must be in a very bad way down there when even your helpful and pacific utterances create such a feeling.[2] I very much fear that the South does not mean, if it can prevent it, to permit education or business or anything else to make of the Negro anything more than an agricultural serf.[3]

I see Georgia has disfranchised the Negro.[4] I wonder how much further the process will go before there is a revival of a liberal spirit. I try to be optimistic about these matters, but conditions are not encouraging.

Yours very truly,
Chas. W. Chesnutt

TLS: DLC

[1]Chesnutt refers to "Two Negroes Lynched," *Boston Evening Transcript*, 12 October 1908, 9; see also "Lynch Two Negroes," *New York Times*, 12 October 1908, 1, and an especially full account, "Lynching at Lula, Miss.," *Memphis Commercial Appeal*, 12 October 1908, 1. African-American brothers Jim and Frank Davis were returning to Memphis, Tenn., from Helena, Ark., after hearing a speech by Washington. They allegedly shot and, according to the *Transcript*, "fatally wounded" John C. "Jack" Kendall (1878?–1908), an Illinois Central Railroad conductor. Kendall had admonished them for their behavior while the train stopped at Lula, Miss. Taken to jail to await the arrival of the sheriff, the Davis brothers were seized by a mob and hanged near the railroad station. James K. Vardaman (1861–1930)—Mississippi state legislator (1890–96), governor (1904–8), and then U.S. senator (1913–19)—was a prominent white supremacist.

[2]In a lengthy reply sent to Chesnutt on 22 October 1908 (TNF), Washington stated that he too would be "desperately discouraged" were the newspapers always to be believed. He confirmed that he "happened to be near the place where the lynching occurred," but explained that his speech in Arkansas had nothing "to do with the lynching of the two colored men." That Chesnutt had been misinformed about the brothers being hanged where Washington would see their corpses is clear in "Bodies Taken Down: Were Not Left Hanging to Be Viewed by Booker T. Washington," *Memphis Commercial Appeal*, 13 October 1908, 6: indignantly reported was the fact that the bodies had been removed for burial by 8:00 A.M. on 12 October 1908, long before Washington passed through Lula, Miss., on his way from Helena, Ark., to Chicago via St. Louis.

[3]Washington agreed with Chesnutt: the lynching was "inexcusable and barbaric in the highest degree." But, while on his tour, he had observed distinctly positive signs as well: "if you had seen what I saw in Mississippi . . . you would agree with me in stating that things are far from going to the bad in that state. . . . I do not believe there are any people in the United States prospering as the people in that state are. I was overwhelmed with surprise. In the getting of property, the building and the keeping of beautiful homes, the

going into all kinds of business, from the merchandise to the banking business, in the maintenance of schools at all grades and characters I have never seen anywhere our people going forward to the extent that these people are."

[4]According to "Georgia Negroes Barred," *New York Times*, 9 October 1908, 4, 95% of Georgia's African Americans lost their voting rights on 7 October 1908, when a disfranchising amendment to Georgia's constitution was approved by that state's electorate.

To Reverdy M. Hall

Oct. 19, 1908.

My dear Doctor Hall:—

I received your letter of October 10th, and read with pleasure all the nice things you say therein. I have no doubt I could have spent a week in Baltimore very pleasantly and profitably.

I think your idea of seeing more of the world and visiting foreign countries a most excellent one. I cannot imagine a pleasanter way for a man in middle life to put in his time, and I quite agree with you that there is no true philosophy in piling up money at the expense of happiness.

I should very much like to take the trip to Jamaica with you, but according to the present outlook I am afraid I shall not be able to spare the time this winter. However, there will be other years and there are other countries which would interest us, and I hope to get together with you some time. If I change my mind any time soon I will let you know.[1]

Mrs. Chesnutt and the girls join me in regards to you and Mrs. Hall. Helen was sure I would enjoy my visit, because she had such pleasant memories of her sojourn in your city.[2]

Sincerely yours,

TCU: TNF

[1]On 6 June 1907 (TNF), Hall—apparently aware that Chesnutt enjoyed excursions of the kind without his family—made a similar proposal, inviting Chesnutt to accompany him to Europe.

[2]See 9 October 1908 to Hall and to Edwin J. Chesnutt, n. 3.

To Hugh M. Browne

Oct. 23, 1908.

My dear Professor Browne:—

I have your favor of October 20th.[1] I also have received, though I seem to have mislaid it, a previous communication from you.[2] I quite agree with the committee as to the wisdom of the steps proposed, and that it will be a good thing to keep Mr. Carnegie interested. If ever the Negro needed friends it is at this moment.

If I can think of any instances along the lines suggested by you I shall be glad to furnish them.[3] Just at this moment I am feeling somewhat pessimistic about the situation, but doubtless my natural optimism will come to the front before very long and I can find something to say. If so, I shall hasten to do so.[4]

Sincerely yours,

TCU: TNF

[1]On 20 October (TNF), Browne requested from Chesnutt information on "at least one instance" either of African-American success or of cooperation between whites and African Americans to be used in a possible new publication by the Committee of Twelve as a way of extending the "far-reaching, convincing, and inspiring effects" of the Andrew Carnegie speech published by the Committee of Twelve (see 22 April 1908 to Browne, n. 1).

[2]Chesnutt refers to a letter of 12 October 1908 (TNF) in which Browne suggested that the Committee of Twelve should circulate in the form of a pamphlet an article to be entitled "Self-Help in Hospital Work," which Chicago surgeon and lecturer George C. Hall (1864–1930) had agreed to write.

[3]See n. 1.

[4]See 25 November 1908 to Browne.

To Booker T. Washington

Nov. 25, 1908.

My dear Dr. Washington:—

I was duly in receipt several weeks ago of a long and interesting and cheerful letter from you in answer to mine of a prior date and somewhat pessimistic vein.[1] What you say is very interesting and gives great ground for hope. I fear that there is not much hope for the negro's rights in the South except along that line, for from recent indications he is going to get very small aid or comfort through the Constitution or the Supreme Court or Congress. I quite agree with the *Evening Post*

that the decision in the Berea College case was almost another Dred
Scott decision; it practically amounts to an absolute abandonment of
any Constitutional protection of many of the negro's rights anywhere,
for what one state may do another state may do.[2] I am delighted to see
that Justice Day, from Ohio, with whom I am personally acquainted,
dissented from the opinion of Justices Brewer, Holmes *et al.*[3]

I hope that the new President, who is also an Ohio man,[4] will use his
influence in favor of the fair and just and Constitutional thing.

I return herewith the newspaper cuttings which you were good
enough to send me.[5]

Very truly yours,
Chas. W. Chesnutt.

TLS: DLC

[1]See 19 October 1908 to Washington, n. 3.

[2]Berea had been racially integrated from 1866 to 1906. On 9 November
1908 the U.S. Supreme Court in Berea College v. Kentucky, 211 U.S. 26
(1908), affirmed an October 1906 ruling by the Kentucky Court of Appeals
(Berea College v. Commonwealth, 123 Ky. App. Ct. 209) that prohibited the
integration of white and African-American students in any Kentucky school.
The editorial to which Chesnutt refers is "The Berea College Decision," New
York *Evening Post*, 11 November 1908, 8. It made the same point Chesnutt
does here: "The Supreme Court's opinion that the Kentucky law forbidding
the co-education of blacks and whites is Constitutional, might almost be described as a latter-day Dred Scott decision." Further, "Once the right to dis-
criminate against any section of our citizenship is established, no one can tell
where the line will be drawn." In the Dred Scott decision—Scott v. Sanford,
19 Howard 393 (1857)—the U.S. Supreme Court ruled against the slave Dred
Scott (c.1795–1858), maintaining that Scott was property rather than a citizen
and therefore could not plead his case in court.

[3]William R. Day (1849–1923) was Associate Supreme Court Justice (1849–
1923). In the minority as well was Associate Justice John Marshall Harlan
(1833–1911)—known as the "great dissenter" of the Supreme Court (1877–
1911). David J. Brewer (1837–1910) was another Associate Justice (1889–
1910), as was Oliver Wendell Holmes, Jr. (1841–1935), who served on the
court from 1902 to 1935.

[4]Chesnutt refers to recently elected William Howard Taft who served as
U.S. president from 1909 to 1913.

[5]Washington had enclosed with his 22 October letter "a few newspaper
clippings from the white press that will give you some idea of their attitude"
on the state of African Americans in the South.

To Hugh M. Browne

Nov. 25, 1908

My dear Professor Browne:—

I am in receipt of your several letters with reference to the work of the Committee of Twelve.[1] I have been unusually busy for several weeks, in a matter which absolutely demanded my undivided attention, and I have not been able to write a "paragraph" along the lines suggested in your last communication and in the previous one. I am so far out of touch with the South that I don't know really what is going on there except as I get it from the newspapers, and the race question is very little agitated around this neighborhood. Please consider that I approve of everything which has been decided upon, including the papers which were submitted to me, and I will endeavor to contribute something to some future publication. I hope hereafter to be able to give prompter attention to your communications.

Sincerely yours,

TCU: TNF

[1]On 5 November (TNF), Brown forwarded a copy of the study of Jackson, Miss., authorized by the Committee of Twelve (see 6 June 1908 to Browne, n. 1), and Chesnutt did not acknowledge receiving it. On 4 and 19 November 1908 (TNF), Browne reminded Chesnutt of his 20 October request for a "paragraph" on an example of African-American progress or interracial cooperation (see 23 October 1908 to Browne, n. 1). No information of the kind provided by Chesnutt was included in the Committee of Twelve pamphlet subsequently written by Robert E. Park (1864–1944), *Some Examples in Self-Help and Success among Colored People and of Co-Operation and Cordial Relations between the Races in America* (1910).

To Robert E. Park

Dec. 19, 1908.

My dear Dr. Park:—

I have your letter of December 4th in reference to the free colored people in North Carolina.[1] You ask for names. Of course the term "families" in relation to colored people who lived in the South before the war must be taken very broadly; and you must look for gaps now and then where the descent must be traced through the maternal line.[2]

One family I have in mind was that of Matthew Leary, who lived at Fayetteville, N.C., before the Civil War.[3] He was the owner of much land, of some slaves, of a brick store in the business part of town, and of a handsome residence in a good neighborhood. He was compelled by stress of circumstances to throw in his fortunes with those of the Confederacy—at any rate I understand that he was constrained to contribute to the cause and to purchase Confederate bonds, and some at least of his property was lost, including his slaves—how many he had I do not know, but probably not many. He was a "light mulatto", say about three-fourths white. His sons were more or less conspicuous in North Carolina during the reconstruction era. Matthew Leary, Jr., went into politics in a small way and the last I knew was a clerk in one of the Government departments at Washington; I think he has since died, leaving some children. A younger brother, Hon. John S. Leary, was the first colored man in North Carolina admitted to the Bar, of which he remained a respected member in active practice until he died a year or two ago at Charlotte, N.C.; he was at one time a member of the North Carolina Legislature I think.[4] Mr. Leary was a storehouse of information concerning the colored people of the state, and I regret exceedingly that he has passed to a sphere where it would be difficult for you to get into communication with him—unless you could secure perhaps the cooperation of your gifted neighbor, Mrs. Piper.[5]

Possibly a letter addressed to his widow, Mrs. John S. Leary, at Charlotte, N.C., where I presume she resides, might get you further information.[6]

Another such family was that of Hon. John P. Green, a well known Cleveland citizen, who was for twelve years a justice of the peace, four years a member of the Ohio House of Representatives, two years a member of the State Senate, and for nine years at the head of the Postage Stamp Distribution Bureau of Washington, filling in the intervals of his public service with active practice at the Cleveland Bar. His father was a master tailor in Newbern, N.C., and a free man, and he certainly dated back into the eighteenth century, which after all is only 108 years ago. Mr. Green lives here in Cleveland and is in active practice at the Bar.[7]

I belong in the same class. I know my pedigree for a hundred and fifty years. It would make, I suspect, a somewhat ragged family tree in spots, but at any rate in the legal line of descent it was always free on both sides, so far as my knowledge goes.[8]

I have been out of immediate touch with North Carolina for so long that my information is a little vague with reference to the Croatan Indians, but there are a great many of their descendants still living around Robeson County, N.C.—the county seat is Lumberton. On reference to the North Carolina Statutes, which you will find in any good law library, you will probably find some legislation with reference to the Croatan Indians.

The misfortune of color in the United States, which no amount of optimism can minimize, has made many colored people, when they neared the line which divided them from the white race, step over it, where they had the opportunity and the courage. Several of my own near relatives, as nearly related to me as uncles and aunts, have taken this course. Some I have kept track of, others have been swallowed up in the great majority. I hope they have won distinction; I am sure that their children will have a better opportunity in life, other things being equal, than had they taken a different course. Of course this is personal and not for publication.

If I can think of anything else that would interest you or be of value to Mr. Washington, I will be glad to write it to you, as well as to answer any other questions which you may see fit to ask.

Sincerely yours,

TCU: TNF

[1]Robert E. Park, who later became a professor of sociology at the University of Chicago, assisted Booker T. Washington with the composition of some of his books, including *The Story of the Negro* (1909), *My Larger Education* (1911), and *The Man Farthest Down* (1912). While residing in Boston, Park visited Tuskegee frequently after 1904 when he first met Washington.

[2]Park at this time was performing research for Washington's *The Story of the Negro*. Having read Chesnutt's "The Free Colored People of North Carolina" in *Southern Workman*, 31 (March 1902), 136–41, Park wrote on 4 December 1908 (TNF), requesting the "names of some of the free colored people or their descendants who are now living, who have distinguished themselves." He was particularly interested in Croatan Indians in Robeson County, N.C., and African Americans who had intermarried with them, and in the "colored workmen" who built the statehouse in Raleigh, N.C. Chesnutt had referred to these groups in his article; see *Essays and Speeches*: 173–79.

[3]Much of what follows in this paragraph concerning Matthew N. Leary, Sr. (1811?–?) and his sons appears almost verbatim in Chapter X of *The Story of the Negro*, the chapter entitled "The Free Negro in Slavery Days." Leary served as a commissioner in Cumberland Co., N.C., in 1869 as well as a justice of the peace in 1874. His son, Matthew N. Leary, Jr. (1842–?), also held minor political offices during Reconstruction.

[4]John S. Leary (1845–1904) was the second African American admitted to

the North Carolina bar, practicing law in Fayetteville following his graduation from Howard University Law School; he later became dean of the Law
School at Shaw University.

[5]New England spiritualist Leonore Evelina Simonds Piper (1859–1950)
enjoyed widespread fame for her psychic abilities from the mid-1880s through
the first two decades of the 20th century.

[6]Leary married Nannie E. Latham of Charlotte, his second wife, in 1886.

[7]John Patterson Green (1845–1940), Chesnutt's cousin, moved to Cleveland in 1857 with his widowed mother, Temperance Green (?–1911); his father, John R. Green (?–1850), was the Newbern, N.C., tailor Chesnutt described in "The Free Colored People of North Carolina." Following graduation from Union Law School, John Patterson Green was admitted to the South
Carolina bar, returning to Cleveland in 1872, where he began a successful career in Ohio politics as Cleveland's first African-American justice of the peace
(1873–82), a member of the Ohio House of Representatives (1882–86), and
the first African-American member of the Ohio Senate (1893–95). He was appointed U.S. postage stamp agent (1897–1905) in 1896. *The Story of the Negro* included much of the information in this paragraph on Green.

[8]For information on Chesnutt's ancestry, see Frances Richardson Keller, *An
American Crusade: The Life of Charles Waddell Chesnutt* (1978).

To Hugh M. Browne

December 29, 1908.

My dear Professor Browne:—

Replying to your favor of December 28th, will say that I have no
objection to the introduction by Mr. Carnegie and to the insertion of
the remarks of Mr. Page on the occasion of Mr. Taft's address.[1] I think
I read Mr. Page's remarks,[2] and I am sure Mr. Carnegie would not say
anything objectionable. They are both very good friends to the cause.[3]

Sincerely yours,

TCU: TNF

[1]Browne informed Chesnutt (TNF) that the Committee of Twelve intended
to publish an address by President-elect Taft with an introduction by Andrew
Carnegie. Intended also was the insertion of Walter Hines Page's introduction
of Taft "on the occasion of his notable address." He asked whether Chesnutt
objected to the plan.

[2]Page's remarks had been published in "Breaking the Solid South," *Outlook*, 90 (19 December 1908), 874–75. Anticipating one of Taft's major
points in his speech, Page argued not for "party politics" but for a "National
and patriotic theme" by which the South under president-elect Taft may
"return . . . to its old-time part in the constructive work of government and

the end forever of its political isolation from the achievements and glory of the Union." The full text of Taft's address appeared in "Blacks Can't Rule, Taft Tells South," *New York Times*, 8 December 1908, 1.

[3]The Committee published Taft's speech as *Address Before the North Carolina Society of New York by William H. Taft* (1909).

To Small, Maynard & Co.

Jan. 4, 1909.

Dear Sirs:—

Replying to your favor of December 29, 1908, with reference to a reduction in price in Beacon Biographies from $.75 net to $.50 net per volume, and a corresponding reduction in the royalty on my *Life of Frederick Douglass*, I will say that I will accept the reduction, joining with you in the hope that the increased circulation of the volume will more than make up the difference in the royalty.[1]

Yours very truly,

TCU: TNF

[1]Originally published *circa* 28 November 1899 and priced at 75¢, the *Frederick Douglass* volume in Small, Maynard's "Beacon Biographies" series was in its second printing (1904) at this time. A third printing was made in 1912; a fourth (undated) was the last to appear during Chesnutt's life.

To Robert E. Park

January 14, 1909.

My dear Dr. Park:—

I was duly in receipt of your letter of recent date, and I thank you for the helpful and hopeful suggestions therein. *Weltschmerz*[1] is not altogether an uncommon complaint, but on the whole, even the least optimistic of us, with the rare exception, seems to prefer to stick it out rather than to lay down the burden.[2] You are fortunate in your association with Mr. Washington;[3] he is about the most consistent optimist I know, and it is certainly a cheerful attitude to take toward the world.

In answer to your question I would say yes, that I am entirely willing to write for gain, nor would I call so necessary a thing vulgar gain. Immortality and the *Atlantic Monthly* are all right in a way, but in order to sustain our mortal part we must have money. I should very cheerfully undertake to write any articles for which anyone would express a wish, upon any subject which I am competent to handle, and will appreciate any suggestion of that kind from you.[4]

Sincerely yours,

TCU: TNF

[1]A term associated with the Romantic sensibility, denoting profound disappointment and sadness.

[2]On 28 December 1908 (TNF), Park responded to Chesnutt's long letter detailing the histories of prominent African Americans who lived in North Carolina; see 19 December 1908 to Park. Among other matters, Park described his difficulty in maintaining a positive point of view when he was a young man.

[3]See 19 December 1908 to Park, n. 1.

[4]On 28 December, Park indicated that he might "be in a position soon to place an article or two on a subject" that either Chesnutt or he might name.

To Robert E. Jones

Jan. 18, 1909.

My dear Mr. Jones:—

I enclose you herewith the article on Lincoln's Courtships.[1] I had already partially prepared the article when I got your second letter, and have n't since had any time to write up any other phase of Mr. Lincoln's life.[2] You are at liberty to blue-pencil this to any extent you choose.

Hoping you may find it suitable,[3] I remain,

Yours very truly,

TCU: TNF

[1]Robert Elijah Jones (1872–1960), an A.M.E. minister and later bishop, began editing the *Southwestern Christian Advocate* in 1904. Informing Chesnutt on 24 December 1908 (TNF) of his intention to devote an issue to Abraham Lincoln (1809–65), Jones solicited an article on "the great Emancipator," suggesting the courtships topic. Chesnutt accepted the invitation on 5 January 1909 (TNF).

[2]On 9 January (TNF), Jones replied to Chesnutt's 5 January letter, relating that he need not write on Lincoln's love life if he preferred to treat another subject.

[3]"Lincoln's Courtships" was published in *Southwestern Christian Advocate*, 43 (4 February 1909), 10; see *Essays and Speeches*: 271–74.

To Roscoe Conkling Bruce, Sr.

March 9, 1909.

(Personal.)

My dear Mr. Bruce:—

Your letter came duly to hand and gave me much pleasure. I appreciate the fact that you are a very busy man, and your letter gave me some idea of the magnitude of your interests. It is the common experience that the needs, both of schools and of individuals, generally outrun the revenue. But you should be philosophic as you say you are, and patient, and keep whacking away.[1]

I am delighted to know that you were pleased with your visit to Cleveland.[2] My wife was talking a few days before the inauguration, of running down to Washington, but I saw a moving picture show of the inauguration, yesterday, and have convinced her that she was better off at home. Mr. Taft certainly had bad weather.[3]

I have shown your letter to Mr. Williams and he told me yesterday that he has not yet received the pamphlets containing information about schools and conditions of appointment.[4]

I have read with great care your letter to Mr. Taft, and return herewith the copy you sent me. I think you have stated the situation in a very condensed and tactful and convincing form. Mr. Taft has made some very friendly utterances concerning the negro, and I am hopeful that his administration will mark an advance in the treatment of this seemingly complicated but really very simple problem.[5] If you have not read it, read the article by Quincy Ewing in the March *Atlantic* on "The Heart of the Race Problem". It is the whole thing in a nutshell, and to my mind presents it hopefully; if, as Mr. Ewing says, there is no subjective reason why the negro should not enjoy equality, he can very reasonably hope to overcome the mere prejudice of the white people.[6]

Mrs. Chesnutt and my daughters join me in cordial regards to you, and I remain, with best wishes,

Sincerely yours,

TDU: TNF

[1]Roscoe Conkling Bruce, Sr. (1879–1952), son of U.S. Senator Blanche Kelso Bruce (1841–98), distinguished himself academically at Phillips Exeter Academy (1894–98) and Harvard (1898–1902) before becoming director of the academic department at Tuskegee Institute (1902–6). In 1906 he was appointed supervising principal of the tenth division of the public schools in the District of Columbia; in 1907 he became the assistant superintendent of pub-

lic schools there. Chesnutt had invited Bruce to stay at his home when visiting Cleveland; Bruce accepted the invitation on 24 January (TNF), and Chesnutt acknowledged the same on 8 February (TNF).

[2]That Bruce was to be entertained by Chesnutt, "a life-long friend of the Bruce family," was announced two weeks before his visit in "About Town," *Cleveland Journal*, 6 February 1909, 5. Bruce arrived on 18 February, scheduled to speak the next day before the Minerva Club (Bruce to Nahum D. Brascher, 8 February 1909, TNF). The evening of 19 February, he was the guest of honor and principal speaker at the annual Lincoln-Douglass Banquet of the Attucks Republican Club; see "Lincoln-Douglass Banquet of Attucks Republican Club," *Cleveland Journal*, 20 February 1909, 1.

[3]William H. Taft's presidency was inaugurated on 4 March 1909.

[4]Western Reserve University librarian Edward C. Williams, husband of Chesnutt's eldest daughter Ethel, was seeking employment in the District of Columbia. In September 1909 he became the principal of the M Street High School. He later served as university librarian (1916–29) and head of the Department of Romance Languages at Howard University (1924–29).

[5]Chesnutt did not make a copy of Bruce's letter to President Taft.

[6]Quincy Ewing (1867–1939), an outspoken advocate of racial equality, was an Episcopal priest in Napoleonville, La., and the author of "The Heart of the Race Problem," *Atlantic Monthly*, 103 (March 1909), 389–97. What he explained, "in a nutshell" according to Chesnutt, was "the foundation" of the race problem: the white Southerner's conviction "that the Negro as a race, and as an individual, is his inferior: not human in the sense that [the white Southerner] is human, not entitled to the exercise of human rights in the sense that [the white Southerner] is entitled to them."

To Hugh M. Browne

March 10, 1909.

Dear Prof. Browne:—

I am in receipt of your letter of March 9th. It is very interesting to know that the publications of the Committee of Twelve are in demand. I find that I have a few copies of the pamphlet *What a Colored Man Should Do To Vote*, and I am sending them to you by this mail, under a different cover.[1]

I beg to acknowledge receipt of your letter of March 2nd, containing list of the Committee of Twelve; also copy of your letter to me of May 20, 1905. Perhaps I ought to apologize for putting you to unnecessary trouble, as I undoubtedly have that former letter in my files. I did not know, however, but what there had been some change in the personnel of the committee.[2]

Sincerely yours,

P.S. I also acknowledge receipt of yours of March 1st with reference to the circulation of the committee's literature.

TDU, revised by hand: TNF

[1]Browne (TNF) had reported on the interest shown by whites in the publications of the Committee of Twelve, citing William Donne (1845–1914), Chaplain to the King of England, and Wightman F. Melton (1867–1944), poet, critic, editor, and professor of English at Emory University. He requested extra copies Chesnutt might have of one such publication, *To the Colored Men of Voting Age in the Southern States* (see 8 January 1906 to Booker T. Washington, n. 3), in order to replenish the Committee's depleted stock.

[2]Expressing his surprise that Chesnutt did not know the names of the members of the Committee of Twelve, Browne had forwarded them to him on 2 March 1908 (TNF), along with a copy of his 20 May 1905 letter (TNF) containing the same names. They were: Booker T. Washington, chair; Hugh M. Browne, secretary; Archibald H. Grimké, treasurer; T. Thomas Fortune; Chesnutt; Elias Camp Morris (1855–1922), a Baptist minister and president since 1894 of the National Baptist Convention; Charles W. Anderson (1866–1938) who served in a variety of New York State and federal positions and was presently U.S. Collector of Revenue in the Second District of New York (1905–15); Kelly Miller (1863–1939), professor of sociology at Howard University and the author of *An Appeal to Reason on the Race Problem* (1906) and *Race Adjustment* (1908); Hightower T. Kealing (1859–1918), an educator who began his 16-year tenure as editor of the *African Methodist Episcopal Review* in 1896; George W. Clinton (1859–1921), A.M.E.Z. bishop since 1896, founder of *A.M.E.Z. Quarterly Review* (1889), and editor of *Star of Zion* (1902–6); and John Wesley Edward Bowen (1855–1933), professor of theology at Gammon Theological Seminary.

To John Patterson Green

April 8, 1909.

My dear Senator:—

I received your interesting letter of March 12th in due course. I am glad to learn that you and Mrs. Green are enjoying yourselves on your travels and that you have received such courteous and friendly treatment on all hands.[1]

The family are well and Mrs. Chesnutt and the girls were at Atlantic City and New York for ten days, taking a little rest, but returned last Monday morning much refreshed.

I am quite interested in what you say about the musical people over there. Miss Walker had a beautiful voice many years ago and doubtless time has ripened and mellowed it. It will be a great pleasure to hear her sing in her own country.[2]

I note what you say about hard times in England. I gather from general reading that there must be something of the sort. In fact if the country does n't get over the Dreadnaught scare, it will bankrupt itself and impoverish the people in preparing for war, which would be expensive enough if it ever happened, to ruin any country in a month. I sincerely hope there will be no great war in my time or any other time for that matter, although a lot of military and naval cranks would like no doubt to see one.[3]

Our energetic friend Mr. Roosevelt has gone to Africa. Doubtless we will be able to rest a little during his absence and be prepared to welcome him on his return.[4] Doubtless you have read Mr. Taft's deliverance in his inaugural address, concerning the Negro, and I suspect that you, like a good many others, are waiting to see what there is to it.[5] At first blush it looks as though he had joined the rest and read the Negro out of official life in the South as he has already been read out of the franchise.[6]

Give my regards to your friends and mine whom you meet, especially Mr. Coleridge-Taylor.[7] I hope that you and Mrs. Green[8] will enjoy the remainder of your visit, and look forward with pleasure to seeing you again.

Sincerely yours,

TCU: TNF

[1]The Greens were then touring England.

[2]Rachel L. Walker Turner (1873–1943) was born in Cleveland and taught at Central High School for several years (1889–93). At Green's suggestion, she moved to New York City in 1895 for voice studies. Soon earning the sobriquet "the Creole Nightingale," she successfully launched her career with the support of Cleveland financier, industrialist, and philanthropist John D. Rockefeller (1839–1937). She moved to London in 1897 and remained there for eighteen years, returning to Cleveland at the outbreak of World War I. Chesnutt was not the only recipient of a letter concerning the singer. In a 22 March 1909 letter published in the *Cleveland Journal*, Green related that she "has won an enviable reputation as a singer in the palaces of the nobility, the drawing rooms of the wealthy, and some of the leading music halls of Paris, London, Glasgow, and other leading cities of Great Britain and the continent" ("Cleveland Making Fame in Europe," *Cleveland Journal*, 10 April 1909, 1). Whether Chesnutt was personally acquainted with her at this time is not clear;

they later shared billing in a program of the Du Bois Literary Club at which he read a story from *The Conjure Woman* and she sang ("Social and Personal," *Cleveland Gazette*, 8 January 1916, [3]).

[3]England's launching of the oversized battleship *Dreadnaught* in 1906 marked an escalation in its naval armaments competition with Germany. It was the first of many fast-moving, heavily armored warships with unprecedented firing ranges.

[4]Having succeeded in seeing Taft elected as his successor in the White House, Theodore Roosevelt went to Africa to enjoy a vacation as a big game hunter.

[5]In his inaugural address, Taft promised that "so long as the statutes of the [Southern] States meet the test of the [Fifteenth] amendment and are not otherwise in conflict with the Constitution and laws of the United States," the federal government has no intention of interfering with "the regulation by Southern States of their domestic affairs." For the text of the address, see "Taft Wants Tariff on Revenue Basis," *New York Times*, 5 March 1909, 4, and "Inauguration Address of President Taft," *Cleveland Journal*, 6 March 1909, 2.

[6]Chesnutt refers to political appointments. One of the pressing questions of the day had to do with whether the new administration would continue Roosevelt's practice of appointing African Americans, especially in the South. Taft hedged in his inaugural address: "it may well admit of doubt whether, in the case of any race, an appointment of one of their number to a local office in a community in which the race feeling is so widespread and acute as to interfere with the ease and facility with which the local government business can be done by the appointed, is of sufficient benefit by way of encouragement to the race to outweigh the recurrence and increase of race feeling which such an appointment is likely to engender. Therefore, the Executive, in recognizing the negro race by appointment must exercise a careful discretion not thereby to do it more harm than good."

[7]Samuel Coleridge-Taylor (1875–1912) was a London-born violinist and composer most famous for his *Hiawatha* trilogy of oratorios. Chesnutt and his wife attended two concerts conducted by him in the District of Columbia on 16 and 17 November 1904. Coleridge-Taylor and Chesnutt met again during another U.S. tour in 1906 when, on a visit to Cleveland for a "short recital," Coleridge-Taylor stayed with the Greens ("Famous Musicians Visit Cleveland," *Cleveland Journal*, 8 December 1906, 1). See also 14 September 1912 to Mrs. Jessie F. Coleridge-Taylor.

[8]Annie Walker Green (?–1912).

To Hugh M. Browne

May 24, 1909.

My dear Professor Browne:—

I have been unavoidably delayed in answering your two favors of earlier date.

I have read Dr. Du Bois's article in the *World's Work*; it makes an excellent showing for the colored people of Georgia, and is well worth reproducing; I should entirely approve of it.[1]

As to Professor Coon's paper, it is illuminating, and coming from the source whence it emanates, ought to impress those who read it.[2] Prof. Coon seems to be one of the growing advance guard of Southern white men to whom, in the long run, the Negro in the South must look for justice.

I would suggest, in case the latter paper is published, that a note be appended, making it clear that Mr. Coon is a white man, (this is not a joke, although it savors of one), and also making clear who and what he is.

I also beg to acknowledge copies of *Work of the Colored Law and Order League at Baltimore*, and *Self-Help in Negro Education*,[3] both excellent subjects, admirably treated.[4]

Sincerely yours,

TCU: TNF

[1]Chesnutt here approves Browne's proposal to publish as a Committee of Twelve pamphlet Du Bois' "Georgia Negroes and Their Fifty Millions of Savings," *World's Work*, 18 (May 1909), 11550–54. The article focuses on progress made by African Americans, *e.g.*, those in Georgia who own 2,220 square miles of property, more land than is contained in the entirety of Delaware. Further, an ever-increasing number are artisans, businessmen, and professionals rather than farmers.

[2]Charles Lee Coon (1868–1927), a Southern educator, had recently served as superintendent of North Carolina Negro Normal Schools (1904–7). His long experience in education informed the paper he read at the 12th Annual Conference for Education in the South, 14–16 April 1909, which was subsequently published by the Committee of Twelve as *Public Taxation and Negro Schools* (1909).

[3]Chesnutt refers to two Committee of Twelve pamphlets by James H. N. Waring (see 16 September 1908 to Browne, n. 1) and Richard R. Wright, Jr. (1878–1967), respectively. Wright's was published in 1908.

[4]This is the last known letter addressed to Browne and the Committee of Twelve.

To James D. Corrothers

June 1, 1909.

My dear Dr. Corrothers:—

Permit me to thank you for the copy of your poem dedicated to Senator J. B. Foraker.[1] It is indeed a fine tribute in honor of a fine deed. Our friends seem to have fallen off somewhat in numbers, or in zeal, and it behooves us to show our appreciation of those who speak out in meeting. This you have done very eloquently and beautifully, and more than that, you have shown, with poetic phrase and feeling, that the race in whose behalf Senator Foraker stood so valiantly, was worthy of his friendship and support. Permit me to congratulate you and thank you.

Sincerely yours,

TCU: TNF

[1]Clergyman James David Corrothers (1869–1917) began writing dialect poetry at the suggestion of Paul Laurence Dunbar (1872–1906). He was the author of two collections, *The Black Cat Club: Negro Humor and Folklore* (1902) and *Selected Poems* (1907). He is now best known for "At the Closed Gate of Justice," *Century*, 86 (June 1913), 272. Carrothers sent Chesnutt a copy of his poem concerning Foraker on 11 May 1909 (TNF), asking if, in his opinion as "a literary man," it "is as good as several . . . friends thought it to be."

To Wendell P. Stafford

June 25, 1909

Dear Sir:

My friend Mr. James A. Cobb, an attorney of your city, has kindly sent me a copy of your recent address at Cooper Union, New York, upon the subject of Negro rights.[1] I had read it in the newspapers, I believe in the New York *Evening Post*, as an item of news, and have read it again more carefully in the form in which Mr. Cobb sends it.

Permit me to thank you as one equally interested, in a broad and general way, and more directly in a personal way, in the problem which you discuss. You have sounded a very high and noble note, striking at the very root of the matter. The brotherhood of man—the unity of mankind; equal citizenship; justice and equal opportunity for all men; respect for the Constitution and the laws; the danger of class discrimination; a patriotism broad enough to embrace all the people; a humanity wide enough to include the whole world—these are the principles which you advocate, and what better weapons with which to right a civic wrong and to complete the emancipation of both black and white from the lingering effects of the old system?

It has often been said that the future of the Negro in America lies in his own hands. This is only a half truth. A man cannot breathe without air, or eat without food, or develop without opportunity. And the future of the Negro will depend in great part upon the extent to which men like you and the other enlightened spirits who participated in the recent New York convention can influence public opinion to make for every man in this country the conditions under which alone the rapid elimination of the race problem is possible.

Thanking you again, I am

Yours very truly,

Charles W. Chesnutt

Pioneer: 231–32

[1]On 1 June 1909 at the Cooper Union in New York City, Wendell P. Stafford (1861–1950), Associate Justice of the U.S. Supreme Court (1904–31), presided over and spoke at a session of the National Negro Conference. He identified white complacency as the cause of African-American "ignorance and criminality" ("Whites and Blacks Confer as Equals," *New York Times*, 1 June 1909, 2).

To Reverdy M. Hall

November 6, 1909

Dear Doctor Hall:—

Some one writes me from Washington that the Baltimore *Sun* of I think it was Friday, October 29th, had an article on the front page containing an excerpt from some speech made or article published by me in Boston several years ago, and put forward by the *Sun* as an argument in favor of disfranchisement.[1] I am unable to find a copy here. Will you kindly procure and send me one?

Permit me to congratulate you and all decent citizens of Maryland on the defeat of the disfranchising amendment.[2] There are a few signs of growing decency in the South, which give me great pleasure. Governor Brown of Georgia[3] in refusing to commute the sentence of that aristocratic gentleman who blacked himself up and outraged a relative of his own wife was one, the finding of the arbitration board on the colored firemen's case at Atlanta was another;[4] the decision of the Mississippi Supreme Court a few days ago that a bill for the establishment of agricultural colleges or schools for "white youth only" was unconstitutional because it did not make equal provision for colored youth.[5] These are good things. The Negro will ultimately get his rights through the conscience of the white people.

The family are well. Kindly give my regards to yours, and believe me
. . . .

TCU, incomplete: TNF

[1]"An Appeal to the White Women of Maryland," urging support of the Democrat effort to "disfranchise the ignorant and vicious portion of the colored population," appeared on the first page of the 29 October 1909 issue of the *Baltimore Sun*. It related that one should vote for disfranchisement, first, because "the exercise of the suffrage by the ignorant negro alongside of the white man encourages the latent desire that already possesses him of social equality. This desire is manifested and proclaimed by the most intelligent of his race. Charles W. Chesnutt, of Cleveland, Ohio, one of the best-known colored authors, in an address delivered in Boston as far back as June, 1905, among other things said: 'I not only believe the mixture in races will in time become an accomplished fact, but will be a good thing for all concerned. It is already well forward, and events seem to be paving the way to embrace the negro in the general process by which all the races of mankind are being fused together here into one people. *Millions of foreigners, much nearer the negro in some respects than our native whites*, are pouring into the country. Perhaps in the economy of Divine Providence they may help to solve our problems, by furnishing a bridge with which to pass the race chasm.' " The piece was signed by Murray Vandiver (1845–1916) of the Democratic State Committee. The 1905 speech by Chesnutt quoted was entitled "Race Prejudice"; see *Essays and Speeches*: 214–38.

[2]Following the defeat of the Poe Amendment in 1905 (see 8 January 1906 to Washington, n. 2), Maryland Democrats at their 1907 state convention adopted a new disfranchisement plan. The amendment of the state's constitution was approved by the Maryland General Assembly in 1908 and defeated at the polls by over 15,000 votes on 2 November 1909, in part due to the efforts of the League of Foreign-Born Voters and the Negro Suffrage League.

[3]Joseph M. Brown (1851–1932) began his first term as governor in June 1909 after defeating the incumbent, white supremacist Hoke Smith (1855–1931).

[4]On 17 May 1909 white firemen, members of the Brotherhood of Locomotive Engineers, began a strike against the Georgia Railroad because of its employment of African-American firemen, who were barred from union membership because of race. The railroad's position was that it was entitled to hire

non-union firemen, both white and African-American, on its lines. Both parties submitted to mediation by the Federal Board of Arbitration, which ruled that all firemen shall receive equal pay for equal work ("Georgia Firemen Satisfied," *New York Times*, 29 June 1909, 2).

[5]In 1908 the Mississippi state legislature passed an act providing for the establishment of a county agricultural high school for whites only to be supported by taxation of African Americans and whites alike. To prevent such taxation in Jasper County, a bill was successfully filed in chancery court; and representatives of the county appealed. In McFarland, Tax Collector, *et al.* v. Goins (96 Miss 67, 50 So. 493), the state supreme court affirmed on 2 November 1909 prior decisions sanctioning the separation of the races in public schools and railway carriages, and asserted that civil rights "do not mean social rights." But it ruled in favor of the appellees, finding the act passed by the legislature in violation of the Fourteenth Amendment of the U.S. Constitution.

To Joseph Garner

[6 November 1909]

Dear Sir:—

Replying to your letter of November 4th, I take pleasure in sending you herewith a list of my books.[1]

I have copies of the articles I wrote for the Boston *Transcript* at the time you refer to, but they are pasted in a scrapbook; I have no copies of the newspapers, and the articles never appeared in any other form. I understand that parts of those letters were quoted by the *Baltimore Sun*, during the late campaign, as an argument for disfranchisement. If so, I am happy to note that the argument was not effective. I have asked a Baltimore friend to send me a copy of the paper, but have not seen it yet.[2]

The Boston letters could of course be reproduced upon the typewriter, but they are quite lengthy.[3]

Sincerely yours,

TCU: TNF

[1]Joseph Garner (1877–?) taught in the Baltimore public school system (1899–1902), served as Director of Physical Training at the Frederick Douglass Social Center in Chicago (1906–8) and at Hampton Institute (1908–9), and was presently the proprietor of Garner Art Co. in Baltimore. In 1912 he would become a reporter for the Baltimore *Times*. Wanting to sell Chesnutt's books, he wrote him on 4 November (TNF), asking for the names and addresses of the publishers. He also requested copies of Chesnutt's three "The

Future American" essays that appeared in the *Boston Evening Transcript* in 1900 (see *Essays and Speeches*: 121–36).

[2]See 6 November 1909 to Reverdy M. Hall.

[3]On 12 November (TNF) Garner authorized production of typed copies: "I need them for a work I am about to project and am willing to pay for the cost of typewriting." Chesnutt replied on 26 November (TNF), enclosing "a spare copy of the third of the series of articles" and informing him that typed copies of the first and second installments will cost $2.

To William M. Brown

November 7, 1909.

Dear Sir:—

I beg to acknowledge, somewhat tardily, the receipt of an autographed copy of your book, *The Crucial Race Question*, and to thank you for the courtesy.[1]

For the book itself, I am quite sure that I dissent radically from its views. I could not imagine myself approving a book which condemns to infamy and all kinds of hopeless inferiority so many of my fellow creatures, my fellow citizens, my fellow Christians, and my friends.

The fact that race prejudice is prevalent, north, south or anywhere else, is no argument at all to my mind to establish its justice, its wisdom, or that it has the divine sanction.

I do not know whether it ever occurred to you—it certainly has to me—that if the Creator had intended to prevent the inter-mixture of races, he might in His infinite wisdom have accomplished this purpose by a very simple method, as he has by the physiological laws which prevent the confusion of genera in the lower animals. I think it very fortunate for humanity that not all the ministers of God agree with you in your views in regard to the Negro. If so, his future fate in the country of his birth and citizenship, would be very sad and very hopeless.[2]

I take pleasure in sending you a copy of a book from my own pen, which treats the same general subject in a very different manner. With hope that you may read it with interest, I remain

Sincerely yours,

TCU: TNF

[1]William Montgomery Brown (1855–1937), Episcopal Bishop of Arkansas (1900–1912), had informed Chesnutt on 15 October 1909 (TNF) that he was sending him a copy of *The Crucial Race Question* (1907) under separate cover and mentioned his "pleasant remembrances of their meeting" when he lived in

Cleveland. Brown's analysis of the race problem is a vigorous restatement of the white supremacist perspective on the inferiority of the Negro, the franchise, miscegenation, and the need to maintain the segregated status quo.

[2]Chesnutt had long been familiar with Brown's anti-African-American point of view. In his 1904 speech "The Race Problem" (*Essays and Speeches*: 196–205), he referred critically to a lecture Brown had given in Boston, reported in "The Week," *Nation*, 78 (25 February 1904), 140–41. Brown had described lynching as justifiable in certain cases: "I extenuate the offense of lynching, for it is the only remedy for attacks on women"; "the South is obliged to lynch because women would not appear in court"; and "lynchers are justified in the sight of God, because lynching is a form of self-protection." In the 1905 speech "Race Prejudice" (*Essays and Speeches*: 214–38), Chesnutt alluded to him as "a renegade Northerner," that is, an enlightened man who had regressed to the Southern perspective on African Americans.

To Edwin J. Chesnutt

March 8, 1910

. . . I have your letter of the 3rd. Pardon my delay in not having answered it sooner. Whether the Washington offer amounts to anything depends somewhat on what you are doing there.[1] Two or three fellows have made good under Mr. Washington's wing, but I imagine he is a very absorbing kind of person and uses his assistants for all they are worth. Of course this is good business on his part. Whether you could get anything out of it or not would depend upon several contingencies. I don't think the salary offer is anything to speak of. I don't know that you are worth any more, but Ethel went down there for a year[2] on the same basis and I had to pay her fare either one way or both—in other words she didn't get enough out of it to keep her and pay her railroad fare both ways.

Of course if you had the literary faculty and could write nice letters and get up nice literature you might be valuable to Mr. Washington.[3] On the other hand, if you go down there you will forego any chances of getting admitted to the bar. I judge from your previous letters that you are aiming at this.

I hesitate to advise you. I don't know what sort of future Tuskegee would hold out for you. You would in any event be only a small satellite of a great man, and I notice that those who are ambitious for themselves sooner or later break away from him. I hesitate to advise you really. I want to see you get nailed down somewhere sometime, if not in some place at least in some pursuit or profession. I have been hoping you might qualify for the bar. If I had thought in the beginning that you were going to adopt shorthand as a profession I should have seen that you were trained in it years ago. Perhaps I made a mistake in that regard. But think it out and do the best you can for yourself. . . .

Pioneer: 234–35

[1]Emmett J. Scott invited Edwin on 26 February 1910 (TNF) to work at Tuskegee Institute at a salary of $50 per month including "board, fuel, light, laundry, etc."

[2]See 8 January 1906 to Booker T. Washington, n. 1.

[3]Edwin's sole known skill qualifying him for a position was stenographic; see 20 July 1906 to Edwin J. Chesnutt.

To Houghton Mifflin Company

April 13, 1910.

Dear Sirs:—

I am in receipt of a letter, which was addressed to me at your office and by you forwarded to me at Cleveland, from Mrs.—I presume it is Mrs.—Marie Louise Péris,[1] of Geneva, Switzerland, requesting my permission to translate some of the stories in my *The Wife of His Youth* into French. I have written to her that I should be very much pleased to have her do so, if she wishes, subject of course to your consent, which, I judge from her letter, she has already.[2]

Very truly yours,

TCU: TNF

[1]Emended is Chesnutt's misreading of "Péris" as "Preis."

[2]On 14 April 1910 (TNF), Houghton Mifflin Company granted permission for the translation that was subsequently published. See 10 December 1910 to Francis J. Garrison.

To William English Walling

April 18, 1910

My dear Mr. Walling:

I am in receipt of your letter of April 17th suggesting that I address the National Negro Committee during its approaching meeting in May, on "The Effect of Disfranchisement in the Courts."[1] I see no reason why I should not, in fact many reasons why I should do all that I can to further the work of this organization, and I will very cheerfully undertake to deliver such an address provided you think it worth while. As I

have spent very little time in the South for a number of years, I could
have little to say about actual experience in southern courts, but I have
kept in close touch with the southern situation, and since the argument
would in any event be largely upon principle, I have no doubt I can
find something to say.

I am reasonably familiar with the proceedings of the conference at
the meeting in 1909; at least I followed them closely in the rather full
report which was published in the New York *Evening Post*, and I read
the address by Judge Stafford, of which Mr. Cobb was good enough to
send me a copy, and of course I am familiar with the views and utterances of, I think, every speaker on the last year's program with the exception of two or three.² If there was a complete report of the proceedings published I should be much obliged if you would kindly advise
me where I can procure a copy of same; and of course I should like a
copy of the program for the May meeting as soon as it is completed.³

Cordially yours,
Charles W. Chesnutt

Pioneer: 235

¹At the 12–14 May 1910 conference in New York City, Chesnutt presented
a paper entitled "The Right to Jury Service" on 13 May; see *Essays and
Speeches:* 274–81.

²The first annual conference took place in New York City on 1 June 1909.
See 25 June 1909 to Wendell P. Stafford.

³On 4 May 1910 (TNF), Walling sent to Chesnutt both a copy of the program for the conference and an admission card.

To Benjamin G. Brawley

April 29, 1910.

Dear Sir:—

Please accept my thanks for the beautifully written and printed
pamphlet on *The Negro in Literature and Art*, of which you were good
enough to send me a complimentary copy.¹ It is marked by taste, discrimination, and to my mind a very just estimate of the relative literary
value of the books which you comment upon. I must thank you especially for the very full reference to my own works.²

Is this little work for sale? If so, I should like to know where it can
be procured and at what price.³

Cordially yours,

TCU: TNF

[1]Benjamin Griffith Brawley (1882–1939) was the author of *The Problem and Other Poems* (1904) and was, at this time, a professor at Atlanta Baptist College (later renamed Morehouse College). He taught Latin and English and, by the 1920s, had become an important social and cultural historian who focused on the achievements of African Americans. See 24 March 1922 to Brawley.

[2]On pp. 21–28 in *The Negro in Literature and Art* (1910), Brawley sketched Chesnutt's literary career through 1905, summarized and evaluated his novels and some of his short stories, and concluded that Chesnutt "is today the foremost man of the race in pure literature."

[3]On 30 April 1910 (TNF), Brawley sent Chesnutt an advertisement answering these questions. He thanked Chesnutt for the "kind words" allaying his concerns about what Chesnutt's "opinion of [his] little book might be."

To William English Walling

May 19, 1910.

Dear Mr. Walling:—

I want to thank you again for your invitation to visit New York and participate in the proceedings of the National Negro Committee.[1] As organized and with the men who have been selected to head it, it offers a prospect of effective work in the channel outlined.[2] I also wish to thank you and the ladies associated with you for the personal courtesies which I received at your hands. Assuming that you are the proper person to whom to make the remittance, I enclose herewith a New York draft to my order endorsed to you, for $50.00, on account of the sum which I subscribed to the work. I will send the balance later on.

Cordially yours,

TCU: TNF

[1]See 18 April 1910 to Walling, n. 1.

[2]Among those who addressed the conference were attorney Clarence Darrow (1857–1938), anthropologist Franz Boas (1858–1942), historian Albert Bushnell Hart (1854–1943), educator and pragmatic philosopher John Dewey (1859–1952), W. E. B. Du Bois, Ida Wells-Barnett, and Horace Bumstead.

To Booker T. Washington

July 21, 1910.

My dear Dr. Washington,

I have been intending to write you for some time, but a rather severe illness which kept me confined to my bed for four weeks and from which I am only now convalescing, has interfered with my intention.[1]

I want to thank you for your interest in and kindness to my children. Helen enjoyed her visit to Tuskegee very much indeed, and has had nothing but fine things to say about the place and people since her return.[2]

Edwin seems to be very well pleased with his work and his outlook, and I sincerely hope that you will find him worthy of your confidence. My daughter Ethel is enjoying her visit to Tuskegee, and I hope is making herself useful.[3]

Mrs. Chesnutt and Helen join me in kindest regards to yourself and Mrs. Washington.[4]

Sincerely yours,
Chas. W. Chesnutt.

TLS: DLC

[1]In early June 1910, Chesnutt collapsed in his office and was taken to the Huron Road Hospital where he was diagnosed as having suffered a stroke (*Pioneer*: 238). When Washington replied to Chesnutt on 27 July 1910 (TNF), he related his happiness over the news that Chesnutt's health was "improving" and extended an invitation to visit him at his summer residence at Huntington, Long Island.

[2]Washington had visited Cleveland in April. Helen M. Chesnutt was then suffering a "digestive disorder" that made it impossible for her to continue teaching, and Washington invited her to visit his wife at Tuskegee. Pleased with her experience there, Helen encouraged her brother Edwin—then working in Welch, W.Va., as a stenographer for a local legal aid organization for miners—to give positive consideration to the position offered him at Tuskegee (*Pioneer*: 236–38). See 8 March 1910 to Edwin. Upon her return to Cleveland, Helen thanked Washington on 1 July 1910 (DLC).

[3]Edwin announced to his father on 29 May 1910 that he had decided to accept the position offered him at Tuskegee (*Pioneer*: 237). Chesnutt's daughter Ethel, having taught for a year at Tuskegee (1901–2), returned to teach there "for several summers" (see 21 November 1910 to W. E. B. Du Bois).

[4]Mrs. Margaret J. Murray Washington (1861–1925).

To Ethel Chesnutt Williams

September 1, 1910

. . . Your interesting letter was forwarded to me at Sea Isle City, New Jersey. At that time I was just beginning a month of recuperation and was not as well as I am now.[1] We spent a delightful month by the seashore, and I find myself at the end of it rejuvenated and ready for my fall business. The sea breeze was delightful, the surf bathing was bracing, and the town was quiet and more or less interesting. There was a board walk two or three miles long; the beach was delightful for walks; there were small towns in the vicinity, and Atlantic City was not a great distance away.[2] We managed to put in four weeks very pleasantly, and I was sorry to feel obliged to come away. Your mother and Helen and Dorothy profited equally by the vacation and they are all in fine health and spirits and join me in love to you. . . .

Pioneer: 238–39

[1]See 21 July 1910 to Booker T. Washington, n. 1.
[2]On 8 August 1910 (TNF), Chesnutt wrote to his son-in-law, Edward C. Williams, describing the conditions there similarly: "Plenty of cool sea air, fine sea bathing, comfortable rooms and plenty of well cooked food. . . . There is fishing and crabbing and boating."

To Sherman, French & Co.

September 15, 1910.

Dear Sirs:—

I beg to acknowledge receipt of a copy of *Songs of Life* by George Reginald Margetson,[1] also of your letter of recent date with reference thereto.

I have read the little book with interest and pleasure. It is very well written and sounds a true note. The writer has a fine grasp of poetic form and expression, and I hope his book is but the forecast of better work to come, of riper work.

Yours sincerely,

TCU: TNF

[1]George Reginald Margetson (1877–?) was born in St. Kitts and emigrated to the United States when he was 20 years old. Prior to the publication of *Songs of Life* (1910), he had produced two other books of poems, *England in the West Indies: A Neglected and Degenerate Empire* (1906) and *Ethiopia's Flight: The Negro Question, or the White Man's Fear* (1907).

To William English Walling

October 13, 1910.

My dear Mr. Walling:—

I am in receipt of your letter. I am glad that you had a successful meeting in Chicago. I am sorry Miss Blascoer could not have come on, for I was counting on her cooperation in working up a certain end of this meeting.[1] I am afraid we are going to fall down on the white side. Cleveland is a great and prosperous city, the sixth in the Union, but there is a surprising dearth of people like Miss Addams, Dr. Hirsch and our friends in New York.[2] Racial conditions in Cleveland are peculiar, as I can explain to you when I see you, and I find it difficult to think of half a dozen white people who would take an active, not to say an aggressive part in our movement. However, I think we will have a large meeting for you on Sunday afternoon, and will do what I can toward carrying out your suggestions.[3] If you will call me up by telephone, Bell Main 2164, when you get to Cleveland on Saturday, I shall wait on you at the Hollenden and we can talk the matter over.[4]

Very sincerely yours,

TCU: TNF

[1] On 24 September 1904 (TNF), Chesnutt wrote Frances Blascoer of the Frederick Douglass Social Center in Chicago, requesting her assistance in arranging an October speaking engagement for Walling in Cleveland.

[2] Jane Addams (1860–1935) was co-founder and head (1889–1935) of the Hull House social settlement in Chicago; her *Twenty Years at Hull House* was published in 1910. Emil G. Hirsch (1851–1923) was a rabbi and civic leader whose work in Chicago began in 1880; from 1891 to 1923 he was the editor of *Reform Advocate*. The friends in New York were those associated with the National Negro Conference and the founding of the N.A.A.C.P.

[3] Walling arrived in Cleveland on 15 October 1910. Chesnutt and he delivered addresses the next day, Sunday, at St. John's A.M.E Church, located at the corner of East 40th Street and Central Ave.

[4] In pencil, Chesnutt wrote *"See some fellows—"* at the bottom of the carbon copy of this letter.

To W. E. B. Du Bois

November 21, 1910

My dear Dr. Du Bois:

I have your letter of November 15, enclosing copy of paper entitled "Race Relations in the United States," and asking whether I would care to sign it.[1] In view of the very close relations of members of my family with Tuskegee—my son is in Mr. Washington's office, one of my daughters has taught there for several summers, and another was Mrs. Washington's visitor for a number of weeks this year[2]—and in view further of the fact that I am a nominal member of the Committee of Twelve and signed my name to Mr. Washington's latest appeal for an increase of the Tuskegee endowment,[3] I question whether it would be quite in good taste for me to sign what in effect is in the nature of an impugnment of Mr. Washington's veracity, or at least which it would be only human in him to look upon in the light of a personal attack.

As to the merits of the case—I have read the interview in the *London Morning Post*, which I presume is the expression of Mr. Washington's upon which the protest is based.[4] After all, it is only the ordinary optimistic utterance, to which we are all well accustomed. Mr. Washington is a professional optimist, avowedly so. I imagine the English as well as the Americans understand this fact and take his statements with a grain of salt. The utterances of Mr. Archer, Sir Harry Johnston and Mr. H. G. Wells would indicate that the English understand the situation pretty thoroughly.[5] But after all, it is largely a matter of the point of view. Mr. Washington says in that interview, "The Negro problem in the United States will right itself in time"; this I think we all hope and believe to be the fact. He says further, "I believe that when America comes to a more accurate understanding of the difficulties which the masses of the working people in other parts of the world have to struggle against, it will have gone far towards solving what is called the race problem." I see nothing wrong about that; it is a philosophic reflection which ought to have a great deal of truth in it.

He says further with regard to the racial problem in America, "I know that some writers draw alarmist pictures, but I look forward to the future with hope, and confidence." Well, I think we all look forward to the future with hope, though the degree of confidence varies so far as the immediate future is concerned. Mr. Washington says further, "any one who lives in the South, where the black men are so numerous, knows that the situation, so far from becoming more difficult or dangerous, becomes more and more reassuring." This is a matter of opinion, and Mr. Washington lives in the South, while not more than one or two of the signers of the protest do, unless Washington be regarded as part of the South. Personally, I have not been any farther South than Washington but once in twenty-seven years.[6]

Mr. Washington says in this interview that "in America as in Europe and elsewhere the worst happenings are those that get talked about." You have recently published a newspaper letter in which the same statement is made (apropos of the condition of the colored soldiers in the west). Mr. Washington's statement in this interview about the business relations of white and black people is, I think, a little optimistic, but he knows more about them than I do. "Great industrial concerns" is rather a large term to apply to such ventures among colored people;[7] the recent failure of the True Reformers is a case in point.[8] "The racial feeling in America is not nearly so strong as many persons imagine." This may or may not be true; I should like to think that it is. On the whole, if the protest is based solely on this interview, it hardly seems sufficient to bear it out.

If I were inclined to criticize the wording of the protest, I might ask, does it not lean too far the other way; is it not at least equally as pessimistic as Mr. Washington's interview was optimistic? Nowhere does Mr. Washington say that the condition of the Negro in the United States is satisfactory. The protest says among other things that "because of his dependence on the rich charitable people, he has been compelled to tell, not the whole truth but that part of it which certain powerful interests in America wish to appear as the whole truth." Admitting the fact, is the reason clear? If the word "interests" is used in the ordinary sense of political magazine controversy, I am unable to imagine what "powerful interests" could wish to keep the Negro down. The statement is at least a little obscure.

Mr. Washington does not deny in terms that the Negro problem is the greatest of American problems; it is quite consistent with its gravity that conditions should be improved. The statement[9] that "black men of property and university training can be, and usually are, by law denied the ballot" is scarcely correct. They are in many cases denied the ballot, but hardly "by law," as covered by Mr. Ray Stannard Baker's article in the November *Atlantic*, which I read with interest.[10]

There is, it seems to me, a little inconsistency in another respect. In one place the protest states, "No sooner had we rid ourselves of nearly two-thirds of our illiteracy," etc., than the ballot was taken away. Is it true that even in the very narrowest sense of the term illiteracy as used in the census, namely the mere ability to read and write, two-thirds of the Negroes had reached that point fifteen years ago? In a later statement it is stated that "not one black boy in three in the United States has a chance to learn to read and write." This may be true, but if so, it shows in comparison with the former statement a very disastrous falling off. Mr. Washington states in his interview that education is "general"; he does not state that it is universal—as it ought to be. I think that the statement about our women in the South is a little broad. Also the statement about the courts. The wording of the protest would seem to imply that universally throughout the South the courts are used "not to prevent crime and to correct the wayward among Negroes, but to wreak public dislike and vengeance, and to raise public funds." I should hate to think that this is true. Negroes, as we all know, do not always, perhaps rarely, get equal justice in the courts, especially where the question of race is involved. But it would be a libel on humanity to charge all the courts of always having such an attitude of mind. The collection of revenue by levying fines is not confined to the South; it is a practice of criminal law everywhere, and our police courts are largely used as a means of revenue North as well as South.

The protest speaks of Mr. Washington suffering daily insult and humiliation. Insult and humiliation are largely subjective, a matter of personal feeling, and I have no idea that Mr. Washington feels himself daily insulted and humiliated. Whether he ought to is a question. As a fact, I imagine he thinks that he is daily honored and uplifted. It is possible that, visiting a foreign country as a distinguished American, he may have thought that the reception accorded to colored Americans visiting Europe would not be improved by making such a statement as that contained in the appeal. We know that our rights in the North are affected by the knowledge of the North of the manner in which we are treated in the South. Possibly Mr. Washington may have been, consciously or unconsciously, influenced by such a point of view. Moreover, the protest is signed by a number of gentlemen, most of whom hold or have held positions of honor and profit, political and otherwise, which they certainly could not have attained without the good will and sense of justice of white people, however imperfect that sense of justice may be in some other respects.

I have always believed that the Negro in the South will never get his rights until there is a party, perhaps a majority, of southern white peo-

ple friendly to his aspirations. If Mr. Washington can encourage the
growth of such a feeling in the South, he will have done a good work
even though he should fall short in other respects.

I think the reason first given by me is sufficient for my declining to
sign the protest. The other reasons I think will justify me in feeling that
I have not failed in my duty in so declining. It would be a lamentable
thing to believe that all the money and all the effort on the part of the
colored people since the war had not resulted in improving their condition; and if it is improving, it is on the way to favorable solution. There
are many things yet to be done; some of them, of which Mr. Washington has fought shy, the NAACP seeks to accomplish. There is plenty of
room and plenty of work for both. I make no criticism of any of the
gentlemen who have signed the appeal, but personally I should not, as I
say, like to "pitch into" Mr. Washington.

With sincere regards and best wishes,

Charles W. Chesnutt

Pioneer: 240–44

[1]While visiting Europe for six weeks in August-October 1910, Booker T.
Washington made several speeches in which he opined that "The Negro Problem" was on its way toward being resolved in the United States. On 26 October
1910, Du Bois produced a statement addressed "To the People of Great Britain
and Europe" that was entitled "RACE RELATIONS IN THE UNITED STATES"
and signed by 23 prominent African Americans. It was published under the same
title in the *Cleveland Gazette*, 12 November 1910, 1.

[2]See 21 July 1910 to Booker T. Washington, nn. 2 and 3.

[3]Washington was the chairman of the Committee of Twelve. On 1 March
1910 (DLC), Chesnutt agreed to add his name to the list of those encouraging
support of Tuskegee.

[4]The *London Morning Post* interview was reprinted as "Washington on
Race Problem in America" in a weekly newspaper to which Chesnutt sub-
scribed, *New York Age*, 22 September 1910, 1.

[5]William Archer (1856–1924), whose writings dealt mainly with drama
and acting, was the author of *Through Afro-America: An English Reading of
the Race Problem* (1910). Harry Hamilton Johnston (1858–1927) was the author of *A History of the British Empire in Africa* (1910); his *The Negro in the
New World* (1910) reflects a positive point of view on South and Central
Americans of African descent that is similar to Washington's and Chesnutt's
on African Americans. Chesnutt understood novelist H. G. Wells's point of
view on the American race problem as almost identically his own; see 9 October 1906 to Booker T. Washington.

[6]Chesnutt refers to his February 1901 lecture tour and visit at Tuskegee Institute.

[7]Washington had focused positively on African Americans building colleges, opening banks, and organizing "other great industrial concerns." About business relations between African Americans and whites Washington declared that the "Negroes are employed by the best white people in practically every occupation. There is not, in business matters at least, practically, any friction between the two races. Negroes may run real estate agencies or factories or banks, and they are patronised by blacks and whites alike."

[8]The United Order of the True Reformers was founded by the Reverend William Washington Browne (1849–97) who emphasized the economic necessity of self-reliance and mutual support among African Americans. Numerous True Reformers lodges were established in the eastern United States. Chesnutt refers to the failure of the organization's bank in 1910.

[9]That is, Du Bois' statement.

[10]"Negro Suffrage in a Democracy," *Atlantic Monthly*, 106 (November 1910), 612–19.

To Francis J. Garrison

Dec. 10, 1910.

My dear Mr. Garrison:—

Mrs. Marie Louise Péris, of Geneva, Switzerland, has sent me several copies of the *Journal de Genève*, of Geneva, Switzerland, containing her translation of my story "The Wife of His Youth,"[1] contained in the volume of the same name published by you. She expresses a desire to translate the *House Behind the Cedars*, and in case I am willing wishes to know on what terms.

Have you any objection, and if not, and leave the matter to me, can you make any suggestions as to what terms I might name? I can't imagine there would be very much in it, but I should be very glad to have what there is.[2]

Yours very truly,

TCU: TNF

[1]Francis J. Garrison (1848–1916) was a Houghton Mifflin Company editor with whom Chesnutt corresponded concerning the publication and publicizing of his books at the turn of the century. "*L'Epouse de sa Jeunesse*" appeared in installments in the *Journal de Genève*, No. 301 (4 November 1910), 4; No. 302 (5 November 1910), 4; and No. 303 (6 November 1910), 2.

[2]Garrison responded on 17 December 1910 (TNF), informing Chesnutt that the fee for permission to produce a French translation would be no more than $25.

To Frederick H. Goff

December 10, 1910.

My dear Mr. Goff:

I have your kind note, and thank you very much.[1]

A month or two ago, Ginn asked me one day if I would care to join the Rowfant Club, observing that he thought there would be no difficulty about it this time.[2] I replied that if they could stand it, I could, but that I would like to have him feel pretty certain about the matter before he put my name up, as I would not care to go twice through the same experience. It went through all right, and I anticipate considerable pleasure from the company of the gentleman with whom I am at last found worthy to associate.

Sincerely yours,

TCU: TNF

[1]Frederick H. Goff (1858–1923) was the president of the Cleveland Trust Company (1908–23), an attorney, the librarian of the Cleveland Law Library, and a trustee of Western Reserve University and the Hiram House settlement. He became a member of the Cleveland bibliophile club, the Rowfant, in 1894. Goff wrote Chesnutt the previous day (TNF) to congratulate him on his election to the club, which had flung "its entrance door wide enough to include a man of your standing and ability." Chesnutt was elected as member 231 on 3 December 1910.

[2]Frank H. Ginn (1868–1938), corporate lawyer and patron of the arts, was also a Rowfant Club member, joining in 1895 and serving as the president in 1910–12. Chesnutt here refers to the failure of his first nomination to membership in 1902.

To Benjamin P. Bourland

Dec. 10, 1910.

My dear Professor Bourland:—

I am in receipt of yours of the 8th notifying me of my election to membership in the Rowfant Club, a privilege which I appreciate very much.[1] I enclose herewith my check for $52.08, in payment of the enclosed statement.[2]

Yours very truly,

TCU: TNF

[1]Benjamin P. Bourland (1870–1943), a professor of modern languages at Western Reserve University and a Rowfant Club member since 1909, was the

secretary-treasurer of the club until 1927 when he served for two years as president.

[2]Bourland wrote to Chesnutt on 8 December 1910 (TNF), formally inviting him to become a member and enclosed an assessment of dues.

To Frederick R. Moore

December 15, 1910.

My dear Mr. Moore:—

Replying to yours of November 29th,[1] I have n't the remotest idea how many people in this vicinity voted the Democratic ticket, and would therefore be unable to state their reason for doing so. I do not imagine, however, that they were very many, and the chief criticism that I have heard of the present administration has been Mr. Taft's announcement that he would not appoint colored men to office in the South.[2]

Replying to your letter under another cover, requesting my opinion concerning the proper method for celebrating the fiftieth anniversary of the freedom of the Negro in 1913,[3] I hope you will not think me indifferent in matters pertaining to the welfare of the race, but in this town the Emancipation Proclamation is celebrated by the colored people every year, and I have sometimes thought that it might be well if they could forget that they were slaves, or at least give the white people a chance to forget it. At any rate, there are gentlemen much better qualified than myself to make suggestions upon this matter.

I read the *Age* every week with interest and pleasure.

There is probably nothing in this letter that would be of public interest.

Wishing you continued success with the *Age*, I am

Yours very truly,

TCU: TNF

[1]Moore wrote to Chesnutt in his capacity as the editor of the *New York Age*.

[2]See 8 April 1909 to John P. Green, n. 6.

[3]Effective 1 January 1863, the Emancipation Proclamation freed the slaves in the Confederate states.

To Booker T. Washington

December 28, 1910.

My dear Dr. Washington:—

I wish to thank you very much for the handsome and characteristic calendar which you were good enough to send me, and which reached me in excellent condition. It conveys a sentiment which should be taken to heart by everyone that is privileged to receive it. I shall give it a place of honor in my library, and refer to it whenever I feel in a pessimistic mood.

My son Edwin tells me that he likes his place with you, and finds the surroundings congenial and inspiring. I hope you are making him useful and that his usefulness will increase.[1]

We keep track of your movements through the newspapers. Mrs. Chesnutt and Helen join me in wishing you a New Year equally as successful as your past career.

Cordially yours,
Chas. W. Chesnutt.

TLS: DLC

[1]Edwin remained at Tuskegee until 1912, when he announced on 4 August that he would resign in 30 days because of poor health. On 10 August 1912 (TNF), Washington suggested to Edwin that after "a month or two months of complete rest" he might change his mind. On 19 September 1912 Washington again wrote to Edwin (TNF), expressing his regret that Edwin had decided not to return to Tuskegee and his gratitude for the services he had rendered.

To Carrie W. Clifford

January 2, 1912.

My dear Mrs. Clifford:—

Mrs. Chesnutt and I wish to thank you very much for the handsome copy of your *Race Rhymes*, preceded by the handsome portrait of your smiling countenance.[1]

I have read over your *Rhymes* and wish to congratulate you on your effort to put into the form of verse the sentiments which you and all the rest of us must feel upon the subjects of which you treat. You have done it very well indeed, your words will touch a responsive chord, certainly in every heart in sympathy with yours, and I hope your prayer that "They may change some evil heart, right some wrong and raise some arm strong to deliver", may find an answer commensurate with the labor to be accomplished. I don't know whether we can really expect it, but it is pleasant to cherish the hope.

I wish, while I am writing, to thank you for courtesies extended to my daughters, of which they have written us.

Wishing you, Mr. Clifford and your family a very happy and prosperous new year,

Sincerely yours,

TCU: TNF

[1]*Race Rhymes* was privately printed in the District of Columbia in 1911. Clifford would find a commercial publisher for a second volume of poetry, *The Widening Light*, in 1922.

To Theodore E. Burton

February 10, 1912

My dear Mr. Burton,

I presume you have noted the fact that a flood of protest has been pouring into Washington[1] against the appointment of Judge Hook to the Supreme Bench, because of an unfriendly and prejudiced decision of his in a "jim crow" railroad case.[2] I have spoken with you at times about this matter, and you seemed to feel that any agitation in behalf of the rights of colored men was a hopeless cause. I judge from recent newspaper items that this particular protest is likely to prove effective, and I trust that if you have any influence in connection with this appointment, as you certainly will with its confirmation, if made, that you will use it in accordance with the traditions of your party, of your State, of your city, and, as I fondly believe, with your own personal convictions.[3]

Yours respectfully,

TCU: TNF

[1]Burton was presently a U.S. senator from the state of Ohio.

[2]William C. Hook (1857–1921) of the federal Eighth Circuit Court of Appeals was not the primary judge on the panel of three; and so he was not the author of the decision handed down for McCable *et al.* v. Atchison, T. & S. F. Ry. Co., *et al.* (186 F. 966, 8th Cir.) on 10 February 1911. But he did side with the primary judge and against the dissenting one, agreeing that the Four-

teenth Amendment of the U.S. Constitution was not violated in Oklahoma by the way in which the "separate but equal" rule was applied to railway transportation of African Americans and whites.

[3]Burton did not have to act upon Chesnutt's request. Hook was, by 9 February, removed from President Taft's list of possible U.S. Supreme Court appointees; see "No Show for Hook, Nagel Out of It, Too," *Cleveland Leader*, 10 February 1912, 1.

To Henry J. Davies

March 11, 1912

My dear Henry:

I am enclosing herewith my application, duly signed, for membership in the Chamber of Commerce.[1] If I am elected, I shall take pleasure in my membership largely because of the fact that I shall be associated with you.[2]

Sincerely yours,
Charles W. Chesnutt

Pioneer: 246–47

[1]Henry Joseph Davies (1859–1921), a Cleveland stenographer, worked in partnership with Julius G. Pomerene (1846–1903)—Chesnutt's one-time business associate. Davies, a member of the Chamber of Commerce, also served as chair of the Progress Committee of the Electrical League of Cleveland, organized in 1909 and comprised of electrical contractors and manufacturers. Like Chesnutt, he was a member of the Rowfant Club (1895–1921).

[2]Chesnutt was elected to membership in the Chamber.

To William W. Hudson

March 11, 1912.

Dear Mr. Hudson:

I received in due course your favor of January 3rd, enclosing card of the season's greetings, and thank you very much for your kind offer to look over anything that I might submit to you.[1]

As I remember you made several suggestions about the development of my story *The House Behind the Cedars* as it appeared in your magazine, which no doubt contributed to its success.[2] It is still the most popular of my books and still has the largest sale.[3]

When I write some more, I shall not hesitate to call on you for suggestions if I feel the need of them.

Give my regards to Mrs. Hudson. I remember our acquaintance and association with much pleasure and should be very glad if circumstances should at some time in the future permit me to renew it.

Sincerely yours,

TCU: TNF

[1]William W. Hudson had written in behalf of the Waverly Company, an Indianapolis book publishing firm, enquiring about the availability of a new work by Chesnutt.

[2]Hudson was the editor of the monthly magazine *Self Culture*, the name of which was changed to *Modern Culture* during its serial publication of *The House Behind the Cedars*. The installments appeared as follow: *Self Culture*, 11 (August 1900), 497–510; *Modern Culture*, 12 (September 1900), 22–41; 12 (October 1900), 125–37; 12 (November 1900), 251–62; 12 (December 1900), 355–63; 12 (January 1901), 464–71; and 12 (February 1901), 560–68.

[3]The Houghton Mifflin sales record for *House* (MH) indicates that 3,680 copies were purchased between 1900 and 1911. In 1912 the sales totaled 67 copies.

To Leslie P. Hill

April 20, 1912.

My Dear Mr. Hill:—

Mrs. Chesnutt and I are in receipt of your favor of April 8th. We are very glad to think that we contributed, in any degree, to make your stay in Cleveland pleasant.[1] You and Mrs. Hill[2] made a very good impression upon the people whom you met. Mr. Paul Feiss made some complimentary remarks concerning you to me a few days after your departure, and I remember specially his saying that Mrs. Hill was a charming woman.[3]

Don't worry about the Mark Twain bust, or put yourself to any trouble to replace it. It had long since ceased to be ornamental, if indeed it ever had been, and my library really looks better without it.[4]

With regards to Mrs. Hill, and best wishes for the prosperity of your work, I remain

Sincerely yours,

TCU: TNF

[1]Leslie Pickney Hill (1880–1960) was an instructor at Tuskegee Institute (1904–7) and served from 1907 to 1913 as principal of the Manassas Industrial School for Colored Youth. His collection of poems *The Wings of Oppression* would appear in 1927 and his play *Toussaint L'Ouverture* in 1929.

[2]Jane Clark Hill.

[3]Paul Lewis Feiss (1875–1952) was a tailor who involved himself in a wide variety of entrepreneurial ventures in Cleveland. He became a member of the Rowfant Club in 1907, served as president (1921–22), and delivered one known lecture, "Some London Booksellers of the Eighteenth Century," to the Rowfanters on 23 December 1911.

[4]In 1905, editor and publisher Walter Hines Page secured for Chesnutt an invitation to the celebration of Mark Twain's seventieth birthday at Delmonico's restaurant in Manhattan. The keepsake given to the invitees was a bust of Twain, which was broken by one of the Hills during their visit.

To Mary White Ovington

May 21, 1912.

My dear Miss Ovington:—

You must either have been puzzled or have deemed me singularly lacking in courtesy when you were in my office the other day, or else have considered me something of a liar when I expressed my regret at not knowing of your presence in the city over Sunday—because I made no reference to your letter of May 17th from Indianapolis.[1]

Your letter came duly to hand and was on my desk when you were in the office. As it happened however, there was inclosed with it a little printed pamphlet containing the second annual report of the N.A.A.C.P., and on opening the envelope my eye caught only the printed enclosure. This morning however in going through my desk, I find your letter, and hasten to apologize for my seeming neglect and lack of courtesy and interest.

Sincerely yours,

TCU: TNF

[1]Mary White Ovington (1865–1951) was one of the founders of the N.A.A.C.P. She lived in New York City and apparently visited Chesnutt in connection with an impending speaking engagement, rather than N.A.A.C.P. business. (The Cleveland branch of the N.A.A.C.P. was not formed until 25 January 1914.) That "Miss Mary W. Ovington, Prof. Du Bois, Mr. Chas. Chesnutt and others will speak in Engineers' Hall, cor. of Ortiner St. and St. Clair Av., on Monday [17 June 1912] afternoon" was announced in "Purely Personal," *Cleveland Gazette*, 15 June 1912, 3.

To Susan Utley Chesnutt

July 3, 1912

. . . This is the last evening on the ship.[1] Helen has written you a 12-page letter today, and has doubtless told you all about the trip. We have had a smooth passage, warm weather up to the last three or four days, and an uneventful voyage. There are about 125 passengers, most of them teachers and college students, a great many of them Southerners. Helen was very skittish for awhile, and held me rigidly down; but I had a copy of *The Conjure Woman* with me and lent it to a passenger, and when they were getting up a program for the concert, I was asked and had to read a story, which I did with great success, receiving many compliments, and developing into quite a character.

The trip has been quite long—two weeks less a day or half a day, before we land. We are now in the English Channel having passed the Scilly Isles this morning at breakfast, and the Isle of Wight early this afternoon.

The meals have been fairly good, though we have sighed more than once for home cooking. There is a fairly good library on board of which I have read many books, and with bathing and eating and walking the deck and conversation with the passengers, we have put in the time very pleasantly, though we shall be very glad to land in the morning, as we hope to do. It has really been much less monotonous than I anticipated. There are one or two interesting men on board.

We had a field day—obstacle races, bun-eating contest, broad grin contest, relay races, shoe races, tug of war, needle-threading contest, etc., and a concert with eighteen numbers, of which, as I say, I contributed one. We have had pleasant table-mates, and roommates, and all in all, have enjoyed the first stage of our journey. We reach Antwerp tomorrow, and shall go from there to Bruges; Helen, I imagine, has told you the rest. By the time this reaches you, you will be at the seashore, and I hope enjoying yourselves. . . .

Pioneer: 248–49

[1]On 21 June Chesnutt sailed with Helen for Europe on the *S.S. Marquette*, arriving at Antwerp and touring Belgium, Holland, Germany, Switzerland, Italy, France, England, and Scotland.

To Susan Utley Chesnutt

[July 8, 1912]

. . . This is our 5th day in the Netherlands. We have been to Antwerp, Bruges, Brussels, and are now at the Hague, where we arrived yesterday. The clock is striking 10 in the evening, and the air is full of the chimes from a neighboring church. It has been so in every city; the chimes are wonderful. Helen has gone upstairs, and I am writing this in the writing room of the hotel, which is a very clean and pretty one, with an excellent cuisine and good beds, though the bedrooms are rather small here. In Belgium we spoke French and ate coffee and rolls for breakfast. Here, since few speak French and we don't know any Dutch, we speak very little and have Dutch breakfasts—this morning it was veal loaf and sliced dried beef, bread and butter, cheese, stewed strawberries and coffee. Then we went through a couple of museums and saw some very fine pictures of Rembrandt, Rubens, Paul Potter, Van Dyck,[1] etc., etc.

Afterwards we took a street car and went out to Scheveningen, the Dutch "Atlantic City," stayed there a couple of hours on the beach and had tea at a restaurant overlooking the sea. We heard part of a concert on a long pier like those at Atlantic City and Cape May; then took the car back to the Zoological Garden, where Helen took snapshots and raved over the flowers. Dutch flower gardens are wonderful; the woods are beautiful. The houses, the streets and public places, the hotel rooms, all are kept spotlessly clean, and the cheeses and sausages, etc., displayed in the windows are simply out of sight and keep us hungry all the time looking at them.

Tomorrow we go in the morning, by electric railway, to Rotterdam, and back in the P.M., stopping at Delft. The following morning we will finish up the Hague and go on to Amsterdam, our last stop in Holland. Belgium and Holland are very interesting countries, and we shall come home loaded with impressions and interesting reminiscences. . . .

Pioneer: 249–50

[1]Dutch painter Rembrandt van Rijn (1606–69), Flemish painter Peter Paul Rubens (1577–1640), Dutch painter Paul Potter (1625–54), and Flemish painter Anthony Van Dyck (1599–1641).

To Dorothy K. Chesnutt

July 18, 1912

. . . I am answering your letter written before you left for the sea-side, where I suppose you are now cooling yourself in the same waves that we sailed over for fourteen days; at least I saw a great many of them headed towards America, where I suppose they have arrived ere this.

Helen and I have quite a bit of fun, chasing from city to city. We can't stay long anywhere and cover our itinerary. Day before yesterday we left Cologne at 8 P.M., arrived in Frankfurt at 10, to find the city in full possession of a *Schützenfest* or convention of gunnery clubs.

Today we visited Schloss Heidelberg—the castle—and the University, which is coeducational—that is, women attend the lectures and take the academic degrees, and degrees in everything I understand, except law. The students belong to different corps, which are distinguished by different colored caps. For instance, Helen and I dined today at a restaurant frequented, for the midday meal, by students who wear the red caps. Besides the red caps, most of them carried canes, some of them had bull dogs, and most of them had badly scarred heads and faces, the results of the student duels. They're extremely courteous—indeed it is the custom of the country—and take off their caps to one another, all the way down.

At six P.M.—it is now 5:45—we shall take the train for Baden-Baden, after that, tomorrow, to Schaffhausen, arriving at Lucerne for Sunday, where we shall stop for several days, have some laundry done, and rest up for Italy. Helen is "doing noble"—can stand almost as much hard sight-seeing as I can. . . .

Pioneer: 250

To Susan Utley Chesnutt

July 23, 1912

. . . We are on the eve, or rather the morning of our departure from this beautiful city, set in the bosom of the mighty Alps, by the side of a beautiful lake, flanked by imposing hotels and pretty villas all along its shores from one end to the other. The principal business of the country is hotel-keeping, so far as I can see.

This is our fourth day in Lucerne and we are leaving this morning for Italy. We have steamed from one end of the lake to the other, had some beautiful drives, heard some inspiring music, both sacred and profane, climbed—I should say ridden-up Pilatus, the highest, most rugged and most imposing mountain in these parts, seen the famous Lion of Lucerne,[1] spent four days in a very beautifully situated and well-conducted *pension*,[2] the first we have tried. It has more of the social atmosphere than a hotel—you get acquainted with people and talk to them and they to you. There are people here of all sorts—Mexicans, Italians, Irish-Americans, Scotch-Americans, plain Yankees, Southerners, and Helen says two new arrivals are colored people from the U.S., tho I don't believe it. . . .

We had a delightful trip here down the Rhine from Cologne, through Frankfort, where we saw Goethe's[3] house and a Zeppelin dirigible airship in flight—we have an aeroplane stabled right across the lake here and have seen it several times in flight, once very near, over a boat on which we were riding. . . .

Pioneer: 251

[1] Mount Pilatus overlooks Lake Lucerne. The Lion of Lucerne is a sculptural monument commemorating 700 members of the Swiss Guard who died defending King Louis XVI (1754–93) and his family during the French Revolution.

[2] A small hotel or boarding-house.

[3] Johann Wolfgang von Goethe (1742–1832), German poet.

To Susan Utley Chesnutt

August 13, 1912

. . . This is our fourth day in Paris. Your letter of July 28 met us on our arrival, and was very welcome. Glad you are enjoying yourself; we certainly are having an elegant time. It has rained every day but one. But we have "done" the Louvre and Luxembourg Museums, the Invalides,[1] Notre Dame and the public squares and places. Helen took me to the Maison Boudet, where we had luncheon. We have been to several shows. We called on the Braxtons, and invited them to dine with us last night.[2] Tonight we dined with them. They gave us a nice dinner with champagne. They have a beautiful boy baby, just learning to walk. They live in a fine large apartment, beautifully furnished and decorated, have two servants, and seem to be perfectly happy. I wore my evening clothes and Helen her best. On leaving we took a taxi and on the way home had the *cocher*[3] drive out the Champs-Elysées and back by the theatres and cafes to our hotel.

On Sunday, Braxton called and took us for a drive in the Bois[4] and we had tea at the Cascade Restaurant.

Paris is a beautiful city and I wish we had more time and more money. This Continental is a fine and expensive hotel, but Helen wanted to stop here and enjoys it very much.

Have met several Cleveland people. One of the Rowfanters is stopping at this hotel, and we have shaken hands several times. Ran across Mr. Emil Joseph at the American Express office Saturday.[5] He is at the Majestic and invited us to call, which we haven't done as yet.

Tomorrow we go to Fontainebleau, with a young woman we met on the boat, a Georgia girl by the way. We will be here a couple of days yet, during which we shall visit some more public places, call on Mimi Goulesque, leave a card on the American Ambassador, Mr. Herrick,[6] possibly Mr. Simmons,[7] the Cleveland artist from whom I hope to learn the address of Mr. Tanner,[8] whose name does not appear in the directory.

We shall leave here for London Thursday or Friday night, and put in the rest of our time there and in getting up to Glasgow, whence we shall sail to meet you September 1, when we will exchange greetings and have a grand lovefeast.

Am addressing this to the place where Helen says you will be when it arrives, or shortly thereafter. Much love to you. . . .

Pioneer: 254–55

[1]The Invalides was originally constructed in the 17th-century as an "old soliders home." It became a complex of monuments and museums; Napoléon I (1769–1821) is entombed there.

[2]Possibly John Henry Braxton (1873–?) and Mattie Tinsley Braxton. Braxton founded and was the head of a real estate company in Richmond, Va.

[3]Coachman.

[4]Bois du Boulogne, a park bordering on the Paris suburb of Neuilly-sur-Seine.

[5]Emil Joseph (1857–1938) was a lawyer, bibliophile, philanthropist, and member of the governing board of the Cleveland Public Library.

[6]Myron T. Herrick (1854–1929), fellow Rowfant Club member, was the president and chairman of the board of Cleveland's Society for Savings. Active in Republican politics, he was governor of Ohio in 1903–5; he served as the U.S. ambassador to France in 1912–14 and in 1921–29.

[7]Freeman W. Simmons (1859–1926) was a portraitist and landscape

painter. He was associated with the Cleveland School of Art and was a member of the American Art Association in Paris.

[8]Henry Ossawa Tanner (1859–1937) was a Philadelphia painter who moved to and spent the rest of his life in France. His specialties were biblical and North African local color subjects.

To Jessie F. Coleridge-Taylor

September 14, 1912.

My dear Mrs. Coleridge-Taylor:—

Imagine the surprise and shock of my daughter and me upon seeing in the first newspaper which we picked up on our arrival at New York, the notice of your husband's death.[1] It had been little more than a week since we had seem him in your pleasant home, the very picture of robust health and high spirits. None of the newspaper items which I have seen gave the cause of his death.

Mrs. Chesnutt, my daughter[2] and all the members of my family who have had the pleasure of meeting you and Mr. Taylor, join me in sincere regrets and expressions of sympathy with you in your bereavement. Mr. Coleridge-Taylor's death was a loss not only to his family, but to the world, and especially to the art which he practiced so beautifully.

I trust that your son's health has improved since we were at Croydon,[3] and that you are all bearing up bravely in your affliction.

Sincerely yours,

TCU: TNF

[1]Musical composer Samuel Coleridge-Taylor died on 1 September 1912; see 8 April 1909 to John P. Green, n. 7.

[2]Helen, with her father, visited the Coleridge-Taylors at Croydon, England, in August. Edwin, Dorothy, and she made Mrs. Coleridge-Taylor's acquaintance there in 1906. Chesnutt and his wife had previously met her; see 8 April 1909 to John Patterson Green, n. 7.

[3]Hiawatha Bryan Coleridge-Taylor (1900–?).

To James Weldon Johnson

Jan. 18, 1913.

My dear Mr. Johnson:—

I wish to thank you,[1] or some friend of yours, for sending me marked copies of the *N.Y. Times* of January 1st and 2nd, the first containing your magnificent Emancipation Anniversary poem, "Fifty Years,"[2] and the second containing the very appreciative editorial tribute to the quality of your work and the letter signed "Caucasian."[3] I can only add, after endorsing all they say, that it is the finest thing I have ever read on the subject, which is saying a good deal, and the finest thing I have seen from the pen of a colored writer for a long time—which is not saying quite so much.

If you can find themes which will equally inspire you, why may you not become the poet for which the race is waiting? The deaths of Dunbar and Coleridge-Taylor[4] have left a large gap in the ranks of men of color who have gained recognition in the world of creative thought, and certainly no aspiring author could claim that the field was overworked.

You have rendered a service to your race and to humanity by giving to the world this beautiful poem, and I hope the appreciation it must have received has given you as much pleasure as the poem has given your readers.

Cordially yours,
Chas. W. Chesnutt.

TLS: CtY

[1] James Weldon Johnson (1871–1938) was an educator, lyricist, and poet. He is now best known for his performance as field secretary and then general secretary of the N.A.A.C.P. (1916–30) and for his quasi-autobiographical novel *The Autobiography of an Ex-Colored Man* (1912). In this earliest known letter to Johnson it is not clear whether the two men had yet met or if Chesnutt was aware of his novel. Chesnutt did not refer to Johnson in his writings until 1918 when he delivered a speech on "Negro Authors"; see *Essays and Speeches*: 458–61. Even then *The Autobiography* was not mentioned by name. They may have encountered each other for the first time in 1916 at the Amenia Conference on race relations (Amenia, New York): in a 25 October 1916 letter to Johnson (TNF), Chesnutt closed by referring to "pleasant memories of our brief association at Amenia."

[2] This poem celebrating the progress made by African Americans since 1863 appeared in the *New York Times*, 1 January 1913, 16.

[3] The editorial entitled "A Negro Poet Speaks for His Race" appeared on p. 10 of the 2 January 1913 issue. It praised the "excellence of the verse" and celebrated Johnson's "elevation of sentiment, his power of creative imagination, and his thorough knowledge that for the production of strong emotional effects simple language is the best." It noted, however, that "the poem was not a full statement of the 'race problem'—that it in effect ignored a full half of the problem. . . . The telling of the whole truth [Johnson] properly left for others and through another medium." The letter signed "Caucasian" appeared

on the same page. It declared that "there are few Caucasian versifiers who can summon the spirit and give the swing to their lines that [Johnson] does. The African is a born melodist," and Johnson's "rhythm and rhyme prove that he has the full measure of the quality which cannot come from all the training of all the schools quite as nature gives it."

⁴Paul Laurence Dunbar enjoyed success as a contributor to periodicals prior to 1896, but that year he obtained national visibility as an author with the publication of *Lyrics of Lowly Life* by Dodd, Mead and Company. Less renowned as a short story writer and novelist, he was through the time of his death in 1906 the most widely celebrated African-American poet. Chesnutt never corresponded with or, it appears, met Dunbar. He did, however, know Coleridge-Taylor personally; see 14 September 1912 to Jessie F. Coleridge-Taylor.

To Edward C. Williams

February 18, 1913.

My dear Ed:—

Dorothy will graduate from the College for Women in June.¹ She has prepared herself for teaching, which seems about the only career open to her. There are only three available places for her to teach—at some Southern school, here, or in Washington. The conditions of life in the South are not pleasant for a girl brought up as Dorothy has been; the conditions of life in Cleveland, for a colored girl of culture and of Dorothy's upbringing, are, for other reasons, scarcely less attractive. She would like to teach in Washington, and we should all like to have her do so, if it can be brought about. The place she would naturally think of would be the M Street High School. So I would like to have you write to me as to how best to go about securing this result. You know the ropes.²

Since you have not the appointing power, there could be no savor of nepotism in connection with the matter, and her connection with your family certainly ought not to act against her. I know the Washington people think they ought to have all the places, but the Washington schools are supported in part by the National Government, which interferes with their claim somewhat.

If you think for any reason that the M Street High School is not available, please suggest anything else that may occur to you. She has specialized in English. Help us get the kid placed where she can see a little life, and we will all appreciate it.

Yours cordially,

TCU: TNF

[1]Chesnutt's daughter was graduated on 11 June 1913 at the commencement exercises of the College for Women at Western Reserve University. She was named in "67 Sheepskins Go To College Girls," Cleveland *Plain Dealer*, 12 June 1912, 1–2.

[2]Williams was presently serving as principal of the M Street High School.

To Houghton Mifflin Company

March 3, 1913.

Dear Sirs:—

Referring to the letter forwarded me from your office the other day from Rev. Silas X. Floyd, Augusta, Georgia, I enclose you a copy of my letter to Mr. Floyd.[1]

I see from the check for royalties which I received this morning that my books are still selling. The demand is not large, but seems to be fairly steady. The books represent a little school of their own, in a field where they have hardly any competition. Sometime I should like to add another to them along the line of *The Conjure Woman*. I have a long story, or series of stories connected by a live plot, to which I could add one or two shorter ones, and make a volume as large as the "Conjure Woman." When I get it in shape, I will submit it to you and get your views on it.[2]

Yours very truly,

TCU: TNF

[1]Silas X. Floyd (1869–?) was a Baptist minister who published several compilations of his sermons. The subject of Chesnutt's correspondence with him is not known.

[2]No subsequent correspondence deals with this project.

To Horace Talbert

April 3rd, 1913.

My Dear Mr. Talbert:—[1]

My name seems to give you a good deal of trouble.

With presumably my letterhead in front of you you have spelled it wrong twice in your letter of March 31st. I know it is a very unusual spelling. There is no "t" in the middle but two "t's" are at the end. It should be spelled in the diploma,

Charles Waddell Chesnutt.[2]

I send you under another cover the other diploma.[3] Hoping to correct it will not be a great deal of trouble to you, I remain

Very truly yours,

TCU: TNF

[1]Horace Talbert (1853–1917), an A.M.E. minister and the author of *The Sons of Allen* (1906), had served as the secretary and financial officer of Wilberforce University since 1897.

[2]Chesnutt was to be formally awarded an honorary Doctor of Law degree by Wilberforce University later in 1913.

[3]See 23 May 1913 to Carl Jenkins regarding further difficulty at Wilberforce in spelling Chesnutt's name correctly.

To Newton D. Baker

April 3, 1913.

My dear Mr. Baker:—

Permit me to express the great pleasure your letter in reference to the anti-intermarriage bill has given me.[1] I fear you thought my silence strange, after our interview. I find it a little difficult myself to account for, except that I am naturally of a somewhat dilatory habit of mind. I did not have the literature just at hand, and moreover I have strained my emotions so much on this Race Problem that I was slightly disappointed and a little discouraged at what seemed to be your attitude at the time. I might have realized from the experience of others that you could not be "rushed", and I am sure that a sober, well considered, balanced opinion on any subject, after personal investigation of the facts is worth more as a basis of action than a snap judgment, even on the right side.[2]

I assume, of course, that your decision was on the principle involved, rather than on the particular bill, and I shall take care that it is known among those who are more immediately concerned, who, I am sure, will appreciate the wisdom, the liberality and the real statesmanship of your action.[3]

Sincerely yours,

TCU: TNF

[1]Newton D. Baker (1871–1937), a Cleveland lawyer, was elected mayor of Cleveland in 1912. Bills prohibiting inter-racial marriage had been recently in-

troduced in the U.S. House of Representatives (National House Bill No. 1710) and the Ohio legislature (House Bill No. 27).

²In a 27 March 1913 letter (TNF) acknowledging receipt of and returning the pamphlets Chesnutt sent him, Baker related that he had already looked into the matter on his own following their interview. "Not hearing from you I gave this question some independent investigation with the result that I came to the conclusion that the pending bill in Columbus ought not to be passed under any circumstances, and I have so advised the members of the delegation from Cleveland."

³The *Cleveland Gazette*, having repeatedly urged its readership to fight against the passage of the Ohio anti-intermarriage bill, gleefully reported its defeat in "A Great Victory! The Bill Killed!" 19 April 1913, [2].

To Walter Hines Page

April 3, 1913.

My dear Mr. Page:—

I notice from the newspapers that you have been named by President Wilson¹ as Ambassador to Great Britain. It is a signal honor, worthily bestowed. Considering the men who have filled the office, it calls for all there is in a real big man, and I feel that you can meet the requirements. I hope you may have as successful and brilliant a career as a diplomat and statesman as you have had as editor and publisher.²

I was afraid that Mr. Wilson would not find anybody out of the millionaire class who could afford to accept the position. I hope you are in that class, or that you have made at least money enough in the publishing business to uphold the dignity of the office without embarrassment.

Cordially yours,

TCU: TNF

¹Woodrow Wilson (1856–1924) served as the U.S. president from 1913 to 1921.

²Retiring from the editorship of *World's Work* magazine (1900–1913)—published by Doubleday, Page & Co.—Page served as ambassador from 1913 to 1918.

To William F. King

May 16th, 1913.

Dear Sir:—

I am in receipt of your very interesting letter of May 1st.[1]

The method of training hounds to catch run away negroes described to you by your pupils in 1852–53 is very interesting, and quite consistent with the worst aspects of the slave system. I did not live in the south until after the war, when slavery was only a memory, although a very vivid one, and I do not recall ever hearing any one describe the method that you speak of. It suggests to me a chapter in Sir Harry Johnston's *Negro in the New World*, concerning the cruelty of the planters in the Dutch Colonies. This is a monumental work, and while it perhaps has no direct bearing on your subject, you would undoubtedly find it very interesting and instructive.[2]

Yours very truly,

TCU: TNF

[1]William F. King (1830–1921) was President Emeritus of Cornell College and wrote to Chesnutt from his home in Mt. Vernon, Ia.

[2]See 21 November 1910 to W. E. B. Du Bois, n. 5. Johnston's relatively positive attitude toward the Negro pleased Chesnutt, and he cited and quoted Johnston in two speeches: "A Solution for the Race Problem" (c. 1916) and "The Negro in Books" (1916); see *Essays and Speeches*: 384–402 and 426–41.

To Joseph F. Gould

May 16th, 1913.

Dear Sir:—

I have your favor of May 11th, and note with pleasure that you have read some of my books.[1]

I agree with you that the race prejudice which is most common today, at least most injurious to its victims, is the social prejudice, that is, the prejudice society as a whole has against the negro. This is particularly true at the south, and not equally so in the north. The whole social organism of the south, both public, as evinced by its discriminating laws, and private, as evidenced by social customs, is directed toward keeping the negro in a subordinate and inferior condition, politically, economically, and socially.

I hardly agree with you that there is no personal prejudice against the negro in the south, although southerners have no objection to coming in the most intimate personal contact with colored people as inferiors. The principal difference between the south and north in the matter of race prejudice, is that in the south a white man, though kindly disposed toward his colored neighbor, is not permitted to act as he might otherwise feel disposed to do, while in the north, a white man can, without social odium, be as free in his associations with colored people as with white people.

The prejudice against the Jew, like the Jew himself, is a curious survival. There is a class of Jews who, as you state, claim there is no racial prejudice against them, and who do not admit any difference of race between themselves and other white people. But the prejudice is not religious, because, broadly speaking, there is very little religious prejudice in the present age, certainly no prejudice of the mass of Protestants against others for their religious beliefs, and it therefore must be racial. Unless perhaps, like many other prejudices, it is purely based on tradition. Originally it was perhaps founded on religion, although the Jewish type has always been more or less strongly marked.

Your theory that the negro and Jew are disliked by opposite sects of people, and the reason therefor, is interesting, and I would be glad to read any evidence which would support this view.[2]

Sincerely yours,

TCU: TNF

[1]Joseph F. Gould (1889–1957), then residing at Harvard University's Matthews Hall, became after his graduation a conventional writer contributing articles on international topics to magazines such as *Outlook* and *Nation*. By 1920, however, he had begun a bohemian life in Manhattan's Greenwich Village, where he wrote literary essays, book reviews and poetry but achieved notoriety principally as an eccentric who claimed to be writing a never-found "oral history" of his life and times.

[2]Gould appears not to have replied.

To Carl Jenkins

May 23rd, 1913.

My dear Mr. Jenkins:—

I am in receipt of your favor of May 17th, asking for the subject of my address to the Literary Societies.[1] I think if you will call it "Ideals and their Realization" it will cover it sufficiently.[2]

I notice in the printed program sent me, you have me named as "Hon. Charles M. Chestnutt." This is quite an accumulation of mistakes. In the first place I am not an Honorable, never having held any office or appointment which would entitle me to that designation. In the second place my middle initial is not "M" and in the third place my name is not spelled "Chestnutt." If you will put it "Mr. Charles W. Chesnutt" it will be more correct and quite sufficient.[3]

Yours very truly,

TCU: TNF
[1]Carl Jenkins was secretary to the president of Wilberforce University. The current president (1908–20) was William S. Scarborough (1852–1926).

[2]Chesnutt had been invited to speak at Wilberforce University during commencement week. On 16 June 1913 he read before the school's literary societies a paper with a different title, "Race Ideals and Examples," subsequently published in abbreviated form with that title, *A.M.E. Review*, 30 (October 1913), 101–15. See *Essays and Speeches*: 331–48.

[3]See 3 April 1913 to Horace Talbert, where Chesnutt notes a like mistake: his name had been misspelled on the diploma for the honorary LL.D. degree awarded him by Wilberforce.

To Newton D. Baker

July 29th, 1913.

My dear Mr. Baker:—

I beg to acknowledge receipt of your favor of July 26th, naming me as a member of a committee to arrange for a celebration of the Centennial year of the Battle of Lake Erie.[1] I thank you for the compliment, and it will give me pleasure to accept the invitation and to contribute so far as I can, toward the work of the celebration.[2]

Very truly yours,

TCU: TNF
[1]During the War of 1812, Commodore Oliver Hazard Perry (1785–1819) commanded an American fleet of ten ships on Lake Erie. He defeated a British squadron of six on 10 September 1813, establishing American dominance over the lake and rendering Canada vulnerable to invasion.

[2]Serving as the chairman of the committee to which he was named, Chesnutt directed the organization of the African-American community for the celebration. See "Social and Personal," *Cleveland Gazette*, 13 September 1913, [3], and 15 September 1913 to Charles T. Hallinan.

To Alice Moore Dunbar

August 27, 1913.

Dear Madam,

Replying, somewhat belatedly, for which I trust you will pardon me, to your letter of July 22nd, with reference to the *Masterpieces of Negro Eloquence*, I would say that I have never posed as an orator, and have never even read an essay which would be worthy of characterization as a "masterpiece of eloquence," or even as eloquence at all.[1]

Thanking you for the compliment, I am

Yours respectfully,

TCU: TNF

[1]Alice Moore Dunbar (1875–1935), the widow of Paul Laurence Dunbar, was a teacher, editor, book-reviewer, and short story writer. She requested from Chesnutt (TNF) the text of one of his speeches that might be suitable for inclusion in the anthology she was assembling. The volume was published in 1914 without a contribution from Chesnutt.

To Samuel M. Dudley

Sept. 1, 1913.

My dear Mr. Dudley:—

Replying to your letter of August 26th, I am sending you under separate cover, by parcel post, a half-tone cut of myself.[1] I don't know whether it is the proper size or not; if not I can send you the same photograph, from which a smaller one can be made.

I have never read anything in public on Abraham Lincoln, and although the subject may seem trite, and was threshed out during the Lincoln Centenary several years ago, I think I might say something of interest, in these ticklish times, about a man who believed in the equality of man and proved his faith by his works.[2] Unless the subject is not acceptable, I shall speak on the subject: "Abraham Lincoln: An Appreciation." Of course this will be merely a text, in connection with which I can express a great many other thoughts concerning past and present conditions affecting the colored race.

If you would prefer a different subject, something with a more literary topic, kindly advise me and I shall try to please.[3]

Yours sincerely,

TCU: TNF

[1]Attorney Samuel M. Dudley (1873–1947) was the president of the Bethel Literary and Historical Association in the District of Columbia. On 26 June 1913 (TNF), he invited Chesnutt to give on 7 October the opening address of its 1913–14 lecture series. Chesnutt did not respond, and Dudley wrote to him again on 21 July (TNF); on 22 July, Chesnutt accepted the invitation (TNF). On 26 August (TNF), Dudley requested a photograph of Chesnutt to be used for advertisements.

[2]James 2:26.

[3]Dudley replied on 8 September (TNF), suggesting that Chesnutt choose a different title "to increase our attendance." He added, a presentation "along race lines will be acceptable as we are forced to think on this question every day." Chesnutt, however, delivered "Abraham Lincoln: An Appreciation" .ɔ the Bethel audience on 7 October 1913; see *Essays and Speeches*: 349–52.

To Randolph Y. McCray

September 5, 1913.

My dear Mr. McCray,

I have boiled down the historical facts on colored seamen and soldiers in the War of 1812 into a compact story which I hope, with your approval, will not be too long for the Sunday papers.[1] You can, of course, cut it still further if necessary.[2]

Sincerely yours,

TCU: TNF

[1]Randolph Y. McCray (1879–1951) was a politician elected to the Cuyahoga County Council in 1910 and a journalist who wrote for both the *Cleveland Leader* and the *Plain Dealer*. Chesnutt, as a member of the Perry Centennial celebration committee (see 29 July 1913 to Newton D. Baker), addressed him at the committee's headquarters at the city hall.

[2]Chesnutt's "story" was radically abbreviated; see 15 September 1913 to Charles T. Hallinan, n. 4.

To Houghton Mifflin Company

September 12, 1913.

Dear Sirs:

I enclose you herewith a letter from Mr. R. R. Wright, Statistician and Director of Exhibits for the Emancipation Proclamation Commission of Pennsylvania. Mr. Wright is well known as a man of character and integrity, and if you can consistently send the books to the number suggested, 25 copies of each of my books, to him at Philadelphia, I have no doubt they will either be paid for or returned, perhaps to our mutual advantage. I have written to Mr. Wright that I would make that suggestion to you. If you decide to send them, it should be done at once, so that they would be on hand as near the 15th as possible.

Yours very truly,

TCU: TNF

To Charles T. Hallinan

September 15, 1913.

My dear Hallinan:—

Pardon my not having acknowledged sooner your letter of September 6th, but I have been up to my ears in work of a pressing nature.[1] I shall be glad to do what you ask about Miss Fauset's article,[2] and look forward, when I get it, to making the acquaintance of Mr. Richard, with whom I am not as yet acquainted.[3] I hope he is a newspaper man of your own stripe, as your description would seem to indicate that he is.

I have lately had some experience with the languidness of newspapers in our case. As chairman of one of the committees for the local Perry Centenary Celebration, in the throes of which Cleveland now is, I prepared and submitted to the publicity department of the Centennial Committee an article setting forth what part was played by colored sailors and soldiers in the War of 1812. It appeared in the Cleveland *Plain Dealer*, but the publicity agent informs me that the *Leader* would not print it.[4] The *Plain Dealer* is much the more public-spirited of the two papers, in other respects as well as particularly in this one.

Cordially yours,

TCU: TNF

[1]Charles T. Hallinan was a journalist working for the *Chicago Evening Post* and a member of the Board of Directors of the Chicago Branch of the N.A.A.C.P.

[2]Jessie Redmon Fauset (1882–1961), a writer who would later succeed as a novelist associated with the Harlem Renaissance, was then teaching at the M Street High School in the District of Columbia. Hallinan apparently asked Chesnutt to evaluate Fauset's article on racial discrimination and, if appropriate, recommend its publication by the Newspaper Enterprise Association syndicate.

[3]Livy S. Richard represented the Newspaper Enterprise Association syndicate. Both Hallinan and Chesnutt initially referred to a Mr. Richards, rather than Richard; see 24 September 1913 to Hallinan where Chesnutt observed the misspelling.

[4]Chesnutt's article (see 5 September 1913 to Randolph Y. McCray) was reduced to a news story in which he was merely quoted: "Negroes to Walk in Perry's Parade," Cleveland *Plain Dealer*, 8 September 1913, 3. The article was very likely a condensation of the speech he wrote for the Perry Centennial Celebration; see "Perry Centennial," *Essays and Speeches*: 322–30. The speech was commented upon in "Social and Personal," Cleveland *Gazette*, 20 September 1913, [3]: "Chas. W. Chesnutt's paper at St. Andrew's P[rotestant]. E[piscopal]. Church, Sunday evening [14 September 1913], was . . . worthy of a much larger audience, only 53 being present. It was the best thing of the kind given in that church in years."

To Newton D. Baker

Sept. 24, 1913.

My dear Mr. Baker:—

I received and read with pleasure your note in reference to the Perry Centennial Celebration. I agree with you that it was a great event of which all of us who participated in it have a right to feel proud, and I hope it may have, as you say, the effect of softening race animosities and prejudice of all kinds among our citizenship.

I wish to express, on my own behalf and that of those whom I represented in this celebration, a high appreciation of the courtesy and consideration which was extended by yourself, the general committee, and all with whom I came in contact, toward our colored citizens, in the sincere effort to have them believe that their co-operation was desired in this civic demonstration, not only as citizens, but in appreciation of the part which colored seamen played in Perry's Victory. I know that they appreciate these things, and that some of them will find another way than by mere words to express that feeling in the case of Mr. Baker.

Very sincerely yours,

TCU: TNF

To Jessie Redmon Fauset

Sept. 24, 1913.

My dear Miss Fauset:—

Pardon me for not having acknowledged sooner receipt of your article. It came in due course, and I have seen Mr. Livy S. Richard, of the Newspaper Enterprise Association in regard to it, and have written a letter to our friend Mr. Hallinan giving the result of my interview, of which I enclose you a copy. The letter went forward to Mr. Hallinan today.[1]

Permit me to say personally that your article impresses me as a very well written and convincing statement of the conditions as they exist in the capitol city of this land of the free under the administration of "The New Freedom".[2] I hope that Mr. Wilson, when he gets his tariff and currency bills passed, will not tamely submit to the domination of the Bourbon[3] Southern congressmen upon these vital matters of civil liberty.[4]

Respectfully yours,

TCU: TNF

[1]See 15 September 1913 and 24 September 1913 to Charles T. Hallinan.

[2]"New Freedom" was the term Woodrow Wilson used during his 1912 presidential campaign when describing the salutary actions he would take if elected, *e.g.*, lowering tariffs, reforming the monetary system, and imposing stricter controls upon trusts.

[3]Reference to the House of Bourbon, which ruled France from 1589 to 1792. Following the French Revolution, those determined to reestablish the Bourbon monarchy called for a return of the old order. After Emperor Napoléon I's abdication in 1814, Bourbons again ruled until 1848. "Bourbon" in Chesnutt's time was the pejorative term used to describe U.S. Southerners seen as attempting to restore the antebellum status quo.

[4]Wilson was a Southerner. Born in Virginia, he studied law at the University of Virginia and practiced for a brief period in Atlanta, Ga., before earning a Ph.D. at Johns Hopkins University in Baltimore, Md.

To Charles T. Hallinan

Sept. 24, 1913.

My dear Mr. Hallinan:—

I received Miss Fauset's article several days ago and have submitted it to Mr. Livy S. Richard, which is the correct name of the gentleman to whom you referred.[1] The article was written with pen and ink, and he glanced over it casually, and suggested that it was written rather in an argumentative vein than in the simple and direct style in which they put out their Newspaper Enterprise Association matter. He suggested that if the article were re-written and put in simple narrative form, stating the personal experiences of a colored woman in the matter of discrimination, with the resultant effect upon her mind and her feelings,[2] and then taken up with their editor in Chicago, Mr. Sam T. Hughes,[3] 102 North 5th Ave., who would in any event have to endorse it, it would receive respectful consideration and probably be sent out, if in acceptable form. Mr. Richard asked me to have the manuscript typewritten and send him a copy, so that he might read it more carefully, which I have done, and also send you a typewritten copy with the original.

I found Mr. Richard to be about the type of man you suggest in your letter, sound at bottom on the race question. That is to say, he thinks it our greatest national problem, and that it ought to be settled. He was inclined to think at the beginning of our interview, that agitation was not the method that would produce the best results, but while that by persistent agitation on his own part and that of his friends the Negro might obtain his civil rights, it would be of no value in improving his social status. I think I convinced him that all the friends of the Negro are asking for at present is respect for his civil and political rights, after which and conditioned upon which lies his own hope of social advancement. I think Mr. Richard is good material to work on. He referred to conversations he had had in Boston with Mr. Villard, Mr. Pillsbury, and Mr. Moorfield Storey[4] on the subject, in which, as I say, he expressed a keen interest, fully appreciating and I fear slightly overestimating the difficulty of dealing with it.

If I can be of any further service in connection with Miss Fauset's article, in any other way that may occur to you, I shall be glad to do so.

Yours sincerely,

TDU: TNF

[1]See 15 September 1913 to Hallinan, n. 3.

[2]In the typed draft of this letter Chesnutt canceled here "—such stories, I presume he has in mind, as the *Independent* sometimes publishes—" and then added a comma after "feelings." Though he gives no clear indication of this, Chesnutt was perhaps recalling the publication of a similar, unsigned article, "What It Means to Be Colored in the Capital of the United States," *Independent*, 62 (24 January 1907), 181–86.

[3]Sam T. Hughes (1868–1948), like Richard, was employed by the Newspaper Enterprise Association syndicate.

[4]Oswald Garrison Villard was a vice-president of the N.A.A.C.P. Albert E. Pillsbury (1849–1930) was, like Chesnutt since 1912, a member of the Advisory Board of the N.A.A.C.P. Moorfield Storey (1845–1929) was the N.A.A.C.P. president.

To Charles T. Hallinan

October 18, 1913.

Dear Mr. Hallinan:—

Replying to your letter of October 14th, I assume that when you wrote it you did not have at hand my letter enclosing Miss Fauset's article, and I quote a paragraph from it:[1]

> Mr. Richard suggested that it was written rather in an argumentative vein than in the simple and direct style in which they put out their Newspaper Enterprise Association matter. He suggested that if the article were rewritten and put in simple narrative form, stating the personal experiences of a colored woman in the matter of discrimination, with the resultant effect upon her mind and her feelings, and then taken up with their editor in Chicago, Mr. Sam T. Hughes, 102 North 5th Ave., who would in any event have to endorse it, it would receive respectful consideration and probably be sent out, if in acceptable form.

According to the suggestion in your former letter, the manuscript not being available[2] in its present form I sent it to you, thinking that you would revise it or send it to Miss Fauset for that purpose.[3]

I do not know why Mr. Richard wanted a carbon copy, except perhaps with a view to referring to the facts at some time in an editorial or article from his own pen.

I have not heard anything from him since my last letter to you.[4]

Very sincerely yours,

TCU: TNF

[1]See 24 September 1913 to Charles T. Hallinan.

[2]An "available" manuscript in Chesnutt's time was one that an editor had accepted for publication.

[3]When Chesnutt wrote to Hallinan on 24 September he enclosed the holograph and a typed copy of Fauset's article. On 29 September (TNF), Chesnutt again wrote to Hallinan, relating that Livy S. Richard (see 15 and 24 September 1913 to Hallinan) had sent him a clipping of an editorial and a note; Chesnutt enclosed copies of them and of his reply to Richard. Receiving Ches-

nutt's 29 September letter, Hallinan discovered that he had misunderstood what had transpired with regard to Fauset's article. He explained on 14 October 1913 (TNF) that he assumed Richard would make a publication arrangement with Sam T. Hughes. That is, Hallinan neither revised Fauset's article nor sent it to Fauset for revision. Wrote Hallinan to Chesnutt, "I think now that I misread your letter and that it is up to me to convince Mr. Hughes of the serviceability of the article for the syndicate. Am I right?"

[4]Fauset's article did not see publication.

To Charles E. Bentley

November 1, 1913.

My dear Doctor Bentley:—

I have your favor of October 25th.[1] I had not forgotten that you had asked me to come to Chicago, and rather expected to hear from you, in spite of the fact that I tried to head you off when I was in Chicago.

So far as I can see ahead for a year, I shall be very willing to address your class of Nurse Graduates at this time next year.[2]

Mrs. Chesnutt joins me in thanking you for your kind invitation to spend Thanksgiving with you and Mrs. Bentley.[3] The outlook does not seem very good for either of us availing ourselves of the invitation this year, but if I come next fall, Mrs. Chesnutt says that she will be delighted to go with me.

I hear from my son pretty regularly, and he says he is working hard and learning a great deal. I hope he will succeed in qualifying himself to practice your very honorable profession.[4]

                                        With regards to Mrs. Bentley,
                                                    Cordially Yours,

TCU: TNF

[1]Charles E. Bentley (1859–1929), a dentist and member of the N.A.A.C.P. Board of Directors, was associated with the Provident Hospital in Chicago. He had asked Chesnutt to address the graduating class of nurses, and wrote on 25 October (TNF) to say that the graduation ceremony had been canceled. Bentley invited Chesnutt to perform the same service in 1914.

[2]Chesnutt delivered the graduation address, entitled "The Ideal Nurse," on 4 May 1914. See *Essays and Speeches*: 371–83.

[3]Mrs. Florence Lewis Bentley.

[4]Bentley had related on 25 October that Chesnutt's son Edwin, living in Chicago, "is progressing splendidly" in his study of dentistry. Edwin was licensed to practice by the state of Illinois in 1915.

To Adin T. Hills

February 18, 1914.

My dear Mr. Hills,

Replying to the question you asked me the other day,[1] as to how benevolently disposed people could go about social settlement work among the colored people of Cleveland, it has occurred to me, as I said to you in conversation, and also to Mr. Amos B. McNairy,[2] who spoke to me about the same matter, that perhaps the most effective instrumentality would be a social settlement up in the colored district, on Central Avenue or some intersecting street between Cedar Avenue on one side and Scovill Avenue on the other. It is a little out of the way of Hiram House[3] or Alta House[4] or Goodrich House,[5] and a similar institution in the neighborhood would find a wide field for usefulness. The settlement houses above mentioned do not deny their privileges to colored young people, but the Y.M.C.A. and Y.W.C.A. do not welcome them with open arms, if at all, and an institution conveniently located, which would combine the facilities of these institutions for young people of all ages, would be, it seems to me, an ideal thing.

As to the lines on which such an institution should be conducted, I would suggest, should it be undertaken, that it not be conducted on race lines. A great many colored people object, and very properly so, to the policy of segregation which seems to regard them as unfit to associate with other human beings, and seeks to drive them back upon themselves entirely, and it would be difficult to reach many of them, even with a good thing, coupled with such a suggestion. Of course, they would probably constitute the chief beneficiaries of a settlement house in their district, as do the Orange Street Jews in the case of Hiram House, and the East End Italians in the case of Alta House, and the work could be laid out along lines which might especially apply to their particular needs, so far as these could be distinguished from those of people in general.

Such an institution, if undertaken on the right plan, would probably run into money, not only to build a house but keep it running. It could only hope for success if promoted by white people, because the colored people are poor, and while they would no doubt contribute according to their means, the bulk of the money would have to come from the same sources which support the other benevolent institutions of the city. There ought to be, to secure the best results, a building somewhat similar to those of the other settlement houses of the city, similarly equipped for the different kinds of work which a social settlement carries on, and it should have at its head an experienced social worker, in sympathy with the needs and aspirations of its chief beneficiaries, and who would see that it was conducted along right lines. If such a plan should seem too large for the contemplation of your committee, the same work could be conducted on a smaller scale. There are also several institutions conducted by the colored people themselves, which are worthy of encouragement. One of them is the Colored Old Folks' Home,[6] which is doing a good work, and another the Phyllis Wheatley Home for Colored Working Girls,[7] located on 40th Street, which I am informed is well conducted and serving a very useful purpose.

I don't know that what I have said will be of any assistance to you, but if I can make any investigations in order to answer any special inquiries you may wish to propose, or if I can cooperate with you in any way, I shall be glad to do so. I am very much pleased to see an interest in this subject on the part of the better class of our citizens, for the colored element of our population has been more or less neglected, which is not to the credit of so great a city as Cleveland, with its exceedingly generous contributions to philanthropic purposes. I have an idea that a suitable plan for social work among them, properly sponsored and promoted, would receive a very hearty response from the community.

Sincerely yours,

TCU: TNF

[1]Adin T. Hills (1854–1923) was a partner in the Cleveland law firm of Hills and Van Derveer.

[2]Amos B. McNairy (1854–1942) was a fellow-member of the Rowfant Club (1902–42), serving as its president in 1909–10.

[3]The Hiram House, founded in 1896, was Cleveland's first social settlement and was located at 2723 Orange Avenue. It originally served eastern European Jewish immigrants; by 1914 Italian Americans were its principal beneficiaries, and African Americans would comprise the primary group served following World War I.

[4]Alta House, a day nursery in 1895, expanded into a full-fledged social settlement by 1900 when it acquired its new building on Mayfield Road and was named after Alta Rockefeller Prentice (1871–1962), the daughter of benefactor John D. Rockefeller.

[5]Goodrich Social Settlement was founded in 1897 by philanthropist Flora Stone Mather (1852–1909). It was located on Bond St. at St. Clair, moving several times after 1914.

⁶The Cleveland Home for Aged Colored People, established in 1896, was then located at 186 Osborne St.

⁷The Phillis Wheatley Home for Colored Working Girls opened its doors in 1911 at East 40 St. and Central Ave. under the direction of social worker Jane Edna Harris Hunter (1882–1971), who studied nursing at and was graduated in 1905 from Hampton Institute.

To Charles T. Hallinan

April 7th, 1914.

My dear Mr. Hallinan:—

I must apologize for not answering sooner your letter of March 12th with reference to the Press Committee of the N.A.A.C.P. I am entirely willing that you should enroll my name among the members of the Committee and from time to time I may be able to say something toward the desired end.¹

I have just written letters to the congressmen from this County, protesting against the bill pending in the House of Representatives prohibiting the intermarriage between white and colored people in the District of Columbia.

I enclose herewith a cutting of an editorial which appeared yesterday in the *Cleveland Press*, one of the Scripps-McRae League newspapers, with which our friend Mr. Richard² is connected. I have also sent copies of it to the *Crisis*, to the Ohio Senators, to the Representatives from this County, and to several fire-eaters in Congress to whom I think it may prove interesting.³

Yours very sincerely,

TCU: TNF

¹Hallinan, the chairman of the Press Committee of the N.A.A.C.P., invited Chesnutt to become a committee member (TNF). "Some of the work—my own in particular—will be straight 'publicity work' for the Association," he told Chesnutt; "but the others [on the committee will] merely endeavor to combat in the daily and periodical press such erroneous statements as appear and so forth and so on. It is precisely what you have been doing yourself for years, probably."

²See 15 September 1913 to Hallinan.

³Chesnutt enclosed a copy of an editorial entitled "Where the 'Blunder' Is," *Cleveland Press*, 6 April 1914, 10. It criticized William H. Borah (1865–1940), a Republican U.S. senator from Idaho (1907–40), for denouncing the Fifteenth Amendment of the U.S. Constitution as a "blunder." The blunder,

retorted the editorialist, was not in its enactment but in the failure of the government to enforce its provisions.

To Benjamin G. Brawley

July 29, 1914.

My dear Professor Brawley:—

Replying to your letter of recent date inquiring with reference to *The Colonel's Dream*, I regret to say that the publishers informed you correctly that the book is out of print. It was not a pronounced success. The plates, however, are in existence, and there is a bare possibility that some copies of the book may be run off at some future time.[1] If so, or if I should run across an available copy anywhere, I shall be glad to send you one.

I remember with pleasure your very flattering comment on my writings in a little book of yours which is in my library.[2]

Sincerely yours,

TCU: TNF

[1] This 1905 novel was not reprinted through the remainder of Chesnutt's life.

[2] See 29 April 1910 to Benjamin G. Brawley.

To Paul L. Haworth

September 2, 1914.

My dear Mr. Haworth:—

Your letter containing enclosure of galley proof of chapter on "The Color Line", from your forthcoming book, reached my office while I was away on my vacation, from which I returned only day before yesterday, and I now give it my prompt attention.[1]

You have treated the matter in a very fair and dispassionate manner, which ought to be a model for others who write upon the subject. It is a very complete and lucid statement of conditions as they exist. In fact, I might have written it myself, though I could not have done it as well.

One or two things I might suggest, which, had you had them in mind when you wrote the chapter, might have been worthy of mention. If you had read or had in mind the article by Theodore Roosevelt in, I think, the April *Outlook*, on "The Negro in Brazil,"[2] you might have referred to a part of the world where the Negro constitutes a large portion of the population—with the Indian element and the various cross-breeds from a third to a half—and where there is no color line; where, indeed, the policy of the nation is the fusion of the races; and where, according to Mr. Roosevelt, greater relative progress has been made in social and political development in the last twenty years than in any other country of the world.

You suggest, in a paragraph with reference to separate cars, etc., in the southern states, that if such separate accommodations are provided, they should be equally clean and comfortable with those provided for white people. Experience and a knowledge of human nature suggests that this is absolutely impossible of accomplishment, except from an academic point of view. The sole motive of the separation is the assumed inferiority of the negro, and where the accommodation is furnished by the assumed superior, consciously or unconsciously, it is sure to be made inferior.

While, like all writers on the subject, you merely state conditions and suggest no radical solution, you make it perfectly clear that the negro is not justly treated, and when you and the rest of us have convinced all the people of the United States of that fact, perhaps they may evolve an attitude toward the negro which will solve the race problem, whatever that solution may be.

In my opinion the only solution is the absolute and impartial treatment of the negro (applying of course the same standards applied to white men) in every walk and relation of life, without regard to race or color, even though it result, as in Brazil, in the fusion of the races. I wish you might read that article by Mr. Roosevelt, even if it were not convenient to refer to it.

I remember with much pleasure our association in the Council of Sociology, and thank you very much for bearing me in mind, and giving me an opportunity to read in advance your views upon a question of such importance to the whole country. I shall make it a point to read the whole book when it appears.[3]

Cordially yours,

TCU: TNF
[1]The forthcoming book was *America in Ferment* (1915). Paul L. Haworth (1876–1936) was an historian who, when he resided in Cleveland, had been a member of the Cleveland Council of Sociology, a local discussion group before which Chesnutt read a paper, "Age of Problems," in 1906; see *Essays and Speeches*, 238–52. Chesnutt served as the Council's president in 1911. Haworth was also the author of *United States in Our Own Times* (1920) and

editor of *The Inside Passage to Alaska, 1792–1920* (1924) by William Watson Woollen (1838–1921).

²"Brazil and the Negro," *Outlook*, 106 (21 February 1914), 409–11.

³On 23 April 1915 (TNF), Chesnutt acknowledged receipt of a complimentary copy of the book. He wrote to the publisher, Bobbs Merrill: "In its treatment of the Color Line it is eminently just and fair in statement, and even where the reader may not agree with the views expressed, he has no doubt of the author's honesty and sincerity of opinion and love of fair play. The same is true of the illuminating discussion of the questions of citizenship and Woman's Suffrage, and indeed of the whole book. It is a valuable contribution to current literature and should be widely read by thoughtful readers."

To Mayo Fesler

December 31, 1914.

My dear Mr. Fesler:—

Acknowledging your letter with reference to Dr. Du Bois addressing the City Club at some convenient future day,¹ I have sent your letter to Dr. Du Bois, requesting him to advise me when he will be coming this way again, and when he does so, to let me know far enough in advance so that arrangements can be made for him to speak before your organization, which I have no doubt he will be glad to do. I am sure he will appreciate, as I do, the wish of the Committee to have him speak.

Yours very truly,
Chas. W. Chesnutt

TCS: TNF

¹Mayo Fesler (1871–1945), who became secretary of the Cleveland Municipal Association in 1910 and worked with Newton D. Baker to secure home rule for Cleveland in 1912, wrote on 16 December 1914 (TNF) regarding Chesnutt's suggestion that W. E. B. Du Bois speak before the City Club of Cleveland. Fesler related that the Program Committee unanimously expressed its interest and wished Chesnutt to schedule the visit. The City Club was organized as a forum for discussion in 1912, when Fesler served as its first secretary. Sponsored by Henry J. Davies and Glen M. Cummings (?–1951), Chesnutt became a member on 9 March 1915.

To Susan Utley Chesnutt

October 12, 1915

... I have your letter of October 10. I cannot say it was unexpected. I quite appreciate that life is expensive, and have no doubt that you have spent your money wisely and I hope you have gotten value for it. I certainly have given value for it, in good work.[1] I am sending you herewith the amount requested by registered letter. It is an awkward way to send money, but is no doubt a little more convenient for you.

I hope you will return by way of New York, so that Dorothy may get a line on it and you both may take in some good shows. I don't know whether the opera is running yet or not, but if so, it might be well to see a good opera at the Metropolitan. I will enjoy it by proxy, through you; you can tell me about it.

I am forwarding to you, by this mail—I see I have opened it and therefore will enclose it with this—an invitation to be present at the consecration of the Rev. Mr. Stearly as Suffragan Bishop of Newark.[2] It takes place at Montclair, N.J., which is very close to New York. If the date, October 21, should correspond with your presence in New York, you might find pleasure in being present; in which event sign and forward the request for admission card as per instructions. I presume this might include Dorothy as the invitation is for two. Hope you will continue to enjoy yourselves, and if this is not enough,[3] let me know and I can probably cough up a little more. ...

Pioneer: 264–65

[1]Susan Chesnutt had taken her daughter Dorothy, then recuperating from pneumonia, to Atlantic City, N.J.

[2]The Reverend Wilson R. Stearly (1869–1941) was the former rector of Emmanuel Episcopal Church, at which the Chesnutts were parishioners. He served there from 1900 to 1909. On 23 September 1909 (TNF), Chesnutt expressed regrets over his resignation from Cleveland's Council of Sociology: "Permit me at the same time to express my regret that you are to leave the city and the parish. While I have not availed myself of your ministrations of late to the extent which I should have done, I assure you that your influence has been felt in my household, and that we all join in the fervent hope that you may find in your new field of labor a larger sphere of usefulness and growth."

[3]That is, the money being sent.

To Frank B. Willis

Nov. 23, 1915.

Dear Sir:—[1]

It has been called to my attention that Mr. F. T. Riddle, of Lima, O., who I understand is connected with the State Agricultural Department, and who is promoting what is called the Buckeye Corn Special Tour, has advertised that as part of the entertainment of the party en route, it will be shown at Philadelphia the film called *The Birth of a Nation*.[2]

Inasmuch as this pernicious picture has been rejected by the Board of Censors of Ohio, after careful consideration, as unfit for exhibition in this State, for reasons with which no doubt you are familiar, and with your entire concurrence, as you have stated over your own signature, it would seem highly improper that it should be shown to a thousand or more young people at the most impressionable age, upon the initiative or with the consent of any one representing the State in any way, or deriving any office or authority from the State.[3]

May I and a number of others of the same mind hope that you will exercise your authority,[4] if you have any in the premises, and if not, your influence, to defeat this effort to do by indirection what the State authorities have decided shall not be done?[5]

Yours respectfully,

TCU: TNF

[1]Frank B. Willis (1871–1928) served in the Ohio House of Representatives (1900–1904) and the U.S. House (1911–15) before he became Ohio's governor (1915–17). He would later be elected to the U.S. Senate (1921–28).

[2]F. T. Riddle had made arrangements for a viewing of this 1915 film directed and produced by D. W. Griffith (1875–1948) by participants in a "Buckeye Boys' Corn Growers' Special Tour" at the Forest Theatre on 2 December 1915 during their visit to Philadelphia.

[3]On 28 September 1915 the Ohio State Board of Film Censors had refused to grant a permit for the showing of *The Birth of a Nation* in the state.

[4]Willis acted upon Chesnutt's call for censorship. On the editorial page of the *Cleveland Gazette*, 4 December 1915, [2], appeared his letter dated 26 November. Willis had informed Riddle by telephone that he "strongly disapproved of placing on the official program of entertainment . . . the exhibition of a moving picture film which the Ohio Board of Film Censors had decided to be improper for exhibition in Ohio." He went on to declare that, if the tour included the film, he would rescind his promise to speak to the group during its Philadelphia visit. (A letter with the same text, dated 24 November,

was sent to Chesnutt [TNF].) Another communication with the editor of the *Gazette* appeared on 11 December 1915, [2]. Willis explained that on 23 November he first became aware of Riddle's plan and that he had since received the assurance that the theater visit would be canceled.

⁵The Ohioans on tour were not, finally, prevented from viewing the film. In a *Gazette* article entitled "The Birth of a Nation!" 18 December 1915, [3], the text of a 17 December letter from Riddle to editor Harry C. Smith (1863–1914) was quoted in full. In it Riddle attempted to exonerate himself by observing that he could not prevent Ohioans on the tour from seeing the film since, although it had been withdrawn as an official part of the program, it had been previously advertised as included. Smith called for Riddle's removal from office.

To Oswald Garrison Villard

April 19, 1916.

Dear Mr. Villard:—

I am in receipt of your letter of April 15th, with reference to my annual subscription, and am enclosing herewith my check for $50.00 in payment of same.¹ I had been wondering why I had not received this call sooner.

I am greatly interested in the outcome of the segregation case pending in the United States Supreme Court. As Mr. Storey, I believe, is of counsel, I have no doubt all the influence of the Association has been brought to bear to have the case presented in such a manner as to bring about favorable decision.² The recent opinion of the Court in the Grandfather Clause cases would seem to be an indication that the Court is leaning towards fair play for the Negro,³ and that perhaps in time, when a body of favorable decisions has been built up, all the southern restrictive legislation will be consigned to the junk pile.

Cordially yours,

TCU: TNF

¹Villard was one of the vice-presidents as well as the treasurer of the N.A.A.C.P.

²Moorfield Storey was one of the attorneys for Buchanan v. Warley (245 U.S. 60, 38 S. Ct. 16), the decision for which would not be rendered until 5 November 1917. Reversed was the Court of Appeals of the State of Kentucky which upheld a municipal ordinance prohibiting a "white or colored person from moving into and occupying [a] house in any block upon which the greater number of houses are occupied by persons of the opposite race."

³Chesnutt refers to decisions handed down by the U.S. Supreme Court on

21 June 1915: Frank McGuinn and J. J. Beal v. United States (238 U.S. 347, 35 S. Ct. 926); and Charles E. Myers and A. Claude Kalmey v. John B. Anderson, v. William H. Howard, and v. Robert Brown (238 U.S. 368, 35 S. Ct. 932). At issue was the "grandfather clause," whereby those eligible to vote before the franchise was given to African Americans, and the descendants of those eligible to vote before the passage of the Fifteenth Amendment of the U.S. Constitution, need meet no special requirements to exercise their right to vote. The Supreme Court concluded that voting qualifications based upon race violate the Fifteenth Amendment.

To Newton D. Baker

July 24th, 1916.

My dear Mr. Baker,

I have been requested to write you a letter on a subject of interest to many Clevelanders and other citizens of Ohio, and I take the present opportunity of doing so.[1]

For a number of years there has been a colored battalion of the Ohio National Guard, of which Cleveland has supplied one company, and there is a strong movement on foot at present to have this battalion increased to a regiment.[2] The state authorities have expressed their willingness, but claim they need the authority or consent of the National Government before they can increase any existing military unit. Adjutant General Hough only recently told Lieutenant Harry E. Davis,[3] of the Cleveland company of the Ninth Battalion, that if the National Government would sanction it, he would give the colored men a regiment right away, not because of their color, but because the existing organization has conducted itself in such a way that it deserves the increase. . . .[4]

TCU, incomplete: TNF

[1]Formerly the mayor of Cleveland (1912–16), Baker was appointed Secretary of War by President Woodrow Wilson in 1916 and served in that capacity until 1921.

[2]Evidence of this will be seen in a letter published in the *Cleveland Gazette*. Written by Charles Young (1864–1922), the third African-American graduate of the U.S. Military Academy at West Point, and dated 29 July 1916, it expressed his hope that Ohio "will have a [National Guard] regiment . . . creditable to black people" ("Lieut. Col. Chas. Young," 12 August 1916, [1]).

[3]Harry E. Davis (1882–1955) was a lawyer and civil rights activist who played a prominent role in local politics. He later served four terms in the Ohio General Assembly (1921–29) and became the first African American ap-

pointed to the Cleveland Civil Service Commission in 1928, serving as its president in 1932–34.

[4]Chesnutt's letter was directed by Baker to the Chief of the Militia Bureau of the War Department. The 3 August reply (TNF) pointed out that it was not possible to increase the battalion to a regiment: "the State of Ohio has already more than its proportion of infantry" under the present organization of the U.S. National Guard. Further, consideration of any application of the kind requires the recommendation of the Adjutant General of Ohio. Chesnutt was assured that the "question of color does not enter into the consideration" since "the War Department makes no distinction between white and colored troops."

To Joel E. Spingarn

Sept. 1, 1916

My dear Dr. Spingarn:—

I wish to express personally and in writing my sincere thanks for the generous entertainment of which I was the recipient at Amenia. I enjoyed every minute of the time.[1] It was a privilege and a pleasure to meet so many interesting and worth-while people and to be associated with you and yours for a few days. I am sure you were pleased, as I was, with the outcome of the Conference, the real and valuable results of which will become apparent later.

Kindly express my thanks to Mrs. Spingarn and to your brother[2] when you see him. To Mr. Nash,[3] whose skill and efficiency contributed so much to the success of the meeting, I have written personally.

If there were many more men like you in the United States, the solution of race problems would be a matter of a very short time.

Cordially yours,
Chas. W. Chesnutt.

ALS: DHU

[1]Joel E. Spingarn (1875–1939) was a poet, literary critic, and civil rights activist. One of the founders of the N.A.A.C.P., he would serve in various offices of that organization, including the presidency (1930–39). On 16 August 1916 (TNF), Spingarn asked Chesnutt to chair on 25 August a session of the 24–26 August race relations conference sponsored by him at Amenia, New York: the subject was "Discrimination, Social." Chesnutt made remarks as he convened the session; see "Social Discrimination," *Essays and Speeches*: 423–26.

[2]Mrs. Amy Einstein Spingarn (1883–?) was Joel's wife; she served on the Board of Directors of the N.A.A.C.P. in 1942–51 and 1956–62. Joel's brother,

attorney Arthur B. Spingarn (1878–1971), was at this time a member of the Board of Directors of the N.A.A.C.P; a rare book collector, he later donated his large collection of African-American literature to Howard University.

[3]Roy Nash was secretary of the N.A.A.C.P. from 1916 to 1918.

To E. J. Lilly

Oct. 16, 1916

My dear Mr. Lilly:

Your letter forwarded to me by Doubleday, Page and Company, gave me much pleasure, not only because of what you say about me and my writings, but as a friendly echo from the old town where I was brought up, and the old State where I made my start in life. . . .[1]

I thank you for your kind words about my writings. I wish I could have convinced the whole reading public as well as I did you, of the merits of *The Colonel's Dream*, but it is the least successful of my books. Unfortunately for my writings, they were on the unpopular side of the race question, and any success they may have had must have been due to their merit. Dixon, who took the other side, was not satisfied to present it fairly, but made a fortune prostituting his talent to ignoble uses.[2] My four books on Houghton, Mifflin and Company's list, sell very well, considering how long they have been out, and my little life of Douglass in the Beacon Biographies is still in active demand. I hope to write more, but a busy life along other lines, in these strenuous times, has given me of late years, little time for literary work.

I do not think I have been in Fayetteville since the occasion on which we met in Colonel Pemberton's office.[3] From my father's letters, however, I have learned of some of the improvements of which you speak,[4] and I imagine the old town is very different from my description of it in *The Colonel's Dream*. My memory of the town as I knew it in my boyhood is vastly more vivid than that dating from my last visit.

You ask about my family and myself. . . . I have enjoyed for many years an ample income, from the standpoint of a moderately successful professional man. . . . Of my four children, all are college graduates, two of my daughters from Smith College, at Northampton, Massachusetts, one from the College for Women of Western Reserve University, and my son from Harvard. . . . My eldest daughter is happily married and lives in Washington, D.C. . . . My second daughter has for some years taught Latin and mathematics in Central High School, Cleveland,

and is a popular and successful teacher. . . . My third daughter is probation officer in the Juvenile Court at Cleveland. My son graduated recently as a dentist from Northwestern University at Chicago, and has opened an office in that city.

Not only have we been well treated in a business and professional way, but in other respects as well. I am a member of the Chamber of Commerce, the Cleveland Bar Association, the City Club, and other Clubs of lesser note, and also of the very exclusive Rowfant Club which belongs among the Clubs, membership in which is noted in *Who's Who in America*, which includes among its members half a dozen millionaires, a former United States Senator, a former ambassador to France, and three gentlemen who have been decorated by the French Government. It is needless to say that it is not wealth or blood or birth that makes me acceptable in such company. One of my daughters is a member of the College Club, composed of alumnae of the better colleges and universities.[5] Indeed in this liberal and progressive Northern city we get most of the things which make life worth living, and this in spite of the fact that everyone knows our origin, and in spite of the fact that this is the United States and that there is plenty of race prejudice right here. . . . In the North, race prejudice is rather a personal than a community matter, and a man is not regarded as striking at the foundations of society if he sees fit to extend a social courtesy to a person of color.[6]

I have read Mr. McNeill's *Lyrics from Cotton Land*, and like it very much, and before that I had run across occasional poems of his in the magazines.[7] He was a real poet, and the Old North State may well be proud of him. As to entering the Patterson Cup Competition, as you suggest, I see from the Introduction to McNeill's *Lyrics from Cotton Land*, that the competition is limited to natives and residents of North Carolina, so I am barred both coming and going.[8] It is, however, a very pretty conceit, and ought to promote literary effort in the State.

Your letter was a long one, and I fear I have written you almost a book in reply. But it was so friendly and expressed such a genuine interest in me and my doings that I have written at greater length and in greater detail than good taste perhaps would call for, or than your patience will enable you to read, but I shall throw the blame on you for stirring me up; for it has been a long time since I had the pleasure of talking, even at long range, with a gentleman of the old town.

With thanks and best wishes,

Sincerely yours,
Charles W. Chesnutt

Pioneer: 267–69

[1]E. J. Lilly made Chesnutt's acquaintance when, before the summer of 1883, they both lived in Fayetteville, N.C. Lilly wrote from Asheville, N.C., to commend Chesnutt for the novel he had just read, *The Colonel's Dream* (TNF). Lilly then reminisced at length.

[2]In his letter, Lilly ranked Chesnutt and Dunbar as the two greatest African-American authors and judged novelist Thomas Dixon, Jr., inferior to Chesnutt.

[3]Lilly recalled Chesnutt's 1901 visit to Fayetteville, during which he spoke with him at the home of Colonel John A. Pemberton. He related that the late Colonel greatly admired Chesnutt. Pemberton was a Confederate officer who in 1861 was appointed captain of Company D of the 10th Arkansas regiment, which saw action through the whole of the Civil War in Kentucky, then Mississippi, and finally Missouri.

[4]Lilly had related that one would hardly recognize the old town, *e.g.*, the "deep sand in the middle of the streets has given place to a modern asphalt drive." Chesnutt's father was Andrew Jackson Chesnutt (1833–1921).

[5]Cleveland's College Club was organized in 1897.

[6]Lilly invited reflection upon the subject of race relations in North Carolina twice. He first observed that there were no tensions between African Americans and whites "of the best class." It is the "low down white trash, poor buckra" for which the African American "has no use." Second, he recalled seeing "Capt. F. J. Golan shoot and kill Archie Beeb," who was accused of committing the "'nameless crime'—its object being the daughter of an old Confederate soldier. You remember the incident do you not? It happened in March 1867. I kept my mouth shut and was not called upon to testify." (Chesnutt used this incident in the first chapter of *The House Behind the Cedars*.)

[7]John C. McNeill (1874–1907); Lilly praised and quoted from this volume published in 1907. The periodicals in which Chesnutt very likely read McNeill's poems were the *Charlotte Observer* and *Century*.

[8]Lilly suggested that Chesnutt enter this competition.

To Richard R. Wright, Jr.

October 16, 1916.

My dear Mr. Wright,

I am in receipt of your letter of September 27th, inviting me to lecture in Philadelphia during the second or third week in December, in order to assist in the promotion of your "Buy a Book Movement."[1]

I am a very busy man, and ordinarily I would say no, but in such a cause I feel that it is no more than justice to my publishers, to say nothing about myself, to do what I can to encourage the dissemination of literature on race questions and by race authors. So unless some very important unforeseen obstruction should arise, you may count on me.[2]

I enjoyed very much our brief association at Amenia,[3] and am sure that we all had an excellent time, and I hope accomplished some good.

Sincerely yours,

Dict. by CWC.

TCU: TNF

[1]Richard R. Wright, Jr., was a Philadelphia clergyman and editor of *The Christian Recorder*. He invited Chesnutt to speak in behalf of his "National Buy-a-Book Campaign in the Interest of Negro Literature."

[2]See 27 October 1916 to Wright.

[3]See 1 September 1916 to Joel E. Spingarn, n. 1.

To William E. Henderson

October 25, 1916.

My dear Mr. Henderson,

I received yesterday your letter of October 23rd, and the parcel containing the record in the case of Moton *et al.*, vs. Kessens, was delivered to me by the postman this morning.[1]

I read with interest the brief which you gave me when I was in Indianapolis, and found it very interesting, and I look forward with pleasure to reading the two volumes which you have sent me, and when I have done so, I will give you my opinion, if I think it is worth anything, on the point which you mention in your letter, that is, the sufficiency of the notice.[2]

My family are all well, and my wife who is also an old acquaintance of yours, joins me in regards to you and your family, who I trust are also enjoying good health.

I had heard of the death of Mr. Tyson's father, and have written him a letter of sympathy. As you say, it is too bad that we must die, yet we have no kick coming if we can live to be as old as Mr. Tyson, Sr.[3]

With regards and best wishes,

Sincerely yours,

TCU: TNF

[1]William E. Henderson, an attorney practicing in Indianapolis, Ind., was, like Chesnutt, a former inhabitant of Fayetteville, N.C. He wrote Chesnutt to

solicit his opinion on how he should proceed with an appeal to the Supreme Court of Ohio. See 24 November 1916 to Henderson regarding the outcome of Moton *et al.* v. Kessens.

[2]See 24 November 1916 to Henderson, n. 5.

[3]H. Clay Tyson, who later moved to the District of Columbia, served as Chesnutt's assistant in 1882–83 when he was the principal of the Fayetteville, N.C., State Colored Normal School. Tyson's father died at the age of 88.

To James Weldon Johnson

October 25, 1916.

My dear Mr. Johnson:—

Some one was good enough to send me a marked copy of the *Public Ledger* containing your editorial published in that journal Wednesday, October 18th. I have also since seen the reproduction of it on the editorial page of the *New York Age*.[1] I wish to congratulate you most heartily upon your success in the competition, and upon the editorial itself as a journalistic production. I think you have stated the case against Mr. Wilson with very great skill and effectiveness. Your characterization of the man is clear and convincing.[2] I hope your picture of Mr. Hughes is equally true, and that he may have an opportunity to demonstrate what the true and traditional American ideal of a president is.[3] Certainly he shall have my vote.

With pleasant memories of our brief association at Amenia,[4] I remain,

Cordially yours,

TCU: TNF

[1]Johnson's editorial "Why Charles E. Hughes Should Be Elected" appeared under the title "Editorials Awarded Third Prize in Public Ledger's Competition" in the Philadelphia *Public Ledger*, 18 October 1916, 1. It was reprinted in the "Views and Reviews" feature written weekly by Johnson as a contributing editor of the *New York Age*, 19 October 1916, [4].

[2]Johnson's invective was directed against Woodrow Wilson's "ingrained traits of . . . character": "timidity," "cowardice," "indecisiveness," and "shiftiness." Receiving attention, too, were the "inaction" and "opportunism" displayed by this "pacifist" and "anti-suffragist."

[3]Charles Evans Hughes (1862–1948) won the 1906 gubernatorial race and served New York State thus until 1910 when he was appointed to the U.S. Supreme Court. In 1916 he resigned to accept the Republican nomination for the U.S. presidency. Johnson described Hughes as a sincere and courageous

man "who speaks right out, who says what he means and means what he says and acts accordingly."

[4]See 1 September 1916 to Joel E. Spingarn, n. 1.

To Richard R. Wright, Jr.

October 27, 1916.

My dear Mr. Wright:—

I had mailed you a letter yesterday just preceding receipt of yours of the 24th,[1] replying to which I will say that I think a good title for what I shall say would be, "The Negro in Books,"[2] my idea being to tell the people something of the way in which colored folks are treated as a subject matter of serious writings and as characters in fiction. No doubt I shall say a great many things that other speakers will say, but perhaps I can give it a turn which may make it of interest. I will keep my remarks within an hour, which I think is long enough to ask an audience to listen to one man.

I sent you a half tone cut yesterday. If you cannot use it, let me know, and I will see if I can dig up a photograph.

My available books are:

The Conjure Woman,	Published by
The Wife of His Youth and Other	Houghton Mifflin Company,
Stories of the Color Line,	4 Park Street,
The House Behind the Cedars,	Boston, Mass.
The Marrow of Tradition,	
Life of Frederick Douglass in	Published by Small,
Beacon Biographies of	Maynard and Company,
Eminent Americans	15 Beacon Street,
	Boston, Mass.

I trust your "Buy a Book Movement," will prove a success, both in the matter of interest and in the results achieved. I have no doubt my publishers will cooperate with you in any way they can.

Sincerely yours,

TCU: TNF

[1]On 26 October (TNF), Chesnutt informed Wright that he would speak in Philadelphia, Pa., on 5 December in behalf of Wright's "Buy a Book" movement; see 16 October 1916 to Wright.

[2]See *Essays and Speeches*: 426–41.

To William E. Henderson

November 24th, 1916.

My dear Mr. Henderson,

I wish to acknowledge receipt of copy of record in the Randolph cases, and have read the brief carefully and most of the record.[1] It is an extremely interesting case, and reads like a novel. The will, in fact the two wills, that of 1821 and that of 1832, which was declared invalid, taken together are a fair indication of the character of this able but eccentric Virginia gentleman of the first half century of our Republic.[2] I thank you very much for the privilege of reading them.

As to the legal aspects of the case, I fear I am not competent to advise. I am not in the active practice, and therefore could be of no assistance to you in the presentation of the case. It seems to me that your surest hope of success would be to establish the trust as an express trust, against which the statute of limitations would not run.[3] The original trust certainly was such a trust. I have n't read the defendants' brief, of course, and don't know whether they claim that the trust has never been an express trust, or claim that it changed its character at some stage of the proceedings, and became an implied trust. I can't imagine when that would be, unless when Leigh[4] appointed Plunkett his attorney in fact, or in the subsequent transfer or transfers. I judge from the cross-examinations of the witnesses that the case may have turned on the question of notice, and there is some little testimony which suggests that some of the Randolph freed slaves knew, at least in a vague way, that property had been bought for them in Mercer County.[5] The equities in a case of this kind are so nicely balanced, even assuming the plaintiff to have made a strong case, that as a rule a very small amount of evidence is necessary to turn the scale. If I were deciding the case, I should hold that the trust was an express trust, against which the statute of limitations did not run, and that purchasers took it subject to the trust. If they did not get an abstract or have the title examined, that was their fault, for which other people not at fault should not suffer.[6] There is nothing in the record which discloses the grounds on which the Court decided the case in the two lower courts.

I sincerely hope the case may have an outcome favorable to you and your clients. It is certainly a prize well worth fighting for, and you cannot afford to drop it at this stage, whatever may be the ultimate outcome.

My family are well and join me in regards to you and yours.

Sincerely yours,

TCU: TNF

[1]John Randolph (1773–1833) of Roanoke, Va., arranged for the manumission of his slaves upon his death. Further, he instructed his executor to purchase land outside of the state of Virginia and to settle those free African Americans thereon. Land was bought for this use in Mercer County, O.; but local whites prevented the execution of the plan, and the executor had to transport the former slaves to other localities. He sold the land in Mercer County, using the proceeds for the costs of resettlement. Henderson, in his appeal, contended that the descendants of the former slaves had been deprived of the benefits specified in Randolph's will.

[2]Chesnutt described the character of John Randolph two months later in a 13 January 1917 paper delivered at the Rowfant Club, "The Will of John Randolph"; see *Essays and Speeches*: 442–48.

[3]Henderson advanced this argument, but his appeal in Moton *et al.* v. Kessens and Moton v. Dwell *et al.* (96 Ohio St. 609, 118 N.E. 1083) failed. On 20 March 1917, the Supreme Court of Ohio ruled that "action based upon violation, if any, of executor's trust, was barred by statute of limitations after more than 50 years."

[4]William Leigh (1778–1858?) was the executor of Randolph's estate.

[5]Touched upon at several points in the decision was the question of whether the executor was obliged to notify the beneficiaries of the will concerning the actions he was taking. Henderson was not able to demonstrate such an obligation or the violation thereof.

[6]That is, those presently owning the land in question do not have a legal right to it by virtue of the executor's improper sale of the land and violation of Randolph's expressed intent. The Supreme Court of Ohio justices disagreed. They ruled that, given the circumstances, the executor's behavior was appropriate and in harmony with the terms of Randolph's will.

To Munson A. Havens

April 3, 1917.

Dear Sir,[1]

The Chamber of Commerce, as the foremost representative body of business and professional men of the community, stands very properly in the forefront of the movement for preparedness, for patriotism and the united action of the people in the crisis at present confronting the United States.[2] In view of this position of the Chamber, I think it proper to call your attention, and through you the attention of the Board of Directors or the proper committees of the Chamber to the following facts.

The moving picture film called *The Birth of a Nation*, because of its vicious and anti-social character was refused approval by the board of moving picture censors, or whatever its title is, of the State of Ohio, during the last administration,[3] but has been pounding at the gates of Ohio for several years, and finally under this administration has been passed by the present board of censors, and is announced for early exhibition in Cleveland.[4] It seems to me a most unwise and unpatriotic thing to permit its production, at this time especially, without protest, for the following reasons.

The picture was made of course to make money, and to make it by stirring up race prejudice and race hatred, which it seems to me is a most unwise and most unpatriotic thing at this juncture in our national affairs. The principal action of the picture is devoted to exploiting the alleged misconduct of colored Union soldiers during the reconstruction period (to say nothing of its glorification of that organization of traitors known as the Ku-Klux-Klan). The principal villain of the story, the would-be rapist, is portrayed as a colored captain in the Union army. There are already four colored regiments in the regular army with a military history in past wars of which they and the nation may well be proud. There are several complete regiments of colored militia, and battalions in several other states, and similar units proposed in other places. With war declared there will undoubtedly be a large accession to these. The colored people are loyal citizens, without perhaps a great deal of encouragement, in some quarters, to loyalty, indeed in spite of serious discouragement; but it seems to me and those on behalf of whom I speak, that such an insult to the national uniform when worn by men of color, as the public exhibition of such a picture as *The Birth of a Nation*, which, as a work of pictorial art is a superb and impressive thing, and all the more vicious for that reason, should not be permitted at this time, when all citizens should stand together to support the honor of the nation.

When it is also taken into consideration that there are numbers of colored men in the community who have recently come to the North because of our disorganized labor market, it would seem a matter of doubtful wisdom to do or to permit anything that is likely to breed discontent and ill feeling among these people.

It has seemed to me and to prominent citizens with whom I have talked, some of them members of the Chamber, that it would be a wise and patriotic thing for the Chamber of Commerce to use its influence with the city administration, or the police department, or whatever authority has power in the matter, to discourage this sort of thing at this juncture, and to prevent, if possible, the exhibition of this film.

I am writing as a member of the Chamber, and as a member of the Executive Committee of the Local Branch of the National Association for the Advancement of Colored People, which, in large part, by its activity, has kept this picture out of Ohio until now, to suggest the hope that the Chamber of Commerce will see this matter in the same light that we do, and will by appropriate action exert its undoubtedly powerful influence to prevent, if possible, the exhibition of this picture in Cleveland.[5]

Sincerely yours,

TCU: TNF

[1]Munson A. Havens (1873–1942) had served as an officer of the Cleveland Chamber of Commerce since 1905. Chesnutt also knew him as a fellow-member of the Rowfant Club and the author of *Horace Walpole and the Strawberry Hill Press* (1901) and *Old Valentines: A Love Story* (1914).

[2]The United States had terminated diplomatic relations with Germany in February 1917. Three days after Chesnutt wrote the present letter, the U.S. Congress formally declared war on Germany.

[3]See 23 November 1915 to Frank B. Willis.

[4]Through February and March 1917, the *Cleveland Gazette* ran articles hotly opposing the screening of the film. At the time Chesnutt wrote to Havens, it was being viewed in Dayton and Cincinnati, O.; and arrangements had been made for its presentation at the Cleveland Opera House.

[5]The matter was also receiving attention in the state legislature. A. Lee Beaty (1869–1936), a member of the General Assembly (1917–20), sponsored what came to be known as the Beaty Bill which, in part, prohibited the showing of motion pictures judged likely to reinforce race prejudice and incite race conflict. Though the House had passed the bill, the Senate would not vote on it until the next session; in the interim, of course, the film could be legally shown. The Beaty Bill was defeated on 17 April 1917.

To William R. Green

November 24, 1917

My dear William,

Mrs. McAdoo was in to see me this morning, greatly exercised over conditions for your battalion at Camp Sheridan.[1] She told me about her son's experience and the incidents connected with it, all of which I had read in the newspapers, and about the order forbidding the colored soldiers to leave the camp; also about their subsequent transfer to the rifle range, which she says is a fever-stricken locality which endangers the lives of the men.[2] She came to consult me about the advisability or propriety of either myself writing or getting some prominent citizen like Mr. Herrick[3] to write Mr. Baker[4] and suggest that he investigate these conditions, and if possible, do something to ameliorate them.

I told her that I had no doubt the War Department, including Mr. Baker, was well aware of all these facts; that they were reported in the newspapers; that I had no doubt the War Department fully appreciated the difficulty of the problem of securing decent treatment of colored troops by the southerners, and that I had no idea that a letter from an obscure civilian, or even from a prominent one, would have any influence upon the general staff or its policies. I told her, however, that I would write you a letter and ask you what you thought about it, and if you could suggest any steps that might be taken by any well disposed person which could possibly have any influence or effect; and that I would be governed by what you might say.

I would like to know, if you can inform me, to what extent the colored soldiers are participating in the benefits of the Red Cross and the Y.M.C.A. and the Knights of Columbus and the other, if there are any other, agencies for the promotion of the comfort and welfare of the soldiers.

If you will write me a letter at your convenience and let me know whether you think of anything that could be done to promote improved conditions among the colored soldiers, I shall be obliged.

Yours very truly,

Charles W. Chesnutt

Pioneer: 275–76

[1]U.S. Army Captain William R. Green (1873–1930) commanded Company D, Ninth Separate Battalion. He was the son of Chesnutt's cousin John Patterson Green. Mrs. Mattie McAdoo (1868–1936) was a civil rights activist who, beginning in 1918, would serve with Chesnutt as an officer of the local branch of the N.A.A.C.P.

[2]Mattie McAdoo's son Myron was at this time stationed at Camp Lee near Petersburg, Va., where he and other African Americans protested their treatment. He became a second lieutenant in 1918; see "Myron McAdoo Wins Commission," Cleveland *Advocate*, 30 March 1918, 1.

[3]Myron T. Herrick; see 13 August 1912 to Susan Utley Chesnutt, n. 6.

[4]Clevelander Newton D. Baker, Secretary of War, subsequently conducted an investigation of the conditions at Camp Lee.

To Archibald J. Carey

December 24, 1917.

Dear Sir:—

Replying to your favor of December 20th, I think I can arrange to appear before your society some time in January.[1] I would rather make the date later in the week than the 22nd, if possible, on Friday the 25th, unless it were possible to arrange it for a Sunday afternoon or evening.

I realize that societies of this kind are not over flushed with money, but I am a business man and my time is valuable, and I should charge you $25.00 and my expenses. If the meeting could be arranged for Sunday some time, I would reduce the amount to $15.00.[2] I have a very interesting lecture on the Negro in Latin America, which I think the society would find interesting. Please let me know what you think about it,[3] and oblige

Yours very truly,

TCU: TNF

[1]Archibald J. Carey (1867–1931) was the pastor of the Institutional Church in Chicago, Ill. On behalf of his church's "Young People's Organization," Carey invited Chesnutt to give a speech (TNF).

[2]Carey had asked Chesnutt when it would be convenient for him to come to Chicago and how much he would charge for his services.

[3]Chesnutt appears to refer to "A Solution for the Race Problem"; see *Essays and Speeches*: 384–402. He is not known to have presented this paper in Chicago.

To Ethel Chesnutt Williams

July 30, 1919

. . . We all read with pleasure your account of your activities in the Red Cross, and real estate, and other lines, and I am proud to have fathered so capable a woman. You are displaying excellent judgment in buying yourself a home; I have no doubt Washington property is a good investment, irrespective of the sentimental side of the proposition.[1] With all of the family earning money,[2] you ought to get ahead rapidly and soon assume the rank of substantial citizens; not only intellectually and socially, but materially.

We got our car back and were able to entertain more or less during the NAACP.[3] Emmett Scott was with us a couple of days. Jim and Grace Johnson[4] were to have been with us, but her mother was taken to a hospital and she was unable to come. Johnson, for business reasons, stopped at the Hollenden, tho he dined with us several times. We entertained at meals a number of the visiting notables, including the Butler Wilsons[5] and your friend Mrs. Gray. On Friday of that week Mr. Villard, Mr. Shillady, Mr. and Miss Grimké, and Miss Ovington[6] dined with us and we took them to the meeting. The following week Helen lent Miss Ovington her cottage, which we hadn't been occupying because Helen and Dorothy have been going to the French Summer School—and she spent what she said was a delightful eight days all by herself in the woods.[7] The summer school is over Friday next, and my vacation begins next week, and we are all going out to Chesterland for the month of August. My car was found after five weeks in Detroit, by the police of that city. The whole family went up on the boat to get it.[8]

We have been somewhat concerned about the Washington race riot, and your proximity to it, but it pales into insignificance beside the Chicago riot, the principal center of which has been right in Edwin's block.[9] I was reasonably certain that neither you nor Edwin would be wildly careening through the streets with guns, shooting or being shot. I hope you were able to keep Charlie[10] in the house. Write us the inside history of the riot, and give my love to Ed and Charlie. . . .

Pioneer: 279–80

[1]Chesnutt's eldest daughter wrote to her mother on 25 June 1919 (*Pioneer*: 278–79), relating that she had been working for the Red Cross Home Service in the District of Columbia since the previous fall. She had recently purchased a new home and noted without further explanation, "Everything is in my name and I am managing. I have proved that I can manage and I am surely delivering the goods. . . ."

[2]Ethel reported that her husband, Edward C. Williams, "has some research work which will bring him a salary all summer."

[3]The 1919 annual conference of the N.A.A.C.P. was held in Cleveland. On Sunday, 22 June 1919, Mary W. Ovington presided at the opening rally, at which clergyman and civil rights activist Archibald H. Grimké received the Spingarn Medal and Emmett J. Scott spoke. Mayor Harry Lyman Davis (1878–1950) officially opened the proceedings the next day; Paul L. Feiss, president of the Cleveland Chamber of Commerce, welcomed the attendees; and John R. Shillady (1875–1943), current national secretary of the N.A.A.C.P., made a speech. Chesnutt presided over the afternoon session. Joel E. Spingarn and W.E.B. Du Bois gave addresses on Monday evening. Sessions were held through

the following Saturday. See "The Spingarn Medal," *Cleveland Gazette*, 28 June 1919, 1, for a full report of the week's events.

[4]Grace Nail Johnson (1885–1976).

[5]Roland Butler Wilson (1860–1939), attorney, educator, and civil rights activist, founded the Boston branch of the N.A.A.C.P., serving as its executive secretary (1912–26) and its president (1926–36). He was married to the former Mary Evans.

[6]Mary White Ovington became chairperson of the N.A.A.C.P. in 1917.

[7]At Chester Cliffs in Chesterland, O. Helen and her father owned cottages there. See 1 November 1921 to Mary Dickerson Donahey, nn. 2 and 6.

[8]Chesnutt had taken his automobile to visit a movie theater in Cleveland, and the uninsured vehicle was stolen. See *Pioneer*: 277–78.

[9]The riots in the District of Columbia and Chicago were equally significant, given that armed African Americans and whites in both locales could not be subdued until military interventions occurred. In the former riot, military personnel on leave invaded an African-American neighborhood after being inflamed by several reports of attacks on white women; and African Americans responded in kind. By 22 July, there were four fatal shootings, and more than 70 were wounded. The riot was ended by 2,000 soldiers on 23 July. At Chicago on 27 July, the firing began after whites and African Americans confronted each other over who could use particular beaches on the city's south side. Again there were fatalities, and 6,000 troops did not restore order until 4 August.

[10]Chesnutt's grandson, Charles Waddell Chesnutt Williams.

To the Micheaux Book & Film Company

August 2, 1920.
Attention Mr. George C. Anderson, Asst. Manager.
Dear Sirs:

Replying to your letter of July 27, 1920,[1] I beg to say that I shall be glad to talk to Mr. Micheaux with reference to filming some of my stories.[2]

I am expecting to be away on my vacation for the greater part of the month of August, but I will not be far from Cleveland and if Mr. Micheaux can let me know what day he will pass through here, I will arrange to be at my office to meet him. Or, if equally convenient for him, he could stop over on his way back to Chicago a little later, which would be entirely satisfactory to me.

Yours very truly,

TCU: OClWHi

[1]George C. Anderson was the assistant manager of the Micheaux Book & Film Company in Chicago (renamed the Micheaux Film Corporation in 1921). On 27 July 1920 (OClWHi), Anderson explained that his firm wanted "to film stories by famous colored authors in the near future." He indicated an interest in several of Chesnutt's stories.

[2]Oscar Micheaux (1884–1951) was a filmmaker and novelist who produced more than three dozen cinematic works between 1920 and 1950. His movies frequently dealt with topics Chesnutt had treated in his fiction: interracial relationships, "passing," and harassment of blacks by whites. Anderson had mentioned that the head of his company would like to stop in Cleveland, when on his way to New York, to interview Chesnutt.

To William B. Pratt

January 20, 1921.

Dear Mr. Pratt:—

Referring to our correspondence with reference to the motion picture production of my books,[1] I beg to say that I have a letter from Micheaux Film corporation, 538 South Dearborn Street, Chicago, in which they make me a proposition to produce *The House Behind the Cedars*. Of course they want to chop it up more or less, and probably change the emphasis on certain characters, and adapt it especially to the class of people from whom they get most of their patronage and to whom they must make their appeal, namely, colored people, since the producers themselves are of that class.[2] But from what I have observed this is no more than the usual fate of a novel which is filmed, and one could only hope that it will be done with reasonable taste and judgment. I have seen one of the films produced by this company, and it was n't at all bad.

They make me the following proposition:—[3]

Having sought now to make it clear as to changes that I would reserve the right to make in the event of an agreement, I am prepared and have concluded to purchase the film rights to this novel with a view to producing it if nothing happens to change my present plans, starting about the latter May or early June. If, therefore, you are agreeable to accepting such changes as I may see fit to incorporate and which are only to make the story more acceptable to a peculiar clientele, I am willing to pay for all screen rights the sum of $500.00 payable, a portion down on acceptance say $25.00, $75.00 in thirty days thereafter or say March 1st, the balance June 15th, or on date of release should it be filmed and released before that time which is not likely, since I have two other pictures to make before I will reach this. And, besides, it is necessary to film this in the summer as you will realize. In the event of agreement the present title will be retained and the photoplay from same approximating most likely seven reels long would be advertised about so, "Oscar Micheaux presents *The House Behind the Cedars* a story of the South by Charles W. Chesnutt, featuring Evelyn Preer."[4]

I know nothing from experience about moving picture productions or authors' royalties in connection therewith, and this does not seem like a very large remuneration.[5] However, I don't suppose the concern itself is making a great deal of money, in fact, I do not see how it could, yet if they pay according to their stated terms, it will be that much better than nothing, and I really don't know whether a film could be made from the story which would appeal to a wider audience; at least no concern has been clamoring for the right to reproduce it.

If this proposition is agreeable to you I will write to Mr. Micheaux accepting it. I imagine that these things are sometimes done on a royalty basis, but the accounting for and collection of royalties is a somewhat uncertain thing, since the author necessarily, in small matters, must be entirely at the mercy of the producer.

If the arrangement is made, or whatever arrangement is made, I will account to you on the basis suggested in your letter of August 12, 1920, that is to say, one-third to you and two-thirds to myself.[6]

Yours very truly,

TCU: OClWHi

[1] William B. Pratt (1886–1961) was employed by the Houghton Mifflin Company from 1907 to 1929. He represented the Special Sales department of its trade division.

[2] On 18 January 1921 (OClWHi), Micheaux described changes of *The House Behind the Cedars* likely to be made for a film adaptation. He would exclude racially defamatory language (though "a very great deal of originality is lost" in consequence); rearrange the chronology of the story, having it begin "about the chapter 'Under the Old Regime'," *i.e.*, chapter 18; make the character Frank more intellectually acute; and alter the dour ending of the story so that an audience will leave the theater "feeling that all good must triumph in the end, and with the words 'Oh want [*sic*] that just wonderful' instead of a gloomy muttering."

[3] Chesnutt quotes Micheaux's 18 January letter (OClWHi).

[4] Evelyn Preer (1896–1932) was an African-American actress who performed on stage as well as in movies. She appeared in Micheaux's *The Homesteader* (1918) and in *The Conjure Woman* (1926). She did not become a member of the cast of *The House Behind the Cedars*.

⁵Metro Pictures Corporation offered $190,000 for the screen rights to a novel by Vincente Blasco Ibáñez (1867–1928), *The Four Horsemen of the Apocalypse* (translated into English in 1918 and originally published as *Los Cuatro Jinetes del Apocalipsis* in 1916). Metro released the cinematic adaptation starring Rudolph Valentino (1895–1926) in 1921.

⁶In the final arrangement, Houghton Mifflin received 25%. See 19 September 1921 to Houghton Mifflin Company.

To the Micheaux Film Corporation

January 27, 1921.
Attention Mr. Oscar Micheaux.

Dear Mr. Micheaux:—

Since receiving your letter of January 18th, I have written my publishers, Houghton Mifflin Company, 4 Park Street, Boston, who own the copyright and all other rights of reproduction, translation, etc., in *The House Behind the Cedars*, and of course any arrangement I make with you will have to be subject to their approval. They think your offer of $500.00 for the motion picture rights is small in comparison with prices offered by other firms, but at the same time they realize that the market for such films is somewhat restricted, and are willing to leave that matter to me. As to the terms of payment, they say that your concern is not listed in the motion picture directory, and they have not been able to find out anything about your financial standing, and then go on to say:

> As the price is so low, I think you could advantageously insist upon the full payment of the $500 on the signing of the contract. This would make it a cash transaction, and would eliminate any possibility of your assigning your rights and never receiving payment for them. If Mr. Micheaux is so situated financially that this proposition would be impossible, I would suggest your giving him an option on the motion picture rights on the payment of say $100, such option extending to June 15, or the actual date of release, if the story is filmed before that time, and then the $400 payment on or before March 15, when the actual contract can be signed and the full motion picture rights granted Mr. Micheaux. This, I feel, would give you better protection than under the proposition as outlined by Mr. Micheaux.
>
> A rearrangement of the story to adapt it for motion picture use, would be essential, and most stories when screened have but slight resemblance to the original. This, if properly handled, should not be detrimental. On the other hand, there is always some advertising value to be gained from the

screen presentation of the story, and it is important that in your contract it be stipulated that in advertising, and in the film itself, the statement be always made that the film is based on *The House Behind the Cedars* by Charles W. Chesnutt, by special arrangement with the publishers, Houghton Mifflin Company.[1]

I agree with them as to the rearrangement of the story and quite appreciate what you say about it at considerable length in your letter of January 18th, and I have no doubt that you will make it an interesting and credible picture. That you can do so I am well aware, from the specimen of your work that I saw in Cleveland several months ago, although I have not yet received the copy of the scenario for your next production which you suggested in your letter that you sent me.

Please let me know what you think of Houghton Mifflin Company's proposition.[2] You ought to have this story on your list, because it is the most popular of my novels, which constitute a small body of literature which is in a way unique in its treatment of race questions.

Yours very truly,

TCU: OClWHi

[1]Chesnutt is quoting William B. Pratt's 24 January 1921 letter to him (OClWHi).

[2]On 29 January 1921 (OClWHi), Micheaux accepted the payment schedule suggested by Pratt with one exception: the $400 balance would be due either on June 15 or the day of release, which Micheaux thought would be in August.

To Robert Levy

February 7, 1921.

Dear Sir:—

I beg to acknowledge receipt of your letter of February 3rd, which was addressed to me as Clerk of the Municipal court, which I am not, but the address was corrected at the post office and I received it.[1]

As you say in your letter *The Marrow of Tradition* is at present out of print due to the high cost of paper during the war, though I trust it will be revived ere long. As I have only a few copies, I do not wish to sell any of them, but I am sending you today by parcel post one of my copies which I shall be very glad to have you read and consider as material for a motion picture, with the understanding that if you do not find it available you will return me the book.

I am in negotiations at the present moment with the Micheaux Film Company of Chicago for another one of my stories for motion picture purposes. They made me a proposition which as revised by me they accepted, although the contract has not yet been signed.

I am of course glad that there is demand for my stories for moving picture purposes and shall be glad to consider any proposition you may make me in respect to this one. I have other stories published and unpublished which would make excellent films; indeed the Micheaux people speak of wanting me to write several others for them. I imagine there is no difficulty about my writing for any one who wants my services, but I should of course consider my own interests, and feel more inclined to deal with the concern which made me the best offer.[2]

Awaiting further advices from you, I am

Yours very truly,

TCU: OClWHi

[1]Robert Levy, president and general manager of Reol Productions Corporation in New York City, first approached Chesnutt about the film rights to *The Marrow of Tradition* prior to 6 April 1920 (OClWHi), when Levy apologized for not maintaining correspondence on the matter. In his 3 February 1921 letter (OClWHi), Levy requested a copy of Chesnutt's difficult-to-find novel.

[2]In his 29 January 1921 letter to Chesnutt (OClWHi), Oscar Micheaux had proposed that Chesnutt write stories of 8,000 to 15,000 words long that could be adapted for the screen, for each of which he would receive $500. Micheaux encouraged Chesnutt to write of "strange murder cases, mystery with dynamic climaxes—but avoid race conflict as much as possible."

To William B. Pratt

February 18, 1921.

Dear Mr. Pratt:—

I have agreed with a Mr. Robert Levy of the Reol Productions Corporation, of New York City, upon the sale of the motion picture rights of *The Marrow of Tradition*, for the sum of $500.00. The amount is no larger than that which Mr. Micheaux has promised to pay for the rights in *The House Behind the Cedars*,[1] but the terms are better, since Mr. Levy is to pay cash upon the execution of the contract.

I assumed that you would assent, and have written him conditioning the contract upon the statement being made in the advertising, and in the film itself, that the film is based on *The Marrow of Tradition* by Charles

W. Chesnutt, by special arrangement with the publishers, Houghton Mifflin Company.[2]

This concern has never yet produced a film, but has at least one picture made which it is going to bring out very soon.[3] Like the Chicago concern, it aims to produce pictures featuring colored actors and appealing to motion picture houses especially for colored people, which are already somewhat numerous and increasing.

Of course while *The Marrow of Tradition* is out of print the advertising would be of no value to you as publishers, and would produce nothing for me in the way of royalties. However, the production of these films might produce a sufficient demand to justify the printing of at least another small edition of *The Marrow of Tradition*, the publication of which was suspended, I was informed by your Mr. Greenough,[4] because of war conditions, principally the cost of paper. I should like it very much if this should prove the case, since my books constitute a small body of literature, if I may call them such, which is in a sense unique.

When I have closed up with the Reol people, I will of course remit to you on the basis suggested with reference to *The House Behind the Cedars*, namely one-third of what I get.[5]

Mr. Micheaux has not yet presented his contract for signature, but I will advise you when he does so and remit when he pays.[6]

Yours very truly,

TCU: OClWHi

[1]See 20 January 1921 to Pratt.

[2]Chesnutt stipulated this in his 18 February 1921 letter to Levy (OClWHi).

[3]Reol's first film was *The Burden of Race* (1921).

[4]Chesnutt very likely meant Ferris Greenslet (1875–1959), who began his long association with Houghton Mifflin in 1902 as associate editor of the *Atlantic Monthly*. In 1907 he became literary advisor to the firm, and by his retirement in 1947 had also served as literary director, vice-president, general manager, and editor-in-chief.

[5]See 20 January 1921 to Pratt, n. 6.

[6]It appears that it was only after Chesnutt wrote the present letter that he noted the postscript of a 29 January 1921 letter from Micheaux (OClWHi), asking Chesnutt to prepare the contract. On 19 February 1921 (OClWHi), Chesnutt informed Micheaux that he had asked his "publishers . . . to prepare immediately . . . a contract in the terms agreed between us." On 3 March (OClWHi), Houghton Mifflin sent two copies of the contract to Swan E. Micheaux (1896–1975), the brother of Oscar and the secretary-treasurer of

the Micheaux Film Corporation. Oscar or Swan was to sign both copies and return them, along with a check for $100, to Houghton Mifflin. They would then be signed by Chesnutt, and one copy would be returned to the Micheaux Corporation.

To Robert Levy

March 12, 1921.

Dear Mr. Levy:—

I have not heard anything further from you in reference to contract for the motion picture rights in *The Marrow of Tradition*, since my letter of February 18th.[1] What is the trouble?[2]

Sincerely yours,

TCU: OClWHi

[1]On 18 February 1921 (OClWHi), Chesnutt asked Levy to send him the contract for his signature.

[2]A cinematic adaptation of *The Marrow of Tradition* was never produced, and the Reol Productions Corporation was dissolved in May 1924.

To the Micheaux Film Corporation

July 27, 1921.

Attention Mr. Swan E. Micheaux.

Gentlemen:

I had been a little concerned about your long silence but ascribed it to the cause which you mentioned in your letter of several weeks since, the business depression throughout the country.[1] It seems to have affected every line of business.

I note what you say about a contract which will include the right to publish *The House Behind the Cedars* serially in a colored newspaper, which of course I would have no objection to see done.[2] In the same mail with your letter came one from the *Chicago Defender*, asking what arrangement they could make for the right to publish *The House Behind the Cedars* serially. You do not mention what newspaper you have in mind and it is quite possible that it might be to my advantage to make separate contracts for the two things, the motion picture rights and the serial publication.[3]

However, I shall be in Chicago next Thursday, August 4th, all day on my way West[4] and shall try and get in communication with you. If I do not find you, we can take up the matter by correspondence.

I had not answered your letter sooner, because I have been very busy and assumed moreover that there was no great rush about it, but I hope we can get together.

Yours very truly,

TCU: OClWHi

[1]Swan E. Micheaux explained his silence thus in his 17 June 1921 letter to Chesnutt (OClWHi).

[2]On 17 June, Micheaux asked Chesnutt to draw up another contract which would grant him the right to serialize *The House Behind the Cedars* in a "colored paper" which would advertise the book upon which the forthcoming film was based. Micheaux then suggested new terms for their agreement: for serial and movie rights he would pay Chesnutt $700, "$100 down on signing the contract, and $100 each month until the full contract is paid."

[3]Chesnutt did not accept Micheaux's proposal regarding the serial rights to *House*. See 19 September 1921 to Houghton Mifflin Company.

[4]Helen M. Chesnutt relates her father and she vacationed together, traveling "west to the Pacific coast," visiting Yellowstone Park, and going "as far as Victoria, British Columbia." They returned by train "through the Canadian Rockies, stopping off at Lake Louise and Banff; then on through Winnipeg and home" *(Pioneer:* 289–90).

To Houghton Mifflin Company

September 19, 1921.

Attention Mr. W. B. Pratt,
Syndicate Manager.

Dear Mr. Pratt:

Replying to yours of September 15th, on my recent visit to Chicago I closed with the *Chicago Defender* for the right to run *The House Behind the Cedars* serially in their newspaper. After discussing the matter with them and with Micheaux, I decided that it was a more desirable proposition to deal directly with the *Defender*.[1] They balked on $200.00 and I finally closed with them for $125.00, which they paid, and I enclose you herewith my check for $31.25, to the order of Houghton Mifflin Company, being one-fourth of the amount.[2]

I think you are mistaken about the circulation of the *Defender*. I do not know where you got the information that its circulation is 16,000, it must have been from some earlier data; I imagine it is much larger.[3] They run a power press, which under union rules requires nine men to operate it, although they use but six; they have their own typesetting machines, a regular stereotyping plant, an artist and a considerable staff. They claim 200,000 circulation, and I imagine it must run up well toward 100,000. They are advertising the appearance of the novel in their paper quite extensively, and seem to think it will boom the circulation of the book. I hope it will have some effect upon it.[4]

I also closed with the Micheaux Film Corporation, on the basis of $500.00 for the moving picture rights of *The House Behind the Cedars*, for which amount they have given me their five cognovit notes, payable September, October, November, December, 1921, and January the 15th, 1922, respectively, with interest at seven per cent. I believe they will meet their obligations, and if they don't pay the notes according to the terms of the contract, their rights are to cease and determine. I sent the first of the notes to Chicago for collection, and was waiting to hear from it before writing you, but my bank has just advised me by telephone, in answer to an inquiry, that their Chicago correspondent has not yet reported on the collection, but that they expect a report perhaps today or tomorrow. As soon as I hear about it I will write you, and will remit your proportion of the money as fast as the notes are paid.

Very truly yours,

TCU: OClWHi

[1]Chesnutt had completed this arrangement by 3 September 1921 when he wrote to the *Defender's* associate editor, Alfred Anderson (OClWHi), enclosing a photograph of himself and copies of press notices of his 1900 novel to be used in conjunction with the serialization.

[2]On 30 July 1921 (OClWHi), Pratt had given Chesnutt a "free hand" in arranging for a serialization, suggesting that $200 "would be a reasonable price for the Chicago rights. . . . In selling newspaper serials it is largely a matter of dickering. . . . Any arrangement . . . that you will make will be satisfactory to us, and as you are doing the bulk of the work . . . I think a fair arrangement would be the same as that we suggested for the Micheaux contract—that is, 25% to us, and the balance to you."

[3]Pratt described the weekly circulation as 16,000 on 30 July.

[4]*House* was serialized in 19 parts in both the "National" and "City" editions of the *Chicago Defender*, published on Saturdays. From 29 October 1921 to 7 January 1922, the installments appeared on p. 8. On 14 January the *Defender* began including a "Part Two" or "Feature Section," and through the 4 March 1922 issue the installments appeared on its p. 2.

To the Micheaux Film Corporation

September 23, 1921.

Attention Mr. S. E. Micheaux.

Dear Sirs:

I am in receipt of your favor of September 29th[1] enclosing me your check dated October 1st for $100.58, in payment of your note due September 15th for $100.00 with interest to October 1st.

Your failure to meet the note led to its being protested, for which I paid a protest fee of $2.31, which you ought to take care of. I will deposit the check on October 1st, and hope it will be taken care of.[2]

The notes which you gave me were made payable at the Union Trust Company, Cleveland. They should have been made payable at your bank in Chicago, and with your permission I will strike out of the notes "The Union Trust Company, Cleveland, Ohio," and insert the name of your bank in Chicago, at which they can be presented for payment.

I shall appreciate it very much if you will try to take care of these notes as they fall due, so that I shall not be annoyed with the trouble and expense due to their having been protested for non-payment.[3]

I visited the theatre on Central Avenue where your picture *The Gunsaulus Case* was shown, and enjoyed it very much.[4] The picture was well made, and gives me reason to feel confident that the *House Behind the Cedars* will not suffer at your hands.

Sincerely yours,

TCU: OClWHi

[1]Swan E. Micheaux's letter to Chesnutt was dated 19, rather than 29, September 1921 (OClWHi).

[2]Micheaux sent Chesnutt a check for $2.31 on 24 September 1921 (OClWHi).

[3]Chesnutt explained the situation to William B. Pratt on 8 October 1921 (OClWHi): "Their note payable September 15th was protested, but they sent me a check payable on the first of October for the $100.00 and the protest fee, which went through in due course." He enclosed his check for the 25% due Houghton Mifflin Company, promising to "keep after [the Micheaux Film Corporation] sharply and try to see that they meet their obligations promptly."

[4]*The Gunsaulus Mystery* (1921) was a film based on actual events that occurred in Georgia: Leo M. Frank (1884–1915), a white factory foreman, was alleged to have raped and murdered a young girl, Mary Phagan (1900–1913). He unsuccessfully attempted to place the blame on an African-American night

watchman, Newt Lee, and was sentenced to life imprisonment by the state. Shortly thereafter he died at the hands of a lynch mob in Cobb County. The focus of the film was on the plight of the night watchman.

To Houghton Mifflin Company

October 8, 1921.

Dear Sirs:—

I wish to offer for publication a novel which I have entitled, tentatively "Paul Marchand, F.M.C.," the manuscript of which I send you herewith. I should have liked to call it "The Honor of the Family," but Balzac has used that title.[1]

I naturally think of your house first in this connection, since most of my other books are on your list. I realize that it has been some years since I published a book, but my name was well and favorably known, and my books, as you know, still sell, and if I have written a good one, I imagine it would sell regardless of the others.

By reference to Mr. Pratt, Manager of your Syndicate Bureau, you will learn that the right to publish serially my *The House Behind the Cedars* has been sold to a Chicago newspaper, and the moving picture rights in *The House Behind the Cedars* to a film corporation.[2] The publicity given by these things certainly ought not to hurt the sale of a new book.

Please let me know at your earliest convenience what you think about it,[3] and oblige

Yours very truly,

TLS: MH

[1]French novelist and short story writer Honoré de Balzac (1799–1850) was the author of *Les Deux Frères* (1842). Clyde Fitch (1865–1909) entitled his 1908 dramatic adaptation of this work *The Honour of the Family*.

[2]See 19 September 1921 to Houghton Mifflin Company.

[3]This letter makes the first reference in Chesnutt's correspondence to his development and completion of a book-length work with this title. (See, however, 5 July 1906 to Susan Utley Chesnutt where he refers to his working on a novel.) Houghton Mifflin Company declined to accept "Paul Marchand, F.M.C.," on 24 October 1921 (MH). The letter of rejection initialed "HRB" termed it "unpleasant" to have to return the manuscript "because on personal grounds we would much rather accept than decline." The problem was that "we haven't been able to see clearly the probable sale for your new story at our hands large enough to make the results pleasing either to you or to us,

and we cannot believe that it would be wise to make the venture in the face of absolute distrust." See 12 November 1921 to Harcourt, Brace and Company for Chesnutt's second submission of the manuscript for consideration.

To the Micheaux Film Corporation,

10 October 1921

Attention Mr. S. E. Micheaux.

Gentlemen:

I deposited October 1st your check of that date to cover your note for $100.00 and interest which was due September 15th, and as I have heard nothing to the contrary, I presume the check went through and was paid and I beg to thank you. I enclose you herewith the note with certificate of protest.

I note what you say about my taking some of your gold notes.[1] Since under my royalty contract with Houghton Mifflin Company I have to pay them part of the money I get from you through these notes, and as I have some pressing obligations of my own to meet here, I am not in a position just now to take any part of the $500.00 in your gold notes, much as I might feel disposed to do so.

I will send forward in due course the note for $100.00 due October 15th and trust payment will be promptly made.

I will be very glad at some time when you may wish it, to attempt to write you a story for a scenario.[2]

Very truly yours,

TCU: OClWHi

[1] In his 24 September 1921 letter to Chesnutt (OClWHi), Swan Micheaux noted that the corporation was issuing "$30,000 worth of gold notes bearing interest of 8% payable October 1st and April 1st due October 1st, 1926." Micheaux was going to use the funds raised thus to produce *The House Behind the Cedars.* He asked Chesnutt if he would want "to take one or two of these hundred dollar notes, which are first lien on the assets of the corporation."

[2] Oscar Micheaux told Chesnutt on 30 October 1921 (OClWHi) that he wanted him to write "two more stories to be filmed in 1922." He asked only for synopses of 35 to 80 typewritten pages each. As to the kind of story he wanted, Micheaux explained, "I prefer stories of the Negro in the south, and while a good intense love story with a happy ending, plenty action, thrills and suspence [sic] is the main thing, a streak of good Negro humor is helpful. I think you could develop a good synopsis from the first story of *The Conjurer* [sic] *Woman.* Write the case of the man and woman in to a good love story,

let there, if possible, be a haunted house, the haunts being intrigueres [*sic*] to be found out near the end, the heroine to have ran [*sic*] off there in hiding— anything that will thrill or suspend, but will have a delightful ending and give oppurtunity [*sic*] for a strong male and female lead."

To Mary Dickerson Donahey

November 1, 1921.

My dear Mrs. Donahey:—

Helen has shown me your letter of October 10th written from Free-mont.[1] I enclose a form of proxy in triplicate, which I think will cover any action which the Chester Cliffs Company may wish to take until the same is revoked.[2] Please sign one form, have Bill[3] sign one and keep the third in your files as a memorandum.

I have been trying hard to get Frank[4] out there to look over the property with me. I have had tentative engagements with him now for three Sundays during the pleasant weather, but every Sunday morning or afternoon as the case may be Eula seems to develop some social en-gagement of which Frank was not aware and it was deferred. However, he is good natured about it and I hope to get him out there, and I don't want to antagonize him at present because we can do this thing easily with his consent and cooperation, whereas, if we did it by an action in court, which could be done, it would involve more or less expense, which we of course would like to save. I will keep after him and am in hopes I can work it out.[5] If the worst comes to worst, and it becomes apparent that he does n't mean to do anything, we can take the other course.[6] In the meantime, of course, we can adopt such regulations as we like as to the use of the grounds, as you suggest. As none of us will use the place before next summer anyway, there is no great immediate haste about the matter.[7]

Helen showed me last night her presentation copy of Bill's and your beautiful edition of *Mother Goose*.[8] I have never seen this old classic put out in better shape. The illustrations are a joy and delight especially the personal one at the beginning of the book. Helen and I have not quite figured out the significance of what the goose is saying, but we have no doubt it is something very pleasant.

With regards and best wishes to both of you,

Yours sincerely,

TCU: OClWHi

[1]Mary Dickerson Donahey (1876–1962) was, before her marriage, a feature writer for the Cleveland *Plain Dealer* (1898–1905). In the early 1900s, she and other Clevelanders with artistic interests founded the Tresart Club, which Chesnutt had joined by 1903.

[2]According to Helen M. Chesnutt, one of the members of the Tresart Club discovered an attractive rural setting in Chesterland, O., to the east of Cleveland; and, by September 1903 a new organization was formed to facilitate the purchase of 11 acres. Thus was the Chester Cliffs Club incorporated as a stock company with 11 members. Mary, then Miss Dickerson, built one of the three cottages erected there, and in 1916 Chesnutt purchased his from one of the original owners (*Pioneer*: 188). Chesnutt is here requesting authorization to cast the votes of Mr. and Mrs. Donahey at a meeting of the corporation.

[3]William Donahey (1883–1970), Mary's husband.

[4]A. Frank Counts (1882–?), a Cleveland attorney, was the secretary and treasurer of the Chester Cliffs Club.

[5]Harmony within the Chester Cliffs Club was broken when Mrs. Eula Counts sold a lot to a party unknown to the Donaheys and Chesnutts, Mary Ellen Delahunte (?–1951). In a 2 September letter to the Chesnutts (OClWHi), Mrs. Donahey fumed over this, as well as the fact that Mrs. Counts had told Delahunte that she would not have to pay her fair share of "the taxes and repairs"; Mrs. Donahey was also upset that Delahunte's dog had "free range" over the whole of the property. Chesnutt is thus attempting to mitigate the problem by having Frank Counts view the property, see for himself what the problem is, and take corrective action.

[6]The other course of action was spelled out by Mary Dickerson Donahey in her 2 September 1921 letter. She wrote that her husband "suggests that [Chesnutt] get the constitution from Frank early and go over it to see what our chances of busting the corporation are. Then that we say nothing about selling to anyone, have our meeting, get Frank to render his account in full as secretary and treasurer, pay him what we owe him, and then elect a new sec. treasurer—Helen [Chesnutt], maybe, . . . and proceed with the breaking up process at once."

[7]Whether Chesnutt succeeded in getting Counts to view the property is not documented in the correspondence. Chesnutt did have the satisfaction, however, of hearing him confess to error in 1922: "that he had made a mistake in selling out, that they ought to have stayed in the club until it was finally dissolved, and he expressed his willingness to do the right thing" (13 March 1922 to Mary Dickerson Donahey, OClWHi).

[8]The Donaheys were the authors of *The Teeny Weenie Man's Mother Goose* (1921).

To Harry C. Gahn

November 1, 1921.

Dear Mr. Gahn:—

I hope you will see your way to vote in favor of the Dyer Anti-Lynching Bill which I understand is pending in Congress.[1] It is intended, as you know, to discourage one of the most popular of American amusements, but which I think you will agree with me is not in accordance with democracy or good morals.[2]

Yours very truly,

TCU: OClWHi

[1] Harry C. Gahn (1880–1962) was a Cleveland resident and Republican U.S. congressman (1921–23). The Dyer anti-lynching bill was sponsored by Leonidas C. Dyer (1871–1957) of Missouri, a Republican member of the U.S. House of Representatives from 1911 until 1933 (unseated for several months in 1914–15 when the election results were contested but returned to Congress in 1915). Dyer's bill proposed a $5,000 fine and/or a maximum of five years in prison for any state or local official who did not "make all reasonable efforts to prevent persons from being put to death" or "failed, neglected or refused to make all reasonable efforts in apprehending or prosecuting any person participating in a mob or riotous assemblage." Anyone who was part of a lynch mob—defined as a group of at least five people whose intention was to take a human life unlawfully—would be subject to life imprisonment. The county in which the lynching occurred would have to pay a penalty of $10,000 to the federal government, and the same would be given to the victim's family. See "The Anti-Lynching Bill," *New York Times*, 5 March 1922, section 6, 2.

[2] Gahn responded to Chesnutt's letter on 3 November 1921 (OClWHi), assuring him that he would "give the bill in question [his] earnest consideration." The Dyer bill was passed by the U.S. House of Representatives but defeated in the U.S. Senate.

To Harcourt, Brace and Company

November 12, 1921.

Dear Sirs:

Enclosed please find MS. of a short novel or romance of old New Orleans entitled "Marchand, F.M.C." which I would like to offer you for publication.[1] I should have preferred the title "The Honor of the Family," but the name has been used by no less a writer than Balzac. Perhaps "The Family Honor" might be a better title than the one I have used.

If you can see your way to put this book on your list, I shall consider myself very fortunate.

I enclose postage for return in case you don't find it available.[2]

Yours very truly,

TCU: OClWHi
[1]See 8 October 1921 for the first submission of the manuscript to a publisher, Houghton Mifflin Company.

[2]See 20 December 1921 to Alfred A. Knopf, Esq., for Chesnutt's next attempt to place the manuscript.

To H. Clay Tyson

December 20, 1921.

My dear Clay:

I have your letter with reference to Will Henderson's[1] ambition to become recorder of deeds in Washington, and shall be very glad to write to the President a letter endorsing him, if that is the proper thing to do. I don't know the President personally, and have no idea how far, if at all, my endorsement would influence him.

The President is very slow about giving appointments to colored men. He made a very fine pronouncement at Birmingham on the rights of the Negro, but he rather offset it in the second part of his speech, which was it seems to me entirely uncalled for, and had no relation to the first part at all.[2] I hope he can be made to see the light.

I am glad your son is prospering so nicely in Charlotte, and hope you left him and his family well. Give him my regards when you write. Also give my love to Jane.[3]

Wishing you both a Merry Christmas and a Happy New Year, I remain

Sincerely yours,

TCU: OClWHi
[1]See 25 October 1916 to attorney William E. Henderson.

[2]Warren G. Harding (1865–1923) was the Ohio-born U.S. president from 1921 to 1923 when he died in office. He spoke before nearly 100,000 whites in Capitol Park, Birmingham, Ala., on 26 October 1921. In the first part of his speech, he paid tribute to Birmingham and the Confederate South. In the second part, after proclaiming that African Americans must have equality in economic and political life, he said: "Men of both races may well stand uncompromisingly against every suggestion of social equality. This is not a question of social equality, but a question of recognizing a fundamental, eternal,

inescapable difference. Racial amalgamation there cannot be" ("Harding Says Negro Must Have Equality in Political Life," *New York Times*, 27 October 1921, section 1, 11).

[3]C. French Tyson was the son, and Jane was his mother.

To Edward C. Williams

December 20, 1921.

My dear Ed.:

I received your letter concerning Miss Lula Allen[1] and her application for a position in Columbus, and wrote the Governor a letter of which I enclose a copy, receiving in reply a letter from his executive secretary, acknowledging receipt of my letter and stating that my endorsement will receive serious consideration when appointments in this department are made, and closes up by saying "Governor Davis wishes to thank you for your interest and your desire to be helpful as indicated in your communication."[2]

Ethel tells us that Charlie is in New York working and studying.[3] Mrs. Chesnutt has been worrying about him more or less, but Ethel tells us not to worry that Charlie is all right. I should like to have seen him go to college. Ethel says he may yet, but I fear that the longer he stays away the less attractive it will seem to him.[4] If you know his address or are in touch with him, I should like to know where to write him a letter.

Cordially yours,

TCU: OClWHi

[1]Lula Allen was a librarian at the Hatch Library, Adelbert College, Western Reserve University, prior to assuming a position held for 11 years at Howard University.

[2]The acknowledgment of Chesnutt's 14 December 1921 letter (OClWHi) was written by William S. Bundy, the Executive Clerk in the Executive Department of the State of Ohio, on 15 December 1921 (OClWHi).

[3]That Chesnutt's grandson, Charles Waddell Chesnutt Williams, was living in New York City was very likely a consequence of Edward C. Williams' development of contacts there: he spent many of his summers working at the 135th Street branch of the public library.

[4]Charles would later matriculate at Howard University; see 11 July 1923 to Ethel Chesnutt Williams.

To Alfred A. Knopf, Esq.

December 20, 1921.

Dear Sir:

I have written a short novel of life in old New Orleans which I submit to you herewith for publication, if you find it available.[1] I am quite aware that it deals with a somewhat remote epoch in our national life and with conditions which have in large part disappeared, but it was a very interesting period, and enough of the old conditions still prevail to make it of interest to thoughtful readers.

I thought of calling it "The Honor of the Family," but Balzac wrote a story of that name. Perhaps "The Family Honor" would be a better title than the one I have given it.

I have thought that the story might close more dramatically with the interview between Paul and his cousins which ends at the bottom of page 177.

If you can see your way to publish this manuscript, I shall consider it an honor and a privilege to have it on your list.

If you do not find it available, I enclose postage for its return.[2]

Sincerely yours,

TCU: OClWHi

[1]Chesnutt is submitting the "Paul Marchand, F.M.C." manuscript for his personal consideration to Alfred A. Knopf (1892–1984)—rather than to the editors at Alfred A. Knopf, Inc., who would normally receive it. See 8 October 1921 to Houghton Mifflin Company and 12 November 1921 to Harcourt, Brace and Company for the previous two submissions.

[2]Chesnutt's fourth known submission of the manuscript was to Alfred A. Knopf, Inc. (*i.e.*, the publishing firm rather than Knopf himself). See 8 June 1928 to Harry C. Bloch.

To the Micheaux Film Corporation

March 9, 1922.

Attention Mr. Oscar Micheaux.

Gentlemen:

I have Mr. Oscar Micheaux' letter of February 28th, in which he states reasons why you have not met your notes for December and January, for motion picture rights for *The House Behind the Cedars*, according to the terms of our contract. I am of course sorry that you have fallen behind in this matter, as I had been relying on this money.[1] I am willing to wait until April 15th, as Mr. Oscar Micheaux suggests in his letter, but I hope I shall not be asked to wait any longer. This is not entirely my money as I have to remit a portion of it to my publishers.

It is, of course, annoying that you cannot conveniently produce your pictures in the South, which of course is the ideal place to make them. I am afraid that for our generation anything like a liberal or generous attitude towards the colored people is a hopeless thing to expect down there, and I hope that you will be able to make your pictures under fairly good conditions in the New York studio.[2]

Trusting that I can rely upon your attention to this matter by April 15th, I am

Yours very truly,

TCU: OCIWHi

[1]Chesnutt had written to Swan Micheaux on 16 January and 23 February 1922 (OCIWHi) and to Oscar Micheaux on 23 February (OCIWHi), enquiring about the two overdue payments of $100 each for the rights to produce the film. (See 10 October 1921 to the Micheaux Film Corporation regarding Chesnutt's previous difficulty in collecting the 15 September installment of the $500 owed Houghton Mifflin Company and him.) In his 28 February 1922 letter to Chesnutt (OCIWHi), Oscar Micheaux explained that he was currently in production with *The Dungeon* (1922) and that it would take all of his available cash to complete that film in three weeks. After he had finished work on that project, Micheaux assured Chesnutt, he would be able to honor the two promissory notes in question. See 28 April 1922 to the Micheaux Film Corporation.

[2]In his 28 February 1922 letter to Chesnutt, Oscar Micheaux related that he had "just returned from Florida where owing to the hatred that exists among our people and the white people, I was compelled to change my plans with regard to producing the pictures down there—not caring to subject our ladies to possible insult which we are most likely to encounter."

To Ernest Angell

March 18, 1922.

My dear Mr. Angell:

Mr. Walter L. Flory has written me a letter, in which he gives extracts of your letter to him concerning the American occupation of Haiti,[1] and asked me to sign the brief drawn up by Mr. Storey, of which he enclosed a copy.[2]

I have kept in pretty close touch through the newspapers, principally the *Nation*, with conditions in Haiti,[3] and sign this brief very willingly indeed, my only regret being that my name cannot add greater weight to it than it will.

I have also secured the signature of Judge F. A. Henry, former Judge of the Court of Appeals of Ohio, of this district.[4] I have spoken to several other gentlemen, but find that some of them do not wish to sign for lack of any information on the other side, and some because they think it would be disloyal to suggest that the United States Government could do anything wrong. I enclose signed copy of brief.[5]

I hope that you will secure all the signatures needed, and that the brief may accomplish its purpose. The United States ought to be able to help the Haitians out of the rut without entirely depriving them of their hard-earned and long maintained independence.[6]

Yours very truly,

TCU: OClWHi

[1]Ernest Angell (1889–1973) was a New York lawyer who later became a regional administrator for the Securities and Exchange Commission and the national chairman of the American Civil Liberties Union. At present he was spearheading a group in favor of congressional resolutions calling for the withdrawal of the U.S. Marines from Haiti and the restoration of Haitian independence. Walter L. Flory, a partner in the Cleveland law firm of Thompson, Hine and Flory, wrote to Chesnutt on 28 April 1922 (OClWHi), quoting from a letter in which Angell was soliciting the support of prominent Ohioans: "The facts of the United States intervention [in Haiti] in 1915 are so clear and so shocking an abuse of power, such an absolute violation of professed American principles, that we are trying by means of this investigation to do something to restore our good name in Latin America as well as to help Haiti. To this end I have written a brief on the facts at the intervention and the present status. . . . I can assure you that the statement of facts is as nearly accurate as I know how to make it and gives an absolutely fair picture of Haiti."

[2]Moorfield Storey, former N.A.A.C.P. president, was a partner in the Boston law firm of Storey, Thorndike, Palmer and Dodge. While Angell wrote the brief, he informed Flory that it should be viewed as "the work of Mr. Moorfield Storey of Boston, former president of the American Bar Association."

[3]Over thirty articles dealing with the situation in Haiti appeared in *The Nation* in 1920–22.

[4]Frederick A. Henry (1867–1949) served as an Ohio Circuit Court justice from 1905 to 1912, when he resumed the practice of law in Cleveland.

[5]On 20 March 1922 (OClWHi), Angell acknowledged receipt of the brief signed by Chesnutt and Henry, informing him that approximately twenty other lawyers from around the country had done the same.

[6]Haiti proclaimed its independence from France on 1 January 1804. See 6 May 1922 to Frank B. Willis regarding Chesnutt's continuing interest in reestablishing Haiti's sovereignty.

To Ethel Chesnutt Williams

March 18, 1922.

My dear Ethel:

I am ashamed of myself for not having written sooner to thank you for the beautiful necktie you sent me for Christmas; I surely ought to acknowledge it before it's worn out, for I have worn it a good deal and like it very much.

I note what you say in your more recent letter about Charlie. I have nothing more to say to him than I have said to you, which I assume you have communicated to him. I hope he is doing well, wherever he is and whatever he is doing, and whenever it is consistent to let me know anything more definite about those matters without imperiling his future, I shall be humbly grateful for the information.[1]

Glad to know that you and Ed are well. I don't know whether or not I wrote you about it, but I read with interest his very readable article of some weeks ago in one of the numbers of *The Crisis*, on Howard University.[2] Give him my regards and believe me as always

Your affectionate father,

TCU: OClWHi

[1]Several months earlier, Ethel had informed Chesnutt that his grandson was "working and studying" in New York City; see 20 December 1921 to Edward C. Williams where Chesnutt related his regret that Charles had decided not to become a college student.

[2]Williams had written a broadly descriptive article on "Howard University," *Crisis*, 23 (February 1922), 157–62.

To the Editor of the *Chicago Defender*

March 24, 1922.

Dear Sir:

I wish to thank the *Defender* and whoever on the staff sent me a cutting from the issue of March 11th,[1] containing the article by Roscoe Simmons, headed "The Week," in which he said some nice things about me. Also please convey my thanks to Colonel Simmons for the kind words, all of which I wish I merited.[2]

I have been keeping track of *The House Behind the Cedars* as it has come out in the *Defender*,[3] and hope you have found that it added to the interest of the paper.

Sincerely yours,

TCU: OClWHi

[1]The *Chicago Defender* was edited and published by Robert S. Abbott (1868–1940), who founded the newspaper in 1905.

[2]Roscoe Conkling Simmons (1878–1951) was a journalist hired by Abbott in 1913 as a sales representative and columnist. After the *Defender's* serialization of *The House Behind the Cedars* had concluded, Simmons lavished praise upon Chesnutt in "This Week," 11 March 1922, 13. He proclaimed that the "heart of man, the star-lit torch of love, the common genius of human hopes and ambitions, this man writing with a pen that even Dickens could not improve on has unfolded to you. Now get the book, and put it on your library table." Chesnutt, he continued, "is the only Negro living who sold his genius to fame as a man. Others traded on being a 'Negro'; still trading." Simmons went on to attribute to Chesnutt the following statement made to his readers: "Look at my pen, . . . examine my manuscript; inquire into such local touches as I have laid upon my works; and then forget my Race." Following a brief biographical sketch, Simmons concluded: "You can't know a book unless you know the man who wrote the book. This information you should have had long ago. Read Chesnutt. Study him. He occupies a fine home; his wife is living and he is father of three [sic] children; two [sic] young ladies—one a noted teacher, and a son, a leading Chicago dentist."

[3]See 19 September 1921 to Houghton Mifflin Company, n. 4.

To Benjamin G. Brawley

March 24, 1922.

My dear Dr. Brawley:

In writing to me last fall you called attention to your two forthcoming books that have since appeared, *A Short History of the English Drama*, and *A Social History of the American Negro*.[1] I have them both in my library and have read, so far, most of them. They give evidence of a tremendous amount of erudition and research, and impress me still further with the very high quality of your intellect. There are some conclusions in the *Social History of the American Negro* which I perhaps would not have arrived at, but it is a real historical document, absolutely without rancor (where so much could be excused), and with no more bias than should naturally be expected from a friendly advocate.

I am especially pleased to see that you were able to get away entirely from the race question in your subject and treatment of the English Drama. As some one else has remarked, it is extremely difficult for colored American writers to write about anything else, nor is this in the main to be deplored, since it is a vast field and has never been any too well written up from the Negro's viewpoint. However, the world is so wide, and life is such a vast complex, that it is well for the colored writer not to segregate himself intellectually.

I presume you have read René Maran's *Batouala*. I think it was first on sale in America in Boston. I have read it and enjoyed it.[2] It is a rather gruesome and gloomy picture or "etching" as he calls it, of conditions which the French domination has as yet removed but slightly from their original—I was going to say barbarism, but I think savagery is the better word. It is written in beautiful French, and has a wonderful charm of style, especially in its treatment of natural objects, like smoke, fog, sounds, the birds, the animals, wild and domestic, the streams, the winds and the woods. While he is not a United States Negro, I think his triumph is one of which all those who share the blood of his race,—for from his portrait he seems to be of the full-blood,— may well be proud.

I congratulate you on your literary progress, and shall look forward to your continuing advance. It is comparatively easy to write one book and get it published, but it is quite a different proposition to get the appreciation and support essential to encourage one to keep on writing. This you have had and I trust will continue to have.

Cordially yours,
Chas. W. Chesnutt.

TLS: DHU

[1]Benjamin Griffith Brawley (see 29 April 1910 to Brawley, n. 1) had recently been ordained and become the pastor of the Messiah Baptist Church in Brockton, Mass., where Chesnutt addressed this letter. He would soon resign from the Brockton church and teach at Shaw University. He wrote poetry, but his major works were historio-cultural and pedagogical. *A Short History of the American Negro* (1913) was superseded in 1921 by the larger version of the work that Chesnutt had read, *A Social History of the American Negro*— wherein Brawley praised *The Marrow of Tradition* as a "faithful portrayal of

[the] disgraceful events" transpiring during the 1898 "race riot" in Wilming-
ton, N.C. *The Negro in Literature and Art* (1910) was revised and expanded
repeatedly, becoming *The Negro Genius* in 1937; in each version, Chesnutt's
career was described. *A Short History of the English Drama* (1921) was not
his only work of the kind. It was followed by *A New Survey of English Literature* (1925), *Freshman Year English* (1929), and *A History of the English
Hymn* (1932).

[2]René Maran (1887–1960) was a prolific poet and novelist born in Mar-
tinique whose *Batouala, Véritable Roman Nègre* was published in Paris in
1921 and awarded the Prix Goncourt. English and American translations were
available in 1922. The novel criticizes French colonial rule in equatorial Africa, but—as Chesnutt next observes—was replete with impressionistic ren-
derings of the natural environment.

To Bernard Quaritch, Ltd.

April 8, 1922.

Gentlemen:

Please send me, as listed in your catalogue No. 368 which you were
good enough to send me,[1] a copy of the "Villon (François) Oeuvres," at
£ 0 10 6, for which I enclose a postal money order.[2] I am not quite
clear from you catalogue whether this includes postage or not, and if
not, kindly advise me and I will pay the rest.

Yours very truly,

TCU: OClWHi
[1]Bernard Quaritch, Ltd., was located in London, England.
[2]François Villon (1431–62?) was a lyrical poet best known for *Le Petit Testament* (1456) and *Le Grand Testament* (1461). Chesnutt had a long-term interest in Villon; in March 1915, he gave a lecture entitled "François Villon,
Man and Poet" before the Rowfant Club—the text for which does not appear
to be extant.

To the Micheaux Film Corporation

April 28, 1922.

Gentlemen:—

I beg to acknowledge receipt of your letter of April 19th covering
two checks of $100.00 each with interest, to meet your two notes
which are long overdue.[1] While of course the checks are not money, yet

as an evidence of good faith they are appreciated. I shall put them through the bank as of their dates, May 15 and June 1, and shall confidently expect them to be honored.[2]

I am glad to know that you will begin the picture soon. I hope it will be a good one, and that the returns from it will more than justify your outlay.

Very truly yours,

TCU: OClWHi

[1]See 9 March 1922 to the Micheaux Film Corporation.

[2]These checks were for the payments due on 15 December 1921 and 15 January 1922. On 27 May 1922 (OClWHi), however, the payment for the second was delayed; pleading problems attending the release of the corporation's latest film, Micheaux's accountant asked Chesnutt not to cash the 1 June check (for the 15 January payment) until between "the tenth and fifteenth of June" when a new, cashier's check would be sent him. On 30 June 1922 (OClWHi), Chesnutt complained that it had not yet arrived, and he enquired again about the cashier's check on 25 September 1922 (OClWHi). See 17 January 1923 to the Micheaux Film Corporation regarding the final payment of $100.

To Frank B. Willis

May 6, 1922.

My dear Senator Willis:

The colored citizens of Ohio supported you, unanimously I imagine, in your election to the Senate, and I as one of them, and reflecting, I believe, the unanimous opinion of the thinking element of that group of our population, am intensely interested in the present situation in Haiti and Santo Domingo.[1] I would respectfully suggest that it would greatly please me and all those who feel as I do, if you would support the conclusions set out at the end of the enclosed report on the military occupation of Haiti,[2] and specifically the three resolutions introduced into the Senate by Senator King[3] and now pending before the Foreign Relations Committee, numbers 219, 233, and 256, calling for the withdrawal of our forces from Haiti and Santo Domingo, for opposition to any loan to Haiti at the present time (the present proposed loan would subject Haitian finances and indirectly the Haitian Government to complete control by the United States for the next thirty or forty years), and finally, provide the practical means for the withdrawal of the

American forces, the restitution of a genuine native government in Haiti and the transfer of governmental functions as now exercised by Americans to a re-constituted Haitian Government.[4]

It is obvious from reading the list of lawyers who signed the enclosed report, that a great many other men besides colored people take the same view of this matter. I can assure you that so far as I and any others whom I can influence are concerned, any action that you may take toward complying with this request will not be forgotten.[5]

Sincerely yours,

TCU: OClWHi

[1]See 18 March 1922 to Ernest Angell. On 20 March 1922 (OClWHi), Angell—fearing that Chesnutt's signature on the brief calling for an end to the American intrusion into Haiti "could be criticized as a not impartial expression of sympathy with the colored Republic of Haiti"—asked Chesnutt to orchestrate "an apparently independent concentration of Ohio influences" on Frank B. Willis, U.S. senator from Ohio. Willis was the political enemy of the other U.S. senator from Ohio, Atlee Pomerene (1863–1937), who served from 1911 to 1923; since Pomerene favored the congressional resolutions for withdrawal from Haiti's affairs, Angell assumed that Willis would not. The language Chesnutt uses in this letter is reproduced verbatim or paraphrased from Angell's 26 April 1922 letter to Chesnutt (OClWHi).

[2]On 26 April 1922, Angell informed Chesnutt that he was sending him "under separate cover a number of copies of the lawyer's report on Haiti."

[3]William Henry King (1863–1949) was a U.S. senator from Utah (1917–41) and previously served in the U.S. House of Representatives (1897–99 and 1900–1901).

[4]Chesnutt made a carbon copy of this letter—the text ending here—from which he derived appropriately modified models for letters to Willis that might be sent by others whom he asked to write. See, for example, 17 May 1922 to Harry C. Smith. Two other known recipients were the Reverend Dr. Horace C. Bailey (?–1942), pastor of the Antioch Baptist Church in 1903–23 (OClWHi), and George P. Hinton, president of the Caterers Association of Cleveland (OClWHi).

[5]Willis replied on 8 May 1922 (OClWHi): "I have your letter in re conditions in Haiti. As you may know a Senate Committee has recently visited Haiti and investigated conditions. This Committee has not yet completed and filed its report and it is probable the resolutions you mention can not be passed upon till this Committee completes its work. This matter will have my most careful attention from a viewpoint most friendly to Haitian independence and welfare."

To Harry C. Smith

May 17, 1922.

Dear Mr. Smith:

I enclose you copy of the pamphlet of which I spoke to you,[1] and also a suggestion of the sort of a letter I would write to Senator Willis if I were in your place. I am not trying to write your letter for you, and I have no doubt you will write a very different and a much better one, but this is merely a suggestion.[2] If you could comment on the matter in the *Gazette* and send the Senator a marked copy, I have no doubt that your letter and editorial would have a great deal of influence. We have got to bring some pressure to bear down there if we want to save the only free colored nations of the western continent.

Very truly yours,

May 17, 1922.

Honorable Frank B. Willis,
U.S. Senate,
Washington, D.C.

My dear Senator Willis:

As editor of *The Cleveland Gazette*, which circulates widely in Ohio, especially among your colored constituents, as well as in other states, I am in a position to keep informed of the prevailing sentiments among colored Americans with regard to matters in which they are interested. I have read the lawyers' report on the *Seizure of Haiti* of which you doubtless have been furnished a copy, and I agree with its conclusions. I express my own opinion and I believe that of the majority of the colored people and of many white people with whom I have talked, when I respectfully urge you as our representative in the Senate, to support Senator King's resolutions pending before the Foreign Relations Committee of the Senate, Nos. 219, 233 and 256, calling for the withdrawal of our forces from Haiti, opposing any loan to Haiti under conditions which would give the United States complete control of the Haitian government, under the color of right, for many years to come, and providing a practical means of withdrawing the American forces and the restoration of the governments of Haiti and Santo Domingo to the people of the island. The United States is in possession of Haiti without any right and we believe without any sufficient excuse, and the continuance of the occupation sounds the death knell of the only two independent colored nations in America. If the U.S. Administration is so interested in orderly government, it might try to find some way, constitutional or otherwise, to stop lynchings and burnings and peonage and enforce the Fifteenth Amendment in the South.

Respectfully yours,
Editor *Cleveland Gazette*.

TCU: OClWHi

[1]The pamphlet stated the case against the U.S. involvement in the affairs of Haiti; see 6 May 1922 to Frank B. Willis, n. 2.

[2]Smith replied by postcard on 18 May 1922 (OClWHi). He deemed Chesnutt's sample letter to Willis "excellent, only a few minor changes necessary." He agreed to contact Willis immediately.

To Nathan C. Newbold

May 24, 1922.

My dear Sir:

Replying to your letter of May 4th, which a press of business has caused me to neglect until now, I am sorry to say that while I at one time taught in North Carolina and was principal of the State Colored Normal School at Fayetteville in the 80's, I am unable at this time to tell you anything about the education of colored people in North Carolina prior to the Civil War.[1] I know, however, that there were schools for free colored people and that my father and mother both attended them and that both of them were fairly well taught. Slaves got their education such as they got, as they could. I was told that my mother had surreptitiously taught slaves, which was against the law.[2] My father died in North Carolina in January, 1921. Had your inquiry come along prior to that period, I might possibly have got you some information from him. He was 88 years old.

After the close of the Civil War, in Fayetteville, N.C., where I was living at the time, schools were first established by the Freedmen's Bureau, which later on were taken over by the State and the school supported from public funds, with some assistance from the Peabody Fund.[3] In the same town and others there were missionary schools established, mainly as I recall by the Presbyterian Church, North. The colored people themselves contributed more or less to these missionary schools.

Robert Harris, formerly of Cleveland, Ohio, was the first colored teacher in the Freedmen's Bureau School at Fayetteville, N.C., continuing as the head of the public school there after it was taken over by the State, and when the State Normal School at Fayetteville was opened, became and continued principal of that school until his death some years later, when I succeeded him.[4] His brother, Cicero R. Harris, who later became a bishop of the A.M.E. Zion Church, and who died a year or two ago, was his earnest and efficient collaborator in this work, teaching with him in Fayetteville for some years, and later serving as principal of the colored public school at Charlotte, N.C.[5] Both these were men of high school education, acquired in Cleveland, Ohio, and were men of splendid moral character and high ideals, and did much to establish standards of conduct and aspiration among their people. Hoping that this information may reach you in time to be of any service you can make of it, I am

Yours very truly,

TCU: OClWHi

[1]Nathan C. Newbold (1871–?) was Director of the Division of Negro Education in the Department of Public Instruction for the State of North Carolina from 1913 to 1950. He wrote to Chesnutt from the Teachers College of Columbia University on 4 May 1922 (OClWHi), enclosing a "circular letter" being "sent to a number of leading negro educators in North Carolina." He sought information that he might use "to help promote negro education." Published in 1939 was his *Five North Carolina Educators*.

[2]Chesnutt's mother was Ann Maria Sampson Chesnutt (1832?–71).

[3]The Freedmen's Bureau was a federal agency established during Reconstruction, in May 1865, to provide relief for and guardianship of emancipated slaves. The Howard School, a free public school for blacks named for General Oliver O. Howard (1830–1909), the head of the Bureau, was established in 1867 under the auspices of the American Missionary Association and received funding from the Freedmen's Bureau; it became the State Colored Normal School in 1877. The Peabody Trust Fund was established by financier George Peabody (1795–1869) to promote free education in the Southern states.

[4]Robert Harris, born in Fayetteville, N.C., was educated in Cleveland, O., and returned to teach in Fayetteville after the Civil War. He died in 1880; and Chesnutt became principal of the Normal Colored School there in November 1880.

[5]In 1872, Cicero Harris (1844–1917) left Fayetteville to teach at the Peabody School in Charlotte, N.C. Chesnutt taught with him there from 1873 to 1877. Harris was ordained a bishop of the A.M.E.Z. Church in 1880.

To Walter D. Sayle

June 12, 1922.

My dear Mr. Sayle:

I have read with great interest and pleasure the little book which you were good enough to send me, *A Trip to the Land of Romance*.[1] It is very well written, beautifully illustrated, and has served to strengthen my desire to visit that part of the world.

I was especially interested to observe that you confirm what I said in my *News* interview with regard to racial conditions in Brazil.[2] It is an exceedingly interesting experiment and seems to be working out all right. There may be a suggestion in it of a method, at some time or other, for the solution of our own race problem. Thanking you again,

Cordially yours,

TCU: OClWHi

[1]Walter D. Sayle (?–1941) was an author of travel books who lived in Cleveland. He wrote Chesnutt on 6 June 1922 (OClWHi) that he "had read in the evening News of June 5th of your desire to visit Latin America" and was sending Chesnutt "a small book which I wrote as a record of my trip thru those countries," *A Trip to the Land of Romance* (1921). "Travel in Latin America," that is, was Chesnutt's reply when asked by an interviewer if there was something he would very much like to do ("Mental Photos, No. 97— Charles Waddell Chesnutt," *Cleveland News*, 5 June 1922, 13).

[2]In "Mental Photos," Chesnutt was asked about race prejudice. He related that there is no significant prejudice in England where a man is judged by his abilities. In France, "there is no prejudice whatsoever; a man of any color, other things being equal, is received and treated upon a footing of equality." Then he turned to South America: "In Brazil, the new president is a mulatto, Nilo Pecamba, one-time premier. He is a Brazilian, per se, and not a Negro." See "A Solution for the Race Problem," wherein Chesnutt gives extended attention to this subject (*Essays and Speeches*: 385–402). With "one-time premier," Chesnutt appears to refer to the presidency (1909–10) of Nilo Peçamba (1868–1951); Peçamba was not the "new president" since he lost the 1922 election.

To Arthur H. Clark

September 1, 1922.

Dear Mr. Clark:

I have your note of August 22nd with reference to the Baer Valentine volume.[1] I left Cleveland August 1st on my vacation, taking with me the material for this book, with the firm intention of having the manuscript ready by my return. But the delights of bass fishing and other amusements at a summer resort have sidetracked my scheme.[2] However, I did some work on it and will get at it again hammer and tongs and will have the manuscript ready for submission in a few weeks.[3]

Yours very truly,

TCU: OClWHi

[1]Arthur H. Clark (1868–1951), formerly associated with Burrows Brothers of Cleveland, founded his own publishing company in Cleveland in 1902. He had made plans to publish an historically arranged volume on valentines with Chesnutt and Frank H. Baer (1864–1940) of the Cleveland Chamber of Commerce. Baer, a fellow-member of the Rowfant Club, was to make available his collection to Chesnutt, who would produce the narrative accompanying the reproductions of particular valentines and transcriptions of texts. That the collaboration was initiated as a Rowfant Club project is made clear in Clark's 22 August 1922 letter to Chesnutt (OClWHi). Clark wrote to ask how "the Baer Valentine volume [is] coming along," and he opined that it "will be of great interest to the club members." Further, when Baer asked about the progress Chesnutt had made on 31 August 1922 (OClWHi), he reminded Chesnutt that if the book was to appear in February 1923 the club's Publication Committee "will soon have to get busy on the mechanical part of the work."

[2]Chesnutt was vacationing in Idlewild, Mich., at an African-American summer resort community whose advertisements appeared in *Crisis*.

[3]The same day, Chesnutt wrote to Baer (OClWHi), informing him of the delay and his plan for returning to work on the manuscript.

To Frank H. Baer

October 3, 1922.

My dear Baer:

I have been rather busy since I was at your house, but I shall be probably through with your valentine material, at least the most of it, by the end of the week, and will return it to you probably next Sunday.[1]

I had n't been able to see Mr. Clark, but I called him up on receipt of your letter, and he said he was going out of town that day and would return Thursday and get in touch with me right away. I will show him the valentines which you think would be suitable for illustrations, and leave with him those which he selects, if he is going to use them right away, and I will report to you the result of our interview.

I quite appreciate your desire to have your valentine matter returned to you as soon as possible, and I shall not keep it any longer than I have to.[2]

Sincerely yours,

TCU: OClWHi

[1]Baer had informed Chesnutt on 30 September 1922 (OClWHi) that he would have no time for another conference about their valentines book for sev-

eral weeks. He asked how many illustrations publisher Arthur H. Clark had decided to include in the volume, and he requested Chesnutt to return the valentines he no longer needed because he "very naturally" wanted "to get them back
under the protection of the insurance policy, which covers the collection."

²No further mention of the valentines project is made by Chesnutt in his
letters. On 11 May 1923 (OClWHi), publisher Clark once more asked how
Chesnutt was "coming along with the Valentine volume." Clark wanted to get
it "into the works this summer"; and he related that he was "having the colored plates made." He hoped for publication in the fall. On 22 May 1923
(OClWHi), Frank H. Baer asked Chesnutt, "How are you getting along with
the manuscript?" While Chesnutt would deliver a presentation on "Valentines" at a 16 February 1925 meeting of the Rowfant Club, the book was
never published—nor, it appears, completed by Chesnutt. The manuscript remains are preserved at OClWHi.

To Judson Douglas Wetmore

October 28, 1922.

My dear Douglas:

I received, several months ago, your and Mrs. Wetmore's card with
the cute little card attached of Frances Lucille Wetmore, whom I presume was your, at that time, newborn daughter.¹ Upon receipt of this I
imagine you will think I was waiting until the young lady grew up before I acknowledged her card. Kindly explain to her, if she has yet arrived at an age to understand it, which, being your daughter, would not
be surprising, that such was not the case.

Permit me to congratulate you and Mrs. Wetmore upon the addition
to your family.

I have not had occasion to visit New York for several years, and
therefore have not seen you. I hope to visit the metropolis again before
very long.² With best wishes,

Yours sincerely,

TCU: OClWHi

¹Judson Douglas Wetmore (1870–1930) was an attorney from Jacksonville,
Fl., who moved to New York City in 1905. His earliest known letter to Chesnutt, dated 29 December 1922 (OClWHi) was a reply to Chesnutt's of 28 October. How Chesnutt met Wetmore is not indicated in the correspondence;
but he was a business associate and long-term friend of James Weldon Johnson, was involved early in the 1900s with Booker T. Washington's National
Negro Business League, and was an acquaintance of W. E. B. Du Bois and
other prominent African Americans in the New York City area. Chesnutt and

he had not seen each other or corresponded for a long while since Wetmore related on 29 December that he was pleased "to find that you [are] still living and able to go to business." Wetmore's historical significance today has to do with the fact that he easily passed for white, and James Weldon Johnson used him as one of his models when writing *The Autobiography of an Ex-Colored Man.* He is in large part the character referred to as "D——." (Johnson scholars consistently cite Wetmore's middle name as "Douglass." His letterhead stationery does not offer clarification since it reads "J. D. Wetmore." But Chesnutt uniformly addresses him as "Douglas," and this is how he signed a 31 May 1930 letter to Chesnutt [OClWHi].)

[2]On 29 December 1922 Wetmore encouraged Chesnutt to visit him for dinner, in part so that he might meet "the most charming wife in New York City" and "the most wonderful baby in the world." Also, there "are so many things I would like to discuss with you, that I will not attempt to write them, but will wait until you come to New York." He suggested that he might come to Cleveland if Chesnutt was not able to visit him this winter: "I have been piling up things in the back of my country brain for about four years, about which I want to talk to you." See 25 July 1924 and 29 May 1930 to Judson Douglas Wetmore concerning their shared interest in real estate and 8 September 1924 concerning Wetmore's troubled relationship with his first wife.

To H. Clay Tyson

November 22, 1922.

My dear Clay:

I have your letter of November 16th, and am delighted to hear from you and to know that you are well and getting a grip on a new business, which at your age or mine is not as easy as it was in earlier years.[1] You must have taken some little time to get accustomed not to have to go to the office at a certain hour and stay until a certain hour. I certainly wish you success in your new venture.

As to my own health, it is in fair condition.[2] I have been troubled more or less a couple of years with a condition of the stomach which kept me feeling rather mean a good part of the time, though it did n't affect my fundamental health. However, I changed doctors recently and find myself very much improved indeed, in fact, I should say that at present my general physical condition is practically normal.

I enjoyed my trip this summer very much indeed. I spent a good part of my time fishing, and I would go up to the Clubhouse to dinner, play cards for an hour or two afterwards, and then dance until the home waltz. I was one of the sights of the place. It is a very delightful summer resort at Idlewild. My wife wants me to buy her a cottage up there but I have n't done so yet. Susie and the girls are well. The girls work hard all the year and then go away to various universities in the summer time to study for degrees of one kind or another. Ned[3] is in Chicago and is coming home for Thanksgiving, the first visit he has paid us for about two years, although we did see him for a week or ten days in Michigan this summer.

Please give my love to Jane and the rest of your folks when you see them. Susie and the girls join me in love to you both, and I hope to meet you again some time in the near future.

Sincerely yours,

TCU: OClWHi

[1]In his 16 November 1922 letter to Chesnutt (OClWHi), Tyson wrote that he had retired from government service and was "trying to build up a business on [*sic*] Real Estate line" in the District of Columbia.

[2]Tyson had related that he recently visited Chesnutt's son-in-law, Edward C. Williams, at Howard University. He gathered from their conversation that Chesnutt's "health is no worse," and he asked if his "trip this summer improved" his health.

[3]Edwin Chesnutt.

To Edwin J. Chesnutt

November 24, 1922.

My dear Edwin:

Glad to know that you are coming home for Thanksgiving, and we will have a good, fat turkey with all the trimmings and will endeavor to make it pleasant for you. The rest of the family are all well, and am feeling pretty fit myself. Hope you are well and prospering.

Your affectionate father,

TCU: OClWHi

To Ethel Chesnutt Williams

December 20, 1922

. . . Enclosed find a small check of which please give Charlie what you like and keep the rest for yourself as an earnest of my love and good wishes for my eldest daughter and my only grandson.

We have done the old house pretty well over during the year. In the late spring and summer we had the old soapstone sink taken out of the kitchen and replaced with a modern sanitary white sink of the approved level for dishwashing; a new toilet and washstand installed in the bathroom and new linoleum to replace the old.

Recently we have had the hall, parlor, library and vestibule refinished in the new sand color, the dining-room ceiling repainted, kitchen repainted and back halls and sewing room repainted or kalsomined.[1] There are new pongee curtains in hall, parlor and library. In the way of furniture we have bought a brown mahogany five-drawer table-desk for the library, Sheraton model inlaid, a dream of graceful beauty, 60 x 30 inches; a large overstuffed chair upholstered in taupe mohair, with a brown mahogany end-table on which to put your book or whatever you like. And the final extravagance, we have just bought an electric victrola, and have been dancing ever since. Up at Idlewild, where your mother and Dorothy and I spent August, I danced every night until the home waltz.

I also spent a lot of time fishing and rowing; caught so many black bass and blue-gills that your mother got tired of cooking them. . . .

Edwin came home for Thanksgiving, his first visit since my operation a couple of years ago.[2] He got in at 11 o'clock in the morning and left by the night train. He is very good looking and seems to be doing very well.

We wonder why he does not get married, but he seems to have no inclination that way. Unless you should get busy, or Dorothy should marry, Charles seems likely to be my only descendant in the second generation. Helen is a hopeless case.[3]

The family all join me in love and the season's greetings. . . .

Pioneer: 291–92

[1]Kalsomine is a white or tinted liquid containing zinc oxide, water, and glue used as a wash for walls and ceilings.

[2]In 1920 Chesnutt underwent an operation for appendicitis and required additional treatment for peritonitis.

[3]Neither Edwin nor Helen married. Regarding Dorothy and the birth of her son, see 26 March 1926 to Charles Waddell Chesnutt Williams, n. 4.

To the Micheaux Film Corporation

January 17, 1923.

Attention Mr. Oscar Micheaux

Gentleman:

What progress are you making with the production of my *The House Behind the Cedars*? I have been patiently awaiting payment of your last note for $100.00, which, according to the terms of our contract is long overdue.[1] I appreciate what you say in your letter of October 7, 1922, with reference to the difficulty and expensiveness of the task,[2] but hope you have been able to get it to the point where you are able to take care of this note.[3]

Kindly let me hear from you.

Yours very truly,

TCU: OClWHi

[1] The last payment was originally due on 15 January 1922; see 19 September 1921 to Houghton Mifflin Company.

[2] In his letter to Chesnutt dated 7 October 1922 (OClWHi), Oscar Micheaux claimed that he had "started production on your *The House Behind the Cedars* three days ago and expect to have it completed in about four weeks, a portion of it, viz[.]: the reception of Rena at Mrs. Newberry's and the storm scenes, will be filmed in New York. We have, as in most books, been compelled for the convenience of our resources to make certain changes, the largest one being to bring it down to the present day which was not as difficult as it might seem. The point being that it is an intricate task, not to say a most expensive one, to film periods gone by. It either has to be done almost entirely in a Studio where all stores, buildings, etc[.], must be erected in accordance with the period, or out in the wild woods where no modern civilization may confuse that period. We are not financially [able] to do that—but in my opinion, it will be more appreciated as I am doing it."

[3] Micheaux concluded his 7 October 1922 letter by telling Chesnutt that he could not pay his note until he completed the film. See 29 January 1924 to the Micheaux Film Corporation, n. 4, regarding the final payment of $100.

To Ethel Chesnutt Williams

January 23, 1923

. . . I don't believe I ever acknowledged receipt of the handsome necktie you sent me at Christmas. I have been wearing it, to the great improvement of my personal appearance.

We have been having quite a lively season since we had the house fixed over. First Dorothy gave a large party, over fifty guests, during the Christmas week. She had a tall Christmas tree in the stair-well in the hall, two pieces of music, dancing, and nice refreshments. Everybody enjoyed it immensely. Then Susan had the new rector and his wife to dinner.[1] Last Saturday night Helen gave a party to all the Central Senior High School women teachers. As soon as it was mentioned her friend Miss Mallory asked permission to join as hostess, which Helen granted. Immediately another friend, Miss Sowers, demanded the same privilege, so the three of them shared the labor and the expense.[2] There were thirty-two guests. The party began at 4 P.M. with music by an orchestra of five of the high school students conducted by Mrs. Parr the musical director. When the music was dismissed supper was served. After this delectable meal the ladies played cards—bridge and five hundred; and after that I gave a victrola concert; and about 11 o'clock the party broke up. Everybody commented on the beauty of the house, the perfect harmony of the lamps and the flowers, and certainly, with the ladies all togged out in their best clothes it was a beautiful sight. The thing this house is best adapted to is social entertainment and I fear now that it has been put in apple-pie order we shall be bankrupted by hospitality. Dorothy's club, The Young Matrons, meets here next Friday afternoon to round out the circle.

I have been reading with interest the newspaper articles concerning Roscoe Bruce and Harvard University. I am glad he raised the question. I don't know that he or anyone else can change President Lowell's decision, but it is a dirty shame to spoil a fine old tradition by a petty surrender to a low and unfair prejudice.[3] All send love and best wishes. . . .

Pioneer: 292–93

[1]The new rector was the Reverend Kirk B. O'Ferrall (1888–?), listed for the first time as such in the Cleveland city directory for 1923; he would officiate at the wedding of Dorothy and John G. Slade (1891–1976) on 29 March 1924.

[2]M. Eleanor Mallory and Caroline Sowers were Helen's colleagues at Central High School, as was B. Marie Parr, mentioned below.

[3]Abbott Lawrence Lowell (1856–1943), an attorney who taught political science at Harvard (1900–1909) before becoming that university's president (1909–33), drew national attention when he would not allow African-American students to live in the freshman halls. Roscoe Conkling Bruce, Sr., a Harvard graduate, unsuccessfully tried to have his son, Roscoe Conkling Bruce, Jr., admitted to one of these dormitories when he was enrolled as a student. Lowell's

14 December 1922 letter denying admission to Bruce's son was quoted in "Harvard Negro Ban Declared Final," *New York Times*, 12 January 1923, 5: "'I am sorry to have to tell you that in the Freshman Halls . . . we have felt from the beginning the necessity of not including colored men. To the other dormitories and dining rooms they are admitted freely, but in the Freshman Halls I am sure you will understand why, from the beginning, we have not thought it possible to compel men of different races to reside together.'" Quoted in the same article was Bruce's response, that he was shocked by this decision: "'It ill becomes a great mother of culture avoidably to accentuate the consciousness of racial differences among Americans—that seedbed of so many strifes and griefs.'" He assured Lowell that his son with Caucasian features, a "'negro by election,'" will not "'ever deny his name or his blood or his tradition.'"

To John A. Penton

February 9, 1923.

My dear Mr. Penton:

I am writing this letter to introduce Mr. R. W. Jelliffe, of whom I spoke to you.[1] Mr. and Mrs. Jelliffe have for a number of years been conducting the Playhouse social settlement at 2239 East 38th Street, and have been doing a much needed work in a somewhat neglected district of the city.[2]

The needs of the neighborhood have grown to such an extent that Mr. Jelliffe is seeking the means to secure larger quarters.[3] Anything you may feel able or inclined to do in this connection I am sure will further a good work and be appreciated by all who are interested in what the Playhouse stands for.[4]

Sincerely yours,

TCU: OClWHi

[1] John A. Penton (1862–1940), a member of the Rowfant Club (1904–32), founded the Penton Publishing Company in 1904. It published a variety of business magazines including *Steel* and *Machine Designs*. Penton was currently serving as the first president of the Cleveland branch of the English-Speaking Union, a national organization which promoted good will among speakers of English worldwide.

[2] Russell W. Jelliffe (1891–1980) was a social worker who founded the Playhouse Settlement in Cleveland in 1915. His wife, Rowena Woodham Jelliffe (1892–1992) who was also a social worker, promoted interracial dramatic performances and thus the name of the settlement—changed in 1941 to Karamu House (Swahili for "place of joyful meeting").

[3]The fund-raising drive for the purchase of a new building was announced in "The Playhouse Drive," *Cleveland Gazette*, 17 March 1923, [4].

[4]See 9 May 1923 to The Playhouse Building Committee for the Chesnutt family's financial contribution to the project.

To Roscoe Conkling Bruce

February 10, 1923.

My dear Mr. Bruce:

Thank you very much for sending me the marked copy of the *Nation* referring to the situation at Harvard College.[1] As I am a subscriber to the *Nation* I had already seen it, but thank you none the less for the kindly thought. I have followed your correspondence and the newspaper comments on the matter with very great interest indeed, and I hope the university will see fit to change its attitude.

I see from the morning paper, however, that the Harvard University has an invested endowment of thirty-one million dollars. It is rather doubtful whether one could reasonably expect anything liberal from an institution which has so great a financial power.[2] The fact that race prejudice is increasing at the North temporarily, let us hope, should have stirred a generous spirit to resist it, but such is obviously not the metal of which President Lowell is made.

I hope you have found a worthy field for the exercise of your very great talents where you are.[3]

Sincerely yours,

TCU: OClWHi

[1]See 23 January 1923 to Ethel Chesnutt Williams, n. 3. Roscoe Conkling Bruce, Sr., appears to have sent Chesnutt a copy of *"Fair* Harvard?" *Nation*, 16 (31 January 1923), 112. It complained that "Harvard, so long as it follows President Lowell's lead in this matter, is accepting and preaching the Southern Doctrine that every man with Negro blood in his veins is inferior to every all-white man. . . . There is a kind of boarding-house snobbery in Mr. Lowell's policy which fits ill the distinction which has been Harvard's. . . . Harvard owes it to herself, to a magnificent New England tradition, and to American democracy to refuse to make any racial discrimination, anywhere, at any time." Under the title "'Fair Harvard,'" the *Cleveland Gazette* reprinted this editorial twice, on 17 February 1923, [1], and 24 February 1923, [4].

[2]Bruce replied on 12 February 1923 (OClWHi): "The situation at Harvard is peculiar. The fact is that Lowell will unquestionably be repudiated, no matter how considerately the action of the governing boards may be phrased. I don't think that great wealth should make a man or an institution illiberal. . . . What

Mr. Lowell will . . . do, it is difficult to guess. He's now in Europe. He ought to resign. I recall that in his book on Governments and Parties in Continental Europe he says somewhere—perhaps in discussing the achievement of Franz Josef—that race is now the recognized basis of nationality. And this is Lowell's fundamental philosophy." Lowell's *Governments and Parties in Continental Europe* was originally published in 1896; Franz Joseph (1830–1916) became emperor of Austria in 1848 and king of Hungary in 1867.

³Following his graduation from Harvard in 1902, Bruce had served as an educational administrator at Tuskegee Institute (1902–6) and in the District of Columbia (1907–21). In 1921 he became the principal of the Brown's Creek District High School in Kimball, W. Va. In his 12 February 1923 letter, Bruce informed Chesnutt that he was ready to exercise his talents elsewhere: "The situation here is pleasant. I am making more money than ever I did. But, to be frank, I am determined to quit school-teaching in the near future forever. I've done my bit. Perhaps, I shall enter the Law School of the University of Chicago."

To Roscoe Conkling Bruce

February 23, 1923.

My dear Mr. Bruce:

My family and I were much distressed to learn yesterday of the death of your mother, which must have occurred shortly after your letter to me of February 12th.¹ Mrs. Chesnutt and our daughters join me in regrets and sympathy with you in your loss. Kindly convey this sentiment to your aunts, Mary and Victoria. So far as I know there are none of your mother's relations now in Cleveland.²

Your statement with reference to Harvard in your letter as to the soundness of the heart of Harvard is very encouraging, and I hope your prediction in regard to the recall of Lowell's ruling on the dormitory will prove to be correct. If Lowell's postulate that race is now the recognised basis of nationality is accepted, what is to become of democracy in a great mixed nation like the United States?³

I should think you would make a success at the practice of the law.⁴ You have a logical mind and an impressive personality, as I can say without flattery. Your success at the law, however, will depend to a large extent on your ability to get business, which is in a measure something apart from legal knowledge. I am sure I wish you entire success in the profession if you enter upon it.

I am pleased to know that you are writing a novel. I shall very much appreciate a copy, especially since it is something new in American writing.⁵ Something new, something different, if it be something good, ought to merit and win success.

With best wishes,

Sincerely yours,

TCU: OClWHi

¹Bruce, in his letter of 12 February 1923 (OClWHi), wrote Chesnutt that his aunts Mary A. Wilson and Victoria A. Wilson had just arrived at Kimball, W.V., "because of the critical illness of my mother." Chesnutt appears to have heard of the death of Josephine Beall Wilson Bruce (1853–1923) from Harry C. Smith, who announced her passing in "Social and Personal," *Cleveland Gazette*, 24 February 1923, [3].

²In the same "Social and Personal" column (see n. 1), the late Mrs. Bruce's brother was identified as Leonidas S. Wilson of Cleveland. Harry C. Smith also related that Bruce's maternal grandfather, Joseph Willson [*sic*] (1817–95) was a dentist from Philadelphia who settled in Cleveland when Bruce's mother was one year old.

³See 10 February 1923 to Roscoe Conkling Bruce, nn. 1 and 2. For the outcome of the Lowell controversy, see 10 April 1923 to Roscoe Conkling Bruce.

⁴Bruce had declared to Chesnutt his intention to study law; see 10 February 1923 to Roscoe Conkling Bruce, n. 3.

⁵On 12 February 1923, Bruce related that he was writing a novel that would be in press by June: "I recall nothing like this book in American writing. I realize, however, that singularity and wisdom are two different things!" Bruce is not known to have seen the publication of this work.

To A. E. Bernsteen

March 8, 1923.

Dear Sir:

Permit me to congratulate you on your appointment to the important and distinguished office of U.S. District Attorney, which you are so well qualified to hold.¹

Might I suggest that if you would give favorable consideration to the application of Mr. Chester K. Gillespie for the position of Assistant U.S. District Attorney, under you, such an appointment would give pleasure to a great many citizens and voters and Republicans in the district?² You are doubtless well informed as to Mr. Gillespie's experience and qualifications,³ and his friends would appreciate very highly any favorable action that you may see fit to take in his behalf.

Sincerely yours,

Chas. W. Chesnutt.

TCS: OClWHi

[1] Prior to his appointment as U.S. District Attorney for the Northern District of Ohio, A. E. Bernsteen (?–1952) was a lawyer whose offices were in the Engineers Building in Cleveland.

[2] Chester K. Gillespie (1897–1985) wrote Chesnutt from his law offices in the Superior Building on 3 March 1923 (OClWHi), requesting a nomination for the position.

[3] Gillespie, a 1920 graduate of Cleveland's Baldwin-Wallace Law School, was a politically active Republican who would eventually become known as a leading civil rights attorney, earning the sobriquet of "Mr. Civil Rights." He served as president of the Cleveland branch of the N.A.A.C.P. in 1936–37.

To S. D. Green

April 10, 1923

My dear Mr. Green:

I really owe you an apology for the somewhat cavalier manner in which I have treated your former letters, although they did reach me at busy moments.[1] I hope the explanation I make in the enclosed letter to the young folks will excuse me to a certain extent.

I have written and take pleasure in enclosing a letter which you can present to my group, and which I hope they will find of some value. I feel confident, from the tone of your letters, that they are being well taught, by teachers who have a proper conception of what education means.

Cordially yours,

My dear young Friends:

Your instructor, Mr. Green, has written me with reference to your desire that I say a word which might be of aid to you in fitting yourselves for the business world which you are preparing to enter. Reading his former letter perhaps somewhat carelessly, I had not quite appreciated that a small group of you had done me the signal honor to select me as a friend and mentor. But this being impressed upon my mind by his latest communication, I thank you very much for the compliment and apologize for my delay in responding. I can think of no better thing than to encourage the young who are aspiring to better things, and of no higher compliment than to be held worthy of their esteem.

I do not know that I can say anything new to you, but sometimes old things when presented in a new way or from a different source, or to those whose attention has not been directed to them before, may have the effect of novelty.

My theory of education has ever been, since I began to think about it at all, that its most important purpose is to teach the pupil to think intelligently, that is, logically, and that its next function in the order of importance is to teach the pupil to express his thoughts clearly. Incidentally, and in order that one may have something to think about, you are taught mathematics, science, languages, literature, and the other branches of a liberal education. These things are all closely related. To be able to think and have nothing to think about would be of no particular value, and to reach conclusions and not be able to express them would be equally futile.

It is quite obvious that if one has learned to think logically, learned to relate cause and effect, he will live honestly and decently and respect the rights of others, because clear thinking will reveal that to do otherwise is to strike at the very foundations of society. And if one learns to express himself clearly, he will be able to impart to others what he has learned and thus help to further the advancement of the race.

In our own day the scope of popular education, without losing sight of these elementary objects, has been greatly widened. We have technical, vocational and business schools, where young people are taught not only to think and to express themselves, but to apply their thinking and their knowledge along special lines which prepare them more directly for their life work, and which puts stress upon doing things—*"faciendo discimus"*—we learn by doing. In an industrial age and a commercial country like our own, the importance of business training cannot be over-estimated. Great opportunities are open to properly trained young people, especially those who can initiate things or invent things. If you have learned in your high school course to think intelligently, to be accurate, to be punctual, to be conscientious in the performance of your duties, to look out for the interests of your employer, realizing in the long run that his interests are yours, you cannot fail to succeed in your business life.

And after you have begun actual work, keep on studying and trying to improve yourselves. Employers do not pay big salaries because you honor them with your presence. And mere ability is of no particular value unless it is applied to produce results. Most young people nowadays want pleasant and lucrative work. If you do not succeed at first in getting this kind of employment, throw yourselves heart and soul into whatever you are able to get. Fall in love with it, deliberately and consciously, and it will win recognition and bring success, or ought to, and what is greater, happiness in your work and in your daily life. Corporations hiring hundreds of clerks and stenographers keep a careful record of their accuracy, the quantity of the work they produce, their eagerness to learn the business, their observation of office rules, their personal appearance and their manners. What you are is the consequence of what you do, therefore the formation of good habits at the beginning of one's career is a splendid aid to success.

Habits, such as tardiness, carelessness, lack of ability to concentrate, are a perpetual source of irritation to an employer. The laxness of one individual can disturb the workings of a whole organization.

The employer who runs his business with an eye singly to the profit, and who serves his patrons only indifferently, invites disaster, and so, too, does the employe who has a single-minded devotion to the pay envelope.

I imagine I have not told you anything new or anything that your competent instructors have not already taught you. But if I have brought out any new points or said anything to emphasize what you have already been taught, I shall have justified you in selecting me as your friend and advisor. Though what I have said may seem prosy or didactic, I have not meant to preach to you but merely to make a few friendly and helpful suggestions. That each one of you may achieve the fullest success in his or her chosen career is my fervent wish.

I shall be glad to hear how you are getting along, and if you wish it, to write to you again sometime.

Cordially yours,

TCU: OClWHi

[1]S. D. Green taught at Trenton High School in Trenton, N.J. In a 5 April 1923 letter to Chesnutt (OClWHi), he reminded Chesnutt of a request he made in the autumn: "I wrote you to the effect that each group of eight students training for business under my supervision in the local Senior High School had taken the liberty of choosing some prominent man or woman as a sort of 'guardian,' believing that a little letter of kindly interest from them would help each student do better work in school as well as aid the individual young man and young woman in being better citizens in the business world for which they are fitting themselves. Your life made its appeal to such a group." He went on to say that Chesnutt's group "will be graduated in June and they are keenly disappointed that you have not had an opportunity to write them."

To Roscoe Conkling Bruce, Sr.

April 10, 1923.

My dear Mr. Bruce:

I see from a news item in the morning paper that the authorities of Harvard University have revoked the order with reference to receiving colored students in the dormitories, and also the proposed method of selecting students by other standards than those of scholarship and character.[1] I have no doubt whatever that this action was brought about largely through your masterly presentation of the case through the New York *World*,—and elsewhere,[2] and I think that not only all colored folks but all Harvard men and good Americans owe you a debt of gratitude. I shall await with interest to learn how many southern students leave the university because of this action of the Governing Board.

I hope this may find you and your family well, and Mrs. Chesnutt and my daughters join me in regards to you and Mrs. Bruce.[3]

Sincerely yours,

TCU: OClWHi

[1] The revocation was reported in "Negro Ban Off," *Cleveland Press*, 10 April 1923, 11. The Harvard Corporation had voted on 9 April not to bar African Americans from residing in the university's freshman dormitories; further, the university reaffirmed its "traditional policy of freedom from discrimination on grounds of race or religion."

[2] See 23 January 1923 to Ethel Chesnutt Williams, n. 3, and 10 February 1923 to Bruce, n. 1. In addition to the coverage given by the *New York Times* to Bruce's protest against barring of his son from Harvard's freshman dormitories, the New York *World* ran a series of pieces on the situation through the rest of the month, beginning with the news story "Harvard Bars Son of Negro Graduate" (11 January 1923, 1, 5) and the editorial "Harvard Loses Its Bearings" (12 January 1923, 12). Bruce's "presentation of the case" occurred only in quotations of his correspondence with Harvard's president, appearing in the first article and in "Harvard's Policy Is to Bar Negroes, Dr. Lowell Insists" (12 January 1923, 1, 6). Subsequent articles focused on the views of a past president of Harvard, members of the board of trustees, alumni, politicians, and civil rights activists.

[3] Clara Washington Burrill Bruce.

To Charles T. Henderson

April 20, 1923

Dear Sir:

I have been a subscriber to *Cleveland Topics* for several years. I began to take it at my wife's suggestion that you had been a classmate of my son at Central High School, and that she had known your mother.[1] It is one weekly paper that all the family have read from beginning to end, and I have for some time been saying to my friends and acquaintances at the Chamber of Commerce, the City Club and elsewhere, that it was the best edited paper in Cleveland, because of its sane and sensible views on public questions, and its outspoken courage in expressing them.

Imagine my feelings therefore, when I opened my paper last week and ran upon the following gem of liberality, broadmindedness, fair play and good taste:[2]

So it has been decided that negroes shall not be excluded from Harvard dormitories. We should like to say what we think of this but there is a constitutional amendment against such language.

Anyway, we are interested to learn that the all wise Harvard overseers voted that "men of the white and colored races shall not be compelled to live and eat together." That must be a great relief to certain gentlemen of color who otherwise might find themselves "compelled to live and eat" with white folks.

If this utterance had emanated from a Florida "cracker" or a Georgia "red neck",[3] or even an Alabama senator, I should not have been surprised; but from a man brought up in Cleveland, educated in its public schools where he went to school with colored children, and with a mother such as yours, who was widely known as a generous and broad-minded woman, who to my personal knowledge has eaten in public with colored people, it came as a surprise, to say the least.

I really cannot understand the basis of your emotional turmoil, which is apparently so great that you cannot find decent language to express it. I suspected that you did not know what you were writing about, which I have verified by ascertaining that you are not a Harvard man. Colored students have always lived in the dormitories and eaten in the dining halls at Harvard; I have paid the bills for one of them and ought to know. The "living together" and "eating with white folks" involves no more intimacy than life in a hotel, and you know or ought to know that colored men, even black men,[4] are received as guests at some of the best hotels in Cleveland, that eight or ten of them are members of the City Club and eat in its dining room, and I have seen brown men eating in the sacred precincts of the Union Club, and at the University Club.[5]

I am quite sure that had you had any such feeling against Jews, you would not have expressed it publicly in any such manner, nor, had you had a hundred subscribers whom you knew to be colored, would you have gone out of your way to insult them, if only as a matter of policy, to say nothing of good taste.

I shall not indulge in the childish gesture of saying "Stop my paper," since I have paid for it in advance, but I shall hereafter take it up with suspicion and qualify my admiration with reflection.[6]

Yours truly,

TCU: TNF

[1]Charles T. Henderson (1883–1951), son of Mrs. Gilbert W. Henderson, had been a classmate of Edwin Chesnutt at Central High School. Currently

editor of *Town Topics*, he became editor of *Town and Country News* in 1926. When he entered retirement, he was the city editor of the Cleveland *Plain Dealer*.

²Chesnutt quotes from "Moths and Stars," *Cleveland Topics*, 64 (14 April 1923), 34.

³Both racial slurs denote rural white Southerners of the lower socio-economic stratum.

⁴When Helen Chesnutt published this letter she omitted the qualification "even black men" (*Pioneer*: 293–94).

⁵The Union Club of Cleveland was incorporated in 1872 to create a venue for free discussion, entertainment, and education. At this time it was located at E. 12th St. and Euclid Ave. The University Club was organized at Adelbert College of Western Reserve University in 1896 as a social club for men with college degrees; incorporated in 1898, it moved to its current building at 3813 Euclid Ave in 1913.

⁶Managing Editor A. Lawson Lewis replied to Chesnutt on 22 April 1923 (TNF), explaining that Henderson's responsibilities began and ended with the magazine's editorials. The "'smart' item" concerning African Americans who may not want to dine with whites was written by someone else, a "rather erratic" fellow who "wrote without reflection." Lewis apologized and promised to "take up the matter" with the author "at the earliest opportunity."

To the Playhouse Building Committee

May 9, 1923.

Gentlemen:

Enclosed please find my check for $100.00, in full payment of subscriptions to the Building Fund, as follows:

Charles W. Chesnutt	$50.00
Helen M. Chesnutt	$25.00
Susan U. Chesnutt	$15.00
Dorothy K. Chesnutt	$10.00

I am delighted to learn that you are going ahead so promptly with the building project and that we are able to contribute in however small a degree to such an excellent work.¹

Yours very truly,

TCU: OClWHi

¹See 9 February 1923 to John A. Penton.

To Anne Joyce Cassidy

May 12, 1923.

My dear little friend Anne:

Miss Moore has just shown me a letter from your mother in which she states how ill you have been, and indeed still are.[1] I can sympathize with you, because I was seriously ill myself a couple of years ago, went through an operation for appendicitis, and was laid up for quite a while.[2] You must not be discouraged or downhearted.

I was an old man and I got over it, and you are—you must be by this time—a young woman, and your power of recuperation ought to be much stronger than mine was.

I often recall our pleasant associations when you used to come up to the office and dance for me. I suspect by this time you are dancing with younger men than I, and I suspect you are a very good dancer. We have a Victrola at our house with some nice dance records, and I hop around quite a bit myself.

Last summer I spent my vacation at a summer resort, and every night I would go up to the Clubhouse where there was a good band and dancing floor, and dance the whole program through to the Home Waltz. I danced only with the young and good looking girls, and if you had been there and had favored me I suspect you would have been the leader of the bunch.

I hope you will get nicely over your illness and be in a position to enjoy the good things to which your youth entitles you. Your Aunt Celia comes to the office now and then when she happens to be in town, and I always inquire about you. When you come to Cleveland again be sure and come up to see us. We shall probably have moved our office by that time to what will be the biggest building in Cleveland, the Union Trust Company's building at the corner of Euclid and East 9th Street.

With all the best wishes in the world,

Your old friend,

TCU: OClWHi

[1]Stenographer Helen C. Moore (1881–1963) was currently Chesnutt's partner in the firm of Chesnutt and Moore. The young girl addressed was the daughter of Leora Easton, according to Helen Chesnutt who also noted at the bottom of Chesnutt's carbon copy that Anne died a few days later.

[2]See 20 December 1922 to Ethel Chesnutt Williams, n. 2.

To H. Clay Tyson

July 11, 1923.

My dear Clay:

I read last night your letter to Susie, and was glad to see that you were in good shape and that Jane is well.

It is a source of deep satisfaction to have you feel about me as you do, and of course you know it is not one-sided. Our friendship is so firmly cemented that neither time nor distance nor infrequent intercourse can affect it. I don't know what Susie wrote you, but as I do not want you to be worrying about me, I am writing to explain that I have been bothered more or less with acidosis, too much hydro-chloric acid in the stomach—which has made me at times very miserable and has impaired my effectiveness somewhat, while not incapacitating me for work. At the time she wrote, I had a sty in one eye, and some slight infection of both eyes, and Susie, who is of a somewhat alarmist disposition, probably wrote you that I was on my last legs, or something from which you might infer as much. I have been taking osteopathic treatments for a couple of months, and other remedies for the acidosis, and my eyes have cleared up so that at present I am feeling quite fit.

The first of August we are going up to Michigan on our vacation and a month of fishing, and boating, and swimming and loafing will, I imagine, bring me back to absolute par.

I note from the newspapers what your southern friends are trying to do at Tuskegee. I hope the president and Mr. Hines will have the "guts" to do the right thing, which is to put that hospital in the hands of a colored personnel.[1]

I enclose a cutting from the New York *World* of yesterday.[2] Please give my love to Jane, and any of your offspring with whom you come in contact, and believe me as always,

Sincerely yours,

TCU: OClWHi

[1] On 3 July 1923, over one thousand Ku Klux Klan members and their sympathizers marched in protest in Tuskegee, Ala. At issue was the question of whether whites or African Americans would manage and serve on the medical staff of the Negro War Veterans Hospital located there. Frank T. Hines (1879–1960), appointed director of the War Veterans' Bureau by President Harding in 1923, asked an assembly of white townspeople on 5 July to appoint a three-member committee to discuss the matter with him. On 15 August, Hines would take the first steps toward doing what Chesnutt deemed

"the right thing": putting the institution under the control of African Americans.

[2]Chesnutt refers to the sole article in that issue dealing with the Tuskegee hospital dispute: "Tuskegee Inquiry Looms; KKK Names Given Justice Men," New York *World*, 10 July 1923, 15. It reported that "Negro organizations" have complained to the U.S. Department of Justice about the intimidation of African Americans associated with the hospital and that an assistant attorney general "rendered an opinion to the Bureau of Investigation that there is sufficient cause for a Federal inquiry."

To Ethel Chesnutt Williams

July 11, 1923.

My dear Ethel:

I have your very nice letter which I read at home last night with great pleasure. I am glad to know that you are all working and earning money. I imagine that your house is either paid for, or will be before very long. As you say, the Social Service work and the hours you mention must be very confining. I know from experience at home what it means. Helen and Dorothy are working women and put in about the same hours, not all in the school room, but necessary school work which has to be done at home. Your mother has not been able this winter to get any competent domestic help. These "refined Colored ladies" from the south, who want three and a half a day or thereabouts and won't work nights or Sundays, or do the laundry work has been about the best that she could do. We had one who stole a lot of things, including most of my little ivory animal collection. At present we are without a maid. Your mother has a washing machine, an ironing machine, a vacuum cleaner and other appliances of that sort, and with Dorothy at home, manages to keep things going, although she is just as busy as though she were engaged in some directly gainful occupation.

Helen has gone east for the summer, and your mother and Dorothy and I expect to go up to Idlewild, Michigan, the first of August for a month where, with fishing, and boating, and swimming and loafing, I hope to be in hundred per cent. shape by the time we return. I have been bothered more or less by acidosis—too much hydro-chloric acid in the stomach—which has made me more or less uncomfortable, though it has n't kept me from work at all. However, I have this very well under control, have taken some osteopathic treatments quite recently, and am feeling quite fit.

Thanks for your kind invitation to visit you. I do not know whether I can make it this fall or not, but I will keep it in mind, and call on your hospitality at some convenient season. You always treated me nicely when I came to Washington.

I am delighted at what you say about Charlie, and to know that he is making good in college. There are some sentimental objections from our point of view to his taking Howard as his Alma Mater,[1] but if he is classified for life and gets as good training there as he would elsewhere, this with the oversight which you and Ed are able to give his studies, will quite compensate for any disadvantages.[2]

Give my regards to Ed when you write.[3] Your mother and Dorothy join me in love to you and Charles.

Your affectionate father,

TCU: OClWHi

[1]Chesnutt refers to his son Edwin having been graduated from Harvard in 1905 and grandson Charles Waddell Chesnutt Williams choosing instead to attend Howard University. Ethel may very well have been confused by this teasing complaint: Chesnutt wrote "Harvard" rather than "Howard"; his unintended reading is here editorially emended.

[2]Howard University is located in Washington, D.C., and thus the reference to Charles's parents being able to oversee his studies.

[3]Ethel's husband Edward was in New York City; see 20 December 1921 to Edward C. Williams, n. 3.

To Helen M. Chesnutt

July 13, 1923.

My dear Helen,

I have read all your nice letters and find them very interesting. Glad to know that you are "all set and off with a good start." You have a congenial group of friends, a congenial subject to study, and I have no doubt you will enjoy every minute of it.[1]

Family jogging along very smoothly. Last Sunday morning I got the car out of the barn before Dorothy was dressed. I had it about halfway up the drive to the house when Dorothy came out the back door, clad in her kimono, like a whirlwind, nearly ate me alive, and said it was an imposition on her that after I had not touched the car for five months I should now want to drive it before she had become an expert, or words to that effect. After my usual fashion, I submitted and let her put the car back. She is driving very nicely. We go on our usual drives. Day before yesterday afternoon John[2] was at the house and she took the car and him out to the country. First she went down west hill on the dirt road, then came back up the hill on the brick road, went down again on the brick road, went up west hill, etc.

Last night we went calling in the car, called on the Heals who have a very nice new home on 86th Street between Euclid and Hough, old Glen Park, I think it is.[3]

Business not very good, but don't expect it nor worry about it during this month. We are going out to the country tomorrow afternoon for the week end, Susie and Dorothy will probably stay over Monday, coming back for the laundry Tuesday. We are rather figuring just now on going to Michigan by train. It is as cheap or cheaper than going in the car. Will write you further about this.

All join me in love to you, and in wishing you a pleasant and successful summer.

Your affectionate dad,

TCU: OClWHi

[1]The only extant letter pertaining to Helen's summer plans is 11 July 1923 to Ethel Chesnutt Williams, in which Chesnutt refers only to Helen as having "gone east for the summer."

[2]John G. Slade.

[3]Family friends William Heal (?–1925) and his wife Leah (?–1933).

To A. Philip Randolph

July 21, 1923.[1]

My dear Mr. Randolph:

Of course, as a reader of the *Messenger*, I know of the series of articles on "These Colored United States." I have read them with interest and find them very good indeed,—so good that I shrink from attempting to write one of them.[2]

I have n't answered your letter sooner, because I thought I might be able to write it, but the fact of the matter is that I am going on my vacation the first of August, and have all that I can stagger under in my office until that time.

Another reason, I really don't think I am the man to write this article. My knowledge of the Negro in Ohio is confined largely to my own city, and in a recent issue of the *Chicago Defender*, Kelly Miller has written, more or less accurately, a large part of what I would be able to say,³ and a certain amount of research for which I have n't the time would be needed for me to write anything I would n't be ashamed of. I am quite sure you can get a better man for the job.⁴ Thanking you for the compliment, I remain,

Sincerely yours,

TCU: OClWHi

¹Misdated "July 25, 1923."

²Asa Philip Randolph (1889–1979), credited with the conception of the 1963 Civil Rights March in Washington, D.C., co-founded with Chandler Owen (1889–1967) *The Messenger* (published from 1917 to 1928). Owen left the magazine in 1923, but Randolph—also serving as the president of The Messenger Publishing Company in New York—remained actively involved as an editor until 1925. Randolph had invited Chesnutt to write about Ohio for his state-by-state series on African-American life entitled "These Colored [or 'Colored'] United States."

³Neither an article on Ohio nor any piece signed by Kelly Miller appeared in recent issues of the *Chicago Defender*.

⁴Wendell Phillips Dabney (1865–1952) was the author of "These 'Colored' United States, No. 19: Ohio—Past and Present," *The Messenger*, 7 (April 1925), 153–55. When he turned to black cultural history in his article, Dabney identified Chesnutt and Paul Laurence Dunbar as the prominent literary figures in the state's history.

To Thomas Jesse Jones

October 5, 1923

My dear Dr. Jones:

I owe you an apology for not having acknowledged sooner the receipt of the copy of your volume on *Education in Africa*, which you were good enough to have sent to me last spring.¹

I read it with great interest and profit. It was indeed a revelation to me. I agree with your point of view that Africa needs industrial education, but in view of your report, taken in connection with an article by a writer in the *Atlantic Monthly* for June of this year—I have n't the magazine before me, and the name has slipped my memory for the moment, from which two sources I learned that substantially all the physicians, lawyers, preachers, teachers and clerks of British West Africa are educated natives, I have an idea that they are not getting too much of the higher education.² They need both, and not the one at the sacrifice of the other.

Considering the curricula of the native colleges as you give them, and the further fact that the boys speak English correctly and prepare for the Cambridge, Edinburgh and Durham college examinations, it leads one to imagine that perhaps when religion and the humanities have entirely disappeared from our American colleges, when under-graduate effort is devoted exclusively to sports and fraternity activities, when modern slang and the English of Ring Lardner have become the American standard of speech,[3] there may turn out to be in Africa, the cradle of civilization, a source upon which, should there be a future re-vival of learning, we can draw for teachers and instructors in pure English, religion and classical learning. This is perhaps a fantastical suggestion, but it has an argument in it.

Thanking you very much for the privilege of reading the book, I re-main,

Cordially yours,

TCU: OClWHi

[1]Sociologist Thomas Jesse Jones (1873–1950), educational director of the Phelps-Stokes Fund (1913–46), was the author of its African Education Com-mission's report entitled *Education in Africa: A Study of West, South, and Equatorial Africa* (1922).

[2]John H. Harris, "Britain's Negro Problem," *Atlantic Monthly*, 131 (April 1923), 544–55.

[3]Ringgold "Ring" Lardner (1885–1923) was famous for his humorous short stories featuring American vernacular.

To Mary Ochiltree Chesnutt

December 20, 1923

My dear cousin Mary:

Enclosed please find New York draft to my order, endorsed to you, which Anne can get cashed for you at the bank, as a token of my love and best wishes at the Christmas season.[1]

My family and I are all well and they join me in regards to you. The weather here has been quite warm for the season, in fact we have had no real winter weather up to date, although I suppose there will be some later on.

I hope you have been well since your visit to Cleveland, and that you remember it with pleasure. I was very glad to see you and hope I may have that privilege again.

Give my love to Anne and wish her Merry Christmas for me. I enclose a card for her. We received the one you and she sent.

Your affectionate son,

TCU: OClWHi

[1]Cousin Mary Ochiltree (1852–?) became the second Mrs. Andrew Jackson Chesnutt, Sr., shortly after the death of Chesnutt's mother in 1871. Anne was, very likely, Chesnutt's half-sister.

To Ethel Chesnutt Williams

December 24, 1923.

Dear Ethel:

Charlie came in Sunday morning.[1] I had rather expected that he would come right away, because when a young man has something to do he is apt to want to get right at it. His train was an hour late, but Dorothy and I waited at the station until we had collected him and then delivered him safe at the house. He is a big, well-grown fellow, and we are glad to see him looking so well and strong.

He seems to be enjoying himself so far, and we are going to try to give him a good time. Helen took him out to see his Uncle Jack yesterday.[2] Jack did n't know him at first, thought he was Ned,[3] but soon got straightened out. Your mother has been calling him Ned all the time, she seems to get her only grandson mixed up with her only son.

I think you must have misunderstood my letter about the check. I meant you to keep all but his fare to Cleveland, for yourself. He says you gave him the whole amount and told him to buy a return ticket, but he could n't get a return ticket and turned over to me what he had left after purchasing his ticket one way. As I meant it for a Christmas present to you, I am sending my check herewith, so that you can get it before the holidays are over. I will pay his fare back home.[4]

Wishing you and Ed again a Merry Christmas and a Happy New Year,

Your affectionate father,

TCU: OClWHi

[1]On 18 December 1923 (OClWHi), Chesnutt invited his grandson, Charles, to visit Cleveland for the Christmas holidays, the same day writing to his daughter Ethel as well to inform her of his having extended an invitation (OClWHi). On 21 December 1923 (OClWHi), Chesnutt acknowledged Charles's accep-

tance and registered the fact that his grandson had studied French: Chesnutt closed his letter with, "Je vous veux bon voyage, et vous assurant que vous serez le bien venu, je reste, [v]otre grandpère affectionné" ("I wish you a pleasant trip, and assuring you that you will be most welcome, I remain, [y]our affectionate grandfather"). Charles arrived on 23 December 1923.

[2]Andrew Jackson "Jack" Chesnutt (1862?–?) was Chesnutt's brother.

[3]Edwin Chesnutt.

[4]With his 21 December 1923 letter to Ethel, Chesnutt enclosed a check to her for $40. He asked her to arrange for Charles's transportation and to keep the remainder as a Christmas present.

To Carmi A. Thompson

January 26, 1924.

Dear Sir:

I beg to acknowledge receipt of your letter of January 18th, advising me of my appointment as a member of the committee of 150 of the Republican convention committee for Cleveland.[1]

I shall be glad to do anything that I can to promote the success of the convention.[2]

Yours very truly,

TCU: OClWHi

[1]Carmi A. Thompson (1870–1942), former Ohio secretary of state (1906–10) and United States treasurer (for six months in 1913), was the chairman of the National Republican Committee for Cleveland. It oversaw local arrangements for the 1924 Republican Convention to be held at the Hollenden Hotel. Thompson, on 18 January 1924 (OClWHi), advised Chesnutt that he would be notified of a forthcoming meeting "to formulate plans by which the Cleveland convention will be made a success."

[2]Chesnutt does not refer to what was transpiring as a group of African-American Clevelanders was acting to ensure its full inclusion in the proceedings of the convention. On 16 January 1924 (OClWHi), a 17 January meeting of "the colored members of the General Committee of One Hundred Fifty" was announced by George A. Myers (1859–1930), the proprietor of the barbershop at the Hollenden Hotel and a prominent African-American figure in Ohio's Republican party. He told Chesnutt that his attendance was "essential." The result of the meeting was a 19 January 1924 letter to Thompson (OClWHi). It asked him to appoint African Americans, "at once," to membership in the following convention committees: Entertainment, Housing, Transportation, Finance, Press, and Reception. The letter specified "Charles W. Chesnut [*sic*]" as the individual who should serve on the Press Committee. On 23 February 1924

(OClWHi), William J. Raddatz (1880–1940) of Cleveland's Stratford Press Co. informed Chesnutt that "the Executive Committee of the National Republican Convention Committee for Cleveland" had appointed him to "the Decorations Committee of the Press Committee."

To the Micheaux Film Corporation

January 29, 1924.

Attention Mr. Oscar Micheaux.

Gentlemen:

In your last letter to me regarding your unpaid note of $100.00 for the picture rights of my *The House Behind the Cedars*, you stated that you would pay the note when you had made the film.[1]

I had the pleasure of seeing your picture of *The Birthright* about a week ago. It was very well done, and was certainly extremely realistic. Neither the author nor the picture flattered the negro one particle, and they both showed up the southern white in his least amiable characteristics, which seem always to come to the front in his dealings with the negro.[2]

I learned from your brother, who was in Cleveland the night I saw the picture,[3] that *The House Behind the Cedars* has been filmed, and that you expect to run it before very long. I am looking forward with interest to see what you will do with it, and in the meantime I am wondering if I may not expect payment of that note before very long.[4]

Hoping that you will relieve my suspense in the matter and give me any further information you may have about the picture, I remain,

Very truly yours,

TCU: OClWHi

[1]See 17 January 1923 to the Micheaux Film Corporation.

[2]*The Birthright*, subtitled *A Story of the Negro and the South*, was a film adaptation of the 1922 novel of the same name written by Thomas S. Stribling (1881–1965). It was shown at the Temple Theatre in Cleveland, 6–12 January 1924. In a promotional pamphlet (OClWHi), Micheaux advertised the film as "a grim, gripping story of Negro life in the South today": a Harvard-educated mulatto, Peter Siner, attempts to open a school for African-American youths and suffers numerous indignities such as being removed from a Pullman car and forced to ride in the Jim Crow car. After he buys land for his school, he discovers that the deed contains a "nigger-stopper, prohibiting all colored people from occupying the land."

³Swan Micheaux was in Cleveland for the entire week during which *The Birthright* was shown.

⁴Chesnutt never received from the Micheaux Film Corporation the fifth and final payment of $100 for the rights to produce the *House Behind the Cedars* film. See 16 May 1932 to Ethel Chesnutt Williams. The film was released in early 1925.

To Sampson P. Keeble

March 27, 1924

Dear Mr. Keeble:

I do not know whether I acknowledged receipt of your letter of March 15 or not,¹ but I feel honored at being named as a member of the Press Committee of the Cleveland branch, and acknowledge the appointment with pleasure, especially as I know from previous experience that it does not involve a great deal of work.²

I have sent my subscription of $50.00 to the N.A.A.C.P. for this year, in compliance with pledge made at Mr. Bagnall's meeting, to Mr. Spingarn, Treasurer at the home office, at Mr. Bagnall's suggestion, with the assurance that the local branch will be given due credit therefor.³

Yours very truly,

TCU: OClWHi

¹Sampson P. Keeble (?–1956) was secretary of the Cleveland Branch of the N.A.A.C.P.

²On 15 March 1924 (OClWHi), Keeble added a postscript to his letter informing Chesnutt of his appointment: "This work will not entail any extra or arduous effort. On special occasions I would appreciate your help in reaching the daily press, or in furthering other publicity."

³The Reverend Robert W. Bagnall (1884–1943) organized a Detroit Branch of the N.A.A.C.P. in 1911 and served as the full-time director of such local branches from 1921 to 1930. In a 13 March 1924 letter to Chesnutt (OClWHi), he alluded to a meeting he conducted in Cleveland, thanked Chesnutt for his annual pledge of $50, encouraged him to send his check as soon as possible to Joel E. Spingarn at the New York office, and assured him that the Cleveland Branch would receive full credit for his contribution.

To George W. Chesnutt

April 7, 1924

My dear George,

I have your letter of April 31st.[1] I am sorry to learn that you are in such hard luck.[2] Since hearing from you I have had a visit from a worker of the Associated Charities here in Cleveland, on behalf of the Associated Charities in Brooklyn. She says that you are in need, and made many inquiries about you which I was unable to answer for lack of information, as I have been out of touch with you for many years.

I am not able at present to lend you the amount you ask for, as last week my daughter Dorothy was married,[3] which cost me a round sum of money. And I have made some poor investments which set me still further back. However, I enclose you a New York draft to my order, endorsed to you, for $25.00. Don't lie awake nights worrying about repayment or interest, but if with your various burdens and disabilities you ever have it to spare I will not refuse it.

I have spoken to Lillie and Sarah about your case, and one or the other of them may write to you.[4] My family are all well. I hope you will dig out of your troubles. It was certainly a large contract for a man of your years and resources to have four children in less than seven years.

With best wishes,

Sincerely yours,

TCU: OClWHi

[1] The letter was misdated 31 April 1924 (OClWHi).

[2] Half-brother George W. Chesnutt of Brooklyn, N.Y., announced that he was facing "a serious predicament. I have been ill off and on for the last seven mos. [and] unable to work at all since December. My boy is at present in the hospital. Now my house rent is due tomorrow and I am threatened with a dispossess [*sic*]." He asked for a six-month loan of $75, to be repaid with interest. He closed his letter by referring to the difficulty of supporting a wife and five children, and particularly a son hospitalized for "crooked legs."

[3] See 23 January 1923 to Ethel Chesnutt Williams, n. 1.

[4] Lillie is Chesnutt's sister Lillian Chesnutt Richardson. Sarah may have been his half-sister or perhaps a cousin.

To Joseph I. Bantom

April 22, 1924

Dear Sir,

I am today forwarding to the Lake County Bank at Baldwin, Michigan, New York draft for $700.00, to the bank's order, in payment for lots 8–9–36–37 in block 68, plat F, Idlewild, Michigan, in return for which I shall expect the bank to send me the proper deed and abstract for same as per your letter.[1]

Yours very truly,

TCU: OClWHi

[1]The Chesnutts had vacationed at Idlewild, Mich., since 1922 and would return each summer through the remainder of Chesnutt's life.

To Houghton Mifflin Company

May 23, 1924

Gentlemen:

I have your unwelcome letter of April 28th, with reference to the killing beyond hope of resuscitation of my two books, *The Wife of His Youth* and *The House Behind the Cedars*.[1] I appreciate your attitude in this matter, but the books have had a rather long life I imagine, for novels of minor importance, by a writer who has neglected to keep himself in the public eye.

I do not know what the cost to make the plates was, but I imagine that it was a good deal more than I should be willing to pay the half of for them. There would be a very remote chance of my ever printing from them, but as a matter of sentiment I might be willing to offer you their value as scrap, or what they would be worth to you in the melting pot. If I took them on that basis, I could probably, when I felt disposed, be able to sell them myself for something as scrap metal.

Most of the gentlemen in your firm who encouraged my early literary efforts, such as Mr. Mifflin, Mr. Page and Mr. Garrison,[2] are gone beyond the reach of my thanks, but I can express my appreciation to the present organization for the favors extended to me by them in the past, and if you will let me know the lowest price for which I can have the plates,[3] I will let you know promptly whether I want them.

Yours very truly,
Chas. W. Chesnutt.

TLS: MH

[1]A 28 April 1924 letter from Houghton Mifflin Company (MH) initialed "A.P." informed Chesnutt that the firm was pressed for space in its warehouse where the plates for the printing of their books were stored. In light of the fact that market demand for *The Wife of His Youth and Other Stories of the Color Line* and *The House Behind the Cedars* was "so slight as not to justify" new printings, Chesnutt was offered the plates "at half their cost," as specified by contract. If he did not want them, the letter continued, "we should be glad to hear that you have no objection to our disposing of them with others of our books which we are sending to the melting pot."

[2]George H. Mifflin (1845–1921) was a partner in the firm; Walter Hines Page was the editor of its magazine, *Atlantic Monthly*, in 1895–99; and, as Page also did, Francis J. Garrison served as an editor of Chesnutt's book-length manuscripts.

[3]See 4 August 1924 to Houghton Mifflin Company, n. 1.

To Judson Douglas Wetmore

July 25, 1924.

My dear Douglas:

I have your letter of July 11th, enclosing circular of your magnificent property at Gladstone, New Jersey, and offering it to me for sale.[1] I presume your letter is a form letter, which was addressed to many gentlemen, but all the same I appreciate the compliment, as the old colored man said when somebody asked him to change a five dollar bill. I should like, of course, to earn a commission by selling it, but I have n't thought of any of my acquaintance who might consider such a proposition. If I think of any I will call their attention to it.

Your letter makes me think I would like to run down there and look it over anyway, just to see what sort of a real estate man you are.[2]

Please give my regards to Mrs. Wetmore, in which, and in regards to you, the family join me. We enjoyed your visit to Cleveland very much.[3]

Sincerely yours,

TCU: OClWHi

[1]In his 11 July 1924 letter to Chesnutt (OClWHi), Wetmore announced that he had taken title of a "gentleman's residence" in Gladstone, N.J. Because he could not himself "afford to live in a house of this size and value," he wanted to sell the main house and a 250-acre tract of land. Wetmore did not specify the asking price of the property, but he claimed that "the house alone could not be built today for less than a million dollars." He attached to his letter a detailed description of the house and land.

[2]Chesnutt acted upon his inclination. On 12 August 1924 (OClWHi), business partner Helen C. Moore wrote to him in New York City, expressing the hope that he was enjoying his visit with the Wetmores and would not develop "any more bad habits" because of "the presence of so many servants" at Wetmore's residence on Riverside Drive. "We can't wait on you any more than we do, you know."

[3]Almost two years earlier, Wetmore had encouraged Chesnutt to visit him in New York City, expressing a strongly-felt need to discuss personal matters with him; see 28 October 1922 to Wetmore, n. 2. He suggested that, if Chesnutt could not come to see him, he would visit Cleveland; not known is when he was entertained by the Chesnutts.

To Houghton Mifflin Company

August 4, 1924

Gentlemen:

Replying somewhat belatedly to your letter of May 28th, in which you make me an offer of the plates and dies for the *House Behind the Cedars* and *The Wife of His Youth*,[1] as it would probably be merely a matter of sentiment if I bought them and the chances are almost nothing that I would ever print from them, I think you may as well let them be scrapped.

With thanks for your past consideration, I remain,

Very truly yours,

TCU: OClWHi

[1]In response to Chesnutt's query of 23 May 1924 concerning how much it would cost to save from "the melting pot" the plates for these two books, Houghton Mifflin's "A.P." replied on 28 May 1924 (OClWHi): "We sympathize with your dislike to see your books disappear beyond hope of resurrection through the destruction of the plates but it is something which we have to face very frequently, and your books have had a longer life than the average. . . . It is usually impossible to revive fiction after the sale has once ceased, but if you care to preserve the plates for possible future use, we are prepared to make you an offer of them for one hundred dollars, this sum covering the plates and dies for both books. This is very much less than the contract option of half the cost, and indeed is much less than half the cost of either one."

To Victor K. Chesnut

August 4, 1924

My dear Mr. Chesnut,

I have your interesting letter of July 23rd. I have noticed your name in *Who's Who in America* more than once, and have often wondered whether I might be related closely enough to claim kin with so distinguished a gentleman.[1]

However, I suspect I must be content to remain in the ranks of those Americans, and their name is legion, whose origin is obscure. My people were not, to my knowledge, connected in any way with the South Carolina Chesnuts, who, by the way, spell their name, if I recall correctly, like your own, "Chesnut". My people for the 150 years of family history with which I am familiar, have spelled it as I do, "Chesnutt".

My ancestors, somewhat prior to 1775, lived in Sampson County, North Carolina, and my great-grandfather was at one time sheriff of that county.[2] I thought at one time that you might be a descendant of a great-uncle of mine who migrated from North Carolina in the 1850's and settled in Iowa, but from what you say, this could not have been.

I guess the best I can do is to feel that I bear a name which, so far as I know, no one has ever disgraced and which a few of us have made at least worthy of mention among those who have done something worth while.

With assurances of my sincere regard, and my appreciation of your courtesy in writing me, I am

Cordially yours,

TCU: OClWHi

[1]An assistant chemist at the U.S. Department of Agriculture, Victor K. Chesnut (1867–1938) wrote to Chesnutt from his home in Hyattsville, Md., on 23 July 1924 (OClWHi). He requested "a brief sketch of your family." He related that his ancestors "in 1798 left western Va. & settled in the Scioto Valley[,] Ohio[,] near Chilicothe."

[2]Possibly Henry E. Sampson; see Frances Richardson Keller, *An American Crusade: The Life of Charles Waddell Chesnutt* (1978): 176–77.

To William Stanley Braithwaite

September 8, 1924

My dear Mr. Braithwaite,

Thank you very much for your fine appreciation of my literary work in the September *Crisis*.[1] When I read something like that, it makes me regret that I stopped writing and resolve to start up again.[2] However, it is not always easy to get the attention of publishers or of the public after one has stopped for so long a time.

There are several reasons why I have not written, some of them psychological, which are most difficult to explain. However, to have written enough to bring forth an article such as yours from such a critic as yourself, is almost enough in itself for any writer, though he never did any more.

It seems a pity that a man, in writing such an article, cannot refer to himself, for your name would have stood very high in the list you have mentioned.

I have not read *The House Behind the Cedars* over recently, but I am fairly familiar with its important incidents, and I have been wondering just what particular incident you had in mind that puzzles you "That human nature betrays its most passionate instincts at a moment of the intensest crisis."[3] I would accept your judgment on the matter as better than my own, though ordinarily one would expect one's deepest instincts to find expression, almost unconsciously, in moments of extreme feeling.

If you will be good enough to enlighten me, I shall thank you still more.[4]

Cordially yours,

TCU: OClWHi

[1] William S. Braithwaite (1878–1962) was a literary critic, poetry anthologist, and poet whose publications include *Lyrics of Love and Life* (1904) and *House of Falling Leaves, with Other Poems* (1908). Focusing on prose fiction produced by African Americans, Braithwaite had celebrated Chesnutt as superior to Paul Laurence Dunbar in "The Negro in Literature," *Crisis*, 28 (September 1924), 204–10.

[2] Braithwaite was fulsome when praising Chesnutt, observing that it was he who supplied what was lacking in Dunbar's works, "the conflict between the two worlds" of African Americans and whites. It was Chesnutt who established "with the precision of the true artist, the fiction of the Color Line." He ranked *The Marrow of Tradition*, "an epic of riot and lawlessness," as Chesnutt's best novel.

³The passage that intrigued Chesnutt reads thus: "Primarily a short story writer, Mr. Chesnutt showed defects in his long novels which were scarcely redeemed by the mastery of style that made them a joy to read. I recall the shock a certain incident in 'The House Behind the Cedars' gave me when I first read the book at the time it was published, puzzled that human nature should betray its own most passionate instincts at a moment of intensest crisis. I realized later, or at least my admiration for Mr. Chesnutt's art, led me to believe that the fault was not so much his art as the problem of the Color Line."

⁴Chesnutt appears not to have received a reply.

To Judson Douglas Wetmore

September 8, 1924

My dear Douglas,

"Man is born to trouble as the sparks fly upwards," was said by Solomon, a man who had many wives,¹ but it seems to me that you who have had only two, have more than your share of trouble, especially for a fellow who tries to make everybody around him happy—a disposition diametrically opposite to Jeannette's, who seems to make everybody around her miserable. It is too bad about your daughter Helen. One would think the mother would at least want to make her happy.² She knew all about you when she married you, the girl is her daughter, and why she should be always rubbing it into either of you is beyond me.³ It must be the Shylock in her regretting the pound of flesh she thinks she lost by not sticking to you,⁴ but she can't very well have two husbands, so why she should be jealous of the present Mrs. Wetmore, is one of those mysteries of the feminine temperament which often puzzle one.

It is a pity you can't get away from the "eternal question."⁵ I think it would be well for you if you could forget it now and then—at least so far as you are permitted to. But since you insist on thinking of it, and before you stop, get the September number of the *New American Mercury*, a green-covered magazine, and read the article on "Some Fads in Health Legislation," the section in reference to the recent Virginia law against miscegenation. Taking the figures quoted, twenty thousand acknowledged "near-whites," and counting them as white under the old law, and averaging them into the one million four hundred thousand white people of the state, I have figured that about one in thirty-five of the white people of Virginia today confessedly have some Negro blood.⁶ If they had wished to preserve the purity of the White race, they should have started three hundred years ago.

I am sure you enjoyed having your daughter Helen with you, no matter how it came about. I should like to see her some time. She ought to be a bright girl since she is her father's daughter, and her mother, except for her fiendish disposition, is no fool.

I enclose the dollar you were good enough to pay William for me— something might happen to prevent me from pressing that suit for you in the future. Never mind about the last letter; it was from Dorothy, and was of no importance except as a message from home.[7]

Regards to Mrs. Wetmore and love to the children, in which Mrs. Chesnutt and the girls join with me.[8]

Fraternally yours,

TCU: OClWHi

[1]The statement was instead made by the character Eliphaz in Job 5:7. King Solomon (c. 973–933 B.C.), as is noted in I Kings 11:3, had seven hundred wives and three hundred concubines.

[2]Wetmore wrote on 29 August 1924 (OClWHi), following Chesnutt's return to Cleveland from his visit at Wetmore's home (see 25 July 1924 to Judson Douglas Wetmore, n. 2). After Chesnutt's departure, a crisis developed. Wetmore's daughter Helen had had an argument with her mother—Wetmore's first wife, Jeannette—with whom she lived. Explained Helen to her father, she finally realized that her mother had long misrepresented Wetmore and his second wife, Lucile. When Helen defended them, Jeannette swore that she was "through with" her daughter "for life." Thus Helen was presently living with her father.

[3]The "it" rubbed in by white Jeannette was Wetmore's—and thus his daughter Helen's—African-American ancestry.

[4]Shylock is a usurer in *The Merchant of Venice* (1600), by William Shakespeare (1564–1616). He lends money to Antonio on the condition that, if the debt is not repaid at the appointed time, Antonio will literally have to forfeit a pound of flesh. States Shylock, "The pound of flesh, which I demand of him, / Is dearly bought; 'tis mine and I will have it" (4:1:99–100). Chesnutt equates Shylock's unwillingness to forgive a debt with Jeannette's determination to punish Wetmore for real or imagined offenses in the past. James Weldon Johnson, in *Along This Way* (1933), relates that Jeannette was, like Shakespeare's character, Jewish. (Chesnutt's observation here and his reference to Jewishness in 29 May 1930 to Wetmore perhaps indicate he was not aware that the second Mrs. Wetmore, too, was Jewish—as was his business partner. This was deemed worthy of comment in a *New York Age* article about Wetmore; see 1 August 1930 to Herman N. Schwartz, n. 1.)

[5]Wetmore had referred to "the 'eternal question'" of race in his 29 August

letter. He explained that he had a "long serious talk with [Helen], and told her more about her mother and her treatment of me, than I had ever done before. Her mother and her mother's family had browbeaten this child all her life on the 'eternal question', and one day she and Lucile had a long talk about it, and Lucile told her she was crazy, if she allowed anybody to convince her, that her father was Colored, or that she was Colored, and that her father was a wonderful man, and that if it had not been for the race question, which her mother had emphasized and brought to the front soon after her father came to New York, that her father might have been one of the most successful men in the city, and I really believe that she has changed this child's entire idea, as to her own value as well as the value of her father, and that for a while, she will hate her mother now, because of the way her mother and her mother's people have always talked about me, and made her feel that she was inferior on account of being my child." When closing his 29 August letter to Chesnutt, Wetmore added, "I have just remembered that Lucile told Helen all about you, and your position in Cleveland, and how little the question meant to you, and of course what Lucile told her, was a great eye-opener to her."

[6]Morris Fishbein (1889–1976), "Fads in Health Legislation," *The American Mercury*, 3 (September 1924), 50–56. The occasion for the article was the 8 March 1924 passage by the Virginia House of Senate Bill No. 219, which was intended to preserve racial integrity by making it legally impossible for virtually all people with "mixed blood" to identify themselves as white in the state of Virginia.

[7]In his letter of 29 August, Wetmore noted that he reimbursed his son for having Chesnutt's suit pressed while in New York. He also informed Chesnutt that, the day after he left New York for Cleveland, a letter for him arrived. Wetmore apologized to Chesnutt for losing it.

[8]Chesnutt received at least two other letters from Wetmore before the end of the year. On 2 December (OClWHi), he informed Chesnutt that his daughter of his second marriage, Frances, still speaks of Chesnutt's stay at the Wetmore home and shows a copy of *The Conjure Woman* to visitors. In the same letter he also noted the publication of one of Chesnutt's short stories in *Crisis* (see 16 September 1924 to W. E. B. Du Bois, n. 1), observing incorrectly that he supposed Du Bois "was short of material for the magazine this month, and therefore they decided to use one of your old stories." On 30 December (OClWHi), Wetmore corrected himself, explaining that during a luncheon at the Civic Club Du Bois informed him that the short story had never before been published. Wetmore waggishly concluded that "Chesnutt [*sic*] has one character [Uncle Julius McAdoo], that he intends using for the balance of his life." He closed his letter with, "Take care of yourself, and do not drink too much New Year's Eve Night."

To W. E. B. Du Bois

September 16, 1924

My dear Dr. Du Bois,

As I said in a previous letter that I would, I enclose you herewith a copy of a story which you may be able to use for the *Crisis*.[1] It is in my earlier manner, but I think has a thread of interest which might be interesting to your readers.[2]

Perhaps it is too long for one number, in which event you could divide it at a convenient point, the middle of page fifteen would be a dramatic point at which to make the division, but if that is n't consistent with the makeup of the magazine, you can probably find one equally as good.

If you do not find the story available, kindly return it, and I will look up another one.

Yours very truly,

TCU: OClWHi

[1] On 8 September 1924 (OClWHi), Du Bois reminded Chesnutt that he had "promised to look among [his] manuscripts and pick out a story for publication in The Crisis." The manuscript Chesnutt enclosed with the present letter was "The Marked Tree," which was published in *Crisis*, 29 (December 1924), 59–64; (January 1925), 110–13.

[2] Uncle Julius McAdoo, the African-American storyteller in the *Conjure Woman* short stories, is a character in "The Marked Tree."

To James A. Flaherty

November 3, 1924

Dear Sir,

I wish to thank you and the Knights of Columbus very much for the copy of Dr. Du Bois's book *The Gift of the Black Folk*, mailed to me recently.[1] I should have acknowledged its receipt sooner, but was waiting until I had read the book. It is a worthy contribution to the effort which the Knights of Columbus are making to combat the racial and religious propaganda of the Ku Klux Klan.

It is needless to say that I hope this campaign will prove effective and that it may result in promoting among all of our people the recognition of the brotherhood of man regardless of race, which the Roman Catholic Church has always taught and sought to live up to.[2]

Sincerely yours,

TCU: OClWHi

[1]James A. Flaherty (1854–1937), the Supreme Knight of the Knights of Columbus (1909–28), and William J. McGinley (1865–1947), the organization's Supreme Secretary (1909–39), sent Chesnutt a copy of Du Bois' 1924 study subtitled *The Negro in the Making of America* on 15 August 1924 (OClWHi).

[2]In their cover letter, Flaherty and McGinley informed Chesnutt that the Knights of Columbus has "arranged for the publication of a series of books telling what the various races have done in the making of the United States, each book written by a competent historian who is of the racial group whose story is related." The intent of the series was "to promote national solidarity and to explain the racial history of the making of America, free from any suspicion of selfish motive."

To the Editor of *The Survey*

March 17, 1925

Dear Sir:

I have read with great interest and pleasure your special number on "Harlem—Mecca of The New Negro."[1] It is in line with the always liberal and indeed generous policy of your magazine. It not only tells the Negro's story, but permits him to tell it himself. It is, in effect, an illuminating discussion of the whole race problem in the United States, which every American man and woman, white or colored, can read with profit.

Yours sincerely,

TCU: OClWHi

[1]On 9 March 1925 (OClWHi), Paul Underwood Kellogg (1879–1958), editor of the social reform-focused *Survey* (1912–52), wrote Chesnutt that he intended a "Harlem number . . . [to be] a contribution to racial understanding." He solicited Chesnutt's comments, which he intended to quote in the magazine. The Harlem number (53 [1 March 1925]) featured distinguished African-American authors such as James Weldon Johnson, W. E. B. Du Bois, Kelly Miller, Alain Locke (1886–1954), Langston Hughes (1902–67), Countee Cullen (1903–46), and Claude McKay (1890–1948).

To W. E. B. Du Bois

August 3, 1925.

My dear Dr. DuBois:

I have read the four stories which you have been good enough to send me, and am prepared to tell you what I think about them.[1] In my opinion the quality of a story depends upon several elements: 1, the theme; 2, the plot and its working out; 3, the language, including the style; 4, the effect on the reader. The theme is important. A motive which in real life is improbable (except of course in fairy tales and others of that sort) does not make a good story. A plot which suffers from the same defect or is not well worked out does not make a good story. Good English or whatever the language may be, which is easily understood by the reader, is essential. But the most important of all is the effect upon the reader. However irreproachable your theme, however well developed your plot, however fine your style or however choice your language, if the story does not ring true and does not convince the reader, it is not a good story.

Applying these principles to the stories you sent me, and which I return herewith, I should say that the story "Three Dogs and a Rabbit" is well conceived, well written, but not convincing. The race motive is dragged into it unnecessarily. There was no dramatic necessity for this fine old woman to betray the secret of her origin, with the extremely probable effect of embarrassing her children and their future. The story would have been, from any standpoint but that of a colored reader, equally dramatic and effective without that disclosure. So the story is not convincing.

"Easy Pickin's" is merely a character sketch in dialect. I suspect this bum's condition was due to more than his wife's misconduct. He could not have been any good or he would have managed his wife better, nor would he have permitted his life to be ruined by a worthless woman. Speaking of dialect, in my view there is no such thing as Negro dialect. Dialect is a form of speech which has become to a certain extent fixed or at least conventionalized, like the Scotch dialect or perhaps the Pennsylvania Dutch speech. Negro dialect is largely if not entirely merely mispronunciation of English. Mr. Octavus Roy Cohen[2] has either dug up or created some forms of speech which savor of dialect, as for instance the phrase of which this would be an example, "Time is somethin' I ain't got nuthin' else but." But, generally speaking, Negro dialect is merely the local corruption of good English, except as it may here and there include some of the Elizabethan allocutions of which Mr. Mencken has collected so many in his *The American Language*.[3] A dialect which is so difficult that the reader has to stop to figure out what it means detracts from the interest of the story, in which respect this writer sins.

"High Yaller", the most ambitious of the four stories, is very well written. Of course an editor reading it with a view to publication could make certain suggestions as to the language and figures of speech here and there. The plot is well worked out, with a heroine and a hero and a villain, and its atmosphere may be a correct reflection of Negro life in Harlem, with which I am not very familiar. But to me at least the theme is not convincing. I have never yet met knowingly a fair colored girl who wanted to be darker. The almost universal desire is, as the advertising pages of the colored newspapers and periodicals bear witness, to get as much whiter as possible. So the story is not convincing.

"There Never Fell a Night so Dark" is in my opinion the best of the lot. The theme is human. It is a simple sketch, with some elements of improbability in the plot. For instance as I read her story, her son was killed in the war, and according to his story his son is in prison, innocent of course, though they turn out to be the man and the woman. But the little story touches the emotions and to that extent meets the essential requirement of a good story.

If I were grading the stories I should make "There Never Fell a Night so Dark" No. 1, "High Yaller" No. 2, "Three Dogs and a Rabbit" No. 3, and "Easy Pickin's" No. 4.[4]

I suspect you only wanted my opinion on the relative merit of the stories and that I have inflicted on you my reasons unnecessarily. If so you will pardon the superfluity.

Your letter found me and my family well,[5] and we all join in sincere regards.

Cordially yours,

TCU: OClWHi

[1]On 8 September 1924 (OClWHi), Du Bois asked Chesnutt to serve as a judge in a prose fiction contest being conducted by *Crisis*: the competition was for the Amy Spingarn prizes to be awarded works in the categories of short story, play, essay, poem, and drawing. On 28 July 1925 (OClWHi), Du Bois reminded him of this and asked for a timely evaluation of four short stories. The other judges of short stories were H. G. Wells, Sinclair Lewis (1895–1951), and Mary White Ovington—as was announced in "Krigwa," *Crisis*, 30 (October 1925), 275–78. René Maran was also consulted, and his opinion of

the submissions was given in "The Looking Glass," *Crisis*, 31 (November 1925), 38–39.

[2]Octavus Roy Cohen (1891–1959) comically caricatured African Americans in novels such as *Polished Ebony* (1919) and *Assorted Chocolates* (1920).

[3]H. L. Mencken (1880–1956) was a journalist, literary and social critic, and essayist whose most important work of scholarship was *The American Language*, his 1919 analysis of English as it had developed in America.

[4]The awards were given on 14 August 1924 in New York City and announced in "Krigwa" (see n. 1). "High Yaller: A Story" by Rudolph Fisher (1897–1934) won the first prize of $100 and was published in *Crisis*, 30 (October 1925), 281–86; 31 (November 1925), 33–38. Chesnutt's preference, "There Was Never a Night So Dark" by Marie French, won the second prize of $50 and was published in *Crisis*, 31 (December 1925), 73–76. The third prize of $20 was won by Anita Scott Coleman (1890–1960); her "Three Dogs and a Rabbit" appeared in *Crisis*, 31 (January 1926), 118–22.

[5]Du Bois closed his 28 July 1925 letter with "I hope this will find you well."

To Thomas L. Dabney

August 13, 1925.

Dear Mr. Dabney:

Pardon me for not having answered sooner your letter of June 10, 1925.[1]

As I do not want to be quoted, I shall not answer your questions categorically, but shall say that the present condition of Mr. Garvey ought to answer most of the questions in regard to his movement.[2] Of course I regard segregation as detrimental and cooperation as helpful to the solution of the race problem in America, and I have no program to suggest for the redemption of Africa.[3] The Riffians are trying to redeem a part of it, but seem to be playing in rather hard luck.[4]

Yours very truly,

TCU: OClWHi

[1]The letter to Chesnutt from Thomas L. Dabney of Ellerson, Va., is not extant.

[2]Marcus Garvey (1887–1940) founded the Universal Negro Improvement Association in Jamaica in 1914 and was its highly visible leader in Harlem beginning in 1916. The organization promoted economic self-sufficiency for African Americans and a "race pride" orientation that Chesnutt saw as counterproductive. (See 7 September 1926 to Carl Van Vechten.) Separatist in its ori-

entation, it was severely criticized by leaders of organizations such as the N.A.A.C.P. that favored integration. In 1923 Garvey was convicted of fraud for his handling of funds being raised to establish a steamship company; his appeal failed on 2 February 1925. The "present condition" of Garvey to which Chesnutt refers was that of a convicted felon who began his prison term on 8 February 1925. (He would receive both a presidential pardon and, as an "undesirable alien," a deportation order in 1927.)

[3]One of the goals of the U.N.I.A. was the formation of an independent black nation in Africa. Garvey was committed to the ideal of seeing all European colonial powers surrender control of Africa to the Africans.

[4]In northern Morocco, the independence-minded Rif had, since 1920, tried to expel the Spanish. In 1923 these Berber tribesmen defeated the Spanish army, began a new campaign into Tangier, and acted to establish a republic. In 1925 the Rif were being challenged by the joint efforts of Spanish and French troops; they would be defeated in 1934.

To Carl Van Vechten

February 23, 1926.

My dear Mr. Van Vechten:

I am a little late in thanking you for your letter, accompanied by the newspaper cutting, in both of which you express in such generous terms your appreciation of my literary efforts, and I have written to Mr. Johnson to thank him for calling your attention to them.[1] I have also read your article in the January number of *Vanity Fair*, in which you make some further comment.[2]

One reason for my delay in writing to you was that I started out to write what threatened to become a dissertation on certain aspects of the race problem as suggested by some observations of your own, but I finally decided that while perhaps you might have found it interesting, it was out of place in a letter of this kind, and that I would let you gather my point of view upon race prejudice and race fallacies from reading my books.

Unhappily, my books are just now all out of print, though I have the melancholy consolation of my publishers' assurance that the average novel seldom lasts more than two or three years, while mine sold for twenty-five. However, they constitute up to date the largest volume of imaginative literature dealing with the race problem by any one writer in the United States, and the time may come when the colored people will want to read them in such numbers as to justify a reprint, especially if I should write another good novel, which is at least possible. In that event, if I am still alive, such appreciation as yours may have more than a sentimental value.

I foolishly neglected to keep any appreciable number of my books on hand, so find I have only a few, in some cases only one in my own library. *The Conjure Woman* was quoted the other day in Meredith Janvier's catalogue, but by the time he received my order it had already been sold.[3] However, I want you to read the two you have n't read, the Douglass[4] and *The House Behind the Cedars*—my most popular work—and send them to you by parcel post, with the request that you return them to me when you have read them, (the reverse of the wrapper is addressed and stamped) as it would be an unspeakable calamity for an author not to possess a complete set of his own works. They have been in an exhibition here of books by members of the Rowfant Club, or I should have sent them to you sooner. When I see you, as I hope to,—I will tell you what a Negro moving picture concern did to *The House Behind the Cedars* to make it appeal to a black audience.[5]

I must, while writing, express my appreciation of your own writings—not only your critical studies but your books, the latest one of which I have read being your *Firecrackers*, in which you have gotten together a collection of odd or at least unusual characters and strung them on a string which makes them exceedingly interesting. It takes all kinds of people to make a world, and writers of genius have often been the first to discover them, if not to create them. I especially love your use of erudite and unusual words, they are like caviar to the everyday English which anybody can use, and are a compliment to the intelligence and culture of the reader. I must admit that when I read your *Tatooed Countess*, I had to refer to a Latin dictionary to figure out the meaning of a few of them.[6]

I thank you again for the kind things you say about my books, and the next time I am in New York I shall certainly make it a point to look you up, and if you should come to Cleveland before that time, call me up when you get here, that I may have the pleasure of meeting you so much the sooner.

Yours cordially,
Chas. W. Chesnutt.

TLS: CtY

[1]Carl Van Vechten (1880–1964) was a novelist, photographer, and both a music and drama critic for New York City newspapers. An enthusiastic participant in Harlem's cabaret night-life, he was an ardent advocate of African-American artists working in various media who were associated with the

Harlem Renaissance. At this time Van Vechten was incorporating his admiration for Chesnutt's art in the manuscript for his novel published later in 1926, *Nigger Heaven*; see 7 September 1926 to Carl Van Vechten.

²Chesnutt refers to Van Vechten's article "'Moanin' Wid A Sword in Ma Han'," *Vanity Fair*, 25 (February 1926), 60, 100, and 102. Therein Van Vechten lamented the unwillingness of most African-American artists to exploit fully the artistic potential of their cultural life and "picturesque" experience, leaving it for whites to acknowledge, appreciate, and use such rich material in their art. Chesnutt is cited as an exception in this regard: "Until recently, the Negro writer has made a free gift of this exceptionally good copy—one should except Paul Laurence Dunbar and Charles W. Chesnutt from this indictment—to the white author."

³Meredith Janvier (1872–1936) was a book seller in Baltimore who specialized in rare books and first editions.

⁴*Frederick Douglass.*

⁵See Chesnutt's description of the cinematic adaptation in 16 May 1932 to Ethel Chesnutt Williams.

⁶Both *Firecrackers: A Realistic Novel* (1925) and *The Tattooed Countess: A Romantic Novel with a Happy Ending* (1924) described in an urbane, witty tone the manners and mannerisms observable in modern American life. Displaying a kinship with decadent prose stylists of the *fin de siècle*, Van Vechten's vocabulary in these works was rich and often esoteric; he was writing with "sparkle"—as Chesnutt terms it in his 7 September 1926 letter to Van Vechten—for fellow sophisticates rather than the popular readership.

To Charles Waddell Chesnutt Williams

March 26, 1926

My dear Charlie:

I don't think I ever acknowledged your letter of some date in February—you did n't date the letter, and the postmark on the envelope is illegible. *Comment ça va*¹ in the dramatic line and otherwise? In your mother's letter, received about the same date as yours, she mentioned two plays in which you were to appear during February, *A Doll's House* and *Lady Windermere's Fan*.² I hope they went well. Some time I hope to see you perform; I am sure it will be worth while. When you were a small boy you could do the "dying soldier" to a turn, and the same spirit would apply to anything else.

I have been wondering about Mr. Cobb's appointment to the vacant judgeship. I understand that it was confirmed by the Senate, but that some Southern senator who was out of town at the time, had asked for a reconsideration of the confirmation, and I have not yet learned what the outcome was.[3] I sincerely hope that it will stick. Cobb is a good fellow and worthy of recognition.

Family all well and join me in love. The baby is a dandy.[4] He is nine months old and full of pep. He already knows one word, and uses it intelligently. When I show him my watch, he says "tick, tick", and when he wants it to play with he says "tick, tick". He reminds me very much of you when you were a baby, and I am enjoying him immensely.

I presume you are now on the home stretch in your senior year.[5] I hope you will make it all right, and get a Phi Beta Kappa key, if that is the right name of it.

Our colored brethren are cutting a wide swath in literature these days. I just bought a book of poems the other day by Langston Hughes, a former pupil of your Aunt Helen in Central High School.[6] It is interesting, but represents promise more than fulfillment. I presume you have seen Mr. Locke's book *The New Negro*,[7] and have kept track of Mr. Fisher's writings.[8]

Give my love to your mother and father, and let me hear from you any time that the spirit moves.

Your affectionate grandparent,

TCU: OClWHi

[1]How's it going?

[2]Henrik Ibsen (1828–1906), *A Doll's House* (1879); Oscar Wilde (1854–1900), *Lady Windermere's Fan* (1892). That Chesnutt's grandson would become involved in drama was very likely a testimony to his father's influence. Edward C. Williams wrote prose fiction and poetry as well as plays; one of the pieces performed by Howard University's theatrical group, the University Players, was an adaptation of his father-in-law's 1889 short story "The Sheriff's Children." (See "Edward Christopher Williams" by Howard University Reference Librarian Dorothy B. Porter [1905–95], *Phylon*, 8, No. 4 [1947], 315–21, which is based in part on an unpublished typescript by his son entitled "Edward C. Williams, 1871–1926.")

[3]James A. Cobb was a member of the faculty of the Howard University Law School (1916–38), for which he served as vice-dean in 1923–29. In 1926 Cobb was appointed judge of the Municipal Court of the District of Columbia, a position he held until 1935.

[4]Daughter Dorothy Chesnutt Slade's son, John Chesnutt Slade (1925–).

[5]Charles would receive a bachelor's degree from Howard University's College of Liberal Arts in June 1926.

[6]Langston Hughes published *The Weary Blues* in 1926 with an introduction by Carl Van Vechten.

[7]Alain Locke, a philosopher and critic, taught in the Teachers College and the College of Arts and Sciences at Howard University from 1912 to 1925. In

December 1925 his celebrative description of the emergence of the sophisticated, post-"Uncle Tom" African American, *The New Negro*, was published,
and he thereafter served as the chief spokesman for "The New Negro Movement."

[8]Fisher would not publish a novel, *The Walls of Jericho*, until 1928. Ches-
nutt knew him at this point as a writer to whom Locke had given attention in
The New Negro and as a contributor to periodicals: "The City of Refuge,"
Atlantic, 135 (February 1925), 178–87; "South Lingers On," *Survey*, 6
(March 1925), 644–47; and "Ringtail," *Atlantic*, 135 (May 1925), 652–60.
See 3 August 1925 to W. E. B. Du Bois for Chesnutt's opinion of Fisher's
1925 short story "High Yaller."

To Carl Van Vechten

September 7, 1926

My dear Mr. Van Vechten:

Thank you very much for the copy of your *Nigger Heaven* with the
complimentary inscription.[1] It shall occupy an honored place on my
shelf of association books. I should have acknowledged it sooner, but
was on my vacation[2] and conditions were not favorable for writing
such a letter as I wanted to write.

Your novel presents a picturesque and arresting cross-section of a
phase of New York life with which I must confess I am not familiar
except from reading of it, as I was never but once, and that quite a few
years ago, in a Harlem cabaret, though in earlier years when around
New York I have several times, in company with colored friends, visited Marshall's in Fifty-fourth Street, referred to by you, at the time
when Cole and Johnson, Williams and Walker and Ernest Hogan were
in their prime.[3]

The name of your book gave me a shock at first, until I reached the
passage in which it first appears in the text, where it is perhaps appropriate to the character using it as well as by way of local color.[4]

As to the literary quality of the work, it is done with your usual
vividness and sparkle. The characters are clearly drawn, in bold outlines which capture the imagination and are consistent throughout.
They are not merely lay figures—they "live and breathe and have their
being."[5] Some of them reflect little credit on their race, but if they are
true to life, that is all that can be asked of an artist. Byron is a poor
fish, but there are many of his kind. I fell in love with your Mary—
there are many like her.[6] She did not lead a very happy life, but the fact

that she had one of my books on her shelves in itself marks her as a woman of taste and discernment—which afford compensations.[7]

Thank you for the overwhelmingly complimentary references to me and my writings. I should like to think I deserve them.[8] Between you and me, I suspect I write like a white man because by blood I am white, with a slight and imperceptible dark strain, which in any really civilized country would have no bearing whatever on my life or career, except perhaps as an interesting personal item. I never had any Negro complex. I was born in the North, of parents of my own type whose ancestors had been free for generations, lived there the first nine years of my life and the last forty-three, in the interim having taught school in the south for some years among colored people. With that exception my business life has been spent entirely among white people, many of whom are my personal friends and associates. These things being so, it is not surprising that I should write like a white man.

I have seen it suggested that Israel Zangwill wrote not as a Jew, but as an ordinary Englishman who wrote about the Jews with perfect understanding and sympathy.[9] I think that would describe very well my attitude of mind in writing of colored people. I wrote as an American studying a certain group, which, as in Zangwill's case, happened to be my own, from the standpoint of a student of life and psychology, and not primarily as a propagandist. I sympathized even with the snobbery of my friend Mr. Clayton, which was based on sound reasoning, though it turned out unfortunately in the particular instance.[10]

You will notice that I use the word "colored." I read what you said in your article in *Vogue*, I think it was, or *The New York World* which you sent me, about the use of the word "Negress," and started to write to you at the time.[11] I think the same reasoning applies to the word "Negro", which I regard as not a proper designation for the mixed group to which it is applied. Whether it should be so used is a moot question, but to my mind there is no good reason for employing it except convenience. That definition had never, until southern scholars got on the editorial staffs, been given in the best dictionaries. Its general application took its rise in the rotten race prejudice of the southern whites, whose obvious and unfaltering purpose has been to degrade all persons of their own blood, if mixed in any appreciable degree with that of the darker race, to the level to which their laws, traditions and social customs have assigned the Negro, thereby showing slight respect for the boasted superiority of their own blood. I see no reason why the word "colored" is not sufficiently comprehensive to embrace all types, including the pure Negroes. As used in common parlance, there could be no question at all as to its meaning. Polite people use it now, even in the South, especially as applied to individuals. I enclose copy of a newspaper cutting which is *à propos*.[12]

The use of the word "Negro" is tied up with the "race pride" propaganda, which the white people have cunningly encouraged to make the colored people satisfied with their status and not want to rub elbows with the whites. Our good friends the Negro leaders—black, mulatto and near-white—whose viewpoint you have deferred to, in stressing these things are simply playing into the hands of their race's enemies. I do not question their motives, but simply their judgment, though naturally they want to enlarge and hold together their following,—which is good logic and good business. Marcus Garvey is a case in point.

The "race pride" of white people has been the Negro's greatest curse. A group consciousness which promotes the self-respect of the group, asserts the essential equality of the Negro as one of its sources, and inspires to worthy achievement, is a very desirable thing, but I should hate to see the colored people develop any such exaggerated and unreasonable conceit as constitutes the race pride of some white people. Between us, the only thing that holds the group together in the United States is the prejudice of the whites, without which it would disappear by absorption as rapidly as it is now doing in South America. There would be a real "Flight,"[13] not to say a stampede.

The race question is a difficult and delicate one to discuss; as Miss Fauset suggests in her novel, *There is Confusion*,[14] and I fear that I am only adding to it in somewhat rashly writing such a letter as this even to a man on whose discretion and good taste I am relying. Most of my friends understand my viewpoint, which does not imply any reflection on the Negro race, nor any claim of superiority for the mixed bloods,— points which I am not discussing—but is merely an impersonal protest against an unsound and illogical designation. I am simply writing you thus because of your interest in and writings on the subject. Perhaps if I had written you this letter before you had finished your novel, it would have given you an additional viewpoint to the many which are presented so admirably through the mouths of your characters.

Thanking you again for the book and hoping it may have the success which its brilliancy and obvious honesty deserve—I am informed that it is being widely read and is highly thought of in Cleveland,—I remain

Cordially yours,

Chas. W. Chesnutt.

TLS: NN-Sc

[1]The inscribed copy of Van Vechten's just-published novel is dated "August 1926" (TNF).

[2]Chesnutt was at Idlewild, Mich., by 23 July 1926 when he wrote to Helen C. Moore, relating that the vacation house he was having built "isn't quite finished but we are all living in it comfortably" (OClWHi).

[3]Chesnutt alludes to references made in the novel. For example, the character Adora Boniface remarks: "I can remember when there wasn't any Harlem, when we used to go to Marshall's on Fifty-third Street for a bite to eat and to listen to Florence [Mills]. . . . Well they've had cabarets and cabaret entertainers since then, but I don't think any of them have quite come up to Marshall's and Florence" (p. 82). Also, Adora asks Mary Love, the main character in the first half of the novel, if she had "ever heard of . . . Ernest Hogan, or Williams and Walker, or Cole and Johnson. . ." (p. 83). Florence Mills (1895–1927) was a torch-singer who starred in several Broadway musical productions. Robert ("Bob") Cole (1863–1911) and John Rosamond Johnson (1873–1954) were composers whose songs and musical productions earned them the nickname "Ebony Offenbachs"; see 18 January 1913 to John's brother, James Weldon Johnson. Egbert Austin ("Bert") Williams (1875–1922) teamed with George Nash Walker (1873–1911) in 1895 to perform comedy routines; their successful partnership lasted until 1907. Ernest Hogan (1865–1909), an actor and singer, performed in minstrel and vaudeville shows and was best known for his song "All Coons Look Alike to Me" (1896).

[4]Chesnutt refers to p. 15 in the novel's prologue where Ruby Silver remarks to Anatole Longfellow (the "Scarlet Creeper"): "Does you know what Ah calls dis? . . . Dis place where I met you—Harlem. Ah calls it . . . Nigger Heaven! I jes' nacherly think dis heah is Nigger Heaven." Later in the novel, Byron Kasson makes a variant, negative use of the term in the context of segregated New York City, where African Americans are separately seated in the balconies of theaters ("Nigger Heaven") just as they, perforce, live in a separate neighborhood: "We sit in our places in the gallery of this New York theatre and watch the white world sitting down below in the good seats in the orchestra. Occasionally they turn their faces toward us, their hard, cruel faces, to laugh or sneer, but they never beckon. It never seems to occur to them that Nigger Heaven is crowded, that there isn't another seat, that something has to be done. It doesn't seem to occur to them either . . . that we sit above them, that we can drop things down on them and crush them, that we can swoop down from this Nigger Heaven and take their seats. No, they have no fear of that! Harlem! The Mecca of the New Negro! My God!" (p. 149).

[5]Chesnutt paraphrases "In [God] we live, and move, and have our being" (Acts 17:28).

[6]Byron Kasson, a college-educated would-be writer who becomes an elevator operator, never realizes his potential or fulfills his ambitions; instead he blames his racial makeup and environment for his failure to achieve artistic success. Mary Love, a librarian at the 135th Street branch of the public li-

brary, takes pride in the accomplishments of her culture and would like to identify more closely with the people of Harlem. But she is critical of the propensity for vulgarity shown by the uneducated as well as the affectations of both affluent and intellectual African Americans. A self-conceived lady, she genteelly recoils from what she sees as signs of moral degeneracy manifested in the behavior of a portion of the local population. Like some of Chesnutt's own positively imaged heroines, that is, she is a sensitive, moral, idealistically-oriented, and eminently respectable representative of the best in African-American middle-class life.

[7]In her personal collection of the works of black writers is an inscribed copy of *The Conjure Woman*.

[8]Van Vechten was, indeed, extraordinarily kind when describing Byron Kasson's appreciation of Chesnutt's art: "How much [Byron] admired the cool deliberation of style, the sense of form, but more than all the civilized mind of this man who had surveyed the problems of his race from an Olympian height and had turned them into living and artistic drama. Nothing seemed to have escaped his attention, from the lowly life of the worker on the Southern plantation to the snobbery of the near whites of the North. Chesnutt had surveyed the entire field, calmly setting down what he saw, what he thought and felt about it" (p. 176).

[9]Israel Zangwill (1864–1926) wrote such ethnically-focused novels as *Children of the Ghetto* (1892), *Ghetto Tragedies* (1893), *Dreamers of the Ghetto* (1899), and *Ghetto Comedies* (1907).

[10]Mr. Clayton is the fair-skinned hero of "A Matter of Principle," which first appeared in *The Wife of His Youth and Other Stories of the Color Line*. His "snobbery" is directed against dark-skinned African Americans.

[11]In his February 1926 article for *Vanity Fair* (see 23 February 1926 to Van Vechten, n. 2), Van Vechten defended a white novelist's use of the term "slipshod Negresses" in the face of criticism he received from an African-American book reviewer for doing so. Van Vechten's point was that, surely, the heroine in question fit the bill; further, the reviewer, dubbing the novelist a "Negro hater," appeared to be embracing the untenable notion that there are "no slipshod Negresses" in existence. Van Vechten then explained exactly what the problem was: the novelist "was surely unaware of the unreasonable prejudice existing against the use of the feminine substantive. I myself, who can scarcely be called a 'Negro hater,' have often employed it, because all its synonyms are exceedingly clumsy." Chesnutt does not mention it, but in *Nigger Heaven* Van Vechten again addressed the matter in a footnote keyed to the word "Nigger": "While this informal epithet is freely used by Negroes among themselves, not only as a term of opprobrium, but also actually as a term of endearment, its employment by a white person is always fiercely resented. The word Negress is forbidden under all circumstances" (p. 26).

[12]The article published in an unidentified newspaper is entitled "OHIO PAPERS ADOPT NEW RACE RULES" (TNF). It announces that three dailies in Toledo, O., will not stress the fact of "color" in articles about individuals;

will never identify one's "color" in a headline; will use the term "colored" rather than "Negro" whenever possible, and never refer to a "Negress" or "Black"; and will uniformly capitalize the "N" in "Negro" when use of that word is unavoidable.

[13]Chesnutt alludes to the color line-focused novel *Flight* (1925) by Walter F. White (1893–1955), a dedicated integrationist who became a N.A.A.C.P. staff member in 1918. He served as assistant secretary and then executive secretary when, in 1931, he replaced James Weldon Johnson. *Flight* deals with the desire of light-complexioned African Americans of the middle class to distance themselves from those with more pronounced race-determined traits. It also features a heroine who passes for white but finally decides to acknowledge her racial makeup. Other noteworthy publications by White are the novel *The Fire in the Flint* (1924) and a study of lynching entitled *Rope and Faggot* (1929); see 1 March 1930 to White, n. 1.

[14]Published in 1924.

To W. E. B. Du Bois

October 15, 1926

My Dear Dr. Du Bois:

Replying to your letter of September 25th inclosing manuscripts which I return herewith, and to your follow-up letter of October 13th, would say that I have read the manuscripts submitted several times with mingled feelings.[1] Almost without exception they are well enough written from the standpoint of construction and dramatic interest, but the theme and the story! Mr. Fisher's sketches[2] and Mr. Van Vechten's powerful and vivid delineation of certain tawdry if not sordid aspects of Harlem Negro life are Sunday school stuff compared with the scenes and subjects which these budding realists have selected. If they are writing about the things they know, as a writer ought to, they must have a wide knowledge of the more unsavory aspects of life among colored people.

I should grade the stories about as follows, although this is of course a mere guess:

1. "The Swamp Moccasin." A clean, simple, dramatic and convincing story, written in a snappy style. 2. "The Death Game." A rather ambitious and well constructed story. The descriptions of places are good, the characters vividly drawn and the story well built up to a dramatic climax. 3. "How Farmville Came to Jesus." Characters well drawn, story well constructed. 4. "The Flaming Flame." 5. "The Wall Between." 6. "The New Dawn." 7. "The House of Glass."[3]

Of course, I realize that these are amateur efforts and as such they are promising. If or when the writers learn how to employ effectively the literary expedients of humor and pathos and apply their tragedy to subjects that appeal, some of them will make good writers. I can see the reason for your concern about themes for colored writers. It is not only a matter of editors and readers, but, if it can be considered separately, a matter of literary quality and human appeal.[4]

It would be interesting to know from how many manuscripts these seven were selected, but I presume that will be announced in *The Crisis*. Hoping that I have not delayed the decision, and with best wishes for you and *The Crisis*, I remain

Cordially yours,
Chas. W. Chesnutt.

The Correspondence of W. E. B. Du Bois, ed. Herbert Aptheker (Amherst: University of Massachusetts Press, 1973), vol. 1, 343.

[1] In his 25 September 1926 letter to Chesnutt (OClWHi), Du Bois asked him to serve as one of the judges of seven short stories selected for final evaluation in the Second Amy Spingarn Contest conducted by *The Crisis*.

[2] Rudolph Fisher won the first prize for a short story the previous year; see 3 August 1925 to W. E. B. Du Bois, n. 4.

[3] The first and second place stories were published in *Crisis*: "Swamp Moccasin" by John F. Matheus (1887–1983), 33 (December 1926), 67–69; and "The Death Game" by E. D. Sheen (1902–?), 33 (January 1927), 34–37; (February 1927), 198–201.

[4] Du Bois was then conducting a "Symposium" on "The Negro in Art." Chesnutt's contribution to the series of articles appeared under that title in *Crisis*, 33 (November 1926), 28–29; see *Essays and Speeches*: 490–94.

To Carl Van Vechten

October 27, 1926

My dear Mr. Van Vechten:

I certainly was under the impression that I had seen somewhere a reference by you to the use of the words "Negro" and "Negress," but in view of your disclaimer I must acknowledge myself mistaken and apologize for inflicting upon you the screed embodied in my letter.[1]

I have read the appreciation of your book by James Weldon Johnson in *Opportunity* for October.[2] Mr. Johnson knows what you were writing about, appreciates your viewpoint and your purpose and his commendation is sufficient to offset any amount of adverse criticism from others less well informed.[3]

I see from the advertisement on the cover of the same number of *Opportunity* that the book has had its third large printing, which leads me to hope that the sale will be such that you may not feel that you have wasted your time on an unpopular theme, and that the success of the book may teach other American writers that there are more than the traditional approaches to the race problem.

Cordially yours,

Chas. W. Chesnutt.

TLS: CtY

[1]On 11 September 1926 (Rowfant), Van Vechten replied to Chesnutt's "charming" letter of 7 September: "you are mistaken when you credit me with having written a piece about the use of the word Negress. I have never discussed this subject in print, no do I in Nigger Heaven." Chesnutt's apology, however, was unwarranted. Van Vechten did comment on the two terms. See 7 September 1926 to Carl Van Vechten, n. 11.

[2]James Weldon Johnson read the proof for *Nigger Heaven* for Van Vechten and wrote a favorable review of the novel in "Romance and Tragedy in Harlem," *Opportunity*, 4 (October 1926), 316–17. He concluded that Van Vechten had "taken the material [life in Harlem] had offered him and achieved the most revealing, significant and powerful novel based exclusively on Negro life yet written."

[3]On 11 September, Van Vechten had summarized the critical reception of his novel: "I have had a great many sympathetic and intelligent reviews, a few bad ones and a few violent attacks from the Negro press. What pleases me most is that my friends in Harlem, without exception, admire the book. It is selling everywhere, even in the South, and I am convinced that it will go a long way toward destroying that pernicious idea that Ernest Hogan put in the title of his song: All coons look alike to me."

To Carl Van Vechten

November 19, 1926

Dear Mr. Van Vechten:

I shall be delighted to inscribe any of my books which you have, if you will forward them to me. It is a very small thing to do for one so highly appreciative of my writings.[1]

I note what you say in your first paragraph about *Nigger Heaven* being read by the Negro masses.[2] I agree with you that if that is true it is the first time such a thing has happened. Up until now the colored people have not been extensive book buyers. Books are expensive and do not appeal to any imperative appetite. The money that one would pay for a book will pay for a hair or facial treatment, for some article of clothing, for something to eat or to drink, or some other form of pleasure.

In my own case I am quite sure that my books are more written about and read about than they are read or ever were read by colored people. Otherwise, in view of the very small quantity of existent fiction written by colored writers during the last twenty-five years, my books would not have been out of print. If I felt that it would pay to reprint them, or could get some publisher to feel that way, it would be a simple enough thing.

With best regards,

Sincerely yours,
Chas. W. Chesnutt.

TLS: CtY
[1]Van Vechten asked for this favor on 7 November 1926 (Rowfant).
[2]The first paragraph of Van Vechten's 7 November letter reads thus: "Thank you so much for your letter. I read A Matter of Principle aloud one evening recently to some of the younger Negro intellectuals to their amazement. 'This ought to be reprinted!' they exclaimed, in some awe. Nigger Heaven, by the way, is doing better than ever. Thanks, I think, to the hostile shafts of the coloured press, it is even being read by the Negro masses. I think this is the first time such a thing has happened extensively and may be regarded as a hopeful sign for future Negro authors." The short story "A Matter of Principle" was first published in 1899 in *The Wife of His Youth and Other Stories of the Color Line*.

To Carl Van Vechten

December 14, 1926

Dear Mr. Van Vechten:

I have kept your books an unconscionably long time, and fear I have spoiled them by my abominable handwriting.[1] However, I return them to you in a separate package, and I hope what I have written in them will cover what you had in mind.

I have recently had some very good photographs made, and my partner,[2] who is a very capable and intelligent woman, and has followed our correspondence, suggests that I ought to send you one of them. I should hesitate to do so without knowing whether you cared for it, and I should appreciate very much an inscribed copy of one of your own photographs, if you have it to spare.

That was a very hot crack that Du Bois handed to you in the December *Crisis* in his review of your *Nigger Heaven*.[3] I thought it was quite severe, even from his viewpoint. Walter White was here the other night,[4] and he tells me that he wrote Du Bois a letter criticizing his review.[5]

With the good wishes of the season,

Cordially yours,
Chas. W. Chesnutt.

TLS: CtY

[1]Van Vechten sent copies of his books by Chesnutt for inscriptions; see 19 November 1926 to Carl Van Vechten.

[2]Helen C. Moore.

[3]The withering review appeared in "Books," *Crisis*, 33 (December 1926), 81–82. Du Bois began with the complaint that *Nigger Heaven* is "a blow in the face. It is an affront to the hospitality of black folk and to the intelligence of white." As to "its fidelity to truth and its artistic merit," it displays neither. "Mr. Van Vechten tried to do something bizarre and he certainly succeeded. I read [the novel] through because I had to. But I advise others who are impelled by a sense of duty or curiosity to drop the book gently in the grate and to try the *Police Gazette*."

[4]See 28 December 1926 to Walter F. White, n. 2.

[5]On 17 December 1926 (Rowfant), Van Vechten commented on Du Bois' review. "I do not consider Dr. Du Bois' article a book review; I call it an attack. Although I know him but slightly, our relations have always been pleasant enough and I am at a loss to explain his excess of emotion, particularly in view of what his colleague, James Weldon Johnson, wrote for Opportunity. Nigger Heaven probably has many faults—what book has not?—but if it be so entirely lacking in virtues as Dr. Du Bois would ask his readers to believe, it seems incredible that its reception would have been so warm." See 27 October 1926 to Van Vechten, n. 2, regarding Johnson's review.

To Carl Van Vechten

December 20, 1926

Dear Mr. Van Vechten:

Delighted to receive your photograph which came today. I had seen your face in the papers occasionally, but the pictures did not do you justice. You do not look your age, which I gather from *Who's Who in*

America is forty-six. May you live a long time and write many more good books, and never look any older than you are.

I note what you say about the English reviews of your *Nigger Heaven*, and the questions they and many of the white reviewers in this country have asked.[1] The answer to the first one as to how many of these colored intellectuals there are would be comparatively easy. What can be done to make their way easier is a more difficult question. What ought to be done the colored intellectuals could answer very promptly and clearly. It is up to you and men like you, to say what can be done, and to do it if you feel so disposed, as what you have written to me and elsewhere seems to make plain that you do.

Wishing you a merry Christmas and a happy New Year,

Cordially yours,
Chas. W. Chesnutt

TLS: CtY
[1]In his 17 December letter (see 14 December 1926 to Van Vechten, n. 5), Van Vechten closed with, "By the way, the English reviewers are extremely interesting. They ask the questions that so many of the white reviewers in this country have asked: Are there many of these colored intellectuals? and What can be done to make their way easier?"

To Walter F. White

December 28, 1926

My dear Mr. White:

I have your letter of December 16th, containing your gentle hint.

I am able to supply you at present with only four of my books, to-wit, *The Colonel's Dream*, *The Wife of His Youth*, *The Marrow of Tradition*, and *The Conjure Woman*. *The House Behind the Cedars* I have not yet been able to procure, but I am on the hunt for it. You might inquire yourself of the second hand New York book sellers. Mr. Van Vechten, I imagine, found his copy in that way, as I did not get it for him.[1]

I will autograph and forward the four that I have within a few days.

I enjoyed our evening together very much indeed.[2] Don't say anything about that new novel, for it may not materialize. What you say, however, about the reception which a new book by me would receive encourages me to see what I can do.[3] Thank you for your offer of services, and I will not hesitate to call upon you if I need to.

Why can't one of us write a book of fiction that will sell like Dr. Durant's *Story of Philosophy*? It was published only last spring, and the copy which I have is one of the 72nd thousand.[4] It is a five-dollar book, and I imagine he will get a royalty of at least 20 per cent., which would make $72,000.00—quite a handsome return, one would think, from any kind of a book.

My family join me in holiday greetings to Mrs. White[5] and yourself.

Cordially yours,

Chas. W. Chesnutt.

TLS: NN-Sc

[1]See 19 November 1926 to Carl Van Vechten.

[2]White's visit to Cleveland, O., was reported in "White on Aiken Lynchers," *Cleveland Gazette*, 18 December 1926, [1]. He addressed the local N.A.A.C.P. chapter on 10 December 1926 at Mount Zion Congregational Church, focusing on a lynching in Aiken, S.C., and the unwillingness of local authorities to prosecute the malefactors.

[3]While Chesnutt may have still had hope for the "Paul Marchand, F.M.C." manuscript circulated unsuccessfully to publishers in 1921, he is more likely referring to "The Quarry."

[4]William J. Durant (1885–1981), *The Story of Philosophy: The Lives and Opinions of the Greatest Philosophers* (1926). In his 30 December 1926 reply (NN-Sc), White informed Chesnutt that Durant's book "has now passed the one hundred thousand mark."

[5]Mrs. Leah Gladys Powell White (1895–?).

To Walter F. White

January 5, 1927

My dear Mr. White:

I have your letter of December 30th and am sending you today by parcel post the four books which I have secured for you, namely, *The Conjure Woman, The Wife of His Youth and Other Stories of the Color Line, The Marrow of Tradition*, and *The Colonel's Dream*. I have preceded my autograph in each of the books by a word or two which will add to their association value. I hope you will succeed in finding a copy of *The House Behind the Cedars*. In the meantime I will be looking for one.

With regard to the South Carolina decision,[1] I looked up one of my scrap books and find that I quoted this decision in an article in the

New York *Independent*, published on May 30, 1889.[2] Unfortunately, I did not cite the title of the case in that article. I am pretty sure it was the case of Polly Anderson against some school or county authority.[3] The quotation which I give in the *Independent* article, and which I copied verbatim from the decision at that time was this:

> The definition of the term mulatto, as understood in this state, seems to be vague, signifying generally a person of mixed white or European and Negro parentage, in whatever proportion the blood of the two races may be mingled in the individual. But it is not invariably applicable to every admixture of African blood with the European, nor is one having all the features of the white to be ranked with the degraded class designated by the laws of this state as persons of color, because of some remote taint of the Negro race. The line of distinction, however, is not ascertained by any rule of law. . . . Juries would probably be justified in holding a person to be white in whom the admixture of African blood did not exceed the proportion of one-eighth. But it is in all cases a question for the jury, to be determined by them upon the evidence of features and complexion, afforded by inspection, the evidence of the rank and station in society occupied by the party. The only rule which can be laid down by the courts is that where there is a distinct admixture of Negro blood, the individual is to be denominated a mulatto or person of color.

In a later case the Court said:

> The question whether persons are colored or white, where color or feature are doubtful, is for the jury to decide by reputation, by reception into society, and by their exercise of the privileges of the white man, as well as by admixture of blood.

Our law library in Cleveland does not have a Digest of South Carolina decisions. There ought to be one in the New York Law Library, if there is such a thing as a South Carolina Digest, in which it would undoubtedly appear, and could be found by looking under the words "Negro, Mulatto, colored persons, schools," or other subjects that might suggest themselves. I am pretty sure I have a memorandum of the case somewhere. I will look further in my library and see if I can find it.[4]

I note with interest what you say about the novel, and I am going ahead with it, but would rather have nothing said about it at present, lest it might fall by the wayside.[5]

Please give my regards to Mrs. White and Jane.[6] I hope to make their acquaintance in the near future.

Yours sincerely,
Chas. W. Chesnutt.

P.S. Enclosed please find statement.[7]
C.W.C.

TLS, with autograph postscript: NN-Sc

[1]In a postscript to his 30 December 1926 letter (NN-Sc), White explained what he had done following a previous communication with Chesnutt concerning a South Carolina legal decision: "I took up with an attorney in South Carolina the school mater [*sic*] and he has replied that he went to the Supreme Court Library and searched the old cases from 1840 to 1880 but was unable to find the decision. I wonder if you can give me a little more information on this case. There were no public schools in South Carolina until the Constitution of 1868 provided for them. At least that is the attorney's understanding of the history of the public schools of the State."

[2]"What Is a White Man?" *Independent*, 41 (30 May 1889), 5–6; see *Essays and Speeches*: 68–73.

[3]State v. Davis, S.C. 2 Bailey 558 (1831).

[4]There is no record of Chesnutt having identified this decision.

[5]Chesnutt refers to the manuscript entitled "The Quarry." White had encouraged Chesnutt on 20 December 1926: "I hope you won't let anything keep you from doing that novel. The more I think of it, the more certain am I that you could do a story which would be of tremendous value as well as of great beauty and importance. . . . Even if it should not measure up to the previous ones in merit (this is a contingency of which I have no fear) the market has so greatly increased since your other books were published, I think it would bring you at least a part of the reward which you so richly deserve."

[6]Jane White, Walter's daughter.

[7]On 30 December 1926, White thanked Chesnutt for securing the four books to be sent to him, adding: "Be sure and send me the bill." Chesnutt enclosed a statement (TNF) specifying the cost of each item: *The Marrow of Tradition*, $3.50; *The Colonel's Dream*, $2.15; *The Wife of His Youth and Other Stories of the Color Line*, $3.75; and *The Conjure Woman*, $1.50. An additional charge of 29¢ resulted in a total of $11.19. On 13 January 1927 (TNF), White sent Chesnutt a check "as per your bill."

To W. E. B. Du Bois

January 11, 1927

My dear Dr. Du Bois:

I have your interesting letter with reference to the Charles W. Chesnutt Honorarium. The instance of Mr. Van Vechten which you cite, and the various other prizes in the awarding of which you and other editors in New York have had a hand, have all been presented in the name of individuals who have put up the money. I am not in a position just at present to offer any prize in any amount for anything.[1] If I had been making any money out of my writings of recent years, I might feel disposed to offer such a prize myself. But since I cannot, the question arises can I, with proper self-respect permit my name to be used in that connection? If I were dead, like most of the authors of the last generation, the situation would be different. You would be honoring one of the worthy dead. I would like to read your argument in connection with this matter, if you think it worth while, before I give you permission to use my name.[2]

I take this opportunity to answer your letter in regard to the Milholland busts.[3] Much the same argument applies. For many years I made more money and lived better than any colored man in my city. I spent my money freely in racial causes. But times have changed, I have grown old, and my earning capacity has declined, and there are today, I imagine, a goodly number of colored men in the city who earn more money than I do. I am not in a position just now to make any substantial contribution to this very worthy object, but when I get out of a certain snarl that I am in just at present, I may be able to make a small contribution.

I had a nice visit with Walter White when he was here at Cleveland a couple of weeks ago, and we talked over many subjects.[4] He is a brilliant fellow, and a worthy collaborator even of yourself. With regards,

Sincerely yours,

TCU: TNF

[1]On 4 January 1927 (TNF), Du Bois wrote: "It is proposed to offer some special prizes for the best articles, published in *The Crisis* during the year 1927. I am writing to ask you if you will permit these prizes to be called the 'Charles Waddell Chesnutt honorarium.' Mr. Carl Van Vechten has offered another colored magazine a prize of this sort and we do not want to lag behind. Two persons, Mr. James Weldon Johnson and myself, have promised to give $50 each and I hope to find five others so as to offer $200 for the best article, $100 for the second, and $50 for the third. The matter of the judges for these can be taken up later. First, I want your consent for the naming of the fund." The competition funded by Van Vechten was conducted in *Opportunity*; see "Award for Published Contributions," *Opportunity*, 5 (January 1927), 6.

[2]Chesnutt agreed to allow his name to be used. Du Bois thanked him on 12 January 1927 (TNF) and added that the award would be described as "an Honorarium and not as a mere prize. I shall not expect any contribution, unless, of course, you get suddenly rich." Du Bois announced "The Charles Waddell Chesnutt Honorarium, $350" in *Crisis*, 33 (February 1927), 193: "In

honor of the first and still foremost novelist of Negro descent in America, seven 'Friends of THE CRISIS' have offered us the sum of $350 to be paid for the three best contributions published in THE CRISIS during the year 1927," as determined by the votes of the subscribers. The three prizes were for $200, $100, and $50; and the winners were announced in "The Charles Waddell Chesnutt Honorarium, 1927," *Crisis*, 35 (March 1928), 96. First place went to Effie Lee Newson (1885–1979) for the monthly "Little Page" column she contributed to the magazine. Receiving $100 was W. E. Matney for "Teaching Business," *Crisis*, 34 (July 1927), 157, 177–78. Zona Gale (1874–1938) took the third prize for the poem "Medals," *Crisis*, 34 (September 1927), 221, 242.

[3]John E. Milholland (1860–1925) was a businessman, writer, and founding member of the N.A.A.C.P. Four reproductions of a bronze bust of Milholland, each costing $250, were to be produced and placed in the New York City offices of the N.A.A.C.P. and at three African-American universities. Du Bois solicited contributions for subscribers in "Lest We Forget," *Crisis*, 33 (February 1927), 181–82.

[4]See 28 December 1926 to Walter F. White.

To Fred Charles

March 23, 1927

Dear Mr. Charles:

I read with interest and pleasure your very flattering "Write-up" in the *Plain Dealer*.[1] Several gentlemen have called me up, commenting on the fact that a newspaper gave me so much space while I was still alive, and many others of my friends have made favorable comment. My family was very much pleased with it.

Our four o'clock tea business has picked up since your article appeared. In fact, we have had quite a rush. Miss Moore and I suggest that you come around to the office some afternoon about that time and have a dish of tea.[2]

Cordially yours,
Charles W. Chesnutt

Pioneer: 297–98

[1]Fred Charles (1887–1947) was a Cleveland journalist and assistant federal works administrator who interviewed Chesnutt at his home on 16 March. His unsigned "Muse Lures Pencil of Chesnutt [*sic*] Anew" appeared in the Cleveland *Plain Dealer*, 17 March 1927, 1, 4. Subtitled "Novelist of First Decade Gives Signs of Returning to Writing from Court Work," it began by calling attention to Chesnutt's not having completely withdrawn from fiction writing. "A growing pile of penciled manuscript on his library table, at which

he has spent most of a week's confinement by illness, gave promise yesterday of a return to the field of letters of Charles W. Chesnutt, Cleveland's foremost literary man of a generation ago." The interview dealt with Chesnutt having come to Cleveland to work as a stenographer for the Nickel Plate Railroad, his flirtation with a legal practice, his opinion of Cleveland mayor Tom L. Johnson, his advocacy of inter-racial marriage as a solution for the race problem, his fame as a writer as of 1905, and his turning away from the writing of books after 1905 for financial reasons.

²Charles closed his article by noting that Chesnutt's business office is in the Union Trust Building and is "one of the few in Cleveland where tea is served each afternoon punctually at 4."

To William J. Walls

April 21, 1927

My dear Bishop Walls:

Practically ever since you saw me in Cleveland I have been confined at home with an attack of gastric influenza, which entirely incapacitated me, and I am just beginning to crawl down to my office to attend to some imperative matters.¹ I have got so far behind with my own work that I fear that I shall not be able to do anything on the paper about Doctor Price.² The fact of the matter is that I was so slightly acquainted with Doctor Price that I am quite sure I would not be able to do either him or myself justice in anything I might write, and I therefore, regretfully return you herewith the manuscripts which you have sent to me, with the hope that you may be able to find some one else who can do the subject justice. I have been away from North Carolina so long and my memory is such that I am entirely out of touch with events of forty years ago.

Hoping that my failure will not embarrass you and that you may get that part of the work done much better than I could do it, if you do not wish to do it yourself, which I am sure would be better than anyone else could do,³ I remain,

Cordially yours,

TCU: TNF

¹William J. Walls (1885–1975) was a North Carolina-born bishop of the A.M.E.Z. church (1924–75) and formerly the editor of its periodical *Star of Zion* (1920–24).

²Requested was an article on the Reverend Joseph Charles Price (1854–93), a widely celebrated public speaker dedicated to the improvement of the Afri-

can American's lot by means of education. He was a founder of Zion Wesley College (1882)—renamed Livingstone College as its focus shifted from the training of missionaries for Africa to the development of a liberal arts curriculum. *Star of Zion* was, at this time, conducting a fund-raising campaign for the erection of a monument honoring Price.

[3]Chesnutt subsequently changed his mind and sent Walls a manuscript. See 5 August 1927 to William J. Walls.

To William J. Walls

August 5, 1927

Dear Bishop Walls:—

Enclosed please find the manuscript which Mrs. Chesnutt promised you. I am sorry to have delayed sending it for so long, but we have been very busy in the office and did not get around to attend to it until today.[1]

In reply to your letter of August 3rd, received this morning, will say we do not have a copy of Mr. Alexander's address at the Christian Endeavor Convention, as he furnished a manuscript to the secretary, and we only reported the extemporaneous speeches.[2]

The literature regarding Dr. Alexander has not yet reached the office, but I thank you for sending it, and will read it with pleasure.

Yours very truly,

TCU: TNS

[1]The manuscript was entitled "Joseph C. Price, Orator and Educator"; see 21 April 1927 to William J. Walls. The essay was not published in the periodical edited by Walls, *Star of Zion*; it was intended by Walls for publication in a book devoted to Price's life and works. See 29 August 1927 to Walls.

[2]The International Society of Christian Endeavor, a youth organization founded in 1881, held its annual conference in Cleveland from 2 to 7 July 1927. The Reverend Will W. Alexander (1884–1956) of Atlanta, Ga., was the director of Atlanta's Committee on Inter-racial Co-operation. On 6 July he delivered an address entitled "Youth and Race Friendship."

To Edwin J. Chesnutt

August 23, 1927

. . . The baby[1] announced last evening at the dinner table that he was "gonna wite a long letta to Unca Ned." Although his intentions were praiseworthy, I knew he had bitten off more than he could chew, so I am writing a letter in his place.

I received your letter at Idlewild[2] inclosing the cutting from the Chicago paper, telling of Mr. Mencken's views on the future of the colored race. I put away the cutting in order to talk it over with you.[3] It is probably in a drawer or pigeon hole of the desk in the living room.

I am sorry I could not wait to see you, as I like to see my only son at least once a year. Perhaps you will find it convenient to come and see us in Cleveland.

I left some bass in the lake for you with the necessary equipment to take them out. However, fishing for bass is a business in itself. I had better luck than last year, but not anything to boast of as it was.

I hope you will enjoy yourself in Idlewild, and will drop me a line from time to time when the spirit moves you. . . .

Pioneer: 298–99

[1]John Chesnutt Slade.

[2]In June the Chesnutts began their vacation at their summer house in Idlewild, Mich. With his daughter Dorothy and his grandson John, Chesnutt returned to Cleveland on 9 August to attend to business matters. Mrs. Chesnutt and daughter Helen remained at Idlewild through August.

[3]The reference may be to a clipping of the unsigned "H. L. Mencken Says New York Color Line Has Gone to Stay," *Chicago Defender*, 23 July 1927, 1–2—which reprinted a portion of a syndicated article by Mencken (see citation below). If so, the matter for discussion between Chesnutt and his son was that New York City, according to Mencken, has become "so cosmopolitan a town that all its old social distinctions and prejudices are in decay and can never be revived. . . . Any one who is presentable may go anywhere. Some of the current Aframerican pets are highly presentable; others are surely not. The latter, no doubt, will soon return to the Harlem whence they came, but the former will survive." Mencken related that "educated Negroes" he knows think that the "social attentions" now being paid the "Colored brethren" who add "a great deal to the charm" of New York represent "only a transient fad." He disagrees: "My belief is that New York, having taken them in, will be very loath to lose them." If the clipping was instead the complete article— "The Colored Brethren," *Chicago Sunday Tribune*, 17 July 1927, Part 7, 1— Chesnutt and his son found Mencken offering as well a less flattering series of observations on "the educated Negro" and his "modest" accomplishments in the fields of music (spirituals remain "naive and crude, like hoe cake") and literature. The poets "have done very little to justify the excessive hospitality with which they have been received"; in prose fiction "there is the same tale to tell"; and even "on the subject of their race's wrongs, they do not write as

well, taking one with another, as the white scriveners who tackle the same subject." Mencken concludes, "It may be that [the educated Negro's] greatest successes during the next generation will be made, not in the arts, but in business. There he seems to be making very rapid progress, and it is no longer factitious and transitory. Booker T. Washington, whose memory is not venerated by the Negro intellectuals, was probably wiser than they think."

To Oscar W. Baker

August 24, 1927.

My dear Mr. Baker:

I have a letter from Mrs. Chesnutt in which she tells me that you are at Idlewild.[1] I regret that I was called away before the grand rush and therefore missed you. She tells me you are interested in my views on Mr. Van Vechten's book *Nigger Heaven*. I was shocked by the name of the book, and there were other respects in which it is not above criticism. James Weldon Johnson speaks in highest praise of it.[2] Dr. Du Bois knocked it very hard as a caricature and a libel on the race.[3] Personally I am disarmed for any very drastic criticism, from the fact that Mr. Van Vechten treated me so handsomely in the book. I am referred to in flattering terms in three or four places, and several pages are devoted to an analysis of one of my stories.[4]

As to the kind of colored people that Mr. Van Vechten selects for his characters, he writes about the same kind of white people in his other novels. In fact, both in theme and treatment the book is quite a Van Vechten work.

In a letter to him I criticized among other things his use of the word "Negro" as applied to all people of color.[5] In a letter which he wrote me in reply[6] he says, "I have employed the word 'Negro' in that book for the reason that the group I was writing about almost insist on the use of that word. The title, of course, is an ironic slap in the face of the white public. 'These are the human beings you call Niggers', is what it says in effect. I have had a great many sympathetic and intelligent reviews, a few bad ones, and a few violent reviews from the Negro press. What pleased me most is that my friends in Harlem, without exception, admired the book. It is selling everywhere, even in the South, and I am convinced that it will go a long way toward destroying that pernicious idea that Ernest Hogan put in the title of his song 'All Coons look alike to me'." . . .

TCU, incomplete: TNF

[1]Oscar W. Baker (1879–?) practiced law in Bay City, Mich., and was a locally prominent Republican.

[2]See 27 October 1926 to Carl Van Vechten, n. 2.

[3]See 14 December 1926 to Van Vechten, n. 3.

[4]See 7 September 1926 to Van Vechten, n. 8.

[5]See 7 September 1926 to Van Vechten.

[6]See 27 October 1926 to Van Vechten, n. 3.

To William J. Walls

August 29, 1927

My dear Bishop Walls:

I have not sent you a photograph sooner for the reason that I was trying to get a better one, but the man to whom I lent it has not returned it, and I am sending you another which is of comparatively recent date and will not slander me. Hope you will be able to make it do. The photographer did n't retouch it so as to bring out my hair very well, but probably the man who makes the plate can retouch that up a little.

I hope I have not delayed the production of your work, and that you found my part of it satisfactory.[1] If I have been of any use to you, I am very glad.

Also wish to acknowledge receipt of the package of literature in reference to the Inter-racial Committee or Committees. It sounds very good and will undoubtedly, if carried out, prove of value. Although I notice that the gentlemen who write make it very plain and distinct that everything must be done in accordance with the established Southern policy, which of course includes the various kinds of discrimination on railroads, railroad stations and other public places which are, after all, perhaps more important than some other things, or at least more keenly resented.

If I could have a copy of the book to which I have contributed, I should very much appreciate it.[2]

Fraternally yours,

TCU: TNF

[1]See 5 August 1927 to Walls, n. 1.

[2]Chesnutt did not receive a copy of Walls' *Joseph Charles Price: Educator and Race Leader*, which was not published until 1943. On pp. 378–81, Walls included only six paragraphs (edited to seven) of the much longer essay that

appears *in toto* in *Essays and Speeches*: 554–65. The photograph sent to Walls was used for a portrait captioned "Charles Waddell Chestnut [*sic*], Famous Negro Novelist"; see the leaf tipped-in between pp. 296 and 297.

To Mayo Fesler

October 19, 1927.

My dear Mr. Fesler:

I have your letter of October 17th with reference to Mr. Clayborne George, a candidate for the office of councilman.[1]

I have known Mr. George for several years and have a very high opinion of him, and I have never heard anything to his discredit.[2] He is better educated than the average city councilman, is a member of the Cuyahoga County Bar in good standing, and is a man of ability and character. I have known him to do, for the sake of the principle involved, a thing which seemed at the time to be very greatly to his material disadvantage. I believe he would make an excellent councilman, and would represent creditably an element of the population which has not been over-represented in previous councils; and while public officials are not supposed to be chosen to represent special groups, when one comes from a certain group it is desirable that he be a worthy representative of it.

I think the Citizens League would make no mistake in recommending the nomination and election of Clayborne George as councilman.

Yours very truly,

Chas. W. Chesnutt

TCS: TNF

[1]Mayo Fesler was an officer of the Cleveland Municipal Association (see 31 December 1914 to Fesler), which became the Civic League, and he was now the Director of the latest manifestation of the same group: the Cleveland Citizens League, which evaluated candidates for public office and made recommendations to voters and to government officials responsible for appointments.

[2]Clayborne George (1888–1970) was graduated from Howard Law School in 1917. He served as a first lieutenant during World War I, came to Cleveland in 1920, and became actively involved in the affairs of the African-American community. He served as the local N.A.A.C.P. president (1924–26), founded the John M. Harlan Law Club, and was elected to the City Council in 1927. In 1934, he became a member of Cleveland's Civil Service Commission and served in that capacity until 1969.

To Emmett J. and Eleonora Baker Scott

November 22, 1927

Dear Dr. and Mrs. Scott:

We only learned some little time after the event of the death of your beautiful and talented daughter, Clarissa,[1] and we were just about to write to you when our minds were sidetracked by what came near being the same thing in our family. Our daughter Helen was taken to a hospital two weeks ago last Sunday and operated upon for the removal of a ruptured appendix. Peritonitis supervened and for the first ten days there was grave doubt of her recovery, but for the last week she has been improving slowly and, barring any unforeseen contingency, will make a good recovery.

It is too bad that these things should happen to those that we can least spare, but, as some one has said, "Death loves a shining mark,"[2] and we can only be resigned, and console ourselves with the thought that we help to make them happy while they are with us.

Rest assured that you have our deepest sympathy in your affliction.

With best wishes,

Cordially yours,

TCU: TNF

[1]Emmett J. Scott was, at this time, Secretary-Treasurer and Business Manager of Howard University. Born while Scott was employed at Tuskegee University, his daughter Clarissa Scott Delany (1901–27) was a promising essayist, poet, and member of Phi Beta Kappa. Graduated from Wellesley College in 1923, she taught at Dunbar High School in the District of Columbia until 1926 when she became Director of the Joint Committee on Negro Child Study in New York City. She died of a "lung infection"—possibly tuberculosis.

[2]Edward Young (1683–1765), *The Complaint or, Night Thoughts on Life, Death, and Immortality* (1742–45), Book 5, line 1011.

To Edwin J. Chesnutt

March 20, 1928

. . . Just returned this morning from a trip to Washington and New York. I went to Washington to appear before a Senate Committee in opposition to a certain bill.[1] Stopped over night with Ethel[2] and found them all well. . . .

In New York I met James Weldon Johnson, who introduced me to some publishers relative to certain designs I have upon the reading world. I also called on Carl Van Vechten at his apartment. I had had some very interesting correspondence with him about the time of the appearance of his *Nigger Heaven*, and found him a very amiable and affable gentleman.[3] He remembered in the course of the conversation that he had met you in Chicago at the home of a Dr. Glenn, if I recall the name correctly.

The family are all well. Helen has recovered superficially from her distressing experience and is back at work, although I am not sure that she is yet entirely out of the woods.[4] They all join me in love to you. . . .

Pioneer: 301–302

[1]Chesnutt and Harry E. Davis, under the aegis of the Cleveland Chamber of Commerce, went to Washington to represent African-American labor in its opposition to the Shipstead Anti-Injunction Bill under consideration in Congress. Chesnutt spoke before the Senate Judiciary Committee, according to a report from Davis in "Shipstead Bill," *Cleveland Gazette*, 24 March 1928, [1]. He objected to criminal (versus civil law) protection being extended to tangible property and argued that African Americans in particular would suffer since the bill strengthened the power of labor unions from which they were excluded because of race.

[2]Daughter Ethel Chesnutt Williams.

[3]Carl Van Vechten lived at 150 West 55th Street. See Chesnutt's letters to Van Vechten: 7 September 1926, 27 October 1926, 19 November 1926, 14 December 1926, and 20 December 1926.

[4]Daughter Helen M. Chesnutt underwent an operation for appendicitis and was subsequently treated for peritonitis; see 22 November 1927 to Emmett J. and Eleonora Baker Scott.

To Harry C. Bloch

June 8, 1928

Dear Mr. Bloch:

I am working on my novel and making very good headway.[1] If I said anything which justified you in gathering that I would have the book finished in six or eight weeks, I must have spoken without due thought.

I have the action of the story practically worked out, the characters well defined, most of the important situations outlined, and several hundred pages written. But it has to be pruned, padded, and polished, and so forth, which is the principal part of the work on anything that I write. I don't believe I can have it ready for anything earlier than fall publication. I hope to be able to submit it to you sometime during the summer.[2]

It is entirely agreeable to me that you keep the manuscript of "Paul Marchand," as you suggest in your letter. With kind regards and thanks for your friendly encouragement, believe me,

Cordially yours,

TCU: TNF

[1]Harry C. Bloch was an editor at the book publishing firm Alfred A. Knopf, Inc. Chesnutt is referring to "The Quarry." In his 6 April 1928 letter to Chesnutt (TNF), James Weldon Johnson related that he had called Bloch about a manuscript submitted by Chesnutt. Bloch told Johnson that he had already received and written Chesnutt about it, referring to "Paul Marchand, F.M.C." rather than "The Quarry." See 20 December 1921 to Alfred A. Knopf, Esq., regarding a previous submission of "Marchand" to Knopf (*i.e.*, to the publisher himself rather than his firm).

[2]Alfred A. Knopf, Inc., rejected "The Quarry"; see 9 February 1929 to Harry C. Bloch.

To Alta M. Bien

June 8, 1928

Dear Miss Bien:

We are enjoying the beautiful flowers which came with your congratulations on our fiftieth wedding anniversary.[1] I can imagine marriages where fifty years would seem like an eternity, but, except when I look at my children and see my gray hairs in the mirror, it does n't seem any time at all, and Mrs. Chesnutt admits that she has n't found it very tiresome; and we are both willing to hang on a while longer yet.

We are fortunate in having a daughter who can gather around her such loyal and devoted friends as Helen's are.[2] Thanking you again and still some more,

Cordially yours,

Chas. W. & Susan U. Chesnutt

TCS: TNF

[1]The Chesnutts were married on 6 June 1878. Alta M. Bien (?–1976) was a close friend of daughter Helen M. Chesnutt and a colleague at Central High School.

[2]The following summer, Helen and Alta would vacation together in Europe. See 15 July 1929 to Ethel Chesnutt Williams.

To James Weldon Johnson

June 11, 1928

My dear Mr. Johnson:

I received your telegram on Friday and answered it on Saturday, expressing my appreciation of the honor and stating that I hoped to be at Los Angeles in person.[1]

I assure you and wish you to assure the committee that I appreciate very highly the honor conferred upon me. I was under the impression that the medal was awarded for current achievement, and am all the more pleased because the committee seems to have made it retro-active in my case. However, I shall try to finish my novel and bring my work a little more down to date.[2]

Mrs. Chesnutt, who has never been to the Pacific Coast,[3] has decided that it has been the dream of her life to visit California and that this is her opportunity. As a married man, you know what this means, and she will accompany me.

A personal question: On these occasions, what kind of clothes are usually worn by the candidate? Is a dinner jacket permissible, or is one supposed to wear a long cut-away or a dress suit? I don't do this every year and I want to do it right.[4]

Is it necessary to make arrangements in advance with regard to entertainment, or will some committee take charge of that, or just what is the situation in that regard?[5]

Please advise me as promptly as possible so that I may know what to do.

Yours cordially,
Charles W. Chesnutt

Pioneer: 303

[1]On 8 June 1928 (TNF), James Weldon Johnson sent Chesnutt a telegram announcing that the Spingarn Medal Award Committee of the N.A.A.C.P. had chosen him as its 1928 recipient for his "pioneer services as a literary artist and [his] distinguished career as a public spirited citizen." The award would be presented on 3 July 1928 in Los Angeles by Lieutenant Governor of California Buron R. Fitts (1895–1973).

[2]Chesnutt refers to the manuscript entitled "The Quarry."

[3]Chesnutt and his daughter Helen visited the west coast during the summer of 1921.

[4]Johnson responded in a letter of 13 June 1928 (TNF) that a dinner jacket would be appropriate dress.

[5]On 13 June, Johnson explained that a committee was in charge of housing

and entertainment; it could either get Chesnutt a room at the Hotel Somerville or in "a nice private home."

To Joel E. Spingarn

September 6, 1928.

My dear Dr. Spingarn:

I have already thanked the National Association for the Advancement of Colored People and the Award Committee for the beautiful medal presented to me at Los Angeles, but I also wish to thank you personally as the original donor.[1] It is a beautiful work of art and means a great deal and I prize it very highly.

I often think of the delightful week I spent on your farm at Amenia.[2] Besides the feast of reason and the flow of soul[3] and the good company, I recall the good fare and especially the cream which was so thick that one could almost cut it with a knife. I also recall your visit to the Rowfant Club[4] and hope that we may meet again, more than once.

Your brother Arthur and his wife,[5] of whom I saw much at Los Angeles and en route thither, are delightful people and I enjoyed their society very much.[6]

Thanking you again, I remain

Cordially yours,

TCU: TNF

[1]See 11 June 1928 to James Weldon Johnson.

[2]See 1 September 1916 to Joel E. Spingarn, n. 1.

[3]Quotation of Alexander Pope (1688–1744), "Satire I," Book 2 of *Epistles and Satires of Horace Imitated* (1733–38), lines 127–28: "There St. John mingles with my friendly bowl / The feast of reason and the flow of soul."

[4]Spingarn's visit to the Rowfant Club was, apparently, an informal one, perhaps arranged by Chesnutt. Anthony W. C. Phelps, archivist of the Club, has found no information concerning such a visit. Spingarn was in Cleveland on 25 January 1914 for a mass meeting of the local branch of the N.A.A.C.P., as was noted in "Should Fight! Be Radical," *Cleveland Gazette*, 31 January 1914, [1].

[5]Mrs. Marion Mayer Spingarn (?–1958).

[6]Chesnutt thanked Arthur B. Spingarn for his kind attentions on 6 September 1928 (TNF), enclosing a copy of his 3 July 1928 Spingarn Medal acceptance speech (see *Essays and Speeches*: 510–15).

To William E. Easton

October 5, 1928.

Dear Mr. Easton:

I have been reading from time to time the copy of your *Christophe*, which you were good enough to give me while I was in Los Angeles last summer.[1] I have read it carefully so as not to miss anything and I wish to congratulate you on a very fine piece of literary work. On reading your book, I have been able to visualize quite clearly the situation which existed during and immediately following the Revolutionary Period in Haiti.

Some months ago I picked up at a second-hand book store a copy of Lamartine's *Toussaint L'Ouverture*,[2] and I find your *Christophe* a very good companion volume. I like the illustrations in your book, they are very beautifully done and worthy of the text.

The liberties of Haiti just at the moment seem to be more or less in a state of confusion. The trouble with Haiti—well, we all know what the trouble has been with Haiti. What it has needed has been a spirit of patriotism, which would make all the people work together all the time for the common good. Too many of their so-called statesmen and leaders never seem to look beyond themselves. Whether the intervention and administration of the United States will work out to their ultimate advantage, is yet to be seen.[3] I am sure we all hope that it may.

Thanking you again for your little book which I will give an honored place in my library, I am

Cordially yours,

TCU: TNF

[1]William E. Easton (1861–?) published *Christophe; a Tragedy in Prose of Imperial Haiti* in 1911. It deals with Henri Christophe (1767–1820), who was born a slave in Grenada and became a lieutenant to Pierre Dominique Toussaint L'Ouverture (1743–1803) in the 1791 Haitian revolution against the French. Following Toussaint L'Ouverture's capture and imprisonment in France, Christophe and Jean Jacques Dessalines (1758–1806), another former aide to Toussaint, drove out the French. Christophe then turned on his ally and, with Alexandre Pétion (1770–1818), assassinated Dessalines, who had proclaimed himself Jacques I, Emperor of Haiti. They divided the island into a northern state and southern republic. The former was ruled by Christophe and the latter by Pétion. In 1811 Christophe became Henri I, King of Haiti, and began a reign of terror there. He fatally shot himself in 1820—with a silver bullet. Prior to the publication of *Christophe*, Easton had published *Dessalines, A Dramatic Tale: A Single Chapter from Haiti's History* (1893). Re-

garding Chesnutt's familiarity with this other work, see 6 May 1930 to William E. Easton.

[2]Alphonse de Lamartine (1790–1869), *Toussaint L'Ouverture: Poème Dramatique en Cinq Actes et en Verse* (1850).

[3]The United States intervened in debt-ridden and politically unstable Haiti's affairs in 1915 for the proclaimed end of stabilizing a country within its sphere of influence and preventing rival nations from bringing it under their control. Chesnutt is referring specifically to the extraordinary number of coups that had occurred since 1806 and the self-serving behavior of each of the successive heads of government. American control was not relinquished until 1930.

To Georgia Douglas Johnson

February 2, 1929.

Dear Mrs. Johnson,

Thank you for your letter of January 16th.[1] I fear I am not the proper person to thank for the Chesnutt award to which you refer. The award was not offered by me, but was conceived and financed in my honor by some gentlemen connected with the N.A.A.C.P. as the "Charles W. Chesnutt Honorarium." I think the thanks should go to the *Crisis* direct, or to Mr. James Weldon Johnson, who was I believe the prime mover in the matter.[2] I am very glad indeed that you were one of the winners.[3]

I have before me an item in the *Cleveland Gazette*, copied from some eastern paper in reference to your *An Autumn Love Cycle*, quoting what the publishers say about it, and what Mr. Braithwaite has said.[4] I concur in all of it, and I am sure that the new book, which I shall take occasion to read very soon, will measure up to if not exceed in excellence your former writings.

I remember your visit to Cleveland and our interesting conversation, and your trip to my home. I hope I may have the pleasure of meeting you some other time.

Houghton Mifflin Company are printing a new edition of my *The Conjure Woman*, with a flattering foreword by Major J. E. Spingarn.[5]

My family join me in compliments and best wishes.

Sincerely yours,

TCU: TNF

[1]Georgia Douglas Johnson (1886–1966) was the author of *The Heart of a Woman and Other Poems* (1918), *Bronze: A Book of Verse* (1920), and

Plume: A Play in One Act (1927). On 16 January (TNF), she expressed her gratitude for "the Chesnutt award which it was my good fortune to receive some time ago. It is a splendid gesture on your part and I did not hope to be fortunate as a winner." She recalled a pleasant visit to Cleveland, "my talk with you and also my trip to your wonderful home."

²See 11 January 1927 to W. E. B. Du Bois, nn. 1 and 2.

³Since 1927 the nature of the competition had changed, as was announced in "Krigwa, 1928," *Crisis*, 35 (March 1928), 76. Instead of three awards being made for works published in one year, Charles Waddell Chesnutt honoraria of $25, $15, and $10 would be given monthly between April 1928 and March 1929. Johnson placed second in July for the poem "Hope," *Crisis*, 35 (June 1928), 196.

⁴*An Autumn Love Cycle* was published in 1928. Chesnutt read William S. Braithwaite's estimate of Johnson as "the foremost woman poet of her race" in "'An Autumn Love Cycle'," *Cleveland Gazette*, 2 February 1929, [1].

⁵Houghton Mifflin Company informed Chesnutt on 14 September 1928 (OClWHi) that *The Conjure Woman* was to be brought back into print.

To Houghton Mifflin Company

February 2, 1929.

Attention Mr. Greenslet

Dear Mr. Greenslet:

Thank you very much for the advance copy of *The Conjure Woman*,¹ the receipt of which I should have acknowledged sooner, but that I have been laid up at home sick for a couple of weeks and I am only just now down at my office.

The format is very pleasing, indeed, and Dr. Spingarn's foreword is quite flattering.² I like that black cover and the use of the title page from the old limited edition,³ which lends an additional note of distinction to the book.

I have seen several references to the new edition in newspapers, and was interviewed last night by the literary editor of *The Cleveland Press*, so I presume the edition has been formally announced.⁴

I could use several more copies, personally, if you can send them. I wish, for instance, to send an autographed copy to the editor of a colored newspaper, in Cincinnati, a great admirer of mine,⁵ whose influence would undoubtedly help sell the book.

I thank you for putting me on the literary map again, and hope the sale of the new edition will justify your enterprise.

Sincerely yours,

TCU: TNF

[1] See 2 February 1929 to Georgia Douglas Johnson, n. 5.

[2] Joel E. Spingarn.

[3] Chesnutt refers to the title page of the "Large-Paper" edition in a special binding, as distinguished from the trade edition also published in 1899. Manufactured were 150 copies for subscription sale principally to bibliophiles in Cleveland.

[4] The interview and review of *The Conjure Woman* by Elrick B. Davis (1895–1960) appeared in "Reading and Writing," *Cleveland Press*, 2 February 1929, 3. Harry C. Smith puffed Chesnutt in "'Conjure Woman' Reprinted," *Cleveland Gazette*, 2 February 1929, [1]: "'The Conjure Woman', earliest novel [*sic*] of Atty. Charles W. Chesnutt of Cleveland, O., who received the Spingarn Medal, last year, for his pioneering in this field, has just been republished by the Houghton, Mifflin Co., with a foreword by Major J. E. Spingarn. In his Foreword, Mr. Spingarn says Mr. Chesnutt's novels 'are the first in which an Afro-American has in any real sense portrayed the fortunes of his race', that 'Mr. Chesnutt was the first Afro-American novelist' and that 'he is still the best.'"

[5] Wendell Phillips Dabney was the editor and publisher of the Cincinnati *Union* from its inception in 1907 to its demise in 1952.

To Harry C. Bloch

[*c.* 9 February 1929]

. . . I am sorry, of course, that you had to decide against my book, but thank you very much for reading it.[1] I note what you say about the central idea in the story, and my failure to carry it out successfully, and the lifelessness of the characters and the "priggishness" of the hero. I suspect you are right about all of this, and in the light of your criticism I shall, before I submit the book elsewhere, see if I can put some flesh on and some red blood in the characters. . . .

Houghton, Mifflin and Company has published a new edition of *The Conjure Woman*, in a very beautiful format, with a foreword by Major J. E. Spingarn. I hope its sale will justify Mr. Greenslet's enterprise.[2] Perhaps I am too old to write another live book, but if some of my first ones could be revived, that would be something. . . .

Pioneer: 307

[1] See 8 June 1928 to Alfred A. Knopf editor Harry C. Bloch. Chesnutt is not referring to the manuscript "Paul Marchand, F.M.C."—also considered by Bloch—but "The Quarry."

[2] See 2 February 1929 to Houghton Mifflin Company.

To Arthur A. Schomburg

March 14, 1929

Dear Mr. Schomburg:

At the instance of our mutual friend Dabney of Cincinnati,[1] I have inscribed and mailed to you[2] a copy of the new edition of my book *The Conjure Woman*, of which he says you are going to write a review for the *Union*.[3] The book is receiving some very good notices, along the line of Major Spingarn's foreword, and I shall be delighted to read what you have to say about it.

I don't believe I have met you since you were here in Cleveland at the same time Dabney was several years ago. I hope we may have the pleasure of meeting again some time in the future.

With regards and wishes,

Cordially yours,
Chas. W. Chesnutt.

TLS: NN-Sc

[1]See 2 February 1929 to Houghton Mifflin Company, n. 5.

[2]Arthur A. Schomburg (1874–1938), president of the American Negro Academy and first secretary of the newly founded Negro Society for Historical Research, amassed more than ten thousand books, pamphlets, and manuscripts by and about African Americans—which became the core of the Schomburg Collection of the New York Public Library.

[3]The issue of the Cincinnati *Union* in which Schomburg's review appeared is not extant.

To Ethel Chesnutt Williams

May 13, 1929

. . . We should like very much to have you with us this summer.[1] The NAACP will meet here June 25 to July 2, I think the dates are, and as soon as it is over we shall trek northward.[2] If you could come to the convention you could drive up with us after it and save R.R. fare.

Your mother and I are getting older every day and you and we live so far apart that we seldom meet, and we should like to enjoy a little of your society while we are still alive—really alive and not just hanging on to save funeral expenses.

Your mother will write, and would have written sooner, but she has been in indifferent health and working too hard because of the rottenly incompetent and unreliable help that she has to put up with. All join me in love and the hope that you can be with us. Please let us know soon. . . .

Pioneer: 307–8

¹At the Chesnutts' vacation house at Idlewild, Mich.

²The annual convention of the N.A.A.C.P. began in Cleveland on Wednesday, 26 June 1929; see "The Great N.A.A.C.P. Annual Conference," *Cleveland Gazette*, 6 July 1929, [1].

To Edwin J. Chesnutt

May 17, 1929

. . . The Clinic catastrophe was a dreadful thing.¹ I have been going to the Clinic this winter for treatment, and was due for a treatment on last Wednesday morning, the day of the explosion, but fortunately had not gone, by which I probably escaped death.

The newspapers have been full of the affair ever since, and I am sending you some papers today.

Dr. Phillips was in the Clinic at the time of the explosion, but he got out.² A friend of his, standing nearby with his automobile, saw him sitting on the steps and went over and offered his automobile to take him home. He had just got in the car when Dr. Crile came out of the Clinic and wanted to look after him.³ Dr. Phillips said no, there were a hundred people in the Clinic who needed attention more than he did. He went home, was taken ill from the gas, and died that night about 8:00 o'clock.

They had moved up to Wade Park Manor a few months ago leaving their house next to ours vacant.

You will see from the list of names that seven or eight of the doctors connected with the Clinic lost their lives. It is all commented on at length in the newspapers, both as news and editorially, and will undoubtedly occupy the public mind to the exclusion of almost everything else for some time.⁴

We all join in hoping that you are well and doing well, and look forward to seeing you at Idlewild this summer. . . .

Pioneer: 308–309

¹The explosion at the Cleveland Clinic occurred on 15 May 1929 and resulted in the death of 123. Nitro-cellulose x-ray film exposed to heat combusted, and those not killed by the explosion died from gas inhalation.

²Dr. John Phillips (1879–1929) was a faculty member of the Western Re-

serve University School of Medicine and one of the founders of the Cleveland Clinic Foundation.

³Dr. George Washington Crile, Jr. (1864–1943), also a Clinic Foundation founder, served as its president from 1921 to 1940. A member of the faculty at the Western Reserve University School of Medicine, he was one of the founders of the American College of Surgeons.

⁴Six physicians died, and another five suffered critical injuries. See "98 Killed By Gas and Fire in Blast-Wrecked Clinic: Bodies Overflow Morgue," Cleveland *Plain Dealer*, 16 May 1929, 1, 3.

To Ethel Chesnutt Williams

July 15, 1929

. . . We are nicely located for the summer¹ and are looking forward to your visit. Helen is in Europe, landed in London yesterday if her boat arrived on schedule. Her friend Alta Bien is with her.²

Your mother hasn't got rested yet but is taking it easy. Dorothy and I do the work, with the assistance (the other way) of the baby.³ Hope the fish will bite when you come, they have been rather shy so far.

Hope your husband and son are well.⁴ Now that you are alone perhaps you can give your old dad a little of your society.⁵

All join me in love in the hope of seeing you. . . .

Pioneer: 309
¹At the Chesnutts' vacation house in Idlewild, Mich.
²See 8 June 1928 to Alta M. Bien, n. 1.
³John Chesnutt Slade.
⁴Edward C. Williams and Charles Waddell Chesnutt Williams.
⁵Ethel's husband was in New York City for the summer; see 18 December 1929 to Ethel, n. 1.

To Ethel Chesnutt Williams

December 18, 1929

. . . No news being good news, and not having heard from you for several days, we are assuming that Ed is improving.¹

Our family is staggering along as usual. Your mother and I are just able to get around; the baby has a bad cold;² and the girls are pretty well tuckered out with their term examinations, and grades, and school parties and plays, and other professional activities. Love to Ed and Charlie.³ . . .

Pioneer: 309

[1] Edward C. Williams was on leave from Howard University and in New York City where he was attempting to complete the work for a Ph.D. at the Library School of Columbia University. He became ill in early December and returned to the District of Columbia. He died at the Freedmen's Hospital on 24 December 1929.

[2] John Chesnutt Slade.

[3] Grandson Charles Waddell Chesnutt Williams.

To Daniel E. Morgan

February 18, 1930

My dear Mr. Morgan:—

I wish to add my name to the list of those citizens who object to the retention in office or reappointment of Mr. Dudley S. Blossom as Director of Public Health and Welfare.[1] The objections of the colored people to Mr. Blossom I am informed have been laid before you in very great detail, and I think they are well taken.[2]

Yours respectfully,

TCU: TNF

[1] Daniel E. Morgan (1877–1949) was Cleveland's city manager. He previously served as a city councilman and had just completed a term as an Ohio state senator (1928–30). The founder and first president of the City Club, he was sensitive to race issues, having designed a policy of considering whites and African Americans equally for all staff positions at City Hospital. Morgan would conclude his career in public service in Ohio as an appellate judge (1939–49).

[2] Dudley S. Blossom (1879–1938) was appointed city welfare director for two years in 1919 and reappointed in 1924. Chesnutt's hope that Morgan would oust Blossom, as he had promised in his campaign, was not realized; Blossom continued in the position until 1932. A philanthropist, Blossom later contributed heavily to various local charities including the Negro Welfare Fund.

To Houghton Mifflin Company

February 26, 1930

Gentlemen:

Attention Mr. Greenslet

I hope you have seen the article in the January *Bookman*, on "The Negro as Writer," in which my writings are given the most space, and I am used to date an era.[1]

I hope the new *Conjure Woman* is still doing well.[2] I hope also that you did not destroy the plates for *The House Behind the Cedars*, for it is the one of my books about which I am most frequently asked.[3] I have an idea that a new edition of this book might go as well as that of the *Conjure Woman*.

Yours very truly,

TCU: TNF

[1]Chesnutt refers to "The Negro as Writer" by John Chamberlain (1902–95), *Bookman*, 70 (February 1930), 603–611. Chesnutt was given the most attention. His strengths and weaknesses were described, and he was credited with high historical importance as a literary pioneer: "Negro fiction in America properly commences with Charles Waddell Chesnutt, a Clevelander who is still living, but whose writing falls mainly into the period of the 'eighties and 'nineties. One goes back to the archaic, quaintly-flavored novels and stories of this pioneer with mingled appreciation and esthetic blankness. Most of the Chesnutt plots hinge on such adventitious circumstances that the works of Thomas Hardy seem the very soul of the natural by comparison, but even in the sketches where the antique machinery creaks the loudest one reads with nothing but admiration for Chesnutt as a man. If his plot structure is definitely dated, the fault resides with the white models with which he worked in that era when the novel was designed to tell a story at all costs; and the spectacle of a Negro of the time working with any models at all and producing fiction with many good points is sufficient to compel applause." Chamberlain noted the republication of *The Conjure Woman* in 1929: "Chesnutt is at his happiest, from a modern point of view," in these folk tales. "The worst side of the writer crops up in the short stories of *The Wife of His Youth and Other Stories.*"

[2]On 10 January 1930 (TNF), Chesnutt acknowledged receipt from Houghton Mifflin Company of a $123.20 royalty check for sales to 1 January 1930. That is, "doing well" meant the sale of 616 copies in 1929. But that many had not actually been sold; see 15 September 1930 to Houghton Mifflin Company, n. 1.

[3]In 1924, Chesnutt was informed that the plates for *The House Behind the Cedars* were to be recycled for the production of plating metal. Offered the opportunity to purchase them, he declined. See 23 May and 4 August 1924 to Houghton Mifflin Company. On 3 March 1930 (TNF), Greenslet replied: "Unfortunately I find that the plates of [*House*] were melted in 1924, at a time when there seemed no prospect of further sale. As a matter of fact, although [*The Conjure Woman*] attracted quite a little attention in its reissue, I am not at all sure that the sale has been large enough to encourage us to take a similar step with [*House*], even [if] we still had the plates." He closed by encouraging Chesnutt to "take advantage of the special publicity which is now being given to your work to write a new book." If it were successful, "it might even be possible to revive [*House*] from new plates."

To Walter F. White

March 1, 1930

My dear Walter:

I see from a newspaper item that you have been raised to the rank of the immortals, like Rousseau, Voltaire, Boccaccio, Theodore Dreiser and others too numerous to mention, by having a couple of your books banned by the Boston censors.[1] If this statement is true, I hope it will make them sell better than ever.

I presume you read the article in the January *Bookman* by Mr. John Chamberlain, on Negro writers. I don't know the gentleman's standing as a critic, though I understand he is on the staff of the *New York Times Literary Review*, but I am glad to see that he gives you and me perhaps the highest place among the colored writers.[2]

I am awfully sorry that Houghton Mifflin Company stopped the publication of my books, as the "uncovering" of them and of me by Carl Van Vechten and others following him might have resulted in the sale of a good many more of them.[3] The new *Conjure Woman* has done very well indeed, and, according to the publishers, has quite justified its reissue,[4] and I hope to persuade them to bring out a new edition of *The House Behind the Cedars*.

Give my regards to Mrs. White, whom I am still hoping to meet. I should probably have been in New York this winter, but the decline in the stock market knocked off a large part of the value of my small holdings, and I have felt too poor to spend the money.[5] However, I will get around to it some time.

Cordially yours,
Chas. W. Chesnutt

TLS: CtY

[1]Chesnutt cites authors notorious for the alleged obscenity of their writings: Jean Jacques Rousseau (1712–78), François Marie Arouet de Voltaire (1694–1778), Giovanni Boccaccio (1313–75), and Theodore Dreiser (1871–1945). Until 2 April 1930 when the governor of Massachusetts signed into law a new, effectively more liberal law, enforcement of a prohibition against the sale of salacious and otherwise morally offensive books had been rigorous for several years. While there was never an official blacklist, 1927 saw at least 60 books "banned in Boston," including Dreiser's *An American Tragedy* (1925); and Carl Van Vechten's *Nigger Heaven* had been banned by, at the latest, 1928. See "List of Books Recently Banned," *New York Times*, 24 January 1930, 16. This list does not cite works by White, nor do lists for other years identified by Ralph E. McCoy in "Banned in Boston: The Devel-

opment of Literary Censorship in Massachusetts," Ph.D. dissertation, University of Illinois, 1956. The explicit sexual content of the 1925 novel *Flight* and White's 1929 study of lynching, *Rope and Faggot*, suggests that these were the books to which Chesnutt refers.

[2]See 26 February 1930 to Houghton Mifflin Company, n. 1.

[3]See 23 February and 7 September 1926 to Carl Van Vechten.

[4]See 26 February 1930, n. 2, and 15 September 1930, nn. 1 and 2, to Houghton Mifflin Company.

[5]Chesnutt is referring to the 1929 stock market crash.

To the Associated Publishers, Inc.

March 12, 1930

Attention Mr. E. E. Dunlop

Dear Sir:—

I received a letter from you several weeks ago, with reference to procuring copies of my books *The House Behind the Cedars* and *The Wife of His Youth*. I regret to say that I have no copies available, either second hand or new.

It is the irony of fate that as soon as my books were entirely out of print, a new demand for them should arise. Neither the publishers nor I anticipated anything of the kind, and were therefore not prepared to meet it.

You know of course that my *Conjure Woman* has been reissued by Houghton Mifflin Co. and has n't done at all badly.[1]

If I hear of any one who wishes to sell a copy of either of those books, I will advise you.

Cordially yours,

TCU: TNF

[1]See 26 February 1930, n. 2, and 15 September 1930, nn. 1 and 2, to Houghton Mifflin Company.

To William E. Easton

May 6, 1930

My dear Mr. Easton:

I am in receipt of a marked copy of the *California News*, containing an item with reference to the stage presentation of your historical drama *Dessalines*, of which you were kind enough to give me a copy during my visit to Los Angeles summer before last.[1] I read it with great interest and have no doubt that its presentation will register success.

Mr. Clarence White who seems to have written some of the incidental music, is a distant relative of mine, and a fine musician.[2]

I shall watch the Boston papers for any mention of the performance.

Thanking you again for the book, and with very best wishes for your success as a dramatist and in all other lines,

Sincerely yours,

TCU: OClWHi

[1]Chesnutt was in Los Angeles, Calif., to receive the Spingarn Award from the N.A.A.C.P. on 3 July 1928. In 1893, Easton published *Dessalines, a Dramatic Tale: A Single Chapter in Haiti's History*, which treats the life of Jean Jacques Dessalines. (See 5 October 1928 to Easton, n. 1.) Albion W. Tourgée (1838–1905) commented upon it in "A Bystander's Notes," Chicago *Inter Ocean*, 8 April 1893, 4, and in an 18 April 1893 letter to Tourgée Chesnutt expressed a desire to obtain a copy. (See *Letters*: 78.) Easton's dramatic adaptation of his work does not appear to have seen publication. See 5 October 1928 to Easton.

[2]Clarence C. White (1880–1960) was a violinist and composer who studied under Samuel Coleridge-Taylor in 1908–11 and was Director of Music at West Virginia State College in 1924–30. With John F. Matheus, a professor of romance languages at that college, he later produced his own operatic adaptation of the Dessalines story, entitled *Ouanga* (1932).

To Judson Douglas Wetmore

May 29, 1930

My dear Douglas:

Answering your letter received yesterday, I drove out to the house at 1035 Linn Drive yesterday afternoon. The janitor was n't in and I went back this morning and talked to him.

Linn Drive is not a fine street, although it has a number of apartment houses of fair quality, comparable to this one. The house was built six or seven years ago, when building costs were very high and large mortgages were easily placed. It is a little old fashioned in appearance, and the janitor says that six suites are in good condition, the rest need repapering.

There are sixteen 3 and 4-room suites, including the janitor's suite. The janitor gets $25.00 a month, and a suite with heat, light, water and telephone. All the suites are rented but two. Heat and hot water are furnished. The rents vary in summer and winter. Four suites rent for $50.00 in winter and $45.00 in summer. Seven rent for $45.00 in winter and $40.00 in summer. One rents for $45.00 the year round; two rent for $35.00 in winter and $40.00 in summer.

The aggregate with all fifteen suites rented the year round would be $8,190.00 a year. You know enough about real estate to know that one never gets the maximum.

The carrying charges, including interest on the two mortgages, taxes, coal, janitor and water, I figure at about $3,298.00. What the decorating will cost, I don't know, but it would make the total run up close to $5,000.00. I have n't had time to look up the tax valuation, but the rate in Cleveland is 2.52. The second mortgage I assume is 6 per cent.

As to the value of the property, I imagine the owner would look a long time in Cleveland to find an $80,000.00 purchaser. Real estate in Cleveland is all shot. There is no market for second mortgages, and the banks are loaded up with defaulted mortgages. You can buy lots of properties for the first mortgage. How much cash you could get quick for the equity on the property I have no idea, but I'm reasonably certain it would n't be anywhere near $30,000.00, in my ignorant opinion. I have an apartment house a few streets away from it, which I can rarely keep filled, and a couple of stores which do not pay over 5 per cent. net.

I don't know what your New York property is worth, and without a Real Estate Board appraisal, I could n't make any reliable estimate on this. But at his price, you would have to stick him pretty hard on the New York property to come out any ahead.

I may be somewhat pessimistic, but indifferent health and shrinkage of income, resulting from the 1929 stock slump, which I have n't time to particularize, may account for it.

I am bothered with an enlarged prostate, and I just recently took up the Thermalaid treatment about which you told me several years ago,[1] and my condition has been improving steadily ever since.

My family are in fair condition. Mrs. Chesnutt fell down last summer and injured her knee, and has been troubled with neuritis ever since, but is improving. Helen was in Europe last summer, convalescing from an appendicitis operation. We are going to Michigan,[2] Monday, June 23rd.

My family joins me in regards to Mrs. Wetmore and the children. Miss Moore got your note and would have been glad to get the information had I not been in shape to undertake it. She sends her regards.

This is a holiday,[3] and I can't see any records to find out the tax assessment on the property. You did n't give me the owner's name, but I am told it is Newsome, who, strange to say, I am told is not a Jew.[4]

Hoping this information will keep you, I remain as ever,[5]

Cordially yours,

TCU: OClWHi

[1]The Electro Thermal Company of Steubenville, O., manufactured and sold electrical stimulation devices for the treatment of hernia, prostate gland enlargement, and related disorders of the genito-urinary system in men and women.

[2]To their vacation house in Idlewild, Mich.

[3]Decoration Day.

[4]Wetmore confirmed the name, P.A. Newsome, on 31 May 1930 (OClW-Hi). He thanked Chesnutt for his trouble, said he was not surprised at the low valuation put upon the Linn Drive property since he had been told that Cleveland real estate is "in bad shape," and explained that he would "make a deal" with Newsome if he was sure that he could get "$8,000 or $10,000 cash out of the Cleveland property, but not otherwise."

[5]In his reply, Wetmore did not touch upon his personal problems, as he had in previous letters. See 28 October 1922 and 8 September 1924 to Judson Douglas Wetmore. Wetmore would commit suicide a short while later; see 1 August 1930 to Herman N. Schwartz. He closed his last known letter to Chesnutt with, "I am glad you are all managing to get around, which I am doing, because I have not been very well for a long time. I hope you enjoy your summer vacation and that you will be very much benefited by it. I am not certain, yet, whether I will be able to take one."

To Wendell Phillips Dabney

June 11, 1930

My dear Mr. Dabney:

The ladies of my family asked me to thank you on behalf of us all for the beautiful box of candy which you were good enough to send us the other day. It is very delicious, and we are stretching out the pleasure of eating it, as there is a little left even now.

I hope you enjoyed your visit in Cleveland.[1] I presume you read what Harry Smith said in the *Gazette*, about the "scrolls of merit," and Mr. Wills' political ambitions. I never knew before that Walter had any, but he would make as good a member of the legislature as a lot of others.[2]

With regards and best wishes from us all,

Sincerely yours,

TCU: OClWHi

¹On 23 May 1930 (OClWHi), Dabney informed Chesnutt that he would arrive in Cleveland on Saturday, 24 May, to attend "The Wills Smoker." He planned to "stay over Monday." To be honored was the senior J. Walter Wills (1874–1971), proprietor of Ohio's largest black-owned funeral home. He was a founding member of the Cleveland Board of Trade, the Cleveland Association of Colored Men, the local branch of the N.A.A.C.P., and the Negro Welfare Association.

²Harry C. Smith derided Wills in "That 'Scroll of Distinction'," *Cleveland Gazette,* 7 June 1930, [2]. Wills had begun awarding "scrolls of distinction" to accomplished African Americans across the country, claiming that he represented a citizen's committee. Observed Smith, this committee chaired by Wills has never really existed but "represents the opinion, as far as Cleveland and Ohio are concerned, of but one or two persons." In the "What's Doing" column in the same issue, on p. [3], Smith addressed Wills' political ambition: "The talk of J. Walter Wills, Sr., as a candidate for State Representative is really amusing," given that Smith could "not recall ever seeing him in a single political meeting."

To John Chamberlain

June 16, 1930

My dear Mr. Chamberlain:

Permit me at this rather late date to say that I read with great interest your article in the January *Bookman* on Negro writers.¹ Your critical judgments seem to me, in the main, just and well balanced (I could n't very well think otherwise, when so large and so complimentary a part of the article is devoted to me and my books). I have always known that my writings had many faults, but since they were those of the age, and are bracketed with those of much better writers, I have no reason to complain.

All my books were obtainable up to 1925. They were covered up by the sand storms of the war—the advancing cost of print paper and other publication expenses, which the small demand for them did not seem to justify. I still own the copyrights under my contracts with Houghton Mifflin Company, though all the plates have been melted down except those of *The Conjure Woman,* the new edition of which has done very well.²

With reference to *The House behind the Cedars,* it is, in a way, my favorite child, for Rena was of "mine own people".³ Like myself, she was a white person with an attenuated streak of dark blood, from the disadvantages of which she tried in vain to escape, while I never did.⁴

I note your comment on the stories in *The Wife of His Youth*, in which I am somewhat ironical about the racial distinctions among colored people and the "Blue Vein Society", but it is very kindly irony, for I belonged to the "Blue Vein Society", and the characters in "The Wife of his Youth" and "A Matter of Principle" were my personal friends. I shared their sentiments to a degree, though I could see the comic side of them.[5]

You refer to the fact that people did not know at first that I was a Negro. When the story "The Wife of his Youth" appeared in the *Atlantic Monthly*, James McArthur, then with the *Critic*, I believe, asked Walter Page, at that time editor of the *Atlantic*, about the author, and, when he learned that I was colored, asked Page if he might announce that fact. Page demurred at first, but McArthur convinced him it was too interesting an item to side step.[6] McArthur took a little of the curse off by referring to me somewhat more correctly as a "mulatto".[7] The fact is that I never wrote or tried to write as a Negro, but, as nearly as possible in the American atmosphere, from an impersonal point of view, seeking the truth without malice, with of course a friendly slant toward my Negro cousins.

I don't know why I am writing you all this, but it is probably because of the very fine personal reference to me in the first paragraph of your article. Hereafter I shall be looking for things from your pen.

Thank you again for what I regard as a very friendly appreciation.

Yours cordially,

TCU: OClWHi

[1]See 26 February 1930 to Houghton Mifflin Company, n. 1.

[2]See 26 February 1930, n. 2, and 15 September 1930, nn. 1 and 2, to Houghton Mifflin Company.

[3]2 Kings 4:13.

[4]Chamberlain described *House* as "an honest attempt to deal with the dilemma of a good-looking white woman who has a streak of Negro blood in her without resorting to the standard happy ending that marred some of George Cable's stories built around similar situations. We can well believe in the situation of *The House Behind the Cedars*, even though the mesh of coincidence that traps Rena Walden in a tragic death is a little too elaborate to swallow. The novel impresses us as true in essence. It might not have happened this way, but it very likely would have happened some other way."

[5]Chamberlain was put off by "The Wife of His Youth" with its "queer twists" in plotting and the absence of "inner conflict" in its hero. He also found repelling the sentimentality of "The Bouquet" and "Cicely's Dream." "The Sheriff's Children," on the other hand, he judged "effective as melo-

drama"; and "saved" from its too-obvious plot manipulations by an effective use of irony was "A Matter of Principle."

[6]James McArthur (1866–1909) disclosed Chesnutt's racial makeup not in *Critic* but in "Chronicle and Comment," *Bookman*, 7 (August 1898), 452.

[7]McArthur wrote, "Mr. Chesnutt has a firmer grasp than any preceding author has shown in handling the delicate relations between the white man and the negro from the point of view of the mingling of the races. Perhaps the most tragic situation in fiction that has ever been conceived in this country is that in which a mulatto finds himself with all the qualities of the white race in a position where he must suffer from the disadvantages of the coloured race. Mr. Chesnutt has for several years treated this subject in a capable and artistic manner, and has proved himself not only the most cultivated but also the most philosophical story writer that his race has yet produced; for, strange to relate, he is himself a coloured man of very light complexion."

To Herman N. Schwartz

August 1, 1930

Dear Mr. Schwartz:

I read in a newspaper the other day that your partner and my good friend Wetmore had committed suicide.[1] I don't know his widow's address, so I have written her a letter addressed in care of the firm, which please forward, and accept my thanks.

I would appreciate any information you could give me in regard to what caused Wetmore to take so rash a step. I know his health was poor,[2] and suspect his finances were none too good, and as his friend I would be glad to know more about it.[3]

If any one in your office knows the address of Miss (or Mrs.) Harriet Butcher Shadd, a close friend of the family, and will send it to me, I shall be grateful.

Thanking you in advance,

Yours sincerely,

(Dictated but not read.)

TCU: OClWHi

[1]Judson Douglas Wetmore shot himself "in the left breast" at his cottage at Indian Head Point, Greenwich, Conn., on 24 July 1930; see "'Doug' Wetmore, Prominent Lawyer, Commits Suicide by Shooting Self at Summer Home," *New York Age*, 2 August 1930, 1.

[2]See 29 May 1930 to Judson Douglas Wetmore, n. 5.

[3]In *Along This Way*, James Weldon Johnson related that Wetmore was de-

pressed because of financial losses resulting from his real estate investments in Florida. The front-page article in the *New York Age* (see n. 1) quotes Wetmore's statement to the physician who unsuccessfully treated his gunshot wound. Wetmore told him that he felt overwhelmed and did not wish to continue to live.

To Robert J. Bulkley

August 25, 1930

My dear Mr. Bulkley:

I have been intending ever since the result of the primary election was announced, to write and congratulate you on your nomination for the United States Senate.[1] I could not contribute to it in the primary without changing my party, and while it is a rotten party, I have not been able to convince myself that the Democratic party is any less putrid—all this of course with many honorable individual exceptions on both sides.

I am quite sure that many colored voters will support you. When it comes to the election, I shall vote for you with very great pleasure, not as a mere friendly gesture, but with the sincere hope that you may win.[2]

The National Association for the Advancement of Colored People is working against McCulloch, and it will influence many voters, and they are sufficiently developed politically to cherish a just resentment and act accordingly.[3] Certainly any influence I can exert among them in my quiet way will be to that end.

With the labor vote, if they will oppose McCulloch, and the colored vote, and the support which your record and your personality will draw from the general electorate, your election, for which you have my best wishes, ought to be secure.[4]

Yours cordially,

TCU: OClWHi

[1]Robert J. Bulkley (1880–1965)—a Democrat—was a banker and Rowfant Club member (1927–65) who had served two terms in the U.S. House of Representatives (1911–15). Senator Theodore E. Burton died in 1929, and Bulkley was a candidate for his seat.

[2]Bulkley's opponent was Roscoe Conkling McCulloch (1880–1958) who had been temporarily appointed to fill Burton's seat in the U.S. Senate. An attorney from Canton, O., he served in the U.S. House of Representatives in 1915–21 and was an unsuccessful candidate in the 1920 gubernatorial election.

[3]That the "Cleveland and Cincinnati branches of the N.A.A.C.P. have voted to oppose U.S. Senator McCulloch" was reported in "McCulloch-Bulkley Contest Hot!" *Cleveland Gazette*, 11 October 1930, [1]. 15 November 1930 to Walter F. White discloses the active opposition of the national office of the N.A.A.C.P.

[4]Bulkley won the election and served in the U.S. Senate until 1939.

To Walter F. White

September 6, 1930

My dear Walter:

I intended to write you some time ago congratulating you on the successful outcome of your fight against the confirmation of Judge Parker's appointment to the Supreme Court bench.[1] It was a great fight, and you won a notable victory. Consider the letter written.[2]

I am writing now in answer to your letter of September 4th, with reference to the candidacy of McCulloch for the Senate.[3] Before answering it I called up Harry Davis, with whom I have just been talking over the telephone, and he takes the ground suggested in your second paragraph, *viz.*, that because McCulloch had n't been absolutely bad in matters concerning the Negro prior to his vote for Parker, he ought not to be opposed, but I stand where I stood at the time. I telegraphed Senator McCulloch that his vote for Parker would hurt him with the colored votes of Ohio, and my individual vote and such other votes as I can influence in a quiet way shall be cast against him.

Unfortunately there was no one else to vote for in the primaries, which would have been the best place to oppose him, but when the election comes I shall vote for Mr. Bulkley, who is a gentleman and a fine lawyer, who has been a personal friend and a patron of mine for many years. His father was an eminent citizen who held a high place in the esteem of Cleveland people,[4] and his son is a chip off the old block.

I sympathize with his views on prohibition,[5] and I have written him that I will support him in the election. I can't imagine him doing anything inimical to the interests of colored people, though of course the party tie is very strong and you can't always tell, but we know what McCulloch did, and though he has explained to Davis the difficulty of his position, he made the wrong decision, and should take the consequences.

I don't see what the colored people owe the Hoover administration, anyway. It has made no effort, so far as I have discovered, to please the

colored voters except in the one instance of the Haytian situation, if
that was the motive.[6] The U.S. diplomats representing Hayti and Liberia are both white men,[7] and if any important presidential offices have
been given to colored men they are so few that I do not now recall
them.

I think the National Association would stultify itself if it supported
or did not oppose McCulloch's election to the Senate. Whether it
would be worth while for it to conduct an active campaign against
him, I don't know. Perhaps it could be done better through the local
organizations, with the suggestions and advice of the National office. I
am not very active in politics or indeed in anything else, but those are
my sentiments, for whatever they are worth.

Sincerely yours,

TCU: OClWHi

[1]Herbert C. Hoover (1874–1964) served as the U.S. president from 1929 to
1933. He had nominated for a seat on the U.S. Supreme Court North Carolinian John J. Parker (1885–1958). When a gubernatorial candidate in 1920,
Parker went on record as being opposed to voting rights for African Americans. White almost single-handedly succeeded in influencing the U.S. Senate to
reject the nomination by a 41–39 vote.

[2]That is, the present letter conveyed Chesnutt's congratulations.

[3]On 4 September (OClWHi), White asked for Chesnutt's opinion on the
senatorial race between Robert J. Bulkley and Senator Roscoe Conkling
McCulloch. McCulloch had voted in favor of Judge John J. Parker (see n. 1),
and White felt that "the N.A.A.C.P. ought resolutely to oppose re-election of
McCulloch." He related that some African-American Ohioans thought
McCulloch should not be opposed since he "has not been absolutely bad, so
far as the Negro is concerned, prior to his vote for Parker." White also asked
Chesnutt for his opinion on whether opposition to McCulloch should be led
by the Ohio branch or the national office of the N.A.A.C.P. White subsequently quoted Chesnutt's statement of opposition to McCullough in "The
Test in Ohio," *Crisis*, 37 (November 1930), 373–74.

[4]Charles H. Bulkley (1842–95) was one of the founders of the Hollenden
Hotel and a member of Cleveland's Parks Commission.

[5]Bulkley was opposed to prohibition.

[6]Hoover wanted to remove American Marines from Haiti, but the Haitian
leaders would not negotiate with a commission intended to facilitate the
withdrawal because the membership included African Americans. The Haitians would negotiate with white officials only. In consequence, Hoover created a separate commission to investigate Haiti's educational system, all of
the members of which were African-American.

[7]On the carbon copy of this letter, Chesnutt inserted an "X" here in 1931 or 1932. The sign was keyed to a handwritten note at the bottom of the leaf: "Colored man appointed Minister to Liberia since this letter was written." The previous minister was African-American William T. Francis (1870–1929) who died from malaria during his tour of duty. Hoover did not immediately replace him; but, when he did, he chose another African American, Charles E. Mitchell (1870–1937?), who had served as the business manager of West Virginia State College from 1904 to 1931. The current minister to Haiti was career diplomat Dr. Dana G. Munro (1892–1990), recently appointed to replace General John H. Russell (1872–1947).

To Houghton Mifflin Company

September 15, 1930

Gentlemen:

There is something wrong about the copyright statement which I return herewith. Royalties on the new issue of *The Conjure Woman* are not due until January 1st.[1]

I have received royalties on the new edition to January 1, 1930, and know that some copies have been sold since then.[2] This statement was probably made from the account of the old edition.[3]

Yours very truly,

TCU: OClWHi

[1]What Chesnutt received was not a royalty statement but a record of correction of his account. In a 20 September 1930 letter from Houghton Mifflin initialed "C.W.B." (OClWHi), clarification of the firm's accounting error was given: 106 copies had been distributed gratis; thus, instead of 616 "only 510 sales should have been credited and . . . we paid you on January 1, 1930, $21.20 too much."

[2]In the same letter from Houghton Mifflin, Chesnutt was brought up to date on sales: "The actual sales during the past year have been 84 copies, a number insufficient to take care of the overpayment with 22 copies still to be sold before this is accomplished." Thus, only 594 copies had been purchased as of 20 September 1930.

[3]Chesnutt was also informed that the "stock of the old edition [*i.e.*, copies manufactured from the sheets of the previous printing] . . . was exhausted two years ago."

To Elmer Adler

September 15, 1930

Dear Mr. Adler:

I have your letter of September 11, 1930, asking me to write, for the *Colophon*, my experiences in writing and publishing my first book.[1] I agree with you that the field for Negro literature has hardly been scratched, and that it is worthy of more general cultivation, and I am willing to do my bit to promote this development.[2]

I am familiar with the *Colophon*. It is a very beautiful publication and is on file at the Rowfant Club, of which I am a member, and I have read the first two issues and am looking forward to the third. I presume you want something along the line of the articles by Hugh Walpole, Henry L. Mencken and William McFee,[3] from 2,500 to 3,500 words long.

The honorarium you mention is not extravagant,[4] but it is an honor to appear in such distinguished company and to labor in so good a cause. I think I can write an interesting article along the lines that you suggest, at least I will give you an opportunity to decide that point.

Please let me know if I am right about the length of the article you wish me to write, and how soon you want it.[5] Thanking you for the compliment, and the opportunity to express myself on the subject in the *Colophon*, I am,

Sincerely yours,

TCU: OClWHi

[1] Elmer Adler (1884–1962) was the editor of *The Colophon: A Book Collectors' Quarterly*, published in New York City. On 11 September (OClWHi), he wrote that it "would be of considerable interest to the readers . . . to know more about Negro literature in America, and we have the hope that you would like to write [about] your experiences in writing and publishing your first book." Apparently prompting the invitation was Walter F. White who "tells us that you are at work on another novel, but perhaps you will find the writing of an article . . . a pleasant diversion."

[2] Adler had written, "We know that there are a few collections of Negro literature, but believe that this could become a field for more general cultivation, and consequently would like to do our share to promote it."

[3] Each of these authors wrote about his experiences as he became a book-author: "Getting into Print" by novelist William McFee (1881–1966) and "On Breaking into Type" by journalist H. L. Mencken appeared in Part 1 (1930), n.p. "My First Published Book" by novelist Hugh Walpole (1884–1941) appeared in Part 2 (1930), n.p.

[4]Adler offered Chesnutt $50.

[5]Adler replied on 16 September 1930 (OClWHi). He approved the length proposed by Chesnutt and asked for the manuscript by 1 December.

To the Editors of *Scribner's Magazine*

October 6, 1930

Gentlemen:

Enclosed please find manuscript of essay entitled "Nursery Tales", which I am offering for publication in *Scribner's Magazine*.[1]

If you do not find it available, please return it in enclosed stamped and directed envelope,[2] and oblige

Yours very truly,

TCU: OClWHi

[1]The manuscript of this essay does not appear to be extant; and the essay never appeared in *Scribner's*.

[2]Declined by a publisher as well was a group of tales for children that Chesnutt had written; see 15 October 1930 to Ferris Greenslet.

To Munson A. Havens

October 7, 1930

My dear Munson:

I have sketched out or rather chopped out a paper which, when revised and abbreviated, would perhaps meet your requirements for an article for *The Clevelander*.[1] It is awfully hard to write a short article about the Negro anywhere—one could write a book on almost any phase of the subject. I spent some little time in procuring the information, although it still needs checking up on certain points.

I could not by any possibility write a "Pollyanna"[2] article about the Negro, because I don't feel that way, but I have tried to keep out sarcasm and irony, and to treat the "uninformed white man's point of view with perfect kindness," though I may have failed to make entirely clear "the modifications of that point of view that a knowledge of the facts brings about."[3]

I called you up this afternoon, only to learn that you were out of town, so I thought I would send you this manuscript so that you may look it over and be in a position to talk to me about it upon your return. It is about twice as long as the article that you want, but I hope to be able, with your valuable suggestions, to boil it down to the two thousand words for which you have room.[4] I have asked your office to call me up when you return to the city, so that we can get together.[5]

Sincerely yours,

TCU: OClWHi

[1]On 20 September 1930, Havens wrote "Charley" Chesnutt on behalf of this monthly magazine published by the Cleveland Chamber of Commerce: "Wouldn't you like to write a clear-headed, non-combative, informative article . . . about negroes in Cleveland—an article that would explain and clarify, by taking as its starting point the uninformed white's point of view, and, while treating that point of view with perfect kindness, make clear the modifications of that point of view that a knowledge of the facts brings about?"

[2]That is, as naïvely optimistic as the heroine of the novel *Pollyanna* (1913) by Eleanor Porter (1868–1920).

[3]Chesnutt quotes Havens; see n. 1.

[4]Chesnutt and Havens discussed the project at some point since Havens did not specify length in his 20 September letter to Chesnutt.

[5]On 17 October 1930 (OClWHi), Havens acknowledged receipt of the manuscript and enclosed with his letter a check for $50. "The Negro in Cleveland" appeared in *Clevelander*, 5 (November 1930), 3–4, 24, and 26–27. See *Essays and Speeches*: 535–43.

To Ferris Greenslet

October 15, 1930

Dear Mr. Greenslet:

I don't know what my standing is with your house,[1] as a business proposition. I fear since the new issue of *The Conjure Woman*, it is not very good, as I imagine the sales have been somewhat disappointing.[2]

I am trying to write the novel of Negro life of which I wrote you some time ago. I don't know whether I have that knowledge of the baser side of Negro life which seems to be necessary these days to interest a publisher,[3] or presumably the public, but perhaps I can strike a balance between that and decency and still have the story vivid enough to make it go.

In the meantime I have been writing from time to time some foolish little stories of which I enclose the manuscript. I have not scanned your catalogue sufficiently to find out whether you have a department of *Juvenilia* or not, if this matter would come under that head.

The stories, of which there are ten, would make of course only a small book, but I could write a few more if deemed advisable. The book might be called "Sickroom Stories" or "Bedside Stories," or some such title.[4] They are foolish, of course, but, as you know, there is lots of foolishness which makes good literature, and some of it has been very popular and very profitable.

The collection is framed somewhat like *The Conjure Woman* stories. The set-up, the location, the people, are all taken from life, of course, with different names. I have tried them on my little grandson and on the other members of my family, who have no prejudices in my favor, and they all seem to like them.

Stuff of this sort is often syndicated. I don't know whether this is quite adapted to that sort of publication, or just where I could send it to find out.[5]

If you do not find the manuscript available for publication, please return it, for which I enclose postage.[6]

With sincere regards,

Yours very truly,

TCU: OClWHi

[1]Houghton Mifflin Company.

[2]See 15 September 1930 to Houghton Mifflin Company, n. 2.

[3]Chesnutt alludes to widespread discussion at the time about the tendency in literature about African Americans to emphasize the sordid and immoral.

[4]Chesnutt had also written recently an essay on "Nursery Tales"; see 6 October 1930 to the Editors of *Scribner's Magazine*.

[5]Greenslet replied on 17 October 1930 (OClWHi), informing Chesnutt that the "children's stories . . . will be promptly and hospitably considered by our Juvenile Department, which is very active and flourishing." About the novelistic manuscript on which Chesnutt was working, he commented: "As I think I have written you before we shall be exceedingly interested in your novel of Negro life." Then, in response to Chesnutt's comments on the poor sales of the 1929 printing of *The Conjure Woman*, Greenslet reassured him, "Although the new issue . . . didn't have a very large sale it was we think an excellent thing to have done and good for the prestige of both author and publisher."

[6]The collection was never published, and the manuscript does not appear to be extant.

To Walter F. White

November 15, 1930

My dear Walter:

I am writing an article for the *Colophon* on "My First Book".[1] In the letter asking me to write the article, Mr. Adler of the *Colophon* mentioned your name. Perhaps I have to thank you for the request to write the article.[2]

I have written for the *Clevelander*, which is the Cleveland Chamber of Commerce magazine, an article on "The Negro in Cleveland",[3] of which I will have some copies in a day or two and will send you one.

I have your letter of September 6th, with reference to the proposed campaign of the N.A.A.C.P., "to secure and protect the Negro's constitutional rights," of which the first point to be taken up is the apportionment of school funds. It is a very serious and important matter,[4] and I hope you will be as successful with it as with the defeat of Senators McCulloch[5] and Allen.[6] It was regrettable in a way that in order to defeat McCulloch it seems to have been necessary to defeat nearly the whole Republican ticket in Ohio, but the party has been courting just such a situation, and except for several of my good friends who got caught in the landslide, I have no regrets.

I am sorry that I did not see you on your last trip to Cleveland, but hope I may have that privilege when you come here again.[7]

Sincerely yours,

TCU: OClWHi

[1] See 15 September 1930 to Elmer Adler.

[2] White replied on 17 November 1930 (OClWHi): "Yes, it was I who suggested to Elmer Adler that you be asked to write the article for the *Colophon*. You owe me no thanks, however, for the suggestion—if anyone is in debt to me, it is the *Colophon*."

[3] See 7 October 1930 to Munson Havens, n. 5.

[4] On 6 September (OClWHi), White announced "an intensive campaign of legal action and education of public opinion to secure and protect the Negro's constitutional rights." The first matter to be taken up was the unequal distribution of state funds and federal apportionments for public education; legal suits were to be simultaneously initiated "in a number of states." White asked Chesnutt for comments and suggestions.

[5] Regarding N.A.A.C.P. opposition to the election of U.S. Senator McCulloch, see 6 September 1930 to White.

[6] In 1929–30, Kansas Republican Henry J. Allen (1868–1950) completed the term of Charles Curtis (1860–1936), who was elected U.S. vice-president.

CU: OClWHi

[1]Attorney Maurice Maschke (1868–1936) was chairman of the Cuyahoga County Republican Committee from 1914 to 1933 and served as a Republican national committeeman from 1924 to 1932. Clayborne George enjoyed a distinguished career in public service (see 19 October 1927 to Mayo Fesler), but he did not receive an appointment to a judgeship.

[2]Frank Phillips (1870–1933) was an attorney and municipal judge in Cleveland.

[3]Maschke replied on 18 November (OClWHi). "Some time ago the Governor agreed that when an opportunity came he would appoint one of the colored group to a judgeship and I believe he will do so. However, a difficulty may arise from the fact that there are so many candidates and that there is a dispute in the group as to who should receive the appointment."

To Wendell Phillips Dabney

November 24, 1930

Dear Mr. Dabney:

My daughter Helen asked me a month or more ago to write and thank you for the beautiful copy of *The Rubáiyát*[1] which you were kind enough to send her. She was very busy at the time, and has been since, and relied on me to do what she asked. It is a beautiful book and a worthy addition to any library. I trust you will pardon us both.

The election I see did not go exactly as you had suggested, but in reading *The Union* since it was over, I don't find any very poignant expressions of regret at the outcome.[2] Senator McCulloch got a proper rebuke and it served notice on white politicians that the Negro vote must be reckoned with.[3]

I voted for Bulkley, but of course I don't take any particular pleasure in seeing my own party[4] smashed all to pieces, although I do think that it laid itself open to just what happened. Mr. Hoover's outlook for the future is not altogether rosy, and the change in the public attitude on prohibition still further complicates it.

Family join me in regards.

Sincerely yours,

TCU: OClWHi

[1]*The Rubáiyát of Omar Khayyám*, trans. Edward FitzGerald (1809–83), first published in 1859 and revised to its final form in 1879.

[2]Issues of the Cincinnati *Union* including discussion of the election are not extant.

On 5 August 1930, Allen was defeated in the primary r
seat. The reason for N.A.A.C.P. opposition to Allen was hi
the nomination of John J. Parker for a seat on the U.S. Sup
September 1930 to White, n. 1).

⁷White's visit to Cleveland on 5 October was noted in "N
Contest Hot!" *Cleveland Gazette*, 11 October 1930, [
N.A.A.C.P. members, advocating the defeat of Senator M
election of Robert J. Bulkley. White, in his 17 November le
regret at not having seen Chesnutt and enjoyed "our usual
with, "I am glad to know your feeling about the election.
Smith says that the N.A.A.C.P. had nothing to do with M
and that my Ohio meetings were poorly attended. I really r
examined because I came away from Ohio believing that I
houses. However, knowing Harry Smith, his animadversions
sleepless nights." Harry C. Smith supported McCulloch and
his insistence that the majority of African-American wards in
same. The piece to which White refers was entitled "Walter
Cleveland Gazette, 15 November 1930, [2]. Smith denied W
that the African-American vote defeated McCulloch: "If M
spoofing, his head should surely be examined. The poorly att
that he, Du Bois, and other N.A.A.C.P. representatives address
during the recent campaign are proof of this fact."

To Maurice Maschke

Novem

Dear Mr. Maschke:

I promised Mr. Clayborne George some days ago to wr
ter asking you to favor his application for an appointment t
judgeships to be filled by the Governor.¹ Several others of
friends have made similar requests.

In spite of the Cleveland *Plain Dealer* and the *Press*, I sus
the leader of the Republican County Committee, you still h
less influence with the Governor, and I am quite sure that t
ment of a colored judge would please the voters of that grou

Others I would favor in this connection are John P. Greer
Davis and Judge Frank Phillips.²

I am writing this a little late in the day, but the appointme
yet announced, and I am sure you will do what you think
matter.³

Sincer

³See 6 September 1930 to Walter F. White.
⁴The Republican Party.

To Myers Y. Cooper

November 24, 1930

Dear Sir:

As a citizen of Cleveland, a member of the Cuyahoga County Bar, and one of the population group to which he belongs, I am writing you to urge the appointment of Alexander H. Martin, to one of the vacant judgeships in this county.¹ The Cleveland Bar Association has recommended him. He is by all odds the best and most favorably known of the colored lawyers who are applying for an appointment, and I am quite sure that to name him would give pleasure to the vast majority of that group.

I have heard it suggested that the difficulty you might find in appointing a colored judge was that there is a dispute in the group as to who should receive the appointment.² Of course no white group has ever been solidly united on any candidate. The best the appointing power can do is to select the name which in his opinion will be most satisfactory to that particular group, and at the same time, satisfactory to the larger group comprising the general electorate.

I sincerely hope that you will see your way clearly to name Mr. Martin to one of these positions, and I am quite sure that neither the bench nor the community nor the Republican Party will suffer in that event.³

Respectfully yours,

TCU: OClWHi
¹Myers Y. Cooper (1873–1958) was the Republican governor of Ohio from 1929 to 1931. Alexander H. Martin (1872–?) began the practice of law in Cleveland in 1897 and served in 1924 as a special assistant to the U.S. attorney general.
²See 15 November 1930 to Maurice Maschke, n. 3
³Martin was not appointed to a judgeship in Cuyahoga County.

To Elmer Adler

November 28, 1930

Dear Mr. Adler:

I am enclosing MS of article for the *Colophon*.[1] I have written more about my race in it than I have ever written anywhere, as I infer from your letter that it was perhaps largely for that reason that you had asked me to contribute the article. My views on the subject are, I think, pretty clearly stated in the paper. I hope it may meet your approval.

I can't think of any illustrative material, unless you could use the title page of the limited edition or the cover illustration of the first trade edition.[2] I don't imagine you use photographs. If you do, if you care for one of me at the time the book was published, or today, I shall be glad to send it.[3]

Yours cordially,

TCU: OClWHi

[1] The manuscript was entitled "My First Book"; see 15 September 1930 to Elmer Adler.

[2] On 16 September 1930 (OClWHi), Adler asked Chesnutt to inform him in advance if any illustrative material would be submitted with the article.

[3] Adler replied on 29 November (OClWHi), "hastening to tell you of my own pleasure in your paper. And I am quite confident that the other editors will be as enthusiastic." He wrote again on 3 December (OClWHi), relating that the managing editors "agreed with me that your paper will be a real contribution" to *The Colophon*. He enclosed a check for $50.

To Fannin S. Belcher

December 3, 1930

Dear Sir (or Madam),

I am addressing you thus because I am not able to determine from your letter of November 20th, whether you are a man or a woman.[1]

I am pleased to learn that the College Literary Club is studying my life and works along with those of other colored authors.

I should be glad to come to your college at almost any time, upon one condition, that you pay my expenses. Owing to unfortunate investments, I have suffered in the recent financial slump, besides being in somewhat indifferent health, so that I am "hard up." If you can meet this condition, or perhaps get up a public reading or lecture which might produce something, I shall be glad to come to you at any time you suggest.

Thanking you and the College Literary Club for the compliment of your invitation, I am,

Sincerely yours,

TCU: OClWHi

[1]Fannin S. Belcher (1908–67) was a professor of English at West Virginia State College who served as the faculty advisor to the College Literary Club.

To Robert J. Bulkley

December 26, 1930

My dear Senator:

I am writing to call your attention to the Vestal Bill for General Copyright Revision—I do not know its number—and to request your aid in seeing that it is enacted into law.[1]

The present copyright law, enacted in 1909, is inadequate and out of date, and it is only by the passage of the bill above referred to that a much needed modernization of the copyright law can be effected.

The main reforms are:[2]

1. Automatic Copyright: *i.e.*, without formality the author, upon completion of his manuscript, establishes ownership of copyright.

2. Divisible Copyright, permitting the author or other owner of copyright to give clear legal title to the various rights in his work which he may wish to dispose of separately, thus enabling the buyer or lessee of separate rights (such as magazine rights to magazines, book rights to book publishers, motion picture rights to motion picture producers) to defend those rights individually without having to take recourse to the author or other owner of copyright in case of infringement suits. The new provision will give clear legal title to every right.

3. International Copyright. American authors, by complying with the provisions of this act, will be able to secure automatic copyright throughout the world without formality. If the United States fails to join the International Copyright Union by August 1, 1931, authors will have little, if any, protection against piracy of their works abroad, as our provisional copyright agreement terminates at that date.

4. Extension of the Term of Copyright from 56 years after publication to the life of the author and fifty years after his death. This is designed to protect authors and their heirs.

This bill seriously concerns authors, of whom I am one. It is endorsed by all associations and industries affected by copyright. It must be passed by the House and the Senate in the short session, or the work of years will be lost.

Hoping, and, indeed, feeling confident that you will lend your aid to the passage of this bill, I remain, with congratulations on your assumption of your new office,[3]

Cordially yours,

TCU: OClWHi

[1]Houghton Mifflin sent Chesnutt a form letter addressed to its authors (OClWHi). It declared that the present copyright law enacted in 1909 is "inadequate and outmoded" and asked for "active help on the Vestal Bill for General Copyright Revision for which all who are affected by copyright must fight for attention and passage in the short session of Congress, commencing December 2."

[2]The four points were transcribed from the Houghton Mifflin form letter.

[3]Bulkley had just been elected to the U.S. Senate; see 25 August 1930 to Bulkley, n. 4.

To Houghton Mifflin Company

December 29, 1930

Attention Mr. Ferris Greenslet

Dear Mr. Greenslet:

I am enclosing MS. of the novel of which I wrote you, and on which I have been working for the past year.[1]

It is a novel about the Negro, but with a difference. I have n't dredged the sewers of the Negro underworld to find my characters and my scenes, but have rather essayed to depict a cross section of the life of the "upper tenth" of the colored people,[2] along the edge of the color line.[3] If you cannot by reading it discover what I have sought to do, and whether or not I have accomplished it, then anything I might say about it would be superfluous.

I am offering it to Houghton Mifflin Company for publication, and hope it may meet your approval. I should like to write a successful novel, not only for my soul's satisfaction, but because I need the money.

Hoping to hear from you at your convenience, I remain,

Sincerely yours,

P.S. I have written an article for the *Colophon*, which will appear in an early number, on "My First Book",[4] in which I have given Houghton

Mifflin Company and its staff credit for everything connected with the modest success of *The Conjure Woman* except writing the text.

TCU: OClWHi

[1]See 15 October 1930 to Greenslet.

[2]Chesnutt echoes W. E. B. Du Bois in his essay "The Talented Tenth," published as the second chapter in the 1903 collection of essays by several authors entitled *The Negro Problem*. Du Bois' point was that a significant portion of the African-American population is capable of intellectual sophistication and need not be limited to the "industrial education" for which Booker T. Washington was an advocate; Chesnutt, in turn, refers to those who have achieved such sophistication.

[3]See 15 October 1930 to Greenslet, n. 3.

[4]The essay appeared under a different title when published. See 25 March 1931 to Elmer Adler, nn. 1 and 2.

To Joel E. Spingarn

January 15, 1931

Dear Colonel Spingarn:

Replying to your letter of December 31, 1930, for which I thank you, I have read some of the ill-advised and unfounded criticism of your election as president of the N.A.A.C.P. I followed at the time the effort to secure Negro officers in the army, and was of the opinion then and am now that opportunism was the only course that could bring this about.[1] It was not the ideal thing, of course, but it was the best that could be done. If the Negro should have to wait for the ideal in all things, he would often have to wait a very long time.

No one could possibly think of race discrimination in connection with you, and in this matter, you had the backing of the gentleman you mention in your letter, whose loyalty to the Negro could not by any possibility be questioned.[2] So I think you need not be in the least disturbed at the ingratitude and bad taste of your critics.

I have just read in the *New York Age* the announcement that the Spingarn Medal for this year has been awarded to Richard Berry Harrison, star of the play *The Green Pastures*.[3] I do not know the gentleman, personally, and have not seen the play, not having been in New York during its run, but I have read such high commendations of Mr. Harrison's art, that I have no doubt he is worthy of this distinguished honor.

I remain with sincere regards

Cordially yours,

TCU: OClWHi

[1]On 29 December 1930 (OClWHi), Chesnutt congratulated Spingarn on his election to the presidency of the N.A.A.C.P.: "I feel quite sure that the Association will be even more vigorous and successful under your administration." In his reply (OClWHi), Spingarn thanked him for this expression of confidence in his abilities, adding: "No one can really replace Moorfield Storey." He went on to relate that he had "recently been attacked by irresponsible persons" for not protesting the training in segregated camps of "a thousand colored men [who] received commissions in the American Army during the World War." His position at that time, he explained, was that a less-than-ideal means justified the end of African-American men having the opportunity to become officers.

[2]In his 31 December 1930 letter, Spingarn related that his position on the training of African-American officers "had the backing of Moorfield Storey, Dr. Du Bois, James Weldon Johnson, William Pickens," and many others associated with the N.A.A.C.P.; "the attack on me is also an attack on them." William Pickens (1881–1954) was an educator and founding member of the N.A.A.C.P who served as one of its field secretaries in 1920–40.

[3]Richard Berry Harrison (1864–1935) distinguished himself as well beyond the realm of popular drama, performing lead roles in the plays of Shakespeare and other classical playwrights. *The Green Pastures* (1930), by Marc Connelly (1890–1980), was based upon *Ol' Man Adam an' His Chillun* (1928), by Roark Bradford (1896–1948); the subject treated in narrative and then dramatic form was the Southern rural African American's conception of Old Testament history.

To Joyce H. Caldwell

February 5, 1931

My dear Miss Caldwell:

I meant to have written you sooner, confirming my telegram canceling my engagement at your school, of January 30th,[1] but this is the first time for a week that I have been at my office where stenography assistance is available. I was all set to leave here Thursday night, and had a little paper prepared on the subject of "The Negro in Fiction," which I like to think you would have enjoyed. But on Wednesday I was taken ill, which generally happens about this time of the winter, the result of a cold which affects certain rather vital bodily organs.

If you should wish me to come to you a little later in the spring, when the weather is milder, I can probably arrange it.[2]

Meanwhile I hope your program was not unduly interfered with and that you were able to supply my place.

With regards and best wishes,

Sincerely yours,

TCU: OClWHi

[1]Professor Fannin S. Belcher had invited Chesnutt to address the members of the literary club at West Virginia State College; see 3 December 1930 to Belcher. On 23 December (OClWHi), the club's president, Joyce H. Caldwell, proposed 23 January 1931 as the date for his appearance. On 13 January (OClWHI), however, Caldwell informed Chesnutt that advertisements for 30 January had been printed: "I trust this misunderstanding won't inconvenience you in any way; and we may look for you on the 30th." On 28 January 1931 (OClWHi), Helen M. Chesnutt informed Caldwell by telegram that her father had become ill on 27 January and was confined to bed.

[2]See 26 March 1931 to Joyce H. Caldwell concerning the possibility of a later visit.

To Otelia Cromwell

February 26, 1931

My dear Miss Cromwell:

I have your letter of February 9th, requesting permission to incorporate my story "The Wife of His Youth," in the text book you and your friends are getting up, and I return the form you sent me giving such permission, duly signed.[1]

This is of course subject to any rights which the publishers of the volume from which the selection is taken, *The Wife of His Youth and Other Stories of the Color Line*, may claim in the matter.[2] Since they are no longer publishing the book, I imagine they would have no objection, but I will leave that up to you.

I think the enterprise is a very worthy one, and I think you have selected for it the very best short story that I have ever written. "Hot Foot Hannibal" is also a good selection. I thank you for the compliment, and shall be glad if I shall help to make your worthy venture successful.[3]

Cordially yours,

TCU: OClWHi

[1]Otelia Cromwell (1874–1972) received her Ph.D. in English literature from Yale University in 1926. She was the co-editor of *Negro Readings for Schools and Colleges, with a Bibliography of Negro Literature* (1931). On 9 February 1931 she requested permission to include "The Wife of His Youth" in this anthology, noting in a postscript that by "a financial arrangement we are securing 'Hot Foot Hannibal' [1899] from Houghton Mifflin Co." The two short stories appeared on pp. 72–84 and 59–72, respectively.

[2]Chesnutt held the copyright for both "The Wife" and "Hot-Foot Hanni-

bal." Why Cromwell did not make "a financial arrangement" with Chesnutt was not addressed in their correspondence.

³Cromwell thanked Chesnutt in a letter misdated 23 February 1931 (OClWHi) for permission to print "The Wife": "We shall be only too happy to acknowledge in the customary way our obligation to you," that is, an acknowledgment in the book of permission to use that story.

To Munson A. Havens

March 6, 1931

My dear Munson:

I got so hard hit financially last year that I find my Chamber of Commerce dues burdensome. I have enjoyed my membership, though it has been rather inactive, a large part of my pleasure being due to the contacts it gave me with you. If you will permit me to resign, my membership to lapse as of February 1, 1931, I shall appreciate it. You will remember I spoke to you about this in January last.

With thanks for your many courtesies and kindnesses and the hope that you may long continue to guide the course of this very valuable public enterprise, I remain,¹

Sincerely yours,

TCU: OClWHi

¹Havens replied to Chesnutt's warm letter in a markedly impersonal manner on 18 March 1931 (OClWHi), addressing Chesnutt as "Dear Sir": "The executive secretary [Havens himself] is instructed to advise you that, at a meeting of the board of directors held today, your resignation as a member of this Chamber was submitted and accepted with regret." He closed by expressing the hope that Chesnutt's withdrawal "may be only a temporary one" and signed himself "Very truly yours."

To Walter F. White

March 11, 1931

My dear Walter:

I beg to acknowledge the honor of your invitation to be present March 22nd, at the presentation of the Spingarn Medal to Mr. Harrison.¹

I regret to say that I was pretty nearly knocked out by the financial slump of 1929–30, and am merely hanging on by my eye-lashes to see if I can possibly save something from the wreck. Under the circumstances, it would be impossible for me to come to New York on the date mentioned, much as I would like to be there.[2]

I see from the press that Mr. Johnson has resigned his secretaryship and is to become connected with the faculty of Fisk University.[3] I have no doubt he will make good in his new connection. Although sorry to see him leave the N.A.A.C.P., I have no doubt that you will carry on the work with your usual efficiency.

Thanking you for your courtesy and hoping that you will have a large and successful attendance at the presentation meeting, I remain with sincerest regards

Cordially yours,

TCU: OClWHi

[1]See 15 January 1931 to Joel E. Spingarn.

[2]The Spingarn Award was to be presented to Richard Berry Harrison on 22 March 1931 at the Mansfield Theater in New York City. Wrote Walter White as acting secretary of the N.A.A.C.P. on 2 March 1931 (OClWHi), "We will be happy to send you reserved seats without charge if you will let us know on the attached blank how many you would like."

[3]James Weldon Johnson resigned on 17 December 1930, and the resignation was announced in "J. W. Johnson Earned It," *Cleveland Gazette,* 10 January 1931, [2]. Related Harry C. Smith, Johnson would serve as a vice-president and a member of the Board of Directors but was miffed because Joel E. Spingarn, rather than he, was elected president of the organization. In October 1930, Johnson accepted the Adam K. Spence Chair of Creative Literature and Writing at Fisk University, a position that was created expressly for him.

To Mayo Fesler

March 11, 1931

My dear Mr. Fesler:

I have your very kind and considerate note of March 6th, in answer to my letter of a previous date, and thank you very much for your courtesy. I shall always be ready and willing to cooperate with the Citizens League in any matter where my service will be of any interest or value, except, as at present, where it would involve the expenditure of money.[1]

Cordially yours,

TCU: OClWHi

[1]Chesnutt had resigned from the Citizens League on 5 March. On 6 March 1931 (OClWHi), League director Fesler replied, "I appreciate your situation . . .

and we are going to continue you on the membership roll so that you will receive our publications until the hard times improve." He recalled that Chesnutt had "always been a good supporter" and assured him that "we want to have your cooperation" with the dues-free arrangement proposed.

To Elmer Adler

March 25, 1931

Dear Mr. Adler:

Permit me to express to the editors of *The Colophon* my sincere appreciation of the very handsome dress in which my contribution was presented, and of the very flattering position it was given in the magazine.[1] The illustration was appropriate, and suggestive, and I like the descriptive name which you gave the article.[2]

This number is a very beautiful one, and I hope there will be many more.

A friend of mine to whom I showed the article inquired of me if it were possible to procure a copy of this number, since he is not a book collector and would therefore not be interested in getting the magazine regularly. I told him I would write and inquire if it would be possible to procure a copy, and if so, at what price. I presume the copy I received was my regular subscription number.[3]

With regards and best wishes,

Cordially yours,

TCU: OClWHi

[1]Chesnutt recalled the beginning his literary career as an author of books and reflected upon his position in American literary history in "Post-Bellum—Pre-Harlem," *The Colophon*, 2, Part 5 (February 1931), n.p.; see *Essays and Speeches*: 543–49.

[2]Chesnutt submitted a manuscript entitled "My First Book"; see 29 December 1930 to Houghton Mifflin Company. The title was editorially changed; see n. 1.

[3]On 26 March (OClWHi), Adler explained that 3,000 copies of the issue were printed for subscribers only and that additional copies were not available.

To Walter F. White

March 25, 1931

My dear Walter:

I presume you read my article in the current number of *The Colophon*.[1] It was in some respects a difficult article to write, but the editors were very much pleased, and I have had some commendatory letters, including one from Carl Van Vechten.

I hope you had a very successful Spingarn Medal presentation meeting.[2] Mrs. Chesnutt is in New York and meant to be present at the meeting, but I had a letter from her yesterday in which she said that the friends with whom she is stopping, at the Dunbar Apartments, had bought tickets for the Paul Robeson recital,[3] which took place at the same time, and she felt under obligation to follow their schedule.

Referring to your letter of the other day, I have no doubt whatever, in view of your past record of achievement, that you will be able to hold down your present job and that you will continue the good work in the capacity of "Secretary" rather than "Acting Secretary."[4]

With the best of good wishes,

Cordially yours,

TCU: OClWHi

[1]See 25 March 1931 to Elmer Adler.

[2]See 11 March 1931 to White.

[3]Paul Robeson (1898–1976) was both a distinguished singer and a widely celebrated actor.

[4]Signing himself as the secretary of the N.A.A.C.P., White had expressed his hope on 13 March 1931 (OClWHi) that "I am going to have your fine support for without the support of my friends I shall be unable to do the great job which is before me."

To Carl Van Vechten

March 25, 1931

Dear Mr. Van Vechten:

Permit me to thank you for your friendly letter in regard to my paper in *The Colophon*.[1] It was a hard paper to write, for several reasons, but the editors were very much pleased with it and I notice gave me the first place in the current number.

I have been in rather indifferent health since I last saw you in New York, and I was badly hit financially by the crash which seems to have knocked nearly everybody out, regardless of whether they exercised good judgment or not, so I have not been either physically or financially in shape to take long-distance vacations.

I shall certainly never visit New York without making it a point to see you.

With best wishes,

Cordially yours,
Chas. W. Chesnutt.

TLS: CtY

[1]Reference to "Post-Bellum—Pre-Harlem"; see 25 March 1931 to Elmer Adler. On 16 March 1931 (Rowfant), Van Vechten wrote to "tell you how much I enjoyed your paper . . . & how very much I appreciated your kind word for me. It has been a long time now since I have seen or heard from you. I hope you will never visit New York without calling upon me."

To Joyce H. Caldwell

March 26, 1931

My dear Miss Caldwell:

I have your letter of March 24th, and in reply thereto would say that I had been hoping that I would be able to come to you on the date you mention, April 26th,[1] but the condition of my health has been such that my family, consisting of my wife and daughters, who have to take care of me when I am ill, think that I should not undertake such a long trip in the spring. I am therefore regretfully compelled to decline your cordial invitation. I regret this exceedingly, as I was looking forward to a pleasant visit to one of the most progressive of the southern schools.

I hope that my inability to come will not mar your program, and shall hope for an opportunity to visit you some time in the not too distant future.[2]

With thanks and best wishes,

Cordially yours,

TCU: OClWHi

[1]On 24 March 1931 (OClWHi), Joyce H. Caldwell reminded Chesnutt that he had promised to speak at West Virginia State College on 26 April; see 5 February 1931 to Caldwell, n. 1, regarding the cancellation of an earlier speaking date. Wrote Caldwell, "It is highly important that we get your final word on the subject as our campus calendar is nearing completion." She closed with, "May we hear from you at once?"

[2]Chesnutt's hope was never realized.

To William T. Couch

April 3, 1931

Dear Mr. Couch:

I beg to acknowledge your letter of March 30th with reference to my story "Sis' Becky's Pickaninny," and thank you for the copy of *Stories of the South* which followed it.[1] It puts me in excellent company, and I am glad to add it to my library.

I notice you give the date of my birth as 1856. This adds two years to my age, which is already uncomfortably old.

If you have seen a copy of the March number of *The Colophon*, you will have observed that in an article from my pen in that magazine I have paid a high compliment to a very distinguished North Carolinian who prompted the publication of *The Conjure Woman*, of which "Sis' Becky's Pickaninny" forms a part.[2]

Cordially yours,

TCU: OClWHi

[1]William T. Couch (1901–88) of the University of North Carolina Press informed Chesnutt on 30 March 1931 (OClWHi) that he was sending under separate cover a copy of *Stories of the South* (1931), edited by Addison Hibbard (1887–1945). The short story "Sis' Becky's Pickaninny" (1899) appeared therein on pp. 294–308.

[2]See 25 March 1931 to Elmer Adler. The North Carolinian celebrated in the essay "Post-Bellum—Pre-Harlem" was Chesnutt's turn-of-the-century editor and publisher Walter Hines Page.

To W. E. B. Du Bois

April 14, 1931

My dear Dr. Du Bois:

I have your letter of April 10th with reference to the republication of my *Colophon* article in the *Crisis*.[1] I am very glad to learn that you liked the article, and have no objection whatever to your reproducing it in accordance with your quotation from the letter of the *Colophon* editors.[2]

My health is not as good as it might be, but is improving as the season opens up. Mrs. Chesnutt had a delightful trip to New York, in the course of which she met Mrs. Du Bois[3] and enjoyed her society very much.[4]

With all good wishes,

Sincerely yours,

TCU: OClWHi

[1]"Post-Bellum—Pre-Harlem" (see 25 March 1931 to Elmer Adler, n. 1) made its second appearance in *Crisis*, 40 (June 1931), 193–94.

[2]In his 10 April letter (OClWHi), Du Bois quoted *Colophon* editor Elmer Adler as follows: "The editors . . . have no objection to your using the Chesnutt article, either in part or in whole, providing, of course, that you have Mr. Chesnutt's consent and protect the Colophon's copyright."

[3]Mrs. Nina Gomer Du Bois (1872–1950).

[4]The same day, 14 April (OClWHi), Chesnutt also thanked Arthur B. Spingarn for the attention he gave to Mrs. Chesnutt during her visit to New York City.

To Oliver LaFarge

June 5, 1931

Dear Mr. LaFarge,

Replying to your letter of recent date asking me to serve as a member of the Advisory Committee of the Du Bois Literary Prize,[1] I shall be glad to serve in that capacity and thereby perhaps lend aid and encouragement to worthy and aspiring authors.[2]

Thanking you for the honor,

Yours sincerely,

TCU: Rowfant

[1]Oliver LaFarge (1901–63) was an ethnologist and novelist whose *Laughing Boy* won the Pulitzer Prize in 1929. The son-in-law of Mrs. E. R. Williams, the donor of the Du Bois Literary Prize for the best book of prose fiction published in 1929–31, he chaired the nominating committee including William Stanley Braithwaite, W. E. B. Du Bois, James Weldon Johnson, journalist-novelist Lewis S. Gannett (1891–1966), and Chesnutt.

[2]LaFarge thanked Chesnutt on 18 June 1931 (Rowfant). The competition was announced in "The Du Bois Literary Prize," *Crisis*, 38 (August 1931), 278. The recipient was to be named in 1932. But no work worthy of the honor was identified; see "The Du Bois Literary Prize," *Crisis*, 40 (February 1933), 45.

To Ida and Fannie Henderson

October 13, 1931

Dear Ladies:

I can only excuse my not having formally acknowledged receipt of the beautiful flowers which you sent me and which cheered my sick room so much by saying that I have been confined at home and practically in bed ever since they came.[1] They were very beautiful and fragrant, and a fine index of the characters of their donors. I think they must have been of some value to me, for I am practically over my illness and am writing this at my office, which I am visiting today for the first time in five weeks.

I certainly had a hectic summer; nine weeks of a delightful vacation, and then after a day or two of relaxation, nearly six weeks of illness. I had a doctor for a week or two to treat me for the stomachache. He gave me everything he could think of, and then suggested an examination at the Clinic, which I underwent—and it was a very difficult and troublesome thing—only to be advised by the surgeons there that there was nothing seriously the matter with me, nothing that was n't easily accounted for by my age. Of course, with this reassurance I immediately began to get better, and in two or three days I was over my illness. However, my strength did not return at once, and after experimenting with one or two tonics, my doctor has finally given me one which seems to have hit the spot. I took two doses and then I jumped into a cab and went to my office, where I have been practically all day. Whether I will be as smart tomorrow, or whether my wife will let me come, I don't know.

Speaking of my wife, she has been extremely faithful and devoted to me, has watched over me and taken care of me as if I were a baby or a small child, and I have assured her how much I appreciate her devotion.

Our old friend John P. has been at the house since I was ill. He is beginning to look his age, and that fall he had did n't do him any good.[2] I guess it broke his Sunday School record, but I hope he will be able to resume it very soon.

I notice from the papers that the city's grand old man, Samuel Mather, is confined at home with heart trouble. I hope he survives, for in these times of depression and hardship we certainly need men of that caliber both in heart and pocket.[3]

Again thanking you for the beautiful flowers, and hoping to see you before very long, believe me, with the thanks and regards of the whole family, I remain,

Faithfully yours,

TCU: OClWHi

[1]In 1931 Ida Henderson lived in Cleveland at 2518 E. 82nd St. Fannie and she were close friends of Susan Utley Chesnutt.

²Chesnutt's cousin, John Patterson Green. On 21 August 1931 (OCIWHi), Green informed Chesnutt that he was injured in an automobile accident on 17 August.

³Samuel Mather (1851–1931) was an industrialist and, like his wife—Flora Stone Mather (1852–1909)—a philanthropist. At the time of his death he had served as an officer or director of at least 25 corporations and was alleged to have been Ohio's wealthiest citizen. Beginning on 10 October 1931, local newspapers reported on Mather's failing health; he died on 18 October.

To Wendell Phillips Dabney

October 13, 1931

My dear Colonel:

This is the first time I have been at my desk for five weeks, and the first thing I take occasion to do is to write you to thank you for your friendly call and for the beautiful flowers which so refreshed my sick room.

I have before me at this moment a copy of *The Union*, and have been chuckling at some of the wisecracks in "Gossip and Reflections". Some of them are not above criticism from the standpoint of a purist, but they are all full of pep, which no doubt accounts for their popularity.[1]

Quite a few things have been happening in the world at large. Mr. Hoover seems to have opened up quite a bit, which will be for the benefit of his popularity.[2] Mr. DePriest and Alderman Anderson seem to be at swords' points, to whose advantage time alone will tell. Whichever one is nominated will undoubtedly be elected from that district.[3] We have already seen what DePriest can do. He seems to have demonstrated one thing that he cannot do, that is to get a colored cadet in either West Point or Annapolis. Perhaps Mr. Anderson would do better in that regard.

I see you are still working away at the N.A.A.C.P.[4] From your point of view it would seem to be justified, but I hope the organization or the labor organization which is fighting for them, one or the other or both together, will succeed in saving the lives of the nine unfortunate colored boys in Scottsboro. Their photographs—and I don't mean their color—are not particularly impressive, but I have no doubt they were framed, and if convicted and executed will be just that many more martyrs to race prejudice. I am glad Clarence Darrow has been secured to aid in their defense.[5]

My family are all well. My wife is pretty nearly tired out nursing me for the past six weeks. A more loyal and devoted wife no man ever had, and I've got my job cut out for the rest of my life to make her feel how much I appreciate her devotion. The young ladies of the family are well, and little Johnnie is full of pep and vinegar.[6] All send their regards and hope to see you when you are around this way again.

Sincerely yours,

TCU: OClWHi

[1]Dabney, editor of the Cincinnati *Union*, was the author of the column to which Chesnutt refers.

[2]Chesnutt is referring to either one or both of the following developments. President Hoover had proposed to congressional leaders a dramatic remedy for the U.S. economic depression: to make more of both private and public monies available as loans. In addition to aiding in the formation of a National Negro Republican League, Hoover was supportive of a newly established Colored Anti-Lynching Congress, promising more vigorous federal involvement in the prosecution of lynchers.

[3]Attorney Louis B. Anderson (1870–?) was an alderman in Chicago's second ward. He unsuccessfully challenged the U.S. House of Representatives incumbent Oscar DePriest (1871–1951), who served as a congressman from 1929 to 1935.

[4]The recent issues of the Cincinnati *Union* in which Dabney criticized the N.A.A.C.P. are not extant. Inferable is his displeasure with the involvement of the International Labor Defense organization; see 10 February 1932 to Walter F. White, n. 10.

[5]Emended is Chesnutt's reference to "Scottsville," rather than "Scottsboro," Ala. The previous March, nine African-American males were accused of having attacked two white women in Alabama. Ruby Bates, 23, and Victoria Price, 19, were in a railroad boxcar with seven white men when the African Americans entered. Alleged was their having forced six of the white men from the boxcar and rendered the seventh unconscious before they attacked the women. They were charged at Scottsboro with "criminal assault on a woman, a capital offense in Alabama" ("Jail Head Asks Troops as Mob Seeks Negroes," *New York Times*, 26 March 1931, 21).

[6]Grandson John Chesnutt Slade.

To Francis X. Cull

October 13, 1931

My dear Frank:

I have a very good excuse for not having acknowledged sooner your letter with regard to Freed's candidacy for Municipal Court judge.[1]

When the letter came and for the five weeks that have followed that time, I have been at home sick, in bed most of the time. This is my first day at the office for six weeks, and one of the first things I am doing is to answer your letter.

Of course I have done what little I could by way of questionnaires and Bar Association ballots, to forward Mr. Freed's ambition, but apparently without success so far. Freed is a nice fellow; I have always liked him; and for his own sake, as well as that of the firm with which he has been connected, I would like to see him succeed.

If he decides to run in spite of the adverse decision of the Bar Association, I shall be glad to vote for him and do anything else for him that I can.

I see, by the way, that the firm has changed recently. I am sorry Mr. Jamison left your firm, and I hope that the return of Mr. Inglis will more than replace his absence.[2]

Otis & Company[3] got soaked in the stock slump, to which they contributed so largely. I know I asked one of their men when a certain stock for which I paid $98.50 was selling at $145.00 if I should sell out. He said no, that he had three times as much as I had and he was holding on—and I held on, and as a consequence my stock dropped from $145.00 to $5.00, and is only a few cents above that now. That was only one rotten apple in the barrel. I had three or four others which I had bought at their suggestion at various prices ranging from $15.00 to $50.00, several of which are quoted anywhere from $1.50 to $10.00.

Hoping that Mr. Freed may decide to run, or at any rate he will not be discouraged by the action of the Bar Association, but will remember that he is comparatively young yet and has plenty of time to distinguish himself in many lines during his probably long duration of life, I remain,

Sincerely yours,

TCU: OClWHi

[1]Francis X. Cull (1881–1965) was a trial lawyer and one of Chesnutt's major clients (see Helen C. Moore to Chesnutt, 7 August 1930, OClWHi). Emmerich Burt Freed (1897–1950) was an assistant Cuyahoga county prosecutor and unsuccessful candidate for a municipal judgeship in 1931.

[2]Robert H. Jamison (?–1965) would be appointed to a federal judgeship in 1940; Richard Inglis (?–1956) had been employed by the investment and banking firm of Otis and Company.

[3]Otis and Company was organized in 1912 by Charles Augustus Otis, Jr. (1868–1953), a Cleveland businessman and industrialist whose seat on the New York Stock Exchange was the first owned by a Cleveland citizen.

To Walter F. White

October 16, 1931

My dear Walter,

I hope you will pardon my not having answered sooner your two letters urging renewal of my annual contribution to the N.A.A.C.P. The first of them, dated August 27th, came to Cleveland a few days after my return from my vacation in Michigan. On the day that the follow-up letter arrived, I went home from my office sick, and have been confined at home and practically in bed until day before yesterday, when I made my first appearance at the office.

The present economic crisis has shot my personal income all to pieces. I had about reached the conclusion that I could retire and live on my dividends, when my dividends disappeared, and with their disappearance my stocks shrank to almost the "irreducible minimum", some for which I had paid $98.00 going as low as $5.00 a share, and some for which I had paid $50.00 a share going down to $1.25, hardly enough to pay the broker's fee for selling them. I have been holding on to them in the hope of a comeback, but so far the hope has proved a vain one. I was never so hard up in my life, and in spite of the noble work of the N.A.A.C.P., I have to confess that I cannot at the present moment contribute anything to it.

Family joins me in regards and regrets. I am living in the hope that things will pick up ere long, although the present prospects are not very reassuring.

Sincerely yours,

TCU: OClWHi

To Mayo Fesler

October 16, 1931

My dear Mr. Fesler:

I have before me your letter with reference to Louise J. Pridgeon, who is a candidate for the office of councilman.[1]

I know Mrs. Pridgeon in a casual way from meeting her in public occasionally. She is an amiable woman of good character, so far as I know. I think she is a college graduate. She is a member of the bar in good standing and of some experience.[2]

As to her fitness for office I should say offhand that she would measure up to the average Cleveland councilman—whatever that amounts to—and in some respects a little better. I do not think the city government would suffer unduly from her election to the council, and personally I should like to see her elected.[3]

Yours very truly,

TCU: OClWHi

[1]Fesler wrote Chesnutt in his capacity as director of the Citizens League of Cleveland, which publicly registered its approval or disapproval of candidates for public office.

[2]Louise Johnson Pridgeon (1891–1932), a 1922 graduate of the Cleveland Law School, was one of the first African-American women attorneys in the city. She served as president of the Women's Civic Organization of the East Side as well as the John M. Harlan Law Club.

[3]Pridgeon's candidacy for a Fourth District seat on the City Council was unsuccessful.

To John Patterson Green

October 16, 1931

My dear John:

I do not know whether I ever spoke to you about it or not or whether I had seen it before, but I picked up from the papers which had accumulated on my desk during my recent illness, a copy of the *Cleveland Bar Association Journal*. My eyes fell first on the very handsome portrait of yourself which adorns the outside page, and next on the very fine appreciation of your public services in the first column of the reading matter.[1]

It is a worthy recognition of a worthy career which I hope may continue for a long time to come.

We all hope you are recovering from you recent accident and will be around as actively as usual in your professional pursuits before very long.[2] The family all join me in these good wishes, and I remain,

Sincerely yours,

TCU: OClWHi

[1]"Hon. John P. Green," *Cleveland Bar Association Journal,* 5 (September 1931), [3], describes Green's career as a Cleveland attorney. Notice of the tribute appeared in "Splendid Recognition," *Cleveland Gazette,* 17 October 1931, [2].

[2]See 13 October 1931 to Ida and Fannie Henderson.

To Jessie Parks

November 17, 1931

Dear Miss Parks:

I beg to acknowledge receipt of the "truckload of sunshine" from you, addressed to me. I have eaten nearly all of the apples, and find my condition much improved.[1]

Yours sincerely,

Dear Jessie:

Having formally acknowledged above the consignment of fruit which you sent me, permit me to say that it was very nice of you to think of me and to wish me good luck. I have had a lot of bad luck in the last two years, so this encourages me a little.

We spent nine weeks at Idlewild, Mrs. Chesnutt, Dorothy, little John and I. We carried a maid with us, which made the summer more endurable for Mrs. C. and Dorothy. Fishing was rather poor for the first month, but picked up a little later on, and I got a good fish picture. We stayed up there nine weeks, and we had a delightful vacation. When we got back, I was taken sick and was away from the office ten weeks, and am just beginning to crawl around there now, cluttering up space and being waited on.

There were some nice New York people there during the summer. Dr. and Mrs. Alexander, whom you undoubtedly know, were very pleasant friends. They were up there a couple of weeks before we left; in fact, we left them up there, but they came away a few days later.

We went up on the boat with the car to Detroit, and Dorothy drove from Detroit to Idlewild. We came home the same way, only Edwin drove us to Detroit at the end of a two weeks' vacation, and then we used our return trip tickets on the boat. Helen was busy all summer at home on some school work, and did n't get up to Idlewild at all.

Dorothy's husband finished his medical studies and his internship last year, and is now a duly commissioned physician, authorized to kill or cure as many of his fellow citizens as he can induce to submit themselves to him. He opened up an office about a week ago,[2] and has already had several patients; as there has n't been any disturbing news from them, I think he will be all right.

Mrs. Chesnutt is well, and little John is full of pep. They all join me in regards to you.

Wishing you the best of luck, believe me as ever,

Sincerely yours,

TCU: OClWHi
[1]Jessie Parks was a resident of Washington, D.C.
[2]At 7819 Central Avenue.

To Langston Hughes

January 12, 1932

My dear Langston,

I wish to thank you very much indeed for the signed copies of your *Dear Lovely Death* and *The Negro Mother and Other Dramatic Recitations*, which you were good enough to send me.[1] The whole family have read them with interest and pleasure, and have found them replete with dramatic interest and poetic feeling.

We have read of your enterprise. It suggests the wandering minstrel of medieval times.[2] You ought, at the conclusion of your journeys, to be able to write a book something like *The Romany Rye* or *The Broad Highway*.[3]

I should have acknowledged the first book sooner, but did not know where to address you.

With best wishes for your future success and happiness,

Yours sincerely,

TCU: OClWHi
[1]Hughes published *Dear Lovely Death* with the Troutbeck Press in a limited edition of 100 copies "for private distribution only" in 1931. The second volume also appeared in the same year.

[2]In October 1931, when *The Negro Mother and Other Dramatic Recitations* was published, Hughes began a performance tour of the American South to be followed by appearances in California in the spring.

[3]*The Romany Rye* (1857) by George H. Borrow (1803–81) and *The Broad Highway: A Romance of Kent* (1910) by Jeffery Farnol (1878–1952) dealt with the wanderings and adventures of their main characters.

To Walter F. White

February 10, 1932

My dear Walter:

I have not hurried to answer your letter of February 2nd in re Newton D. Baker as a possible appointee to the United States Supreme
Court bench,[1] first, because I have been confined at home by illness
since receiving your letter, and, second, because of the difficulty of expressing myself upon the subject.

Mr. Baker is an excellent lawyer and a very fine gentleman. We have
often met, and our relations have always been friendly and cordial. But
Mr. Baker is a Southerner, with all that the word even at its best implies.[2] In saying this, I am not unmindful of the fact that the late Justice
White was a Southerner, to say nothing of Justice Harlan, both of
whom, especially the latter, never to my knowledge let the matter of
race becloud their judgment or color their decisions.[3]

I have often discussed the race problem with Mr. Baker, and only
recently have I had occasion to criticize his attitude. He is a clever advocate, and while he would not consciously, I think, seek to make the
worse appear the better part, he can, as Mr. Villard well said in his recent article in *The Nation* on "The Perfect Secretary of War", make
whatever side he takes on a controverted subject, seem right.[4]

In conversation with him a couple of years ago, he admitted his
having signed the agreement of the Shaker Heights Protective Association, and gave as his reason the fact that practically all the estate he
would leave to his wife and children would be his residence, and that
the immediate proximity of a colored neighbor would decrease the
value of his property at least one-half—which is probably true enough,
I am sorry to say.[5]

When I cited an Ohio case which had held invalid a condition of a
deed against sale to a person of color,[6] he distinguished between such a
condition and an agreement among owners to the same effect, having
in mind, I imagine, the Washington case with which you are no doubt
familiar;[7] and when I insisted that the principle was the same, and the
owners' agreement was simply an evasion which the Supreme Court
could not tolerate, he frankly disagreed with me, and said he thought
they would sustain it. That being so, I leave it to you whether or not
Mr. Baker would be a sound man to pass on a case involving such a
question.

When Thompson was elected mayor of Chicago over Dever,[8] Mr.

Baker was quoted in an interview in I think a St. Louis paper as saying that Thompson had capitalized the ignorance of the Chicago electorate to the extent of thirty or forty thousand Negro votes, to defeat the better candidate.

The late George Myers, who was then alive, took the matter up with Mr. Baker, suggesting, which was true, that even without the colored vote, Thompson would have been elected. Several letters passed between them, but Baker stood his ground, and would not admit any substantial error or misjudgment on his part. Poor George is dead—peace to his ashes!—but I imagine that that correspondence might be interesting. I will call up Mrs. Myers[9] and ask her if she by any chance has any correspondence between her late husband and Mr. Baker.

In a conversation not very long ago with Mr. Baker, as to a probable solution of the race question, I suggested the amalgamation of the races. Mr. Baker said that was absurd, unthinkable, and he said it in a tone of voice and with a flash of the eye, which seemed to class it as akin to incest or sexual perversion. Of course, he probably reflected the opinion of ninety-nine white people out of a hundred, but in the event of a general law forbidding the intermarriage of the races, which is always possible, I again leave to you whether it would be safe to have the question decided by a judge with such a preconceived opinion.

I freely admit that I am prejudiced against Southerners in all matters involving questions of race. Their attitude toward the inviolability of their race, in spite of visible and increasing evidence to the contrary, is like that of a devout Catholic to the infallibility of the pope.

It is a matter on which I imagine we think alike, and it is somewhat difficult to write about, especially where it concerns a man to whom I am indebted for many business favors. I wish it distinctly understood that even the little that I have said here is said in confidence, and that my name is not to be mentioned in connection with any expressions of opinion you may publish. I am like Mr. Baker to this extent, that I am still in business, and would not like to have my interests jeopardized, even in a good cause, by talking too much.

I am sorry to see that the N.A.A.C.P. got out of the Scottsboro case,[10] so that my failure to make a substantial contribution did not affect the matter any.

With regards and best wishes,

Cordially yours,

TCU: OClWHi

[1]Walter White, as secretary of the N.A.A.C.P., noted on 2 February 1931 (OClWHi) that Newton D. Baker was a possible nominee for an appointment to the U.S. Supreme Court. "Naturally, we are checking up very carefully on the record of every person mentioned to date," White wrote. "Because of your intimate acquaintanceship with his [record], would you give me as detailed a picture of his attitude on the race question as you can? I will, of course, treat it as strictly confidential."

[2]Baker was born in the South, at Martinsburg, W. Va. (West Virginia was a part of the state of Virginia until 1863 when it was admitted to the Union.) While technically not a Southerner since he was born in 1871, Baker came from a family that approved of the secession from the Union in 1861, studied for his B.A. degree at Johns Hopkins University in Baltimore, Md., and received his LL.B. degree from Washington and Lee University in Lexington, Va. Before moving to Cleveland, O., he practiced law in Martinsburg. Oswald Garrison Villard had recently given attention to Baker's Southern background; see n. 4.

[3]Edward Douglass White (1845–1921) was born in Louisiana; John Marshall Harlan (1833–1911) was born in Kentucky.

[4]Oswald Garrison Villard had caustically reviewed the two-volume *Newton D. Baker: America at War* by the distinguished war correspondent Frederick Palmer (1873–1958). Villard waxed ironic when he chose to entitle his diatribe "The Perfect Secretary of War," *Nation*, 134 (27 January 1932), 117–19. He criticized Baker as vehemently as he did Palmer; and it is likely that Chesnutt called attention to the book review so that White might read that Baker is "a man of great executive ability and marked eloquence, but without fixed principles or political philosophy. Like his chief, Mr. Wilson, Mr. Baker was able to move from the principles and beliefs he had long advocated, to turn into the complete autocrat" during World War I. Further, if the United States needs a president "of strong autocratic and fascist leanings" during the present economic depression, "we should elect Mr. Baker [who would] cheerfully justify every extra-legal act by a skilful lawyer's and dialectician's argument to prove that every step he was taking was quite within the authority of the Constitution, and in keeping with our finest American tradition." Villard also gave attention to the fact that Baker was a Southerner whose father served the Confederacy during the Civil War.

[5]In his 2 February 1932 letter to Chesnutt, White focused specifically on this matter: "Among the other things we ought to watch, in Baker's record is that he does believe in residential segregation and, if I remember correctly, signed a pamphlet as a member of the 'Shaker Heights Protective Association' during the trouble Charlie Garvin had in Cleveland some years ago." On 31 January 1926, the home of African-American physician Charles H. Garvin (1890–1968) at 1114 Wade Park Avenue was bombed; also in 1926 another African-American, Dr. E. A. Bailey, was harassed by his white neighbors and

finally chose to vacate his home in Shaker Heights. The Shaker Heights Protective Association came into being principally to secure a legally binding agreement among the real estate development's homeowners that they would not sell their properties to African Americans.

[6]Chesnutt may be referring to one of at least two recent decisions rendered by Ohio's Second District Court of Appeals. The first judgment, dated 11 April 1931, declared void a covenant in a deed prohibiting the leasing, renting, selling or conveying a part of, or interest in, the premises to "any colored person" (Williams *et al.* v. Commercial Land Co., 1931 Ohio Law Abs. 314). The second decision, dated 22 April 1931, supported a Columbus, O., common pleas court ruling against a like covenant (Bulen v. Rice, 1931 Ohio Law Abs. 175). Neither case involved covenants entered into by property owners in a neighborhood; see n. 7.

[7]Chesnutt refers to the 1926 U.S. Supreme Court decision for Corrigan *et al.* v. Buckley, 271 U.S. 323, which held that like covenants entered into by owners of property in a District of Columbia neighborhood did not violate the civil rights of those of African descent who were thus prevented from purchasing a home in that neighborhood.

[8]Republican William H. Thompson (1869–1944), who in 1929 received an honorary LL.D. degree from an African-American institution, Wilberforce University, was mayor of Chicago in 1915–23 and 1927–31. Democrat William E. Dever (1862–1929) served as mayor in 1923–27.

[9]Mrs. Maude Stewart Myers (?–1940).

[10]Clarence Darrow had been retained by the N.A.A.C.P. for the defense of the "Scottsboro boys," but he withdrew from the case because of the involvement of the International Labor Defense organization. On 4 January 1932, as preparations were being made for appeal of death sentences before the Alabama Supreme Court on 21 January, the N.A.A.C.P. also withdrew ("Quits Negroes' Defense," *New York Times*, 5 January 1932, 2).

To William Monroe Trotter

March 3, 1932

My dear Mr. Trotter:

I have appreciated very much your courtesy in keeping me on your subscription list, and enclose a small check by way of acknowledgment.[1] I wish it were five times as large, but, alas! I am up to my ears in debt, and find it difficult to live and pay the interest on my loans.

I admire your courage and persistence in a cause which sometimes seems almost hopeless, but which, in the course of time, will no doubt work out all right.[2]

Cordially yours,

TCU: OClWHi

[1]William Monroe Trotter (1872–1934), an old acquaintance of Chesnutt's, was the editor of the Boston *Guardian,* a militant African-American weekly newspaper. He wrote to Chesnutt on 22 February 1932 (OClWHi), apparently having received word from him that he would not be able to afford renewal of his subscription: "I am proud to retain you on my . . . subscription list, in remembrance of the old days when we entertained you at the Boston Literary [and Historical] Society," *i.e.,* in June 1905. (See *Letters*: 224, n. 2.) At the same time, though, Trotter requested an "honorarium" as an "encouragement" for himself as a man now nearing 60 years of age.

[2]Earlier in the century, Trotter was the nemesis of Booker T. Washington, whose conciliatory attitude towards whites infuriated him. His radicalism was again measured when he refused to become involved with the N.A.A.C.P. because of the prominent roles that whites played in that organization. On 22 February Trotter made it clear that he was still a vigorous activist: "I am still agitating for the cause." He closed his letter to Chesnutt with, "Yours against segregation and for the cause."

To Ethel Chesnutt Williams

March 29, 1932[1]

My dear Ethel,

I read yesterday in a local colored newspaper that "Myron McAdoo, who formerly lived in Cleveland, and whose mother was connected with the Loudin Singers," had been convicted of peddling dope in New York, and sentenced to ten years in a federal penitentiary.[2] As I know you are a friend of his mother's, I thought you would probably know whether this statement is true or not. If it is, it must be a terrible blow to his mother, to say nothing of his wife and child. If it is not true, somebody is guilty of a most atrocious libel. The last I heard of Myron he was in the Boston post office. I know that times are most terribly hard, and temptation of the weak-minded or weak-moraled terrifically strong.

Please let me know if you know anything about this.[3]

Saw Charlie's name in the Baltimore *Afro-American* the other day, in connection with a motion for a new trial in his murder case—unless it was another one.[4]

Family still pegging along, and in their average indifferent health. The girls are looking forward to their summer vacation. All join me in love and best wishes.

Sincerely,

TCU: OClWHi

[1]Misdated "March 19, 1932." Chesnutt refers below to a "rumor" reported in the 26 March 1932 issue of the *Cleveland Gazette*; see n. 2. He also alludes to an article he saw "the other day" which was published on 19 March; see n. 4.

[2]Chesnutt is misquoting from memory the following in "Cleveland: Social and Personal," *Cleveland Gazette*, 26 March 1932, [3]: "Current rumor has it that Myron McAdoo, former resident of this city, has been sentenced to ten years in the federal penitentiary in New York for selling dope. His mother was never connected with the Loudin Jubilee singers but on marriage joined the McAdoo Jubilee singers who were abroad."

[3]See 16 May 1932 to Ethel Chesnutt Williams.

[4]Chesnutt's grandson Charles Waddell Chesnutt Williams assisted lead attorney Nathan A. Dobbins according to "D.C. Man is Freed on Murder Charge," Baltimore *Afro-American*, 19 March 1932, 2. Client Robert F. Allen was acquitted of the murder of a white man, Frank Edwards.

To Lessie O. Toler

April 25, 1932

My dear Miss Toler:

I am in receipt of your questionnaire on the subject of the Negro and Communism.[1] I have marked the questions in accordance with your suggestions, and have made some notes on the back of the page, and return the same to you herewith.[2]

Very truly yours,

TCU: OClWHi

[1]Lessie O. Toler was a graduate student in sociology who related on 14 April 1932 (OClWHi) that she was "making a study of the opinions of a selected group of Negro men and women who appear in *Who's Who in Colored America*." Toler's M.A. thesis, "The Negro and Communism," was completed in 1932 at the University of North Carolina, Chapel Hill.

[2]Chesnutt apparently queried his daughter Ethel, a social worker for The Associated Charities, concerning Communist activity in the District of Columbia. On 25 April (OClWHi) she observed: "Communists here, too, are steadily causing commotion. There is something to what they say, too, but I dislike the way they use the lowest and most ignorant alley types as tools." See Chesnutt's noncommittal remark on Cleveland Communists in 16 May 1932 to Ethel Chesnutt Williams. See also "The Negro in Cleveland" wherein in 1930 Chesnutt commented on how African Americans may be attracted to Communism because "it teaches human equality" (*Essays and Speeches*: 535–43).

To Harvey M. Williamson

April 25, 1932

Dear Mr. Williamson:

I have received your letter of April 15th, and since its receipt, the copy of the *Skyline*, which you were good enough to send me, containing one of your stories.[1] This particular story, from my point of view, is well constructed. It has a dramatic theme which is very effectively worked out.

I should not criticize your work because it deals with life on Southern plantations. You are writing about a subject that you know, which is always desirable in a writer. For one to write about an unfamiliar subject is to court literary disaster. A man writes best about what he knows best.

Some of the best American writers have made their reputations writing about Southern conditions. I do not need to mention George W. Cable, Thomas Nelson Page, or, in our own day, Mrs. Julia Peterkin, or the author of *Cane* and other stories.[2]

I think for one who has only been writing a year, your story in *Skyline* is indeed very promising. Unless I hear from you on the contrary, I will keep the copy of the *Skyline* which you sent me, so that I may have your story in my library.

Wishing you every success, I remain,

Sincerely yours,

TCU: OClWHi

[1]Harvey M. Williamson (1908–95) was a student at Western Reserve University who later became the first African-American Clevelander to serve as a principal—at the Rutherford B. Hayes High School. *Skyline* was a literary magazine published by the Cleveland College of Western Reserve University. No 1932 issue is extant.

[2]Chesnutt cites four writers who focused closely on different parts of the South: George Washington Cable; Thomas Nelson Page (1853–1922); Julia Peterkin (1880–1961); and Jean Toomer (1894–1967), whose literary miscellany *Cane* appeared in 1923.

To Wendell Phillips Dabney

May 11, 1932

My dear Brother Dabney:

Thank you very much for the box of delicious chocolates which you were good enough to send me the other day.[1] The family have helped me in eating them up down to the last one, and we enjoyed them immensely.

I see from the morning papers that we have been having a primary election. So far as I have read the returns, prohibition seems to be on the defensive, if not yet on the run. It looks as though the "noble experiment" has not been an entire success.[2]

The A.M.E. General Conference is in session here, last week and this week.[3] It seems as though the dark reverend fathers in God (meaning the bishops), are in a bad way. In addition to the one who was mixed up in the woman scrape several months ago, one, Bishop Vernon, has been suspended for four years, and two others are on the carpet, all for misappropriating the funds which came into their hands.[4] I don't know how many bishops there are, probably a dozen, but four is a very large percentage. They are going to elect two others. Let us hope that they will be at least honest.

Thanking you again, I remain,

Cordially yours,

TCU: OClWHi

[1]Chesnutt's use of "Brother" when addressing Cincinnati *Union* editor Wendell P. Dabney is facetious and keyed to his droll description of A.M.E. Church matters treated below. On 12 May 1932 (OClWHi), Dabney registered the inappropriateness of this form of address, relating that it had been a long time since he was a member of a church.

[2]That the anti-prohibition candidate for the Republican gubernatorial nomination won the primary election was announced in "Ingalls Wins G.O.P. Nomination," Cleveland *Plain Dealer*, 11 May 1932, 1, 6.

[3]The 29th Quadrennial A.M.E. Conference met in Cleveland for nearly two weeks, 2–15 May 1932.

[4]Bishop William T. Vernon (1871–1944), presided at the first morning session of the conference, prior to being suspended for one year: he could not explain the disappearance of more than $17,000 in church funds. The two others "on the carpet" were Bishop William Decker Johnson (1869–1936), who was unable to account for over $50,000, and Bishop Joshua H. Jones (1856–1934), formerly the president of Wilberforce University (1900–1908), who misspent $15,000 ("Convict Two Bishops of Shortages," *Cleveland Gazette*, 14 May 1932, [1]).

then, and somebody is arrested or not, according to how the police
or what takes place.

he A.M.E. General Conference has been in session here for about a
k. They had a halcyon and vociferous time. They tried three bish-
for dishonesty, suspended them for four years each, I think, and
ted three new bishops who were consecrated yesterday.[7] One of the
rnoon papers ran a special edition which was sold around in the
red district and near the church, the front page of which every day
; filled with photographs of persons in attendance. They were a
rd looking lot, comparable as a whole, with a Garvey convention.
1 may not have heard the joke about the United National Improve-
it Association.[8] Some wag around Idlewild says that the initials
J.I.A. mean "Ugliest Negroes in America." I have been at one or
› of their meetings, and I think their description is inapt.[9] However,
y can't help it, and they are doing what they think is best for them-
·es.

Charlie has my sympathy in his hard times. I have found times just
iard, but I am old, with no future, and he is young with his life be-
e him.[10]

School teachers' salaries have been cut here to such an extent, that
len will get $440.00 less a year and Dorothy probably $250.00 less.
I am relying on them to help me pay my bank interest and keep out
the sheriff's hands, this hits me as well as them. However, time will
, and in the meanwhile I try somewhat unsuccessfully to keep up a
erful spirit. School will be out in two weeks from today—I think it's
› weeks—and shortly after that we will endeavor to get started to-
rds Idlewild. Helen wants to go up with us, and Dorothy wants to
y in Cleveland with her husband. I don't know how they will ar-
ige it. I am entirely in their hands.

Family all join me in love, and your mother is very sorry that she
mot accept your invitation to come to Washington.

U: OClWHi
[1]Ethel's letter to her "Dad" (OClWHi) described her viewing of the second
tion picture treatment of *The House Behind the Cedars*, by the Micheaux
ture Corporation, entitled *Veiled Aristocrats* (1932). She related that it was
iite modern in its ending—Rena, instead of dying, meets Frank in a big
o, and he takes her back to Fayetteville to matrimonial bliss. She puts her
d on Frank's shoulder and says 'Don't wake me up until I reach Fayette-
e' and all ends happily. It was played by an all-colored cast. Rena, her
ther, and Miss Molly took their parts very well. It was not artistic, like the

To Ethel Chesnutt Williams

My dear Ethel:

Your mother and I thank you very much for y
cheerful letter of April 25th, and for your invitat
Washington. I regret very much to say that our hea
nancial, will not permit us to accept what would be
cumstances a most welcome invitation. I have rheu
interfere with my locomotion, and your mother is
shape.

I note what you say about the movie *Veiled Arist*
the book advertised in Carter Woodson's publica
times, and thought once of getting it.[2] I sold the n
House Behind the Cedars, to the Micheaux Movin;
of Chicago, and I saw it on the stage once, under t
House Behind the Cedars, and the ending as the ec
was like the story you saw—the young white lover r
time to see her coming down the steps of the house
on the arm of Frank Fuller,[3] evidently at the end of
know whether what you saw was the same or no
Micheaux people got it out. If they did n't, it was ra
they would be liable in a civil action, if I had the m
and they had anything which I could collect. I contra
$500.00, for the movie rights. They paid me four of
$100.00, and the other is still unpaid. When I saw
you that it was very well done, but it was not my s
soundless picture when I saw it.

I note what you say about Myron McAdoo. Susi<
from Washington that there is nothing to the rumc
learned correctly.[4]

I can quite imagine that your work at the Asso
very heavy. We have had all the financial troubles h
plain of there. A special session of the legislature wa
relief bills were passed, which will probably ward off
for the rest of the year. I imagine with you that it
right.[5]

I note what you say about the Communists.[6] The
active around this city. There is a meeting or demons

story, however. Your beautiful English and the soul of the tale were lacking. It was a speaking movie and the actors' voices were all harsh, as they probably are naturally. It was not so bad, though, when you consider the handicaps colored actors have."

[2]Carter G. Woodson (1875–1950) was the editor of the *Journal of Negro History*. The book in question is the novel with the same title as the film, *Veiled Aristocrats* (1923) by Gertrude Sanborn (1881–1928). Chesnutt ordered a copy of the novel from the Warren Book Company in New York City on 16 May 1932 (OClWHi). In an undated reply (OClWHi), he was informed that a copy was not available for sale and could not be located elsewhere. Returned was his money order for $1.50.

[3]Frank's surname in the novel is Fowler. It was Fuller, however, in the never published short story versions of *House* (TNF).

[4]See 29 March 1932 to Ethel Chesnutt Williams wherein Chesnutt enquired about his rumored arrest and imprisonment. On 25 April (OClWHi), Ethel replied, "I do not know anything about Myron McAdoo. I would not ask anyone about him and had not heard."

[5]Ethel had complained at length about the dire conditions in which African Americans in the District of Columbia needing financial assistance and medical care then found themselves. The Associated Charities organization, for which she was a "Visitor," could not obtain the funding it needed to care for them.

[6]See 25 April 1932 to Lessie O. Toler, n. 2

[7]See 11 May 1932 to Wendell P. Dabney. The new A.M.E. bishops were Noah Wellington Williams (1876–?) of St. Louis, Mo., David Henry Sims (1885–?) of Columbia, S.C., and Henry Young Tookes (1882–?) of Jacksonville, Fl.

[8]See 13 August 1925 to Thomas L. Dabney, n. 2. The name of the organization was Universal Negro Improvement Association.

[9]Chesnutt refers to the name of the Universal Negro Improvement Association as "inapt"—rather than to the variant interpretation of the initials U.N.I.A.

[10]Referring to the effects of the economic depression on her son's law practice, Ethel had written that Charles "has had a hard winter but he has had lots of company."

To the Cleveland Museum of Art

September 21, 1932

Gentlemen:

I have not sent in my annual subscription to the Museum because I have been hoping to be able to continue my membership. Things have been breaking in such a way, however, that I find it impossible to do so, and I hereby resign my membership.

I suspect there are others in the same condition, but I hope not enough of them to seriously impair the valuable work of the Museum.

Sincerely yours,

TDU: OClWHi

To Mildred Chadsey

September 21, 1932

My dear Miss Chadsey:

I am sorry that I have not been able to pay my membership fee to the association for the present year.[1] I have been hanging on, hoping that I might be able to pay it some time, but there seems to be no hope, so kindly convey my resignation to the management.

I am glad you were able to raise the money to continue the school, for it is doing a great work, and it would be a pity to have it stop.

Sincerely yours,

TDU: OClWHi

[1]Mildred Chadsey (1883–1940) was the executive secretary of Cleveland's Adult Education Association.

To Vlasta Vavra

October 24, 1932

My dear Miss Vavra:

I have your letter of October 15th, making inquiries about a book which you read some years ago, but of which you have forgotten the title.[1]

The theme is a bit unusual. It generally works the other way. It is the white man who falls in love with a colored woman. I know a number of such books, but I don't at the moment recall such a one as you mention.

I will keep it in mind, though, and if my memory brings it back to me, I will write and let you know.

Sincerely yours,

TCU: OClWHi

[1]Vlasta Vavra wrote from Riverside, Ill., on 15 October 1932 (OClWHi). The story she read, she explained, "pertains to the courtship between a Negro gentleman and a white lady, through correspondence; a final personal meeting; disappointment; and a happy ending."

To Harry J. Warwick

October 24, 1932.

My Dear Mr. Warwick:

I have yours of October 17th, suggesting that I send the autographed books to you at the above address.[1]

I received and have inscribed the three books. There was nothing from which to tell to whom they belonged, so I could not make my inscription personal.[2] I think I did in one instance and probably got it wrong, but you will see that when you get the books. I have sent the books to you C.O.D., to the Hotel Bristol at the above address.

Thanks for your offer to look out for first editions of my books and will be glad to have you write me at length any time you choose.

With best wishes,

Sincerely yours,

TCU: OClWHi

[1] The last known letter written by Chesnutt was a reply addressed to Room 153, Hotel Bristol, 129–135 West 48th Street, New York City. Harry Warwick first wrote him on 1 July 1932 (OClWHi), explaining that a friend and he were collecting "American Negro books" with the intent of someday presenting them "to some Negro university library." He also called attention to a recently published poem of his, an English sonnet in which he describes the experience of an African American accepted by all in downtown Manhattan as white; only at night when the speaker returns to Harlem does he doff the mask ("Passing," *Crisis*, 139 [April 1932], 119). Chesnutt, just returned from his summer vacation in Michigan, agreed on 6 September 1932 (OClWHi) to sign the books. On 17 October 1932 (OClWHi), Warwick thanked him and provided the address to which they should be sent "C.O.D.," *i.e.*, with postage due.

[2] Warwick related on 17 October 1932 that four volumes, rather than three, had been mailed to Chesnutt. Warwick owned two, as did his friend Floyd Miller. Chesnutt could not personalize the inscriptions because he had not been informed as to who owned which books.

Index

Index

In this index an "f" after a number indicates a separate reference on the next page, and an "ff" indicates separate references on the next two pages. A continuous discussion over two or more pages is indicated by a span of page numbers, e.g., "57–59." *Passim* is used for a cluster of references in close but not consecutive sequence.